CRYSTAL REPORTS® 2011 FOR DEVELOPERS: REPORT DESIGN AND INTEGRATION

CYNTHIA MOORE

Course Technology PTR

A part of Cengage Learning

COURSE TECHNOLOGY
CENGAGE Learning·

Australia • Brazil • Japan • Korea • Mexico • Singapore • Spain • United Kingdom • United States

COURSE TECHNOLOGY
CENGAGE Learning

Crystal Reports® 2011 for Developers: Report Design and Integration
Cynthia Moore

Publisher and General Manager, Course Technology PTR: Stacy L. Hiquet

Associate Director of Marketing: Sarah Panella

Manager of Editorial Services: Heather Talbot

Acquisitions Editor: Heather Hurley

Marketing Manager: Mark Hughes

Project/Copy Editor: Kezia Endsley

Technical Editor: Fatisha Coley

Interior Layout Tech: MPS Limited, a Macmillan Company

Cover Designer: Mike Tanamachi

Indexer: Kelly Talbot Editing Services

Proofreader: Kelly Talbot Editing Services

For product information and technology assistance, contact us at
Cengage Learning Customer & Sales Support, 1-800-354-9706

For permission to use material from this text or product, submit all requests online at **www.cengage.com/permissions**
Further permissions questions can be emailed to
permissionrequest@cengage.com

Crystal Reports is a registered trademark of Business Objects Software Ltd. Business Objects is an SAP company.

All other trademarks are the property of their respective owners.

All images © Cengage Learning unless otherwise noted.

Library of Congress Control Number: 2011926581

ISBN-13: 978-1-4354-5796-6

ISBN-10: 1-4354-5796-X

Course Technology, a part of Cengage Learning
20 Channel Center Street
Boston, MA 02210
USA

Cengage Learning is a leading provider of customized learning solutions with office locations around the globe, including Singapore, the United Kingdom, Australia, Mexico, Brazil, and Japan. Locate your local office at: **international.cengage.com/region**

Cengage Learning products are represented in Canada by Nelson Education, Ltd.

For your lifelong learning solutions, visit **courseptr.com**

Visit our corporate website at **cengage.com**

Printed in the United States of America
1 2 3 4 5 6 7 13 12 11

This book is dedicated to the memory of my niece, Jessica A. Moore, who was tragically killed before this project was completed. She was waiting with excitement to see the book in print. I hope I made her proud.

Acknowledgments

I want to thank my family and friends for their patience and understanding during this process. I also want to thank Cengage Learning's team for their support and work on this project. I want to send a special thanks to Heather Hurley, Acquisitions Editor, for her wonderful words of encouragement and Fatisha Coley, Technical Editor, for her hard work and diligence during this long project. I can't forget my Project Editor, Kezia Endsley; thank you so much for all of your hard work.

About the Author

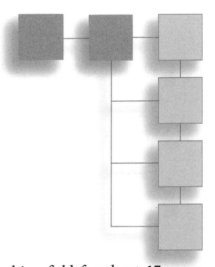

Cynthia Moore has been in the software consulting field for about 17 years, supporting Accounting, HR, and Business Intelligence systems. The enjoyments of supporting these applications include developing reports using Crystal Reports. The majority of her time is spent as a consultant, training and developing products for clients on SAP BusinessObjects products, as well as various Microsoft and Sage Software products. She has a passion for report and database development and enjoys passing that information on to others. Cynthia is also an Adjunct Faculty member for the Community College Workforce Alliance (CCWA) in Richmond, Virginia, teaching computer courses. She has achieved certifications in Microsoft SQL Server and other Microsoft applications as well as certifications in multiple versions of Crystal Reports. She enjoys utilizing her SQL Server querying experience to enhance SAP Crystal Reports capabilities. She has provided training and consulting services in more than 20 states to date. She is based in Prince George, Virginia, which is about 30 miles southeast of Richmond, Virginia.

Contents

INTRODUCTION

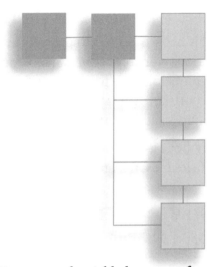

Seventeen years ago I was introduced to Crystal Reports and quickly became a fan of report development. At the time, the billing software that used Crystal Reports had minimal training on the depth of Crystal Reports functionalities. Therefore, I did what other good consultants did; I began to tear it down and find out exactly what this software could do. Crystal Reports functionalities have definitely advanced over the years and with great excitement, I can say it is still conquering new tasks. For the first five years of my experience, I learned through trial and error and managed to produce all of the reports that I needed to. However, now that I have focused on the software and spent years honing my skills and obtaining multiple certifications in Crystal Reports, I can speak about it and design reports with great confidence. With that confidence, it enables me to spend a great deal of time training others on how to develop reports efficiently. With this book, I hope to prevent you from making the development mistakes that I did as an entry-level report developer.

I have taught Crystal Reports in many states now, from beginner to advanced courses, and have found many people who are intimidated by Crystal Reports or quickly decide they don't like it. I credit those thoughts to the possibility that they were given the software and told to make it work as I was as an entry-level consultant. However, my motto is, if you have a strong foundation, you can build a solid product. Your knowledge of the software should be your foundation. Therefore, without the proper training, it is easy to become discouraged with Crystal Reports. With the proper training, you can find report development to be a rewarding career. This reason, among many others, is why I have written this book.

THE PURPOSE OF THIS BOOK

This book is set out to provide an introduction to the report development in the various versions of Crystal Reports. It covers Crystal Reports 2011, Crystal Reports for Enterprise XI 4.0, Crystal Reports for Visual Studio 2010, and Crystal Reports for Eclipse. It does not cover every aspect of Crystal Reports but covers all of the basic fundamentals for developing good analytical reports.

My hope is that as you work through this book, you learn how to develop an efficient, useful, and visually appealing report that your users will find beneficial.

HOW THIS BOOK IS ORGANIZED

I approached this subject as if you knew nothing about Crystal Reports. Each section of the book describes each version of Crystal Reports and the specifics of the report development environment. The first part of the book, through Chapter 10, discusses SAP Crystal Reports 2011. Many of the chapters include exercises to give you additional practice in each area covered in the chapter. The files that correspond with the exercises can be downloaded from www.courseptr.com/downloads.

Chapters 11 through 12 introduce the integration of Crystal Reports into a .Net or Java application. Samples can be downloaded from www.courseptr.com/downloads.

Chapters 13 and 14 take you on a journey through the new SAP Crystal Reports for Enterprise platform and design environment.

The appendix includes the functions you'll likely utilize when you need to create formulas to get your desired results. It also provides a sample Report Requirements Gathering document that you can use as a template for creating your own.

This book is not intended to cover everything, and it does not teach you how to program in Visual Studio 2010 or Eclipse.

THE TARGET AUDIENCE

This book is not intended for everyone. You will get a good, thorough introduction into designing reports in Crystal Reports whether you are using Crystal Reports 2011 standalone version or integrating Crystal Reports into an application that is being developed using Visual Studio. This includes gathering the report requirements, connecting to the various data sources, inserting fields into the report, grouping and creating formulas, and many other topics.

At the end of the first section, you should have a good understanding of Crystal Reports and how to develop more complex reports. As you start to explore the chapters on Crystal Reports for Visual Studio 2010 and Crystal Reports for Eclipse, you will be introduced to the basics of how to integrate Crystal Reports into these applications and understanding the design environment of each.

Finally, the final two chapters introduce you to the new platform for Crystal Reports for Enterprise XI 4.0. These two chapters walk you through connecting to the new semantic layer, the new design window, and give you the crucial information needed to design reports on the new platform.

SYSTEM REQUIREMENTS

At the time of writing, this book references Crystal Reports 2011, SAP Crystal Reports for Enterprise XI 4.0, Crystal Reports for Visual Studio 2010 service pack 1, and Crystal Reports Eclipse. Crystal Reports for Visual Studio 2010 can be downloaded from http://www.businessobjects.com/jump/xi/crvs2010/default. asp. All of the versions covered in this book will run on most operating systems. However, you should check the technical documentation for each application. The specific technical requirements for Crystal Reports 2011 versions are also listed here.

Data Sources

SAP Crystal Reports 2011 can connect to many data sources, including the most popular data sources such as:

- ODBC

- Microsoft SQL Server

- Microsoft Access

- JDBC

- Microsoft Excel

- Oracle

- IBM DB2

- Teradata

- Pervasive

- Salesforce.com

Operating Systems and Disk Space

One of the following operating systems is required:

- Windows 7

- Windows Vista SP2

- Windows XP SP3

- Windows Server 2008 R2

- Windows Server 2008 SP2

- Windows Server 2008

- Windows Server 2003 R2 SP2

- Windows Server 2003 SP2

Disk space requirements:

- 2GB hard drive space (for English language only)

- 4GB hard drive space (for all languages other than English)

SAMPLE AND EXERCISE FILES DOWNLOADS

You may download the exercise files and samples that follow along with the book exercises. You may download the contents from www.courseptr.com/downloads. Please note that you will be redirected to the Cengage Learning site.

Enter the ISBN, the author's name, or the book title to be directed to the appropriate files.

Part I

Using Crystal Reports 2011

CHAPTER 1

INTRODUCTION TO CRYSTAL REPORTS

The objectives of this chapter are to learn the following tasks:

- Become familiar with what's new in Crystal Reports 2011
- Explore the Crystal Reports 2011 interface
- Become familiar with Crystal Reports for Visual Studio 2010 .Net
- Become familiar with Crystal Reports Enterprise XI 4.0
- Become familiar with Crystal Reports for Java developers

INTRODUCTION

Crystal Reports originated under another name in the late 1980s as a report writer for an accounting package that was unable to produce the desired business's needs. Over the years, Crystal Reports has evolved into a powerful multi-language reporting package as a standalone application or as part of a Business Intelligence Suite of products that includes reporting, dashboards, analytical processing, web intelligence, embedding in custom applications, and many other uses.

Crystal Reports has been included in hundreds of accounting software packages as the standard report writer including large Enterprise Resource Planning (ERP) applications such as Microsoft Business Products, Sage Software products, SAP Business products, and Microsoft Visual Studio.

This book covers the basic design of reports for the developer who is just getting started in the Crystal Reports standalone version and then moves into the more advanced functionality as you embed Crystal Reports into web and windows applications to fit your custom needs. For the Crystal Reports for Enterprise XI 4.0 users, this book introduces users to the new platform and discusses how to design reports using the new semantic layer. Enterprise users will benefit from both sections of the book due to the ability to run the standalone and the Enterprise version side by side, which gives users the ability to migrate at their own pace. Throughout this book, you will explore the real-world scenarios of corporations that require total control over reporting or the slight modification of the tool to meet businesses' reporting requirements.

WHAT'S NEW IN CRYSTAL REPORTS

With the release of Crystal Reports 2011, Systems, Applications, Products (SAP) has split the enterprise and the standalone versions again as part of a strategic platform change. Subsequent versions will migrate them back into one version. The new features implemented into Crystal Reports 2011 standalone are few compared to the release of Crystal Reports 2008. However, the Crystal Reports for Enterprise XI 4.0 version is packed full of features for enterprise level users. This book has something for both types of users. The drastic platform change in the Enterprise version allows the developers, advanced business users, and large corporate ERP organizations to take advantage of the semantic layer.

Crystal Reports 2011

Crystal Reports 2011 maintained the Crystal Reports 2008 graphical user interface. SAP developers' primary focus on this release was to start the platform change; therefore, the features in the standalone version are minimal but very beneficial to the everyday business users who export their reports. Fear not; the next release is sure not to disappoint. The new features, shown in Figure 1.1, include:

- Export in a read-only format. (Allows designers to protect their design work.)
- Export into Excel 2007 through the Designer (.xlsx)

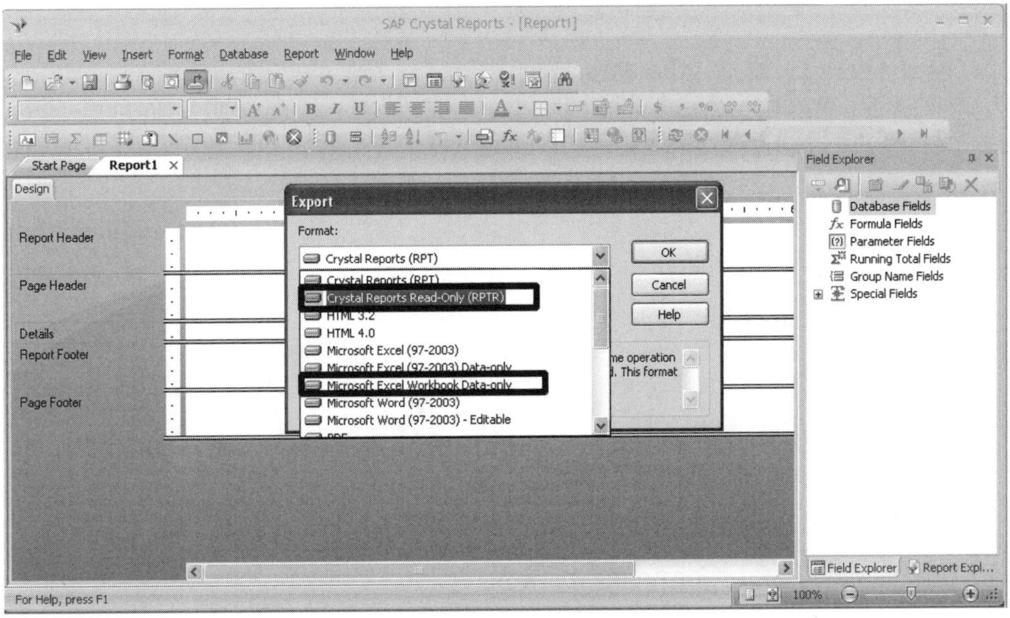

Figure 1.1
New Export features.

- Export into Excel 2007 through the Viewer (.xlsx)
- New tutorial videos on the Start page

Crystal Reports for Visual Studio 2010 .Net

Crystal Reports for Visual Studio 2010 included enhancements for the Windows Presentation Foundation (WPF) Viewer, a set of API enhancements for easier Report Designer Component (RDC) migration. The Crystal Reports .Net version also includes a single runtime engine for embedded reports in .Net applications, whereas earlier versions included two runtime versions. The book covers those enhancements in later chapters.

.Net developers will have the flexibility to program in multiple languages. The improved enhancements of Crystal Reports for Visual Studio allow developers to create custom toolbars, which helps to extend the Crystal Reports Server to meet their custom needs. One important issue to note: You cannot build applications utilizing the .Net SDK with the initial release of Crystal Reports 2011. That feature is expected to be included in the release of version 4.1.

Tip

Crystal Reports for Visual Studio 2010 included many new features for report designers. Crystal Reports 2011 was not included in the out-of-the-box installation of Microsoft Visual Studio 2010, but is provided as a free download from http://www.businessobjects.com/jump/xi/crvs2010/default. asp.

The new features include:

- Parameter panel for Report Consumers
- Sort control
- Saved Data Sort control
- Dynamic Cascading parameters
- Optional parameters
- Multi-Value SQL Command parameters
- More advanced formatting options in the Section Expert
- Flexible pagination
- Easier report viewers
- Embedded Flash capability
- Export to XLSX
- Export to XML
- New WPF Viewer
- Easier to migrate Report Designer Component (RDC) applications
- Dynamic Cascading parameters
- Single runtime engine for embedded reports in Visual Studio 2010

Crystal Reports Enterprise XI 4.0

Crystal Reports Enterprise XI 4.0 encompassed a major update and redesign of the report designer and associated process servers. This version of Crystal Reports 2011 is focused on those corporate users using the Enterprise Server. As mentioned earlier, this version is new and has advanced functionality that will engage the ERP users.

Some of the many new features of Crystal Reports of Enterprise XI 4.0 are:

- A friendlier user interface for designers (shown in Figure 1.2)
- Use of the semantic layer
- Beginning of cross-product harmonization
- Streamlined report design
- Easier transition between business objects Web Intelligence (WebI) to Crystal Reports
- Tabular layout
- Navigation panel
- Extensive new charting features
- Better analysis with OLAP data warehouses
- Multisource common semantic layer
- Tight integration with OLAP BEX query SAP
- True 64-bit native server platform
- Improved multi-lingual capabilities
- Platform-driven alerting

This version has been well designed but excludes several features that can be accessed only through the standalone version. The ability to run the standalone version side by side with the Enterprise XI 4.0 version allows you to still take advantage of the features that are included only in the Crystal Reports 2011 standalone version. The excluded features are:

- No direct to data support
- No direct to OLAP support
- No Java or .Net Crystal Reports SDK for SAP Business Objects Enterprise
- No Live Office support
- No Enterprise search

These features are expected to be included in future update releases.

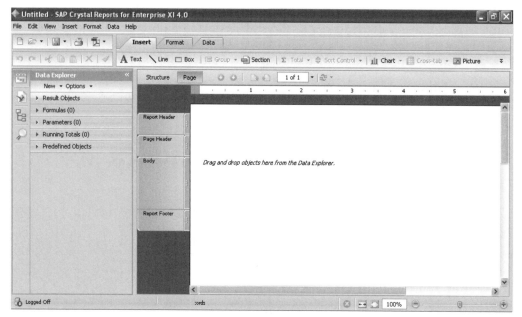

Figure 1.2
SAP Crystal Reports for Enterprise XI 4.0 user interface.

CRYSTAL REPORTS FOR JAVA DEVELOPERS

With the release of Crystal Reports 2008, SAP released a product for Java developers wishing to embed Crystal Reports into a Java application, equivalent to the functionality that .Net application developers have in the new single version. Crystal Reports for Eclipse is an intuitive reporting solution. It contains a runtime solution engine, viewers that can be embedded into thick client or web-based Java applications, a report design tool, and a tooling and software development kit (SDK) to assist in the embedding of the Crystal Reports runtime engine.

Tip

> This software is provided free of charge as a download. You can download Crystal Reports for Eclipse from http://www.businessobjects.com/campaigns/forms/downloads/crystal/eclipse/datasave. asp.

Crystal Reports for Eclipse, shown in Figure 1.3, enables Java developers the full functionality of the standard version of Crystal Reports that was missing in versions prior to Crystal Reports version 2008.

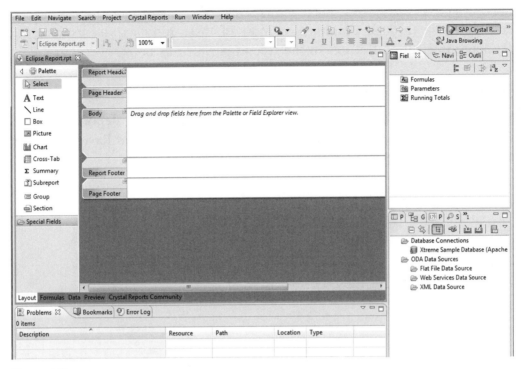

Figure 1.3
Crystal Reports for Eclipse user interface.

This version includes the powerful dynamic and cascading parameters, optional parameters, and the new parameter panel that allows users to change the parameter values without opening the parameter box or accessing the database again. The developers also now have the ability to use the report sort control option, which will give the end user the capability to resort the data in ascending or descending order on the fly. One of the most powerful features enabled with the Eclipse version is the integration capability of the Adobe Flash objects, which allows users to embed interactive visual charts that can be used in a "What If" analysis scenario. All of the previous capabilities included in the Java SDK for Crystal Reports 2008 will remain with version 2011.

With the first release of Crystal Reports 2011, customers will be able to build Java applications to view, manage, and schedule reports. They can use the Java SDK and the Crystal Reports standalone designer or the Crystal Reports for Enterprise XI 4.0 Report Designer.

You will walk through examples of most of these tools as you explore the developer integration features in the second part of this book.

SUMMARY

Now that you have been introduced to the powers of Crystal Reports, the next step is to get to know the Crystal Reports environment and start having fun. The next chapter explores the Crystal Reports environment.

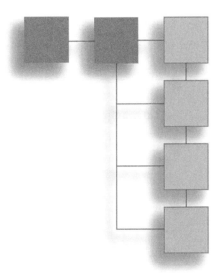

CHAPTER 2

GETTING STARTED

The objectives of this chapter are to learn the following tasks:

- Gather report requirements
- Customize the environment
- Understand the Start page
- Explore the Design window
- Explore the explorers
- Explore the toolbars

This chapter discusses the methodology needed to start designing reports in Crystal Reports. If you are an experienced user, you can skip ahead to Chapter 6 to learn about the more advanced features of the application. If you are a beginner, Chapters 1–5 will get you well on your way to becoming a comfortable designer.

GATHERING REPORT REQUIREMENTS

Many times users have an idea of what they want to create but lack the foundation to build it successfully. The most important part of writing a successful report begins with gathering report requirements. Often people know what they want out of a report but find it difficult to explain the requirements to the developer. There are five basic questions that a report developer should address prior to opening Crystal Reports. They are:

- **What**? – The purpose of the report, the desired end result or distribution method (for example, PDF, Excel export, TXT file, CSV file, email, and so on), aggregations, formulas, grouping, and sorting.

- **Who**? – The audience, as in who will be viewing the data, management versus staff level. Reports should be designed for the user and not for the developer.

- **When**? – Determine the timeframe of the report and frequency. This question will determine the need for a date field or a parameter.

- **Why**? – This question sometime draws a negative response. It's important to ask why the user needs this data in order to ensure the report is pulling the correct data. Often people think they know what they need; however, when it is provided it does not meet their needs. It is imperative that the report developer understand the database that they are utilizing for their reports. This will ensure that they clearly understand the needs of the business users.

- **How**? – Where is the information coming from? What data sources will it be coming from? Is it new data or an existing data source? This will require that you have knowledge of the database, including a data schema or data dictionary that lists and explains the tables and fields.

These answers should be compiled and recorded on a Report Requirements document. There are many sources for a Report Requirements template.

CUSTOMIZING THE ENVIRONMENT

Organizations often have a standard policy for formatting reports. Therefore, users should customize their Crystal Reports environments to meet those standards and not format each report individually. Most users fail to take advantage of this capability. There are Options and Report Options that allow developers to format their systems to meet their business needs. Any feature changes in the Options window will be global and apply to all reports; changes in the Report Options will apply only to that individual report.

There are many useful options to set; I will only highlight some of the more useful ones at this time.

To access the global options, choose File > Options from the drop-down menu, as shown in Figure 2.1.

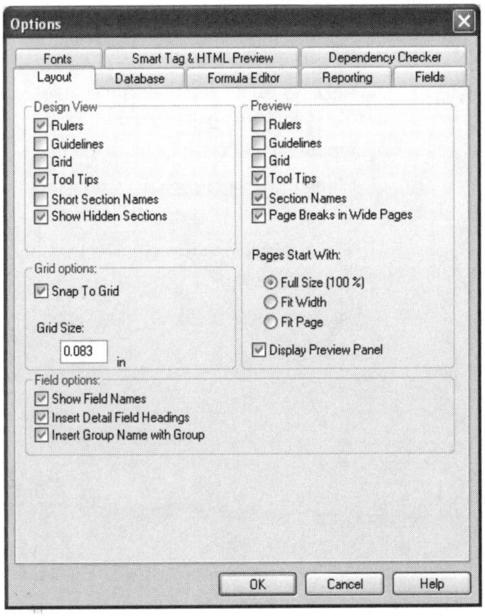

Figure 2.1
Customizing the global options.

The Layout Tab

On the Layout tab, you can format the Design view and Preview screens to fit your comfort level, as shown in Table 2.1. You have the ability to format the Design view differently from the Preview screen based on your desired preference.

Grid Options

You can also format the grid spacing on the report to ensure exact spacing or to allow free-form placement using the Grid Option formatting options shown in Figure 2.2.

Table 2.1 Design View and Preview Format Options

Option	Design View	Preview View	Description
Show Guidelines	X	X	Displays guidelines on the tab.
Grids	X	X	Displays a grid in the background. Used to snap field to the closest dot.
Rulers	X	X	Displays rulers on the tabs.
Show Tooltips	X	X	Displays the name of a button when mouse is hovered.
Short Section Names	X		Displays abbreviated section names. Gives you the ability to see more of the report on the screen.
Show Hidden Sections	X		Hidden and Suppressed sections are shown in the Design tab.
Section Name		X	Shows abbreviated section names on the Preview tab.
Page Breaks in Wide Pages		X	Displays page break in wide report pages.

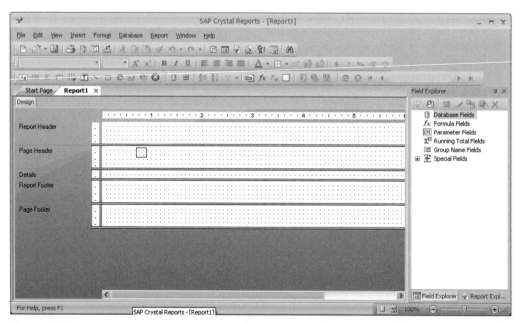

Figure 2.2
Setting the grid's options.

- **Snap to Grid** – When you place a field on the report it snaps to the closest dot on the grid. Uncheck the option and you will have total free-form placement. The field will stay where you place the field on the report. It is checked by default.

- **Grid Size** – If you have Snap to Grid checked, this option will allow you to set the grid increments.

The Database Tab

On the Database tab, shown in Figure 2.3, I recommend developers turn off the default Automatic Smart Linking option located in the Advanced Options section in order to make certain their tables are linked efficiently to extract the desired dataset.

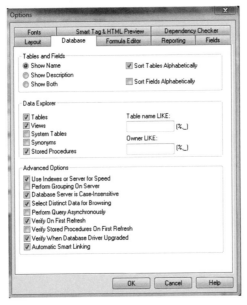

Figure 2.3
The Database tab's options.

Using the Automatic Smart Linking feature allows Crystal Reports to link the tables without user intervention. Crystal Reports will link every common field found. The more fields that are linked, the more restrictive your dataset will be, because all records must have matching criteria to all fields that are linked.

Also, the Perform Grouping on Server option can speed up the processing of your report when available.

The Formula Editor Tab

Many times the default font in the formula workshop appears too small. You can change the font face and size for easier use on the Formula Editor tab, shown in Figure 2.4. One of the most disregarded features is the ability to change the way Crystal Reports handles null values. The default is to force the developer to write an Exception clause using the IsNull function. However, you can change the method to use Default Values for Null. Crystal Reports will then handle null values as a zero or blank depending upon the field's datatype. Certain scenarios will necessitate one null choice over the other.

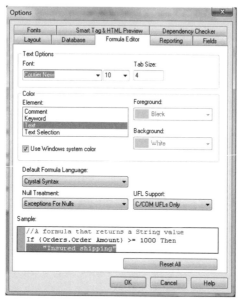

Figure 2.4
The Formula Editor's options.

The Reporting Tab

Depending upon the sensitivity of your data, you may want to consider deselecting the Save Data with Report option on the Reporting tab (shown in Figure 2.5) to prevent the data from being displayed prior to logging in to the database. Otherwise, users without the correct permissions can view the last previewed sensitive data upon opening the report. This also requires users to refresh the report before viewing up-to-date information. This feature can be set in global options or for each individual report using the File > Report Options command.

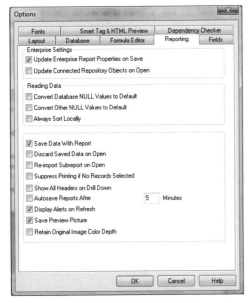

Figure 2.5
Reporting tab's options.

The Fields Tab

Organizations often have a standard format for certain field types. Instead of formatting each of your fields individually on each report, you can set the default formats for each different datatype. For example, the Number field defaults to two decimals but your organization's default is to have no decimals. This can be achieved by changing the default option on the Fields tab, shown in Figure 2.6. All other datatypes can be formatted here as well.

The Fonts Tab

Some organizations have a corporate font to be used in all reports. Based on the types of fields, you can establish a font face, style, and size such as a text object, summary field, or Group Name field, all from the Font tab, shown in Figure 2.7.

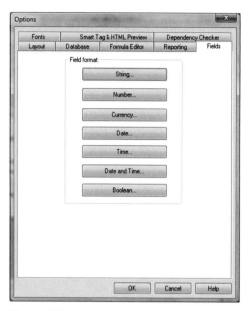

Figure 2.6
Setting the Field tab's formats.

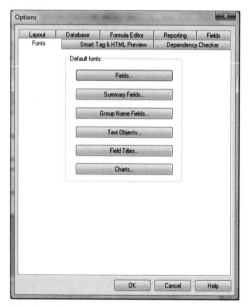

Figure 2.7
Setting the default fonts for your field types.

USING THE START PAGE

The first page that you will see when opening Crystal Reports is the Start page, shown in Figure 2.8. The Start page allows you to start a new report or open an existing one. A new feature of the Start page enables you to access the official tutorials from the eLearning tab located at the bottom of the page.

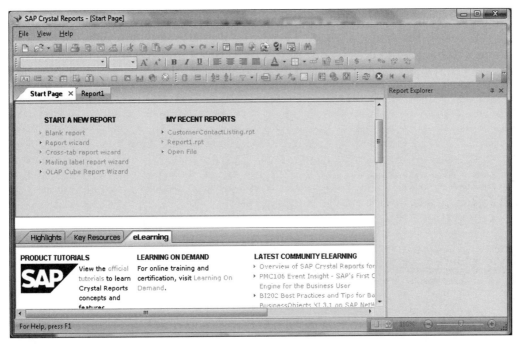

Figure 2.8
Getting familiar with the Start page.

You can create a new report from the Blank Report option or using the Report Wizard. However, I recommend that you create a report using the Blank Report option to fully understand the functionality of Crystal Reports. The wizard walks you through selecting individual tasks but does not require you to understand what and how the system is accomplishing your tasks. Consequently, when your report does not look the way you expected, you may have difficulty modifying the structure because you don't understand the steps of the wizard. For example, if the grouping is incorrect or the filtering of the dataset does not meet your requirements, you'll need to know how to adjust them.

To utilize the Report Wizard, click on the Report Wizard link on the Start page. This wizard will walk you through connecting to your database, selecting fields, grouping, and so on. To open an existing report, use the Open File link on this page or use the Open button on the standard toolbar, shown here.

USING THE DATABASE EXPERT WINDOW

The Database Expert window, shown in Figure 2.9, is the most important window when designing reports. This window controls which data source you connect to in order to create your report. It is important that you understand the proper way to connect to your data source to make sure security and all fields are available.

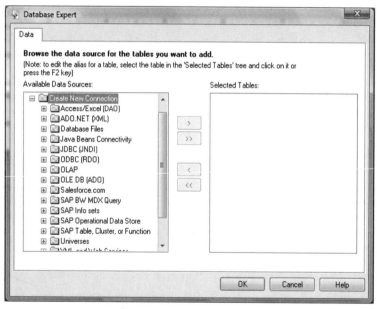

Figure 2.9
Connecting to a data source.

In the Database Expert window, two options are available:

- **My Connections** – Shows all connections you are currently connected to.

- **Create New Connections** – Shows the various data source connections that you can connect to.

An Open Database Connectivity (ODBC) connection is the most common data driver used. The list of available data source connections depends on the features that have been installed on your computer. New available data sources include SAP BW MDX Query, SAP Info Sets, SAP Operational Data Store, SAP Table, Cluster, or Function. Connecting to a data source through the Database Expert window is covered thoroughly in Chapter 3.

Exploring the Design Window

Before you can start to design reports, it's important that you familiarize yourself with the Design window. Crystal Reports includes multiple toolbars. However, the following five toolbars appear by default and will be discussed in more detail in this section.

- The Standard toolbar
- The Formatting toolbar
- The Insert toolbar
- The Expert toolbar
- The Navigation toolbar

The Standard Toolbar

The Standard toolbar, shown in Figure 2.10, allows you to create a new report using the wizard, open an existing report, as well as save, print, print preview, and export the report. You can also access other design-related features, such as the Field Explorer, the Preview panel, the Repository, and the Workbench. These tasks can be accessed from the File drop-down menu or the View drop-down menu.

Figure 2.10
Using the Standard toolbar.

The Formatting Toolbar

The Formatting toolbar, shown in Figure 2.11, allows you to change the font, alignment, borders, and decimal places, suppress objects in your reports, and lock the format, position, and size of the fields. This toolbar is enabled only when a field is selected. These tasks can be accessed from the Format drop-down menu.

Figure 2.11
Using the Formatting toolbar.

The Insert Toolbar

The Insert toolbar, shown in Figure 2.12, is used to insert text objects, logos, lines, boxes, summaries, subreports, and other objects. These tasks are accessible from the Insert drop-down menu.

Figure 2.12
Using the Insert toolbar.

The Expert Toolbar

The Expert toolbar, shown in Figure 2.13, is used to access the Database Expert, Group Expert, Select Expert, and Record Sort, commands, as well as other Expert-related tasks. These tasks are accessible from the Database drop-down menu and the Report drop-down menu.

Figure 2.13
Using the Expert toolbar.

The Navigation Toolbar

The Navigation toolbar, shown in Figure 2.14, holds the page navigator buttons and Refresh button. You can access Refresh option from the Report drop-down menu (choose Report > Refresh Report Data or press F5). The page navigator buttons can only be accessed from this toolbar.

Figure 2.14
Using the Navigation toolbar.

Exploring the Report Design Tab

The Design tab, shown in Figure 2.15, is the template view where the report is designed and organized. You will insert fields, groups, report titles, special fields, logos, and more on the report from the Design tab. You will not see the actual data from your database in Design view, only the templates of the fields.

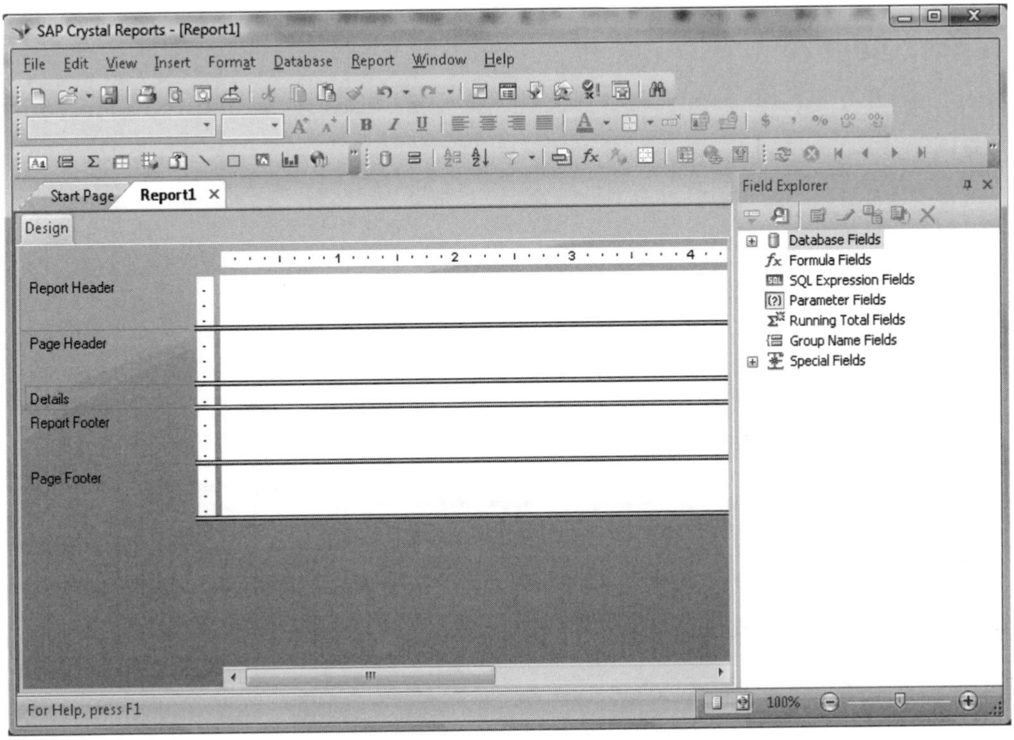

Figure 2.15
The Report Design tab.

You can also zoom in or out of the Report tab using the Zoom level feature located in the bottom-right corner of the design window.

The Preview Tab

 After inserting all fields into the design tab, to see the data from your connected data source you must view the report in Preview. The Preview tab will not be visible until you choose the Print Preview option for the first time

from Design view. To access the Print Preview option, you can choose View > Print Preview from the drop-down menu or using the Print Preview button to preview the report. The Preview tab is considered the old WYSIWYG view. This view will display how the report will print.

As you are now somewhat familiar with the toolbars, it's time to learn where the fields, logos, and more can be placed in the report design template.

Report Sections

There are five default report sections in the report design window, as shown in Figure 2.16.

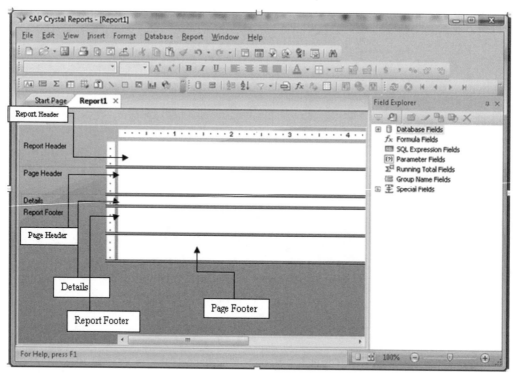

Figure 2.16
The Report Design window.

These default report sections are as defined as follows:

- **Report Header**—Objects placed in the Report header will print only on the first page of the report. For example, report titles.

- **Page Header**—Objects placed in the Page headers will appear at the top of each page of the report. For example, column labels or page titles can be placed in this section.

- **Details Section**—Fields to be read for every record in the database should be placed in this section. The Details section is the most important section in the design view.

- **Report Footer**—Objects placed in the Report footer will appear on the last page of the report. For example, grand totals should be placed in this section.

- **Page Footer**—Objects placed in the Page footer will appear at the bottom of each page of the report. For example, the page number or print date and time normally appear in this section.

There are two additional sections that will appear after you insert a group, as follows:

- **Group Header**—The Group Header section displays the name of the corresponding group or column labels needed for each group.

- **Group Footer**—The Group Footer section displays aggregated totals for the corresponding group.

EXPLORING THE EXPLORERS

There are five explorers that you can use in Crystal Reports to maneuver through the reporting system. They are as follows:

- The Field Explorer
- The Report Explorer
- The Repository Explorer
- The Workbench
- The Dependency Checker

The Field Explorer

The Field Explorer, located by default on the right side of the report's Design window, is the task pane where the majority of your tasks on your report will be performed. It is also the first step to inserting the fields on your report. Under the database folder, you will see the table(s) that you added to your report through the Database Expert. Click the + sign next to the appropriate table; you will see all fields that are available from the corresponding table. See Figure 2.17.

Figure 2.17
The Field Explorer task pane.

The Field Explorer can be docked at the top, bottom, left, or right of your Design window by selecting the title bar of the Field Explorer and dragging to the desired location. You can auto-hide the Field Explorer to view more of the report window by right-clicking on the title bar and selecting Autohide.

You can create and edit formulas, SQL expressions, running totals, and parameters. The Field Explorer also displays any special fields or group name fields in the report. Special fields include the print date and time, file author, file path and name, page numbers, and many other report fields. The Field Explorer can be pinned down using the pushpin, moved to other locations of the window, and docked or closed for more screen view. If the Field Explorer is closed, you can reopen it by using the View > Field Explorer drop-down menu or by clicking the Field Explorer icon on the Standard toolbar.

The Report Explorer

The Report Explorer displays, in a tree-like view, the fields that are on the report and in what section the fields are located. Fields can be modified directly from the Report Explorer by right-clicking on the field and choosing the desired option. For example, if you select a text field, right-click and choose Edit Text, you can change the text of that field. Formulas can be modified, the Select Expert can be accessed, and many other normal operations can be accessed using the right-click context menu. See Figure 2.18.

Figure 2.18
Using the Report Explorer.

The Report Explorer is located on the right side of the window by default but can be moved to other locations on the screen and docked by using the pushpin or closed for more screen view. If the Report Explorer is closed, you can reopen it by using the View > Report Explorer option from the drop-down menu or by clicking the Report Explorer icon on the Standard toolbar.

 The Report Explorer has its own mini toolbar. The Show/Hide Data Fields button allows you to toggle the data fields on or off in tree view. The Show/Hide Graphical button allows you to toggle any charts, OLE objects, lines, and so on, on or off in the tree view. The Show/Hide Grids and Subreports button allows you to toggle any subreports, crosstabs, or OLAP grids on or off in the tree view.

The Repository Explorer

 The Repository Explorer is used to save and share common objects to a central location using the SAP Business Objects Enterprise Repository. Text objects, bitmaps, SQL commands, and custom functions can be saved to the repository. You must have Crystal Reports Server or SAP Crystal Reports Enterprise to use the repository. It requires a logon to the server in order to save objects. If the Repository Explorer has been closed, it can be reopened by using the View > Repository Explorer drop-down menu or by clicking the Repository Explorer button, on the Standard toolbar. The Repository Explorer has its separate toolbar, shown at the top of Figure 2-19.

Figure 2.19
Logging on to the Repository Explorer.

 The View Settings icon on the toolbar allows users to select the items they want to see in the Repository. You can view Text Objects, Report Commands, Bitmaps, Repository Command Groups, or List of Values, as shown in Figure 2.20.

The Advanced Filtering Settings icon on the toolbar allows users to filter the items shown based on a word or author. When the icon is clicked, the filter appears at the bottom of the task pane.

The Delete Item icon on the toolbar allows users to delete the selected item stored in the repository.

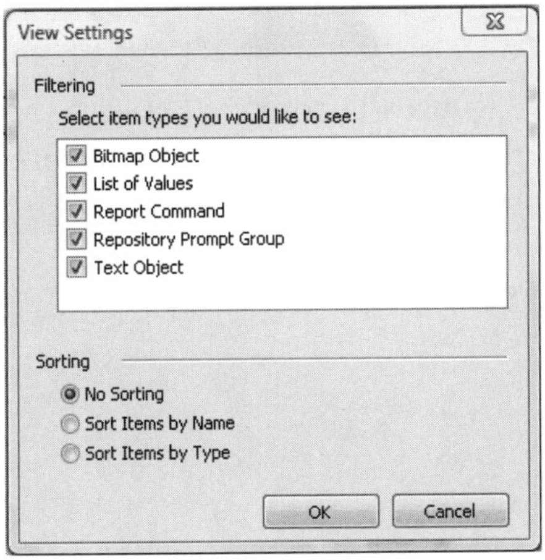

Figure 2.20
The View Settings window.

The Insert New Folder icon on the toolbar allows users to create a new folder to organize items stored in the repository.

Using the Workbench

The Workbench, shown in Figure 2.21, is used to organize your reports in your desired structure. You can create new folders and move, rename or reorganize them into folders, as well as drag and drop reports from Window Explorer into Workbench.

Figure 2.21
You can organize reports in Workbench.

Browsing the Dependency Checker

The Dependency Checker, shown in Figure 2.22, is used in conjunction with the Workbench to verify Report Part hyperlink errors, formula compilation errors, and repository object errors.

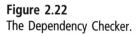

Figure 2.22
The Dependency Checker.

SUMMARY

You should now be familiar with gathering report requirements and the Crystal Reports design window. It's now time to move into creating a new report.

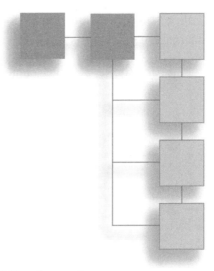

CHAPTER 3

CREATING A REPORT

The objectives of this chapter are to learn the following tasks:

- Connecting to a data source
- Adding tables to a report
- Inserting fields
- Working with objects
- Saving a report
- Previewing a report

Earlier chapters discussed the Design window and all of the toolbars needed to navigate Crystal Reports. Now you'll learn how to create a report. After gathering the report requirements, the first step in creating a report is to connect to a data source. As mentioned before, it's better to design from a blank report than use the Report Wizard.

CREATING AN EXAMPLE REPORT

Consider this scenario. Management has requested a list of customers' information including customer ID, customer name, contact email, and phone number. Due to the fact that this information is constantly updated, it's better to link the report to the database to ensure up-to-date information at all times rather than create a one-time static report.

Follow these steps to begin to create a sample report based on the previous scenario:

1. From the Start page, click on Blank report, as shown in Figure 3.1.

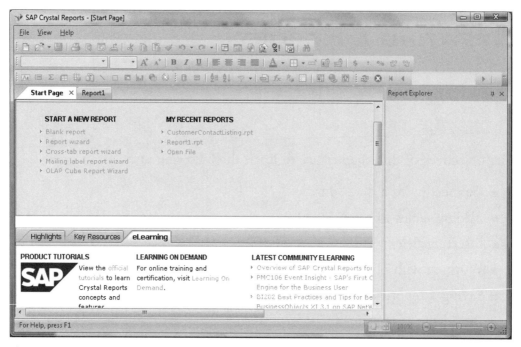

Figure 3.1
The Start page.

The Database Expert window opens. You can connect Crystal Reports to many data sources through multiple types of native or ODBC-type driver connections.

For the purpose of this book, we will use the Xtreme Sample Database and connect through an ODBC connection.

2. Click the + sign next to the Create New Connection option. Scroll down and click the + sign next to the ODBC connection option or double-click the ODBC connection. This will open the ODBC data source

connections that are currently installed on your computer. Locate and select the Xtreme Sample database in the list.

3. Click Next. This window allows you to enter a user ID and password for any secured databases.

Tip

It is not recommended that you enter a user ID and password into the data source connections because it may give unwanted users access to your database.

4. Click Finish. You will see that the Xtreme Sample Database is now connected. The Add Command option and the tree folders—Tables, Views, and Stored Procedures—are listed under the ODBC connection. Each ODBC connection will have the ability to connect to tables, views, and stored procedures. The Add Command option allows you to write an ad-hoc SQL command for the data source. This feature is very handy when you don't have the ability to add a stored procedure or view to the actual database because of a third-party ownership.

Tip

This is when it's a good idea to have the data dictionary or data schema of the database available. As mentioned, the data dictionary will give you a complete view of the database structure. Select the correct tables that store the requested information.

5. Click (+) next to Tables, double-click the Customer table, or click on the right-pointing arrow. See Figure 3.2.

6. Click OK.

7. Once you have connected the data source and selected the tables, the Design window opens. Click on the (+) sign next to the Database Fields option in the Field Explorer to expand the list of tables that you have selected. Click the (+) again next to the table name to see the fields that are available in the table. See Figure 3.3.

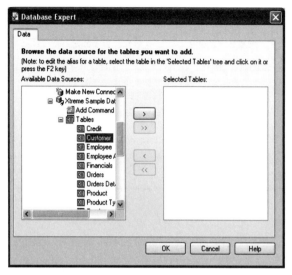

Figure 3.2
Select the table.

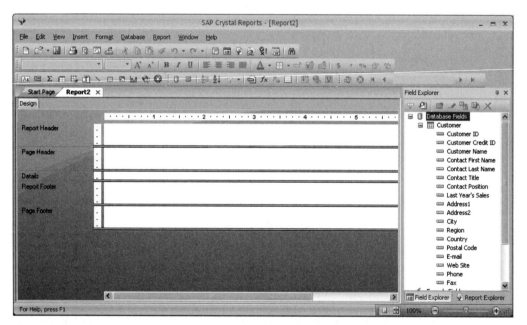

Figure 3.3
The database fields in the Field Explorer.

INSERTING FIELDS INTO A REPORT

There are several ways to enter fields into a report. The most commonly used method is to use the drag-and-drop method.

1. Select the Customer ID field, hold down the left mouse button, and drag over to the left margin of the Details section. Release the mouse button.

2. Select the Customer Name field and then right-click and choose Insert to Report, as shown in Figure 3.4. Move your mouse over to Details and click to the right of the Customer ID field.

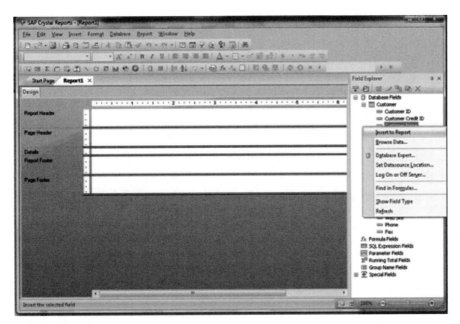

Figure 3.4
Inserting a field using the Context menu.

3. Select the Email field in the Field Explorer, and then go up to the Field Explorer toolbar and select the Insert to Report button, as shown in Figure 3.5.

4. The field is attached to your mouse cursor. Move the cursor to the Details section and click to the right of the Customer name field.

5. Select the Phone field in the Field Explorer and add it to the Details section using any of the methods mentioned previously.

Figure 3.5
Inserting a field using the toolbar.

SAVING A REPORT

Now that you have created your report, it's important to save it. Saving your report at crucial intervals during your design work can save you from losing your work if the application fails. With the Crystal Reports 2008 version, SAP added additional Save options that can help small organizations distribute their reports.

To save your report, choose File > Save from the drop-down menu or click the Save button on the Standard toolbar. The Save As dialog box will appear, as shown in Figure 3.6. You can save the report in any location of your choice on your computer or on the Crystalreports.com server using the CR.COM icon on the left of the window. CrystalReports.com allows up to three named users to distribute reports via the web free of charge for an unlimited time period.

You can save your report to the Repository using the Enterprise connection or My Connection options. You will explore each of these options later in the book.

Tip

Always save your report before previewing for the first time, particularly if you have a report with multiple linked tables. If the tables are not linked together properly, the application will stop responding and you will have to exit the program using Ctrl+Alt+Del. Consequently, you will lose all of your unsaved work.

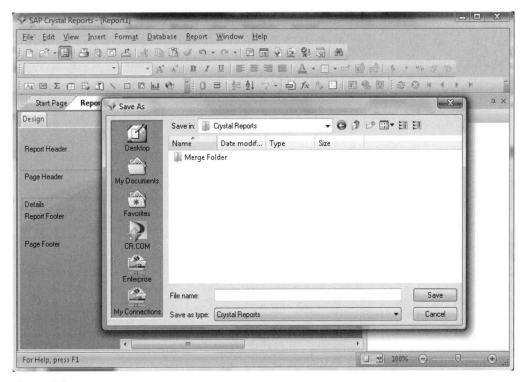

Figure 3.6
Saving a report.

To save the report, follow these steps:

1. Click the Save button on the Standard toolbar.

2. Change the location to the desired folder.

3. Save the report as **CustomerContactListing**. You should always save the report before previewing the data. Notice the Report tab now displays the saved report's name.

PREVIEWING YOUR REPORT

Until the report is previewed for the first time, the Preview tab is not visible. The Preview window shows you exactly how the report will look when it is printed. It shows the WYSIWYG (What You See Is What You Get) view.

To preview the report, you can access Print Preview from the View > Print Preview drop-down menu or from the Print Preview button on the Standard toolbar.

On the left side of the preview window is the Preview panel, shown in Figure 3.7.

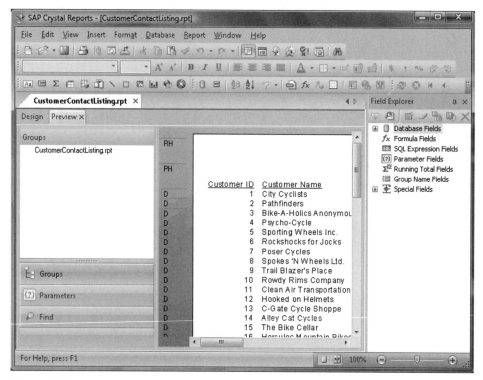

Figure 3.7
The Preview panel.

The Preview panel is made up of three panels. The Groups panel displays all groups included in the report in a tree like view. You can view or hide this Groups panel by using the Toggle Preview Panel button. See Figure 3.8.

The Groups panel is discussed in more detail in the next chapter.

The Parameters panel, which was introduced in Crystal Reports version 2008, allows users to interactively work with parameters without forcing the database to refresh. The user can set up options for each parameter to appear in the panel. The Parameters panel is discussed in more detail in Chapter 7.

Figure 3.8
Using the Preview panel.

The Find Tab allows users to search the report for a specific word. The Find feature works exactly as it does in other applications. Type in the word to search for and then click the magnifying glass.

You can change the options by clicking the drop-down next to the magnifying glass to select Match Case or Match Whole Word Only.

As you preview the report you just designed, you may notice some of your fields are not wide enough to show the complete name of the customer. You can resize and move the fields with ease.

WORKING WITH OBJECTS

There are times when a field is just too wide based on your data or too short to show all the database data, which results in your data being truncated. You can resize the fields by selecting the field; you will notice the active indicators around the field. Put your mouse on the left or right edge of the field to get a two-headed arrow and move right to lengthen the field or left to shorten the field. When you put the mouse on the top-middle or bottom-middle active indicator, you can lengthen or shorten the height of the field.

Caution

If your data from the database is stored in uppercase letters, it will require more space between fields, which might cause the fields to overlap. To fix this issue, ensure that the fields are wide enough to accommodate all uppercase letters or convert the fields to proper case using the `propercase` function in the formulas area.

In this particular report, the customer name field is truncated, so you need to widen the field. However, notice that widening that field will overlap the email field. You'll need to move and reorganize the fields in order to have the correct spacing. You can move fields left or right using *guidelines.* Guidelines are the arrowheads located on the ruler when a field is placed in the report sections. Unless the Global options have been changed to display guidelines in Preview, you must be in Design view to work with guidelines. See Figure 3.9.

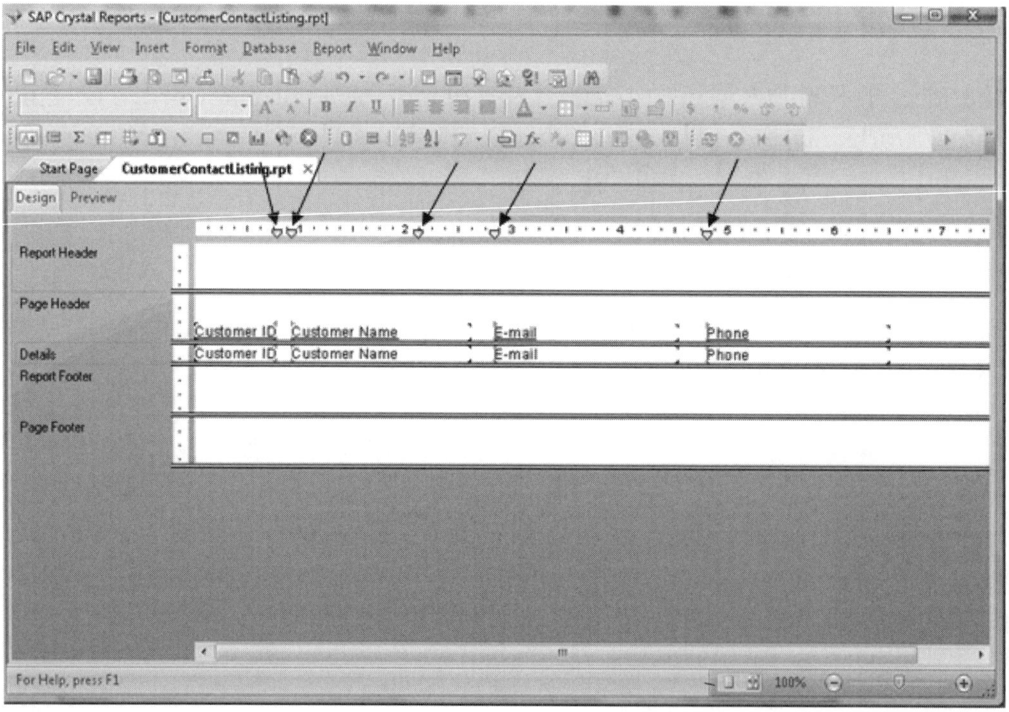

Figure 3.9
Guidelines in Design view.

You will notice the field is attached to a guideline by the red edge on the left side of any text field and right edge of numerical fields. Follow these steps to adjust a field:

1. Switch to Design view of the report.

2. Click the arrowhead on the Ruler for the Phone field and move it slowly to the right, to the 6-inch mark on the ruler.

3. Click the arrowhead on the Ruler for the Email field and move it slowly to the right to the 3.5-inch mark on the ruler.

4. Select the Email field, place your cursor on the active indicator on the right edge of the field, and drag to the right to widen the field.

5. Select the Customer Name field, place your cursor on the active indicator on the right of the field, and widen the field to the 3.2-inch mark on the ruler. See Figure 3.10.

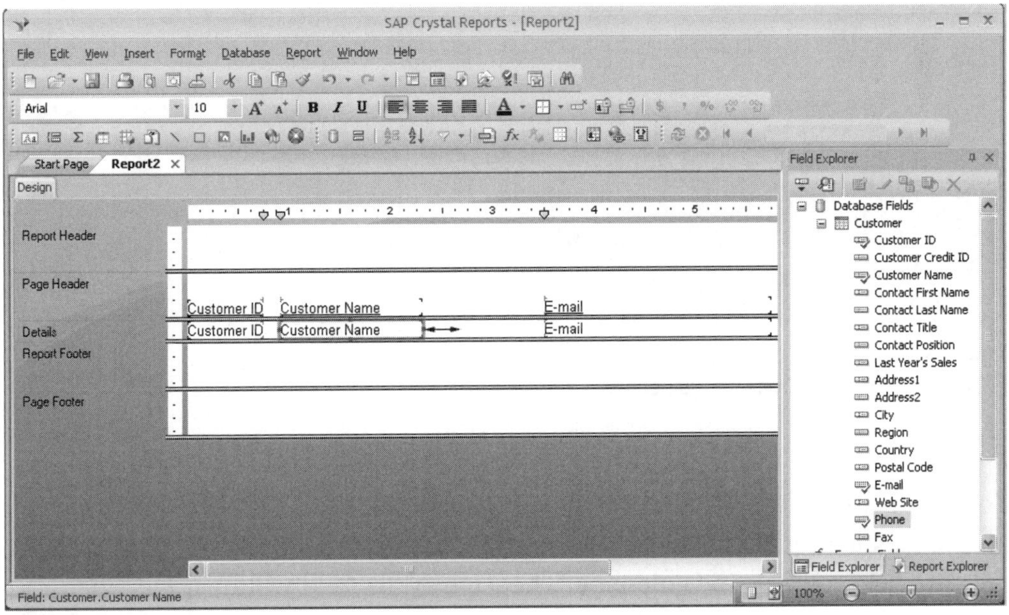

Figure 3.10
Resizing a field using the active indicator.

6. Preview the report now. Notice that the Customer Name field is no longer truncated.

MOVING OBJECTS

At times you may inadvertently move the field away from the guidelines, as shown in Figure 3.11.

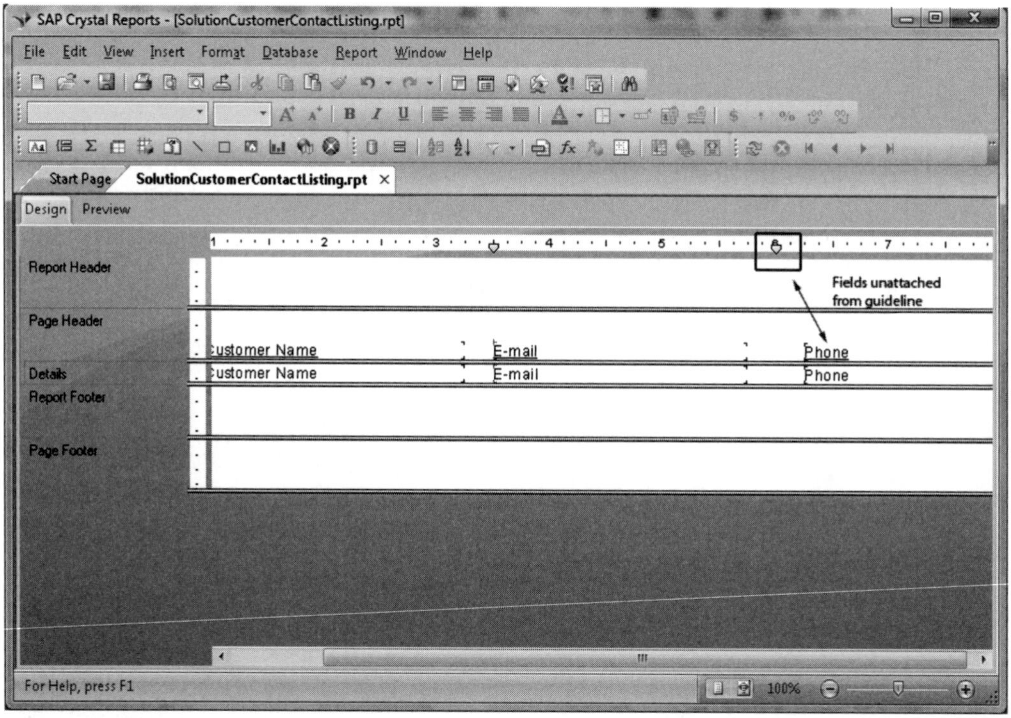

Figure 3.11
Fields are unattached from the guideline.

You can reattach the fields to the guidelines by selecting the field, hovering the mouse cursor over the field until you get a four-headed arrow, and then moving the data field towards the guideline. The edge of the field will turn red when it is attached. Once the fields are attached, you can once again move both the labels and the data field together.

Moving the column label will detach the label from the data field. However, if you move the data field itself, the column label will move in conjunction with the field.

1. Continue using the CustomerContactListing report.

2. Switch to Design view.

3. Move the Customer ID field heading up slightly.

4. Preview the report. Notice the customer ID label is slightly higher than the other column labels on the report.

ALIGNING AND SIZING OBJECTS

When you're inserting and rearranging fields in the report, it's important to maintain proper alignment. Misaligned fields give the report an unprofessional appearance when previewed, as shown in Figures 3.12 and 3.13.

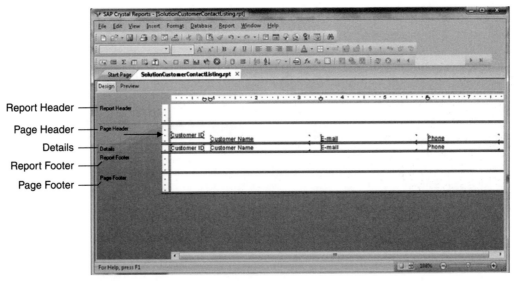

Figure 3.12
A misaligned label.

As you move fields around, you'll find that you'll accidentally move them out of alignment with the other fields in a section. To realign the fields, you should select the field that is out of alignment, hold down the Ctrl key, and then select the field that is properly aligned. Next, release the Ctrl key, right-click and then choose the alignment option you want from the Align options, as shown in Figure 3.14.

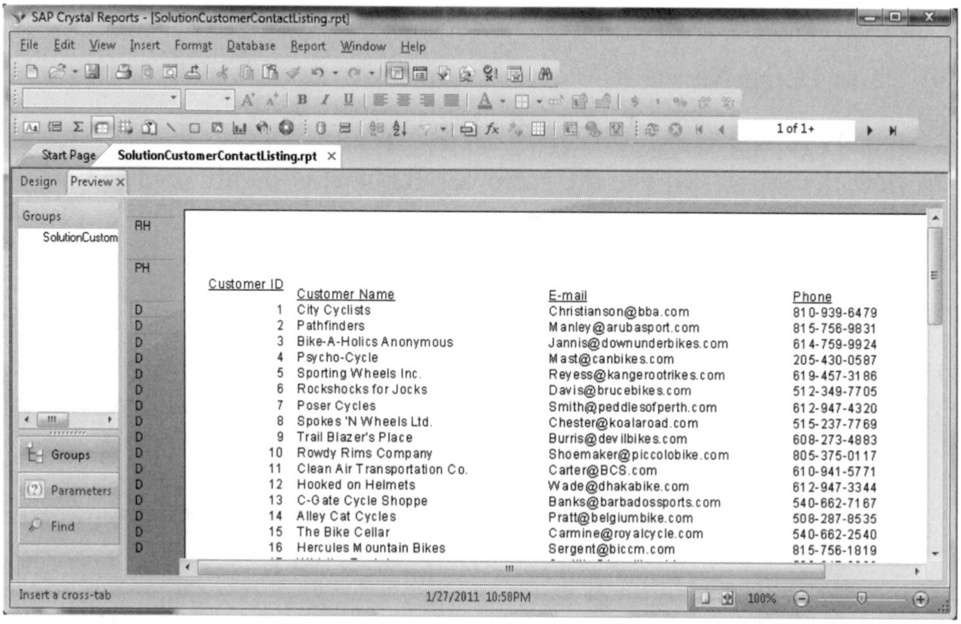

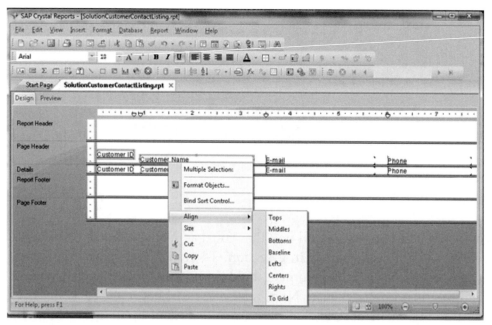

Figure 3.13
The preview of misaligned fields.

Figure 3.14
Alignment options.

Follow these steps to practice field alignment:

1. Switch to Design view.

2. Select the Customer ID label.

3. Hold down the Ctrl key and click on the Customer Name field.

4. Right-click and choose Align > Tops from the context menu. This action will align the column labels again.

5. Preview the report again. Notice the labels are now aligned, as shown in Figure 3.15.

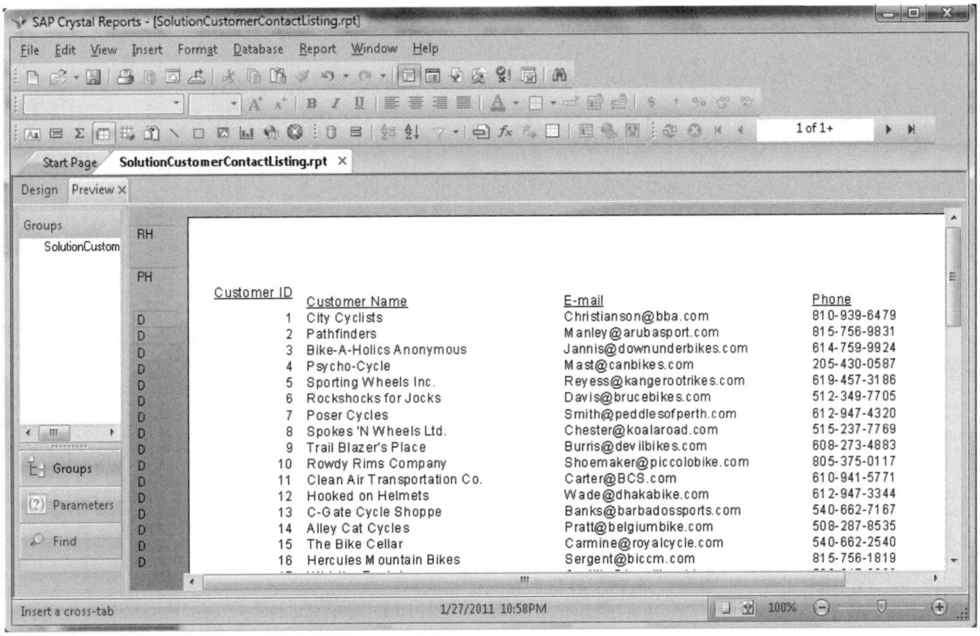

Figure 3.15
Preview of the aligned fields.

The heights of the fields are also an important aspect that a developer must consider. If the heights of all of your fields in the section are not equivalent, the data records may appear out of alignment, as shown in Figure 3.16. Also, if you intend to export your reports to Excel, it is important to make sure the heights are all the same. Otherwise, when the report is exported using Microsoft Excel (97-2003), you will end up with additional rows in the Excel spreadsheet that will require formatting before distributing the spreadsheet.

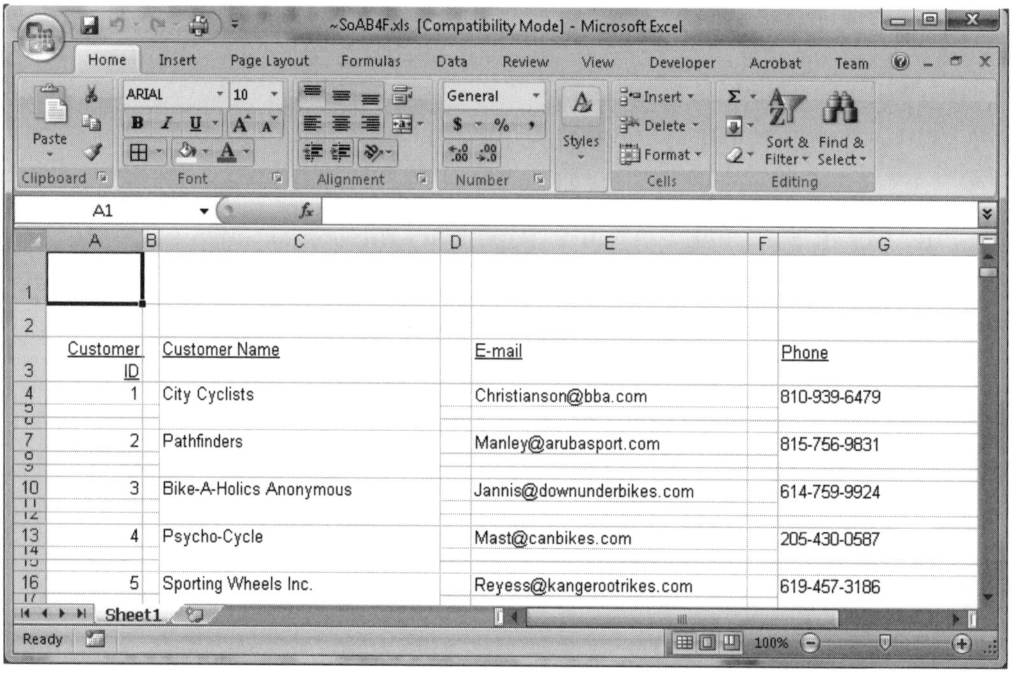

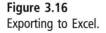

Figure 3.16
Exporting to Excel.

You can modify Height and Width by using the Size feature, which is available only when multiple fields are selected, as shown in Figure 3.17.

The sizing options are listed in Table 3.1.

Follow these steps to practice field sizing:

1. Open Height.rpt, located in the Sample files/Chapter 3 directory.

2. Select the Phone field, Email field, Customer Name field, and Customer ID field.

Tip

Hold down the Ctrl key and click each field or right-click the gray Details section and choose Select All Section Objects.

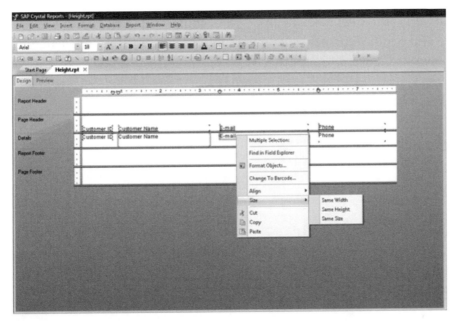

Figure 3.17
Adjust the height of the fields.

Table 3.1 Crystal Reports' Field-Sizing Options

Option	Description
Same Width	Resizes the selected fields to be the same width
Same Height	Resizes the selected fields to be the same height
Same Size	Resizes the selected fields to be the same width and height

3. With the Customer ID as the active field, right-click the Customer ID field and choose Size > Same Height. Notice that all fields are the same height now.

4. Save the report as **Height Modified.rpt**.

5. Preview the report.

6. You can verify the field's height by right-clicking on the field and choosing Size and Position, which opens the Object Size and Position dialog box, shown in Figure 3.18, appear.

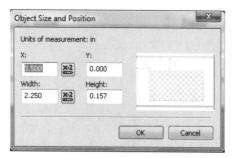

Figure 3.18
Size and Position Window.

The field's width and height properties can be set manually from this dialog box.

7. Close the report.

USING THE REPORT WIZARD

New users may find the Report Wizard to be a quick option to generate a report. As mentioned earlier, it is best to design the report from scratch using a blank report; however, I want to expose you to all options of Crystal Reports, so this section briefly covers the Report Wizard.

From the Start Page, you will be able to choose to create a Standard Report, a crosstab report, a Mailing Label report or a report based on an OLAP cube. Follow these steps to try the Report Wizard:

1. From the Start page, select the Report Wizard link.

2. Connect to the Xtreme Sample Database.

3. Add the Customers table.

4. Click Next.

5. Add the Customer ID, Customer Name, Region, and Phone.

6. Click Next.

7. Group the report by country.

8. Click Next.

9. On the Summaries screen, shown in Figure 3.19, select the Sum of Customer ID field located on the right panel of that screen, and then change the Summary function from Sum to Count.

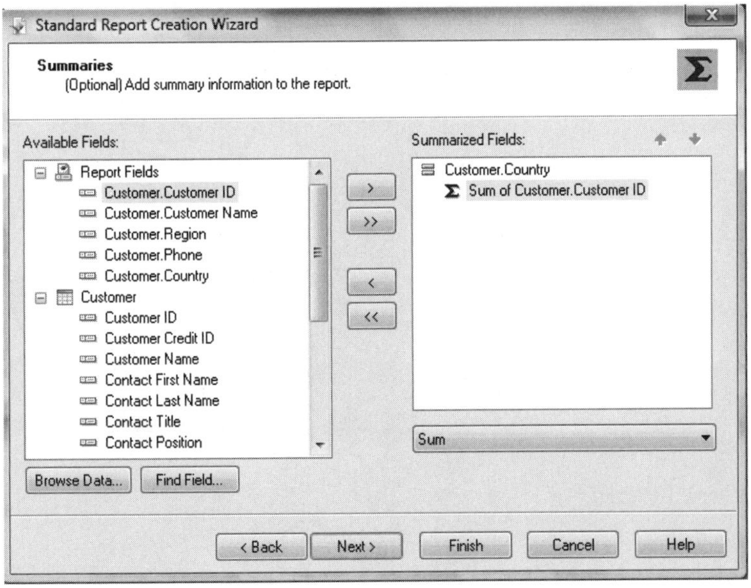

Figure 3.19
Summaries screen of the Report Wizard.

10. Click Next.

11. Leave the default None for Group Sorting.

12. Click Next.

13. Leave the default None for No Chart in Charting.

14. Click Next for Record Selection.

15. Click Finish.

Figure 3.20 shows the final result.

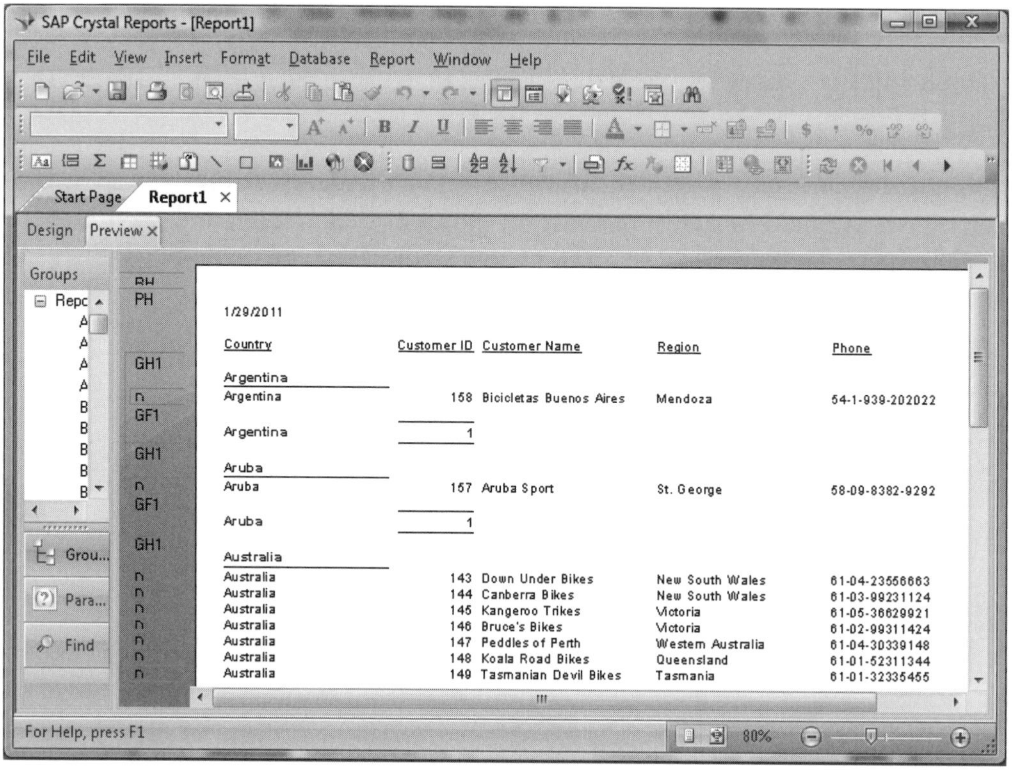

Figure 3.20
Preview of Report using the Report Wizard.

SUMMARY

Congratulations! You have built a basic report. This chapter covered connecting to a data source, inserting fields into a report, moving and resizing fields, saving the report, and previewing the report. As you move into the next chapters, you will start to build upon the basic foundation.

EXERCISES

Exercise 1

In this example, you need to create an employee list with phone number and an emergency contact name and phone number. Follow these steps to do so:

　　1. Start a new blank report.

2. Create an ODBC connection to the Xtreme Sample database.

3. Add the Employees table to the report.

4. Click OK.

5. Insert the following fields into the Details section: First Name, Last Name, Home Phone, Emergency Contact First Name, Emergency Contact Last Name, and Emergency Contact Phone. Tip: You will have to resize the fields to fit all on the report in portrait orientation.

6. Move the Last Name field to the one-inch mark on the vertical ruler and make the field one-inch wide.

7. Move the Home Phone field to the two-inch mark on the vertical ruler and make the field 1.25-inch wide.

8. Move the Emergency Contact First Name field to the 3.5-inch mark on the vertical ruler and make the field 1.25-inch wide.

9. Move the Emergency Contact Last Name and Emergency Contact Phone fields as needed.

10. Save the report as **Employee Contact Listing**.

11. Preview the report. Notice the column labels are truncated for the Employee Contact First and Last Name. Increase the height of the two labels to display the column's heading name on two lines.

CHAPTER 4

FORMATTING AND
ORGANIZING REPORTS

The objectives of this chapter are to learn the following tasks:

- Inserting and changing groups
- Record-level sorting
- Using the Sort Control feature
- Working with summary fields
- Creating drill-down and summary reports
- Creating running totals

This chapter focuses on the organization of the report. Extracting the correct data is the most important aspect of reporting. However, if the report is not organized and formatted in a manner that is easy for users to read, the report will lose its value to them. As you move through this chapter, you will gain the knowledge to develop a report that management can find informational and analytical for their business needs.

A report developer will determine if any grouping is needed based on the specifications documented during the Report Gathering Requirements discussion. One of the keywords used that indicate you must have one or more groups is the word "by." For example, if the user specifies that they need a report by month, you should group the report on a date field. If at any time, an aggregation (average, summary, minimum, maximum, and so on) has to be made, you must group the report by the subject of the aggregation.

INSERTING A GROUP

To insert a single group, access the Insert Group dialog box by using the Insert > Group menu or selecting the Insert Group icon from the Insert toolbar. The Insert Group dialog box is shown in Figure 4.1.

Figure 4.1
The Insert Group dialog box.

A field does not have to be placed on your report in order to group on that field. However, you should always group on a unique identifier field and not on a name field. For example, say you want to group by customer. You have the customer ID field and the customer name field. You should group on the customer ID field because you might have two customers with the same name, for example, John Smith. If you group on the name field, you run the risk of combining records for two different customers in one group. On the Common tab of the Insert Group dialog box, you can select any field that is available in the tables. As mentioned previously, the field does not have to be placed on the report in order to be able to group on it. To select the field to group on, click the first drop-down list for the available fields.

You can choose to sort the group in the manner that best fits your business requirements. The options are in ascending order, in descending order, in specified order, and in original order. Although ascending and descending order are standard, Crystal Reports also provides the In Specified Order option, which gives you the ability to determine the order in which groups are printed on the report. It also gives you the ability to create your own custom groups. For example, if you want to group on territories; however, territory is not a field listed in your database. You can create a new group for each territory and specify which states belong to each territory. The sort order option In Original Order will print the records in the order they were entered into the database. This sort order can be very useful in scenarios where you have no timestamp or when you are working with legacy systems.

1. Choose the Insert > Group menu or the Insert Group icon on the toolbar to access the Insert Group dialog box.

2. Insert a group on the necessary field.

3. From the Insert Group dialog box, change the sort order to In Specified Order. Figure 4.2 shows this process.

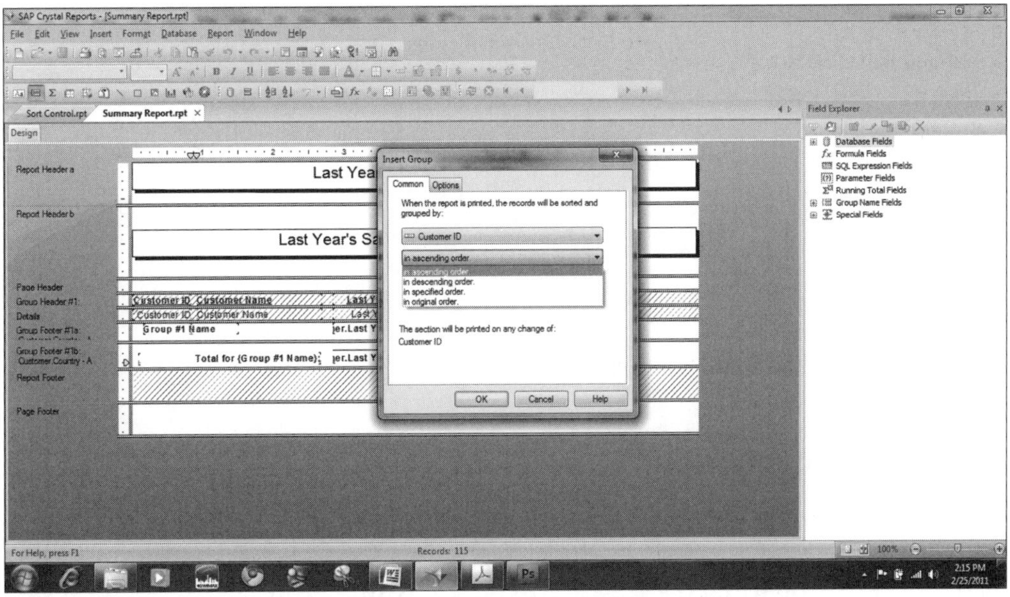

Figure 4.2
Changing the sort order.

4. From the In Specified Order tab, enter the name of the new group.

5. Click New.

6. Define the criteria for the new group. For example, select the products or regions that make up the new group.

7. Click OK to close the dialog box.

EXPLORING THE OPTIONS TAB OF THE INSERT GROUP DIALOG BOX

On the Options tab of the Insert Group dialog box, shown in Figure 4.3, you can customize the format of your group. Each of the options contributes to the visual result of a group on the report. Therefore, spend some time familiarizing yourself with details of each option.

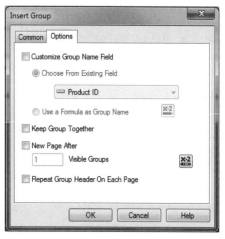

Figure 4.3
The Options tab of Insert Group dialog box.

The Customize Group Name Field

There are times when you need another descriptive name or combination of fields to display on the report as the group name. Crystal Reports allows you to accomplish that by using the Customize Group Name Field option on the Insert Group Options tab. Once the box is checked, you have the option to choose an existing field from the available list to replace the name of the grouped field. For example, if you group the report on customer ID and then preview the report, you'll see customer ID 123244. You have no way of easily identifying who the customer ID belongs to. To correct that issue, you can choose the Customize Group Name Field using the Choose from Existing Field option and selecting the Customer Name option. You have now presented the data in an easy-to-read format. When the users view the report, they will see ABC Company not customer ID 123244.

You have another option, called Use a Formula as Group Name. This option allows you to combine fields to create your own group name. For example, you would like to see the customer ID, a hyphen, and then the customer name, such as 123244–ABC Company. To accomplish this goal, you can create a formula that will combine the fields and separate them with a hyphen. Select the Use a Formula as Group Name option, click the x+2 button to the right of the option, and then write the following formula.

```
ToText({Customer.Customer ID}) + " - " + {Customer.Customer Name}
```

Formulas will be addressed later in the book.

Keep Group Together

The Keep Group Together option allows you to control how the records in the group will break across pages. If you choose the option, and the system cannot print all of the group's records on the same page, it will create a page break and start printing on the next page and continue with any subsequent pages. I recommend you use this option only with small groups unless you intentionally want to ensure multiple groups aren't printed on the same page unless all of the records can be printed.

New Page after Visible Groups

This was a feature, shown in Figure 4.4, first implemented in version 2008. Select this option if you want to control the number of page breaks in a document after a specific number of groups have been printed. For example, perhaps you want a page break to occur after every 5 groups. You would enter "5" in the number box.

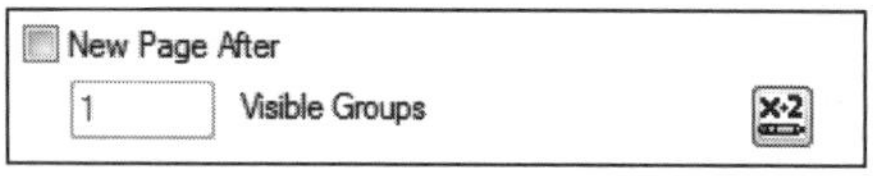

Figure 4.4
Setting page breaks after a specific number of groups.

Repeat Group Header on Each Page

This option, shown in Figure 4.5, allows the group titles to appear across page breaks. Even if your database is initially small, as you continue to enter records the group records are going to grow. The larger your group, the more pages it will take to print the detail records. Therefore, as you design the report you want to turn on these options in order to allow the report capabilities to grow with your business. If your group spans multiple pages, the group will be easily identifiable on each page.

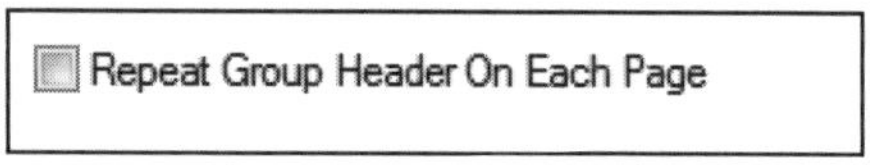

Figure 4.5
The Repeat Group Header option.

INSERTING GROUPS USING THE GROUP EXPERT

You can insert groups from the Report > Group Expert menu or by selecting the Group Expert icon on the Expert toolbar. The Group Expert allows you to insert multiple groups from one window and access the same Options window as in the Insert > Group menu command.

As previously mentioned, you can group the report on any field that is available in the tables that you connected to the report. Select the field that you want to group on and move to the Group By section by double-clicking the field or selecting the right-pointing arrow. Figure 4.6 shows the Group Expert window.

With the field selected in the Group By section, click on the Options button. You can select the sort order and access the Options tab of the Insert Group dialog box.

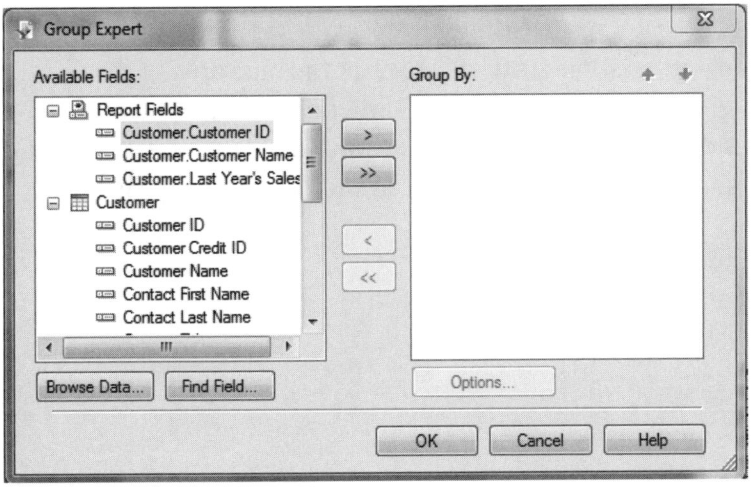

Figure 4.6
The Group Expert dialog box.

You can also change the order of your groups. For example, if you had two groups, Region and Country, their logical order would be Country and then Region. You can use the Group Expert to change the order of these groups, as shown in Figure 4.7.

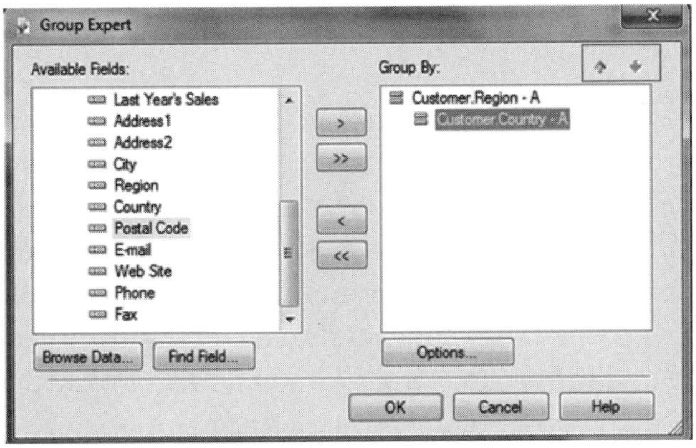

Figure 4.7
Changing the order of your groups.

Modifying an Existing Group

There are times when you have grouped a report on the incorrect field, or you need to change the sort order of the group, customize the group name, or ensure the group name repeats on each page. In these cases, you should use the Change Group option. To modify an existing group, right-click the blue area of the Group Header or Group Footer in the Design window and choose Change Group. The Change Group Options dialog box will appear, as shown in Figure 4.8, displaying the grouped field and sort options that appeared in the Insert Group dialog box.

Figure 4.8
The Change Group Options dialog box.

Deleting a Group

As you develop your report, you may decide you want to delete a group after inserting it into the report. Use caution when deleting the group, because any information that you have inserted into the Group Header or Group Footer will be deleted. This could include information such as formulas, text, and variables that are needed elsewhere in your report. Deleting a group will return the records to a detail level report if no other groups exist. You can delete a group from the Group Expert or by right-clicking on the blue area of the Group Header or Group Footer of the group you want to delete and then choosing Delete Group.

To delete a group using the Group Expert, select the group from the Group By side of the dialog box and click the left-pointing arrow, as shown in Figure 4.9.

You can also delete a group by right-clicking in the blue area of the Group Header or Group Footer section that you want to delete and choosing Delete Group from the shortcut menu, as shown in Figure 4.10.

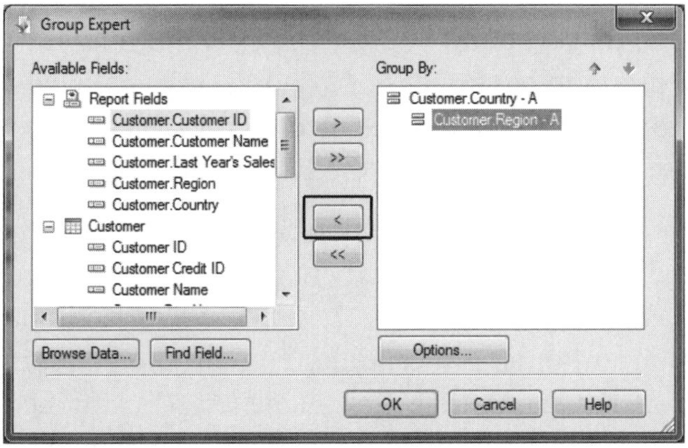

Figure 4.9
Deleting a group from Group Expert window.

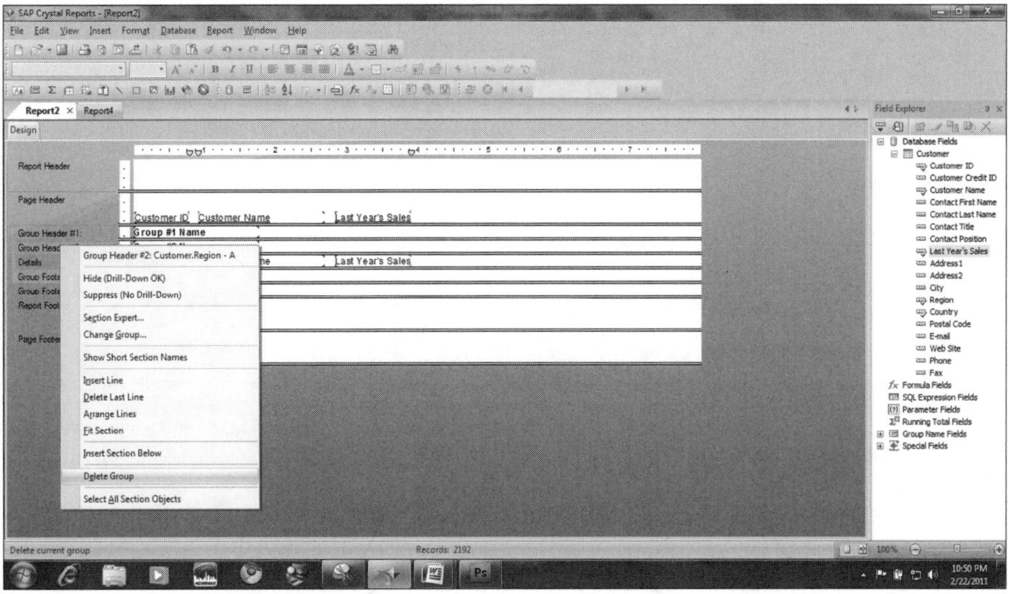

Figure 4.10
Deleting a group using the shortcut menu.

RECORD-LEVEL SORTING

Record-level sorting determines the field you want the detail records to be sorted on when printed. You can sort on any field in the report as well as any other field connected to the report through the Database Expert. If you have grouped your report, the Group will be the first sort and you are only determining how you want the records within the group to be sorted. For example, say you have a report sorted by customer and you want to display the records for the customer by order date. You would choose the Order Date as the Record Sort field.

The Record Sort option is accessed from the Report > Record Sort Expert menu or from the Record Sort icon on the Expert toolbar. The Record Sort Expert window will open, as shown in Figure 4.11; select the sort criteria field and the sort order. The default sort order is ascending. You can choose more than one field to sort on, such as last name then first name. As I mentioned earlier, and will mention many more times throughout this book, you should be developing the report for the audience and not for yourself as the developer.

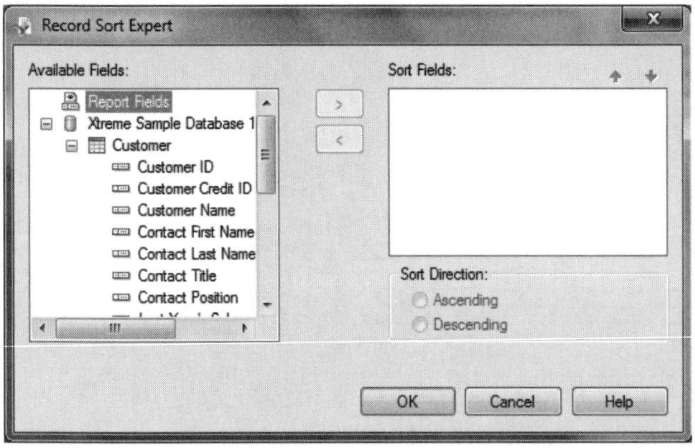

Figure 4.11
The Record Sort Expert dialog box.

USING THE SORT CONTROL FEATURE

Crystal Reports 2008 introduced the Sort Control feature, which allows users to interactively sort fields in ascending or descending order at runtime. This feature eliminates the need to compromise when multiple users are responsible for setting the report requirements. In previous versions, you could allow the sort to be controlled at runtime by using a Sort parameter. The Sort Control is to be used in conjunction with the Record Sort Expert. The fields must be included in the Record Sort Expert in order to bind it to the Sort Control option. The Sort

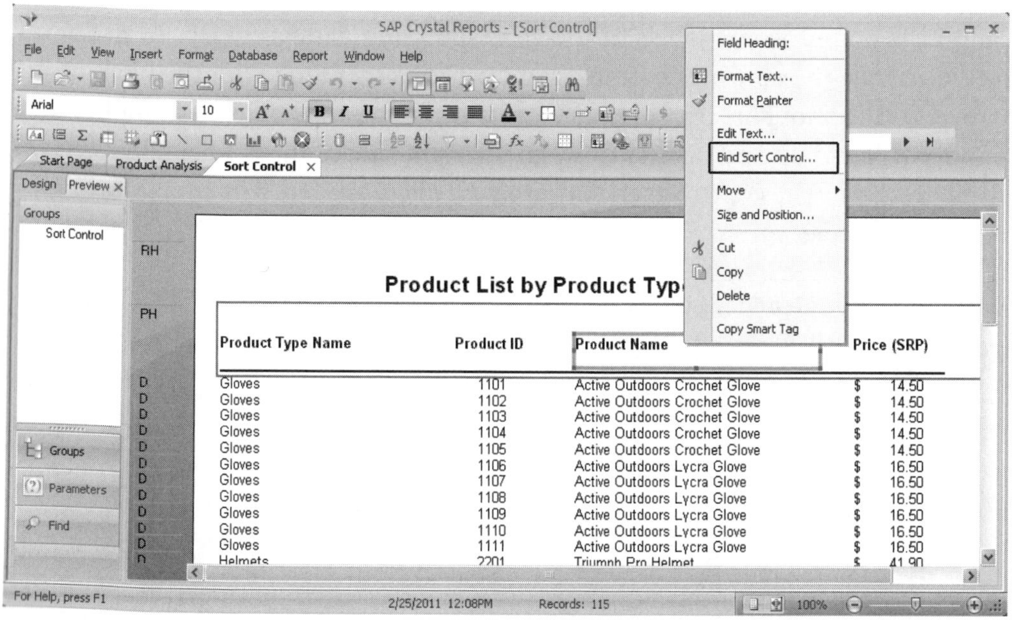

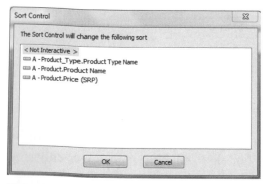

Figure 4.13
Right-clicking to access Bind Sort Control.

Figure 4.14
The Bind Sort Control dialog box.

4. Select the corresponding field name. For example, say you added Product Class to the Record Sort Expert. Right-click on the Product Class field label and choose Bind Control Sort. Choose the Product Class field.

5. Click OK.

Control is bound to the labels of the corresponding database field. It will allow you to change the sort order from ascending to descending with the click of the arrow. You cannot sort on Summary fields or on running totals. Using the Sort Control will add up and down arrows to the right side of the field label, as shown in Figure 4.12. These arrows enable users to click on and sort in ascending or descending order.

Product List by Product Type and Class			
Product Type Name ▲▼	**Product ID**	**Product Name** ▲▼	**Price (SRP)** ▲▼
Competition	101151	Descent	$ 2,939.85
Competition	101152	Descent	$ 2,939.85
Competition	101171	Descent	$ 2,939.85
Competition	101172	Descent	$ 2,939.85
Competition	101181	Descent	$ 2,939.85
Competition	101182	Descent	$ 2,939.85
Competition	101201	Descent	$ 2,939.85
Competition	101202	Descent	$ 2,939.85
Competition	101221	Descent	$ 2,939.85
Competition	101222	Descent	$ 2,939.85
Competition	103151	Endorphin	$ 899.85
Competition	103171	Endorphin	$ 899.85
Competition	103181	Endorphin	$ 899.85
Competition	103201	Endorphin	$ 899.85
Competition	103221	Endorphin	$ 899.85
Competition	102151	Mozzie	$ 1,739.85
Competition	102171	Mozzie	$ 1,739.85
Competition	102181	Mozzie	$ 1,739.85
Competition	102201	Mozzie	$ 1,739.85
Competition	102221	Mozzie	$ 1,739.85
Gloves	1101	Active Outdoors Crochet Glove	$ 14.50
Gloves	1102	Active Outdoors Crochet Glove	$ 14.50
Gloves	1103	Active Outdoors Crochet Glove	$ 14.50
Gloves	1104	Active Outdoors Crochet Glove	$ 14.50
Gloves	1105	Active Outdoors Crochet Glove	$ 14.50
Gloves	1106	Active Outdoors Lycra Glove	$ 16.50

Figure 4.12
Using the Sort Control feature.

The Sort Control option can be accessed by choosing Insert > Sort Control or by selecting the field label you want to sort on, right-clicking, and then choosing Bind Sort Control. See Figures 4.13 and 4.14.

To use the Sort Control option, follow these steps:

1. Open the Record Sort Expert by choosing Report > Record Sort Expert or by clicking the Record Sort Expert icon on the Expert toolbar.

2. Add the data fields you want to sort on in the report.

3. Right-click the label header of the fields you added in the Record Sort Expert and choose Bind Sort Control.

To remove a Sort Control, follow these steps:

1. Right-click on the field label and choose Bind Sort Control.

2. Select <Not Interactive>.

USING SUMMARY FIELDS

Frequently, the purpose of creating a group is to make use of the summary functions to create subtotals, averages, counts, and other available summaries. The summary functions available will depend on the type of the field. You can create different summary types for the same group. For example, say you need the sum of the order amount field and the average order amount to analyze your data. You can create both summaries on the same field. By default, all summary fields are placed in the group footer or in the report footer based on the summary location chosen when inserting the summary. Users often prefer the summary field to be located in the header and not the footer. This can be easily accomplished by moving the summary field to the header.

Inserting Summaries

To insert a summary with no field selected, follow these steps:

1. Σ Choose Insert > Summary or click the Insert Summary icon, found on the Insert toolbar. The Insert Summary dialog box opens, as shown in Figure 4.15.

2. Select the field you want to summarize from the Choose the Field to Summarize drop-down list. The Report Fields list will appear displaying all of the fields inserted in the report. Keep in mind that the field does not have to be placed on the report in order to create a summary field. The available fields will be shown in the corresponding table in the drop-down list.

3. Choose the summary function in the Calculate This Summary area from the available drop-down list. As mentioned earlier, the available summary functions will depend on the field type. For numerical values, sum is the default summary function. For string values, maximum is the default summary function.

4. Choose the desired group for the summary from the Summary Location. The default location is the Report Footer. If you choose the Grand Total

Figure 4.15
The Insert Summary dialog box.

(Report Footer) in the Summary location, a summary field will be inserted in the Report Footer. In order to create a summary for one or more groups, change the Summary Location to the corresponding group.

5. 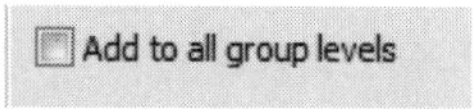 ☐ Add to all group levels   If you have more than one group and want to insert a summary for all groups, select the Add to All Group Levels checkbox. A summary field will be placed in the footer of each group including the Report Footer automatically.

Tip

If you forget to check the Add to All Group Levels checkbox, you can also copy the Summary field from one group footer to another. The value will be recalculated automatically based on the field's location. Use the Ctrl key and drag-and-drop or use the Copy-and-Paste method.

6. You have the option to insert a group directly from the Insert Summary dialog box by choosing the Insert Group button. The Insert Group dialog box will open. Follow the normal steps for inserting a group.

Summary Percentages

Summary percentages are available when the business needs require you to calculate the group percentage of a total, such as the grand total. Percentage summaries are available only when you're working with numeric fields.

To accomplish a summary percentage, after the summary function has been selected and the summary location has been selected, choose the checkbox called Show as a Percentage Of. The option displays the group percentage of the grand total of the summary field.

Click OK when you're done selecting options.

Table 4.1 shows the summary functions available for each datatype.

Table 4.1 Summary Functions

Function	String	Number	Currency	DateTime	Boolean
			Datatypes		
Sum	X	X			
Average	X	X			
Count	X	X	X	X	X
Distinct Count	X	X	X	X	X
Sample Variance	X	X			
Sample Standard Deviation	X	X			
Maximum	X	X	X	X	X
Minimum	X	X	X	X	X
Correlation with	X	X			
Covariance with		X		X	
Median		X		X	
Mode	X	XXXX			
Nth largest, N is	X	XXXX			
Nth smallest, N is	X	XXXX			
Nth most frequent, N is	X		X		X
	X		X		
Pth percentile, P is			X		X
Population Variance			X		X
Population Standard Deviation		X		X	
Weighted Average with			X		X

Inserting Summaries with a Field Selected

You can eliminate the need to select a field from the Insert Summary dialog box by selecting the field in Design view. To do so, follow these steps:

1. Right-click the field from the Design view and choose Insert Summary, as shown in Figure 4.16.

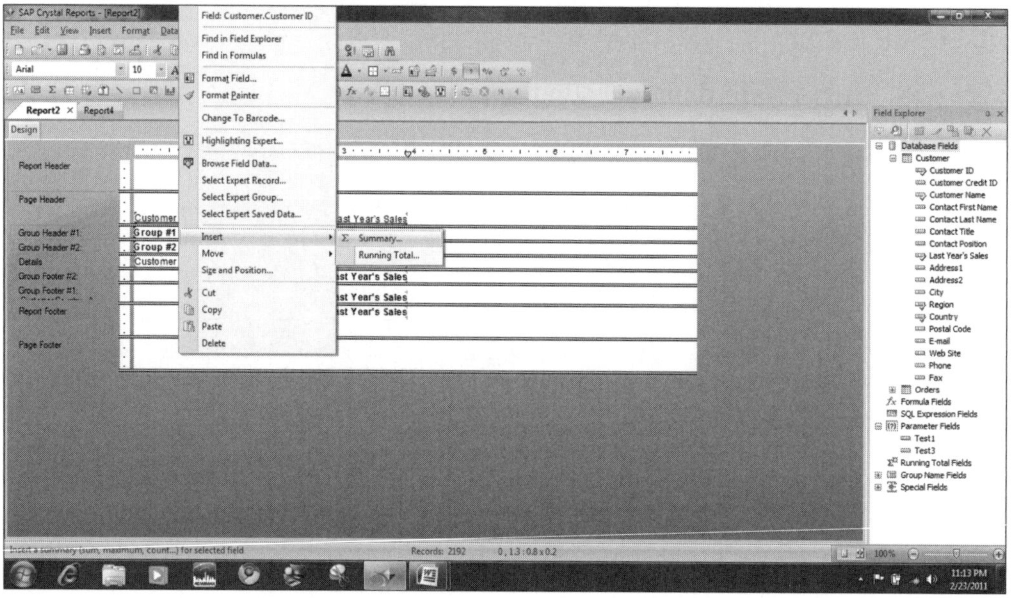

Figure 4.16
Inserting a summary from Design view.

2. Notice the field to summarize is already populated.

3. Select the summary function.

4. Select the summary location.

5. Click OK. Notice the summary field is inserted in the group footer of the group chosen.

Editing a Summary

There are times when you may need to change the field you want to summarize , change the summary function, or change the field as a percentage of the total, all after you have initially created the summary field. You can edit your Summary fields by right-clicking the Summary field and choosing Edit Summary. See Figure 4.17.

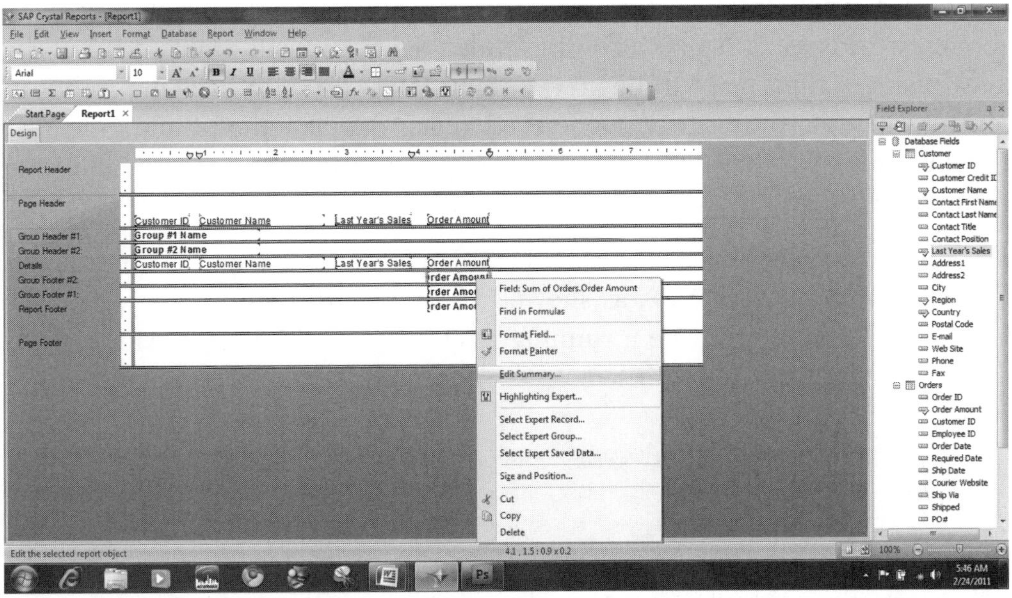

Figure 4.17
The Edit Summary command in Design view.

RUNNING TOTALS

Running totals are much like summary fields but they give you more control over the fields that are calculated, including the point at which the field is included in the summary calculation. For example, there might be times when you need to calculate a summary only when a certain criteria has been met. Say you want to calculate a summary only when the company required margin had not been met or when the sale occurred within the last seven days. You cannot accomplish such a task using a Summary field, even if you hide records, but you can do so using a running total.

The Running Total field gives you the flexibility to determine when the values are to be calculated using a specific field, a group, or a formula. The Running Total field is also used to create an incremental total for every detail line. Think about your bank statement; every time a check or debit card transaction is applied to your account you want to see your balance decrease. When a deposit is made to your account, you want to see your balance increase. That is the functionality of a Running Total feature; it gives you the line-by-line incremental total. Running totals are required when you have created a Top N or Bottom N report and you want to get an accurate grand total of the fields displayed. Summary fields will calculate all of the hidden fields; you will control the records to calculate in the Top N through a running total. You also have the ability to control when the running total is reset. You can calculate the running total for the entire report or have it be calculated only per group and have it reset at the change of each group.

To create a running total, access the Field Explorer. Then right-click Running Total Fields and choose New, as shown in Figure 4.18. You can also select the field that you want to create a running total on from the Design window and then right-click and choose Insert > Running Total.

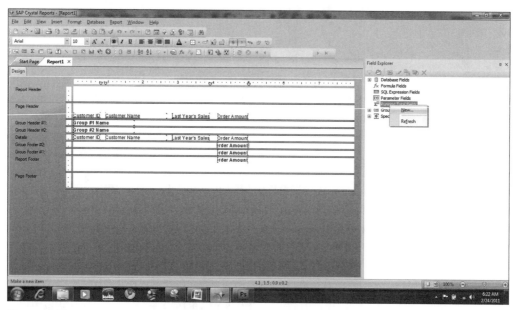

Figure 4.18
Creating a running total from the Field Explorer.

The Create Running Total Field dialog box, shown in Figure 4.19, will appear.

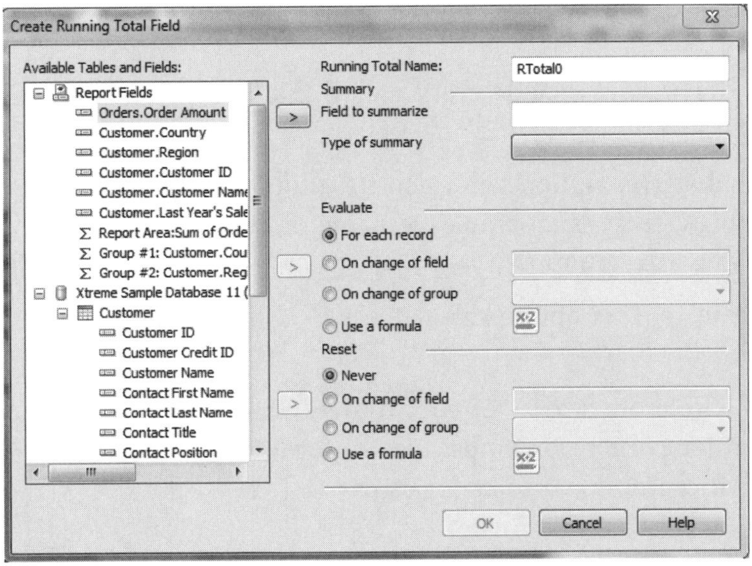

Figure 4.19
The Create Running Total Field dialog box.

To create the running total, type a descriptive name for the running total in the Running Total Name field. There are three sections of the Running Total dialog box and each section has its own functionality. In the next section, you'll take a look at the powerfulness that each section can add to your calculated field.

Summary Field

Select the field to summarize from the Available Tables and Fields list. You must select the field and click on the right-pointing arrow in the Summary section.

You cannot include a running total within a running total. Running totals are calculated in the `WhilePrintingRecords` pass; therefore, you cannot include any formula in the running total that has to be calculated in pass 2 (`WhilePrinting Records`).

Evaluate Section

The Evaluate section gives you the most control over which records are actually included in the calculation.

Your options are:

- **For each record** – This will include every record that is retrieved on the report.

- **On change of field** – This option will calculate a total only when the field selected changes, such as an employee name or customer name. This is not the same as a group.

- **On change of group** – This option calculates a total only when the group changes.

- **Use a formula** – The most flexible option. It gives you the ability to write the actual criteria the record must meet in order to be included in the calculation. For example, {Customer.Region} in ["VA", "NC", "MA"].

Reset Section

The Reset section allows you to control when the value of the running total resets. The options for resetting the calculation are similar to the Evaluate section. They include:

- **Never** – Use when you want the total to run for the entire report.

- **On change of field** – Use when the value must reset on a specific field.

- **On change of group** – Use when obtaining summary values for the group.

- **Use a formula** – Use when you need more flexibility and you have specific criteria the record must meet in order to reset.

Tip

Heavy use of running totals will affect the performance of the report. To minimize the hit, use manual running totals. Manual running totals are covered later in Chapter 8 on formulas.

DRILL-DOWN SUMMARY REPORTS

Summary reports are one of the most commonly used reports. The summary report consists of the grouping field and subtotals only. There is no detail visible in a summary report. In previous versions, Crystal Reports included the drill-down capability of a summary report. You might develop a report and your boss says, "the numbers don't look right." Years ago a statement like that would drive us back to figuring out what records the report was calculating. Well, when Crystal Reports released the drill-down feature it eliminated that problem. The drill-down feature allows the users to double-click on the Summary field or the Group Name field to display all of the detail records that are included in the subtotal for the group. No long periods of data extraction and analysis; it takes seconds to display the data.

Figure 4.20
A Summary report.

To create a summary report, like the one shown in Figure 4.20, you must have a group and a summary field and the detail section must be hidden. Follow these steps:

1. Insert a group from the Insert > Group menu or use the Insert Group icon from the Insert toolbar.

2. Place the fields in the details section.

3. Insert a Summary field for the desired aggregation to be displayed in the summary report.

4. Move the group name field into the Group Footer to the left of the summary field.

5. Suppress any empty sections and hide the detail section. Right-click the blue area of the section and choose Suppress (No Drill-Down) or Hide (Drill-Down OK). The Section Expert will be discussed in Chapter 5.

6. Hide the Details section.

7. Save and preview the report.

To view the drill-down records, you just double-click on the Summary field and then view the detail records. See Figure 4.21.

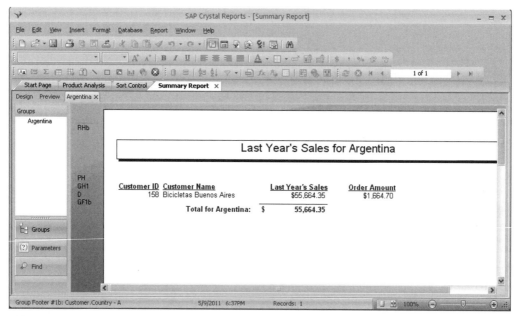

Figure 4.21
Detail records for Argentina's total when using the drill-down feature.

SUMMARY

In this chapter, you learned how to organize your report data through grouping by inserting groups using the Insert Group option or the Group Expert dialog box. You also learned how to use Summary fields and the Running Total function. The Record Sort method and Sort Control give the users more flexibility to control the data sorting at runtime. The use of Summary reports can give you high-level analytical information while providing drill-down capability to view the detail records behind the summary totals.

Exercises

Exercise 1

Create a product analysis report by product that includes the reorder level, units in stock, price and units on order.

1. Start a new blank report.

2. Connect to the Xtreme Sample database.

3. Select the Product and Purchases tables.

4. Save the report as **Product Analysis**.

5. Insert the following fields into the details section of the report: {Reorder Level}, {Units in Stock}, {Price (SRP)} and {Units on Order}.

6. Using the Insert Group Option from the Insert toolbar, insert a group on {Product ID} from the Products table.

7. Save the changes and preview the report. Your report should look similar to Figure 4.22.

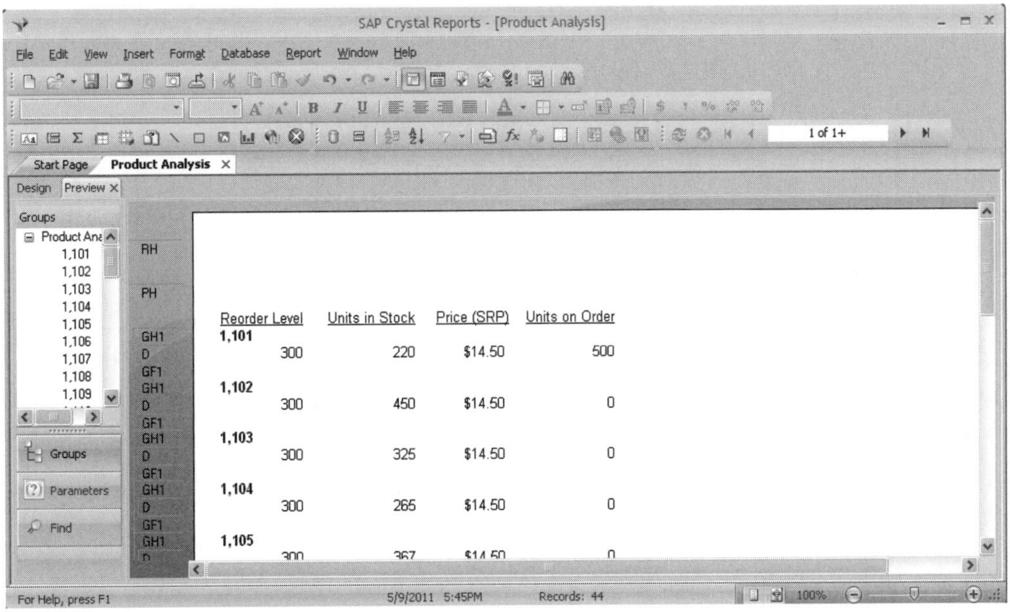

Figure 4.22
Report grouped on Product ID.

Notice the Product ID numbers in the GH1 section of the report. In order to identify the actual product, you need a product list.

1. From Design view, right-click on the blue area of the Group Header and choose Change Group.

2. Select the Options tab.

3. Select the checkbox called Customize Group Name Field.

4. Select the radio button called Choose From Existing Field.

5. Select the field {Product Name} from the Product table.

6. Click OK.

7. Save the report and preview it. You might have to increase the width of the Product Name field to display all of the text. Notice the product name now appears instead of the product ID, thus giving the user the information they need to read the report efficiently. Note that the report needs additional formatting to be in a format that presents a professional appearance but has achieved the exercise goals. See Figure 4.23.

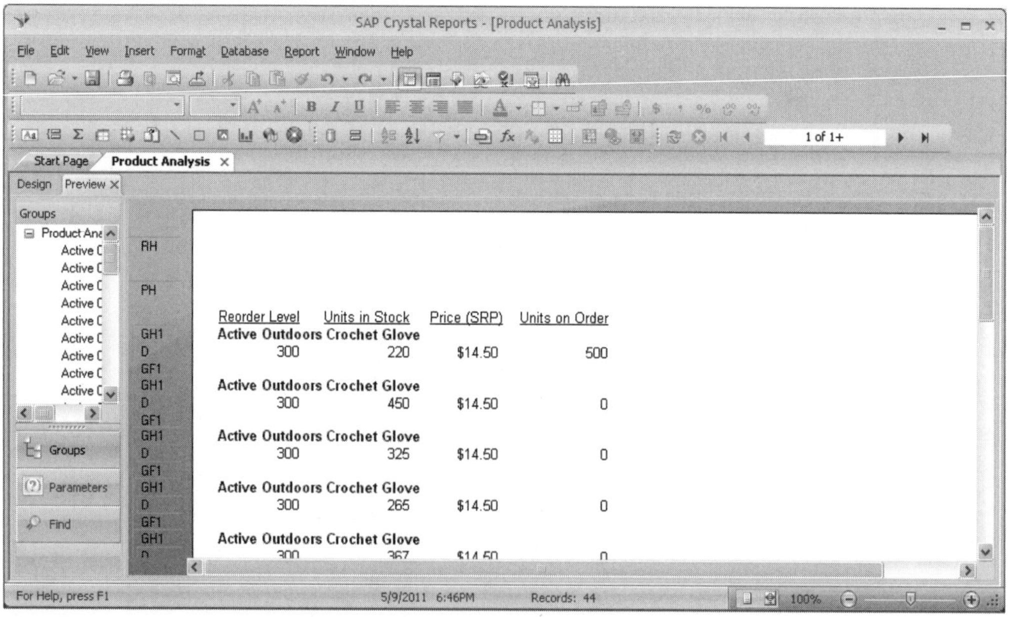

Figure 4.23
The final preview of the report.

Exercise 2

Create a summary report with drill-down capability displaying last year's sales by country.

1. Open the Sales by Country report, located in the sample files under Chapter 4.

2. Insert a group on {Country}.

3. Insert a summary field on {Last Year's Sales} field.

4. Copy the {Group #1 Name.Customer.Country} field from the Group Header to the Group Footer.

5. Move the column labels from the Page Header into the Group Header section below the Group name field.

6. Remove the underline from the column labels and replace it with a line beneath the column labels.

Tip

Using the line tool, draw a line from the left margin to the right edge of the last column label.

7. Hide the Group Header, Details, and Report Footer sections.

8. Save the report as **Sales by Country Summary** and preview it. You can click any field in the Group Footer section to drill down on the group's records.

Exercise 3

Give the users the ability to sort the report on multiple fields at runtime.

1. Open the Sort Control report, located in the sample files for Chapter 4.

2. Preview the report.

3. Switch back to Design view. Click on the Design tab of the report window. See Figure 4.24.

4. Using the Record Sort Expert, sort the report on {Product Type Name}, {Product Name}, and {Price (SRP)}.

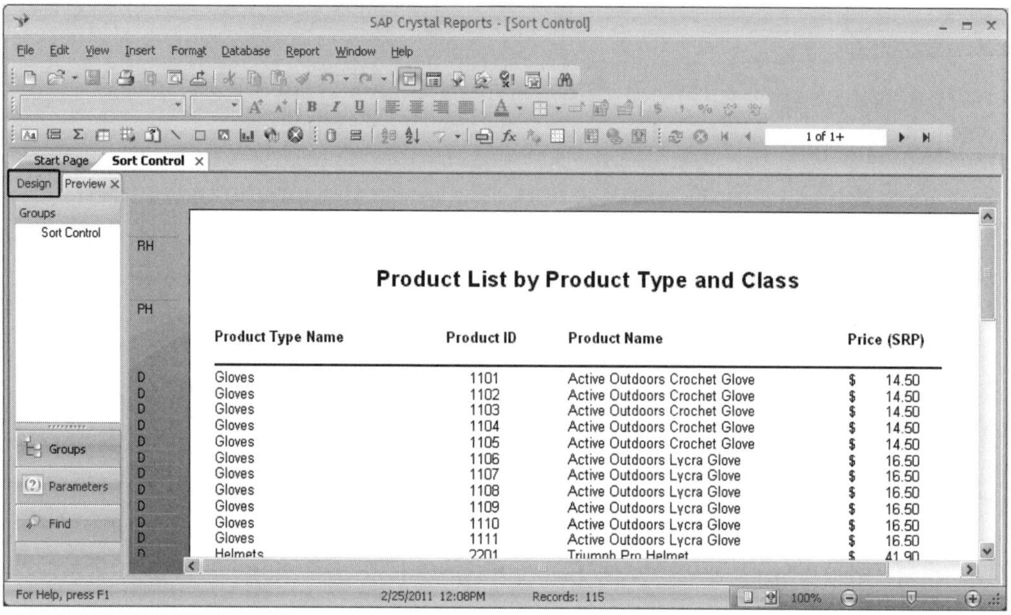

Figure 4.24
Switch to Design view.

5. Right-click on the column label for {Product Type Name} and choose Bind Sort Control.

6. Select the {Product Type Name} field in Bind Sort Control dialog box and click OK.

7. Right-click on the column label for {Product Name} and choose Bind Sort Control.

8. Select the {Product Name} field in Bind Sort Control dialog box and click OK.

9. Right-click on the column label for {Price (SRP)} and choose Bind Sort Control.

10. Select the {Price (SRP)} field in Bind Sort Control dialog box and click OK.

11. Save the report as **Bind Sort Control** and preview it.

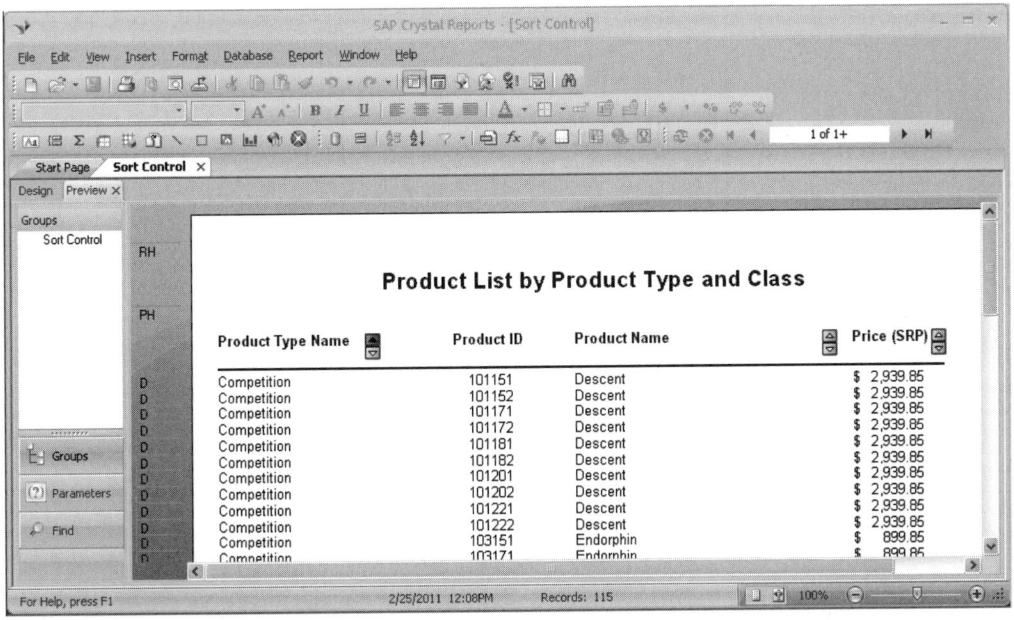

Figure 4.25
Report using Sort Controls.

Notice the sort control arrows on the right side of the column labels. Your report should look similar to Figure 4.25.

CHAPTER 5

WORKING WITH MARGINS AND SECTIONS

The objectives of this chapter are to learn the following tasks:

- Setting page margins
- Working with the Section Expert

As you continue to work with the organization of your report, you will learn how to make the data on your report look professionally appealing. This chapter discusses the use of the Page Setup options to set the margins, page orientation, and other settings. This chapter also covers the use of multiple sections and formatting the report using the Section Expert.

SETTING MARGINS

Report margins are dependent upon the printer driver that you have installed when designing the report. It is important that you take into account the printer drivers of the users who will be printing the report. Crystal Reports will change the margins based on the printer that is being used. Even when the same printer is used but a different printer driver is installed then the report may print differently. You can design a report with no printer driver by choosing the No Printer checkbox at the top of the Page Setup dialog box. The No Printer option should also be used if the report is going to be viewed on the web only. I will discuss what happens if you decide to print the report with the No Printer option later in the chapter.

Margins are accessed from the File > Page Setup menu, shown in Figure 5.1.

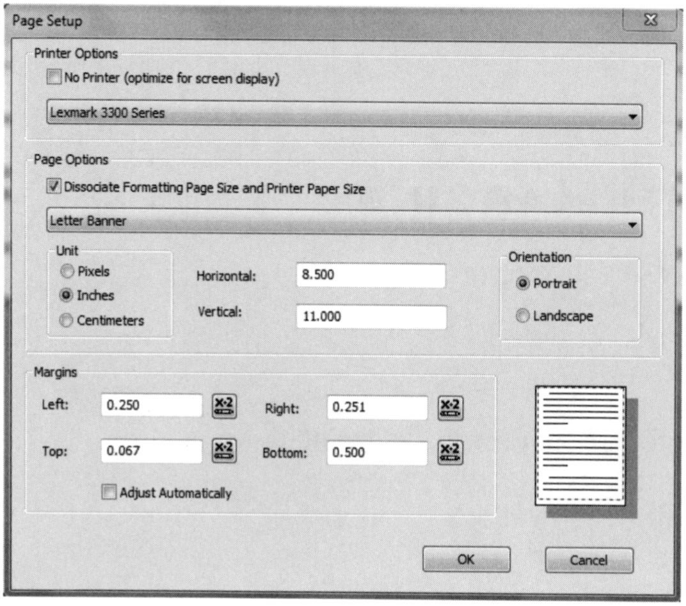

Figure 5.1
The Page Setup dialog box.

Users can manually set the margins of the report from the Page Setup window. You can set the top, bottom, left, and right margins individually. You also have the option to conditionally set the margins based on the orientation of the report. That's useful when the printer drivers may change and a report that has a default orientation of landscape may be printed on a printer that does not allow landscape. By conditionally setting the margins, you have the ability to set the margins if the default printer sets the orientation to portrait.

Crystal Reports has the ability to adjust the margins automatically. This option allows the system to increase or decrease the margins based on the printer. To turn on this option, click the checkbox called Adjust Automatically from the Page Setup dialog box. The Adjust Automatically checkbox is shown in Figure 5.2.

 You can set margins conditionally by selecting the x+2 icon and creating a formula that sets them. See Figure 5.3.

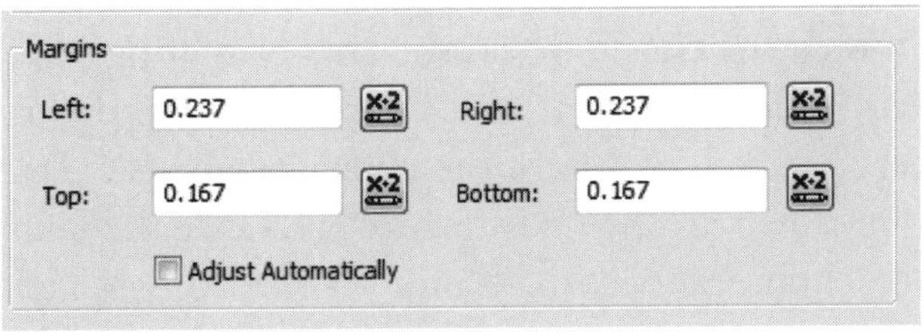

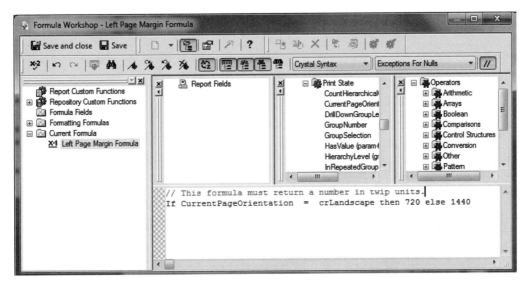

Figure 5.2
The Adjust Automatically checkbox.

Figure 5.3
Formula to conditionally set a margin.

When you're conditionally setting margins, the margin measurement must be specified in *twips*. Twips are measured as follows:

1440 twips = 1 inch

2880 twips = 2 inches

To set the margin based on the page orientation, create the formula for the corresponding margin (top, bottom, left, or right). The following example specifies that the left margin will be .5 inch if landscape and 1 inch if portrait.

```
If CurrentPageOrientation  =  crLandscape then 720 else 1440
```

Occasionally, you may develop reports that require custom sized paper. Custom sized reports require you to manually set the margins and printer orientation.

To set the user defined settings, check the checkbox Dissociate Formatting Page Size and Printer Page Size located in the Page Options of the Page Setup dialog box. Once the checkbox has been enabled, you have the ability to choose User Defined Size in the paper size drop-down, as shown in Figure 5.4. Once the User Defined Size option is selected, choose the correct unit of measure—pixel, inches, or centimeters—and then enter the vertical and horizontal sizes of the paper. Figure 5.5 shows the user-defined settings.

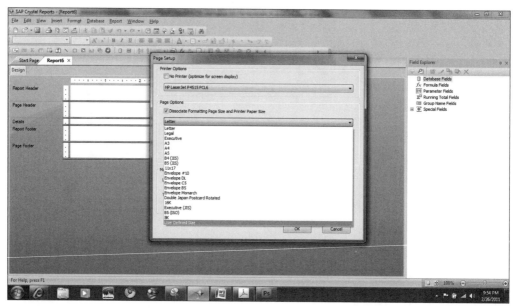

Figure 5.4
Selecting a user-defined paper size.

Setting the Page Orientation

The default paper orientation is Portrait. To change the orientation from Portrait to Landscape, choose File > Page Setup and change the option to Landscape in the Orientation section of the Page Setup dialog box.

Setting the Report to Use No Printer

When the report is going to be viewed online only, you should use the No Printer (optimize for screen display) option. The report will be designed with no printer driver saved with the report. If you decide to print the report later, the

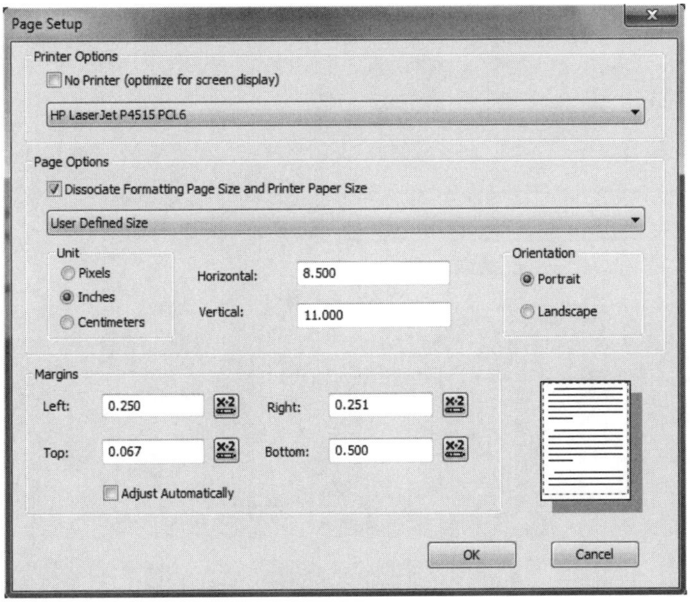

Figure 5.5
Setting the user-defined settings.

default printer driver will be used. If no printer driver is installed, a message will appear asking for permission to configure a printer. Access the No Printer (optimize for screen display) option from the File > Page Setup dialog box.

USING THE SECTION EXPERT

The Section Expert is used to format individual sections of a report. The sections available to be formatted are based on the sections of the active report. As discussed in an earlier chapter, the default sections are the Report Header, Page Header, Details, Page Footer, and Report Footer. If you have one or more groups in your report, you will also have the Group Header and Group Footer sections. The Section Expert allows you to format many options, such as section suppression, inserting page breaks, adding background color to a section, or changing the page orientation of a section. The ability to include both portrait and landscape orientation into the same report was first featured in Crystal Reports 2008.

To access the Section Expert, choose Report > Section Expert or right-click the blue area of the section and choose Section Expert, as shown in Figure 5.6. The Section Expert will then appear, as shown in Figure 5.7.

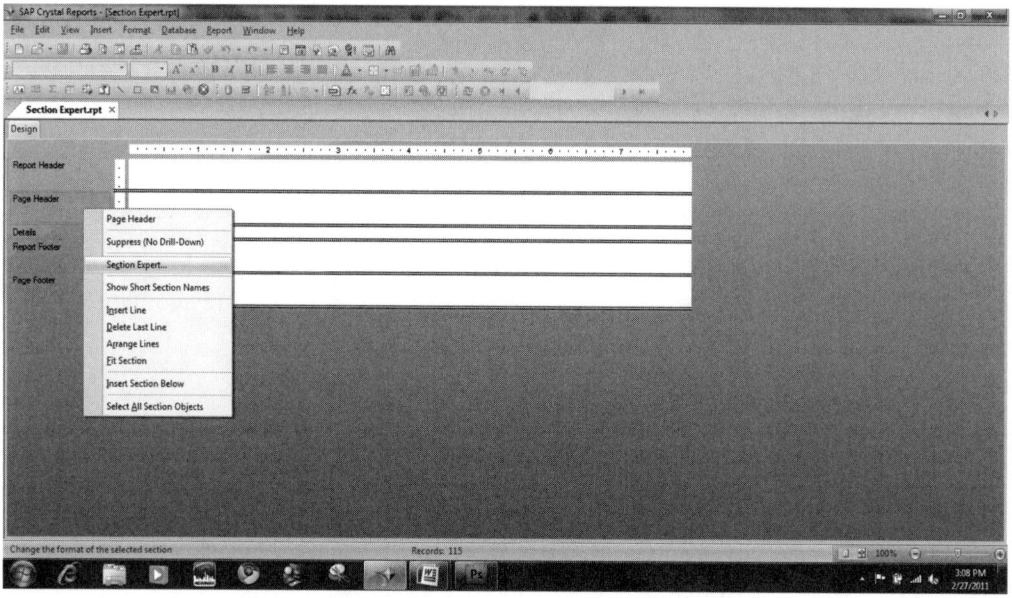

Figure 5.6
Accessing the Section Expert is easy.

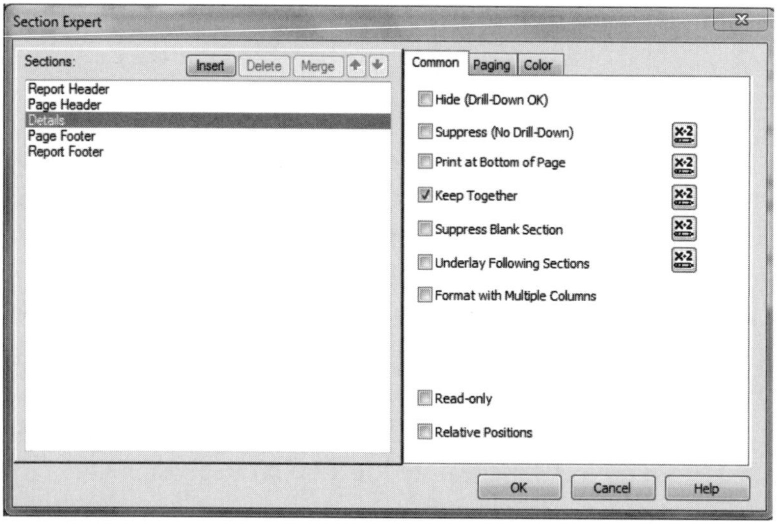

Figure 5.7
The Section Expert window.

The formatting options that are available depend on the section that you are formatting. Not all of them will be available for all sections. With the release of Crystal Reports 2008, three tabs were introduced into the Section Expert, as follows:

- The Common tab holds all of the options that are available for most of the sections.

- The Paging tab allows you to set page breaks and the orientation of each section.

- The Color tab allows you to give the section a background color.

In the Details section, if you choose to format the section in multiple columns, the Layout tab will also be available. You can conditionally set most of the formatting options by using the x+2 button to the right of the option.

The following sections cover each of these Section Expert tabs in more detail.

The Common Tab of the Section Expert

On the Common tab, you'll find the following options:

- **Hide (Drill-Down OK)** – This option hides a section when printed. However, the section can be viewed if included in a group-level scenario such as a Summary report. When the user double-clicks on the Summary field or group name, the section will appear.

- **Suppress (No Drill-Down)** – This option suppresses the section and any fields in it when printed. When suppressed, this section will not appear when any drill-down features are used in the report.

- **Print at Bottom of Page** – Any data in this section is printed at the bottom of the page regardless of how many records are in the section. For example, subtotals and totals should be at the bottom of the page even if two lines appear on the invoice or purchase order. Selecting this option in the Section Expert forces the section to print at the bottom of the page.

- **Keep Together** – Checked by default. This option will ensure the data for a single record will not break across pages. Specifically if text in one field is more than one line and cannot fit on the same page, the Keep Together option will force a page break before the record starts to print. Therefore, the entire record is printed on the same page. This option is ignored in a multi-line and memo datatype field.

▪ **Suppress Blank Section** – This option will help minimize the wasted whitespace. If no data is printed in the section, the entire section will be suppressed. If there is data, the section will print.

▪ **Underlay Following Sections** – This option allows the objects in this section to print behind the other sections that follow. It can be used to insert a watermark, such as the company logo in the background of the report, or to print charts and other data side by side. It can also be used to eliminate the need for pre-printed forms. For example, a purchase order pre-printed form can be scanned and placed in the Report Header or Page Header and the remaining sections will print on top of the image. Therefore, you line up the fields where they fall on the image. See the example in the Chapter 5 sample files.

Tip

The sample files can be downloaded from www.courseptr.com/downloads. Enter the book title, ISBN, or the author's name to be linked to the sample files for this book.

▪ **Read-Only** – This option disables all formatting for the section. All objects in this section become read-only and cannot be moved or formatted.

▪ **Relative Positions** – This option allows you to lock an object in its original position on the report. Regardless of how it is printed, the system will maintain its original measurements on the report. Once this option is checked you can no longer drag-and-drop the fields in this section; you must use the Size and Position option from the shortcut menu of the field.

▪ **Format with Multiple Columns** – This option is available only with the Details section in the Section Expert. It allows you to have multiple columns in the section for purposes of a newsletter, barcode labels, or mailing labels. Selecting this option will enable the Layout tab for further formatting. (You'll read about the Layout tab in a later section of this chapter.)

- **Clamp Page Footer** – This option is available only with the Page Footer in the Section Expert. It is used to remove any extra whitespace at the bottom of the report.

- **Reserve Minimum Page Footer** – This option is available only with the Page Footer section in the Section Expert. It reduces the amount of space reserved for the page footer. It affects the page footer size only if the report has multiple Page Footers.

The Paging Tab of the Section Expert

The Paging tab, shown in Figure 5.8, holds the formatting options relating to page breaks, page numbers, and section orientation. The options that are available depend on the section that you are working with.

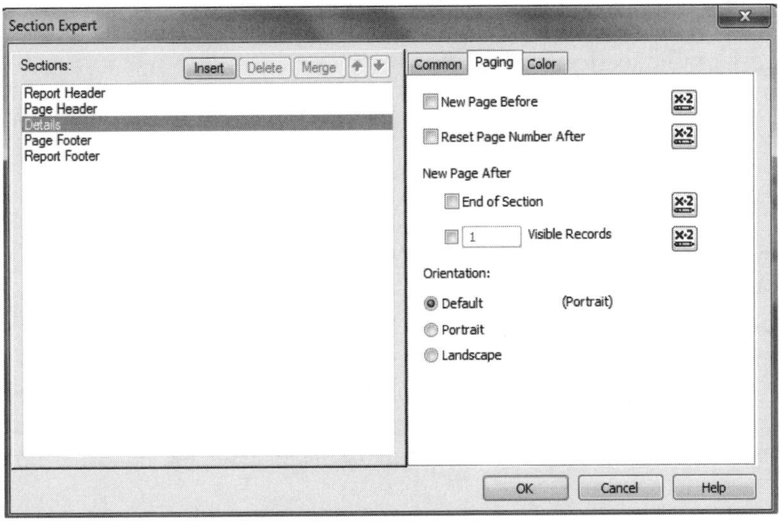

Figure 5.8
The Paging tab of the Section Expert window.

The options that are available are:

- **New Page Before** – Use of this option will ensure a page break is implemented before the selected section is printed. This option is not available with the Report Header or Page Header sections because it would create a blank page in an undesired location in the report.

Tip

When using the New Page Before option with Group Headers, you will need to conditionally set it not to break on the first group. Otherwise, your page header will print and the first page of the report will blank. Use the conditional formatting x+2 option and enter: **not onfirstrecord**.

- **Reset Page Number After** – Use of this option will allow the page numbers to reset to page 1 after the section is printed. This feature is very useful when a report is printed by group and you want to distribute the report individually to each group. Each group will be presented with page 1 to the end of the group's data instead of the continuous incremental page numbers of the report.

- **New Page After** – Visible in the Report Header, Group Header, Details, and Group Footer.

  Available in the Details section only:

  - *End of Section* – This option will force a page break after the section is printed.

  - *# Visible Records* – This option gives you more flexibility and allows you to specify that the page break will occur after a certain number of records are printed.

Tip

When using the New Page After option with the Group Footer, you need to conditionally set it not to break on the last record. Otherwise, the last page of the report will be blank or will list any grand totals on the page alone. Use the conditional format to set the option to **not onlastrecord**.

- **Orientation** – This option will allow you to change the page orientation of the section. This option is available only for the Report Header, Report Footer, and the Details sections. This option is very useful for placement of charts, crosstabs, and data that needs to be in a landscape report when the majority of the report is in portrait or vice versa. If the option is not changed, the sections take on the default orientation of the report.

The Color Tab of the Section Expert

The Color tab, shown in Figure 5.9, has the following option.

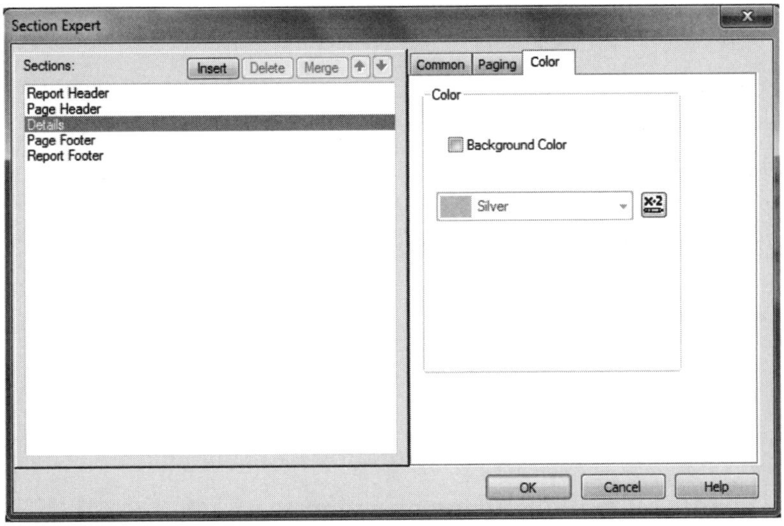

Figure 5.9
The Color tab of the Section Expert.

- **Background Color** – Use this option to set the background color of the section. For example, alternate the background color in the Details section to break the monotony of a large list report.

Tip

This option can be conditionally set in the x+2 button to the right of the option. This example alternates the background color for every second record:

```
If recordnumber mod 2 = 0 then crSilver else crNoColor
```

The Layout Tab of the Section Expert

The Layout tab, shown in Figure 5.10, is active in the Details section only when the Format Multiple Columns option has been checked.

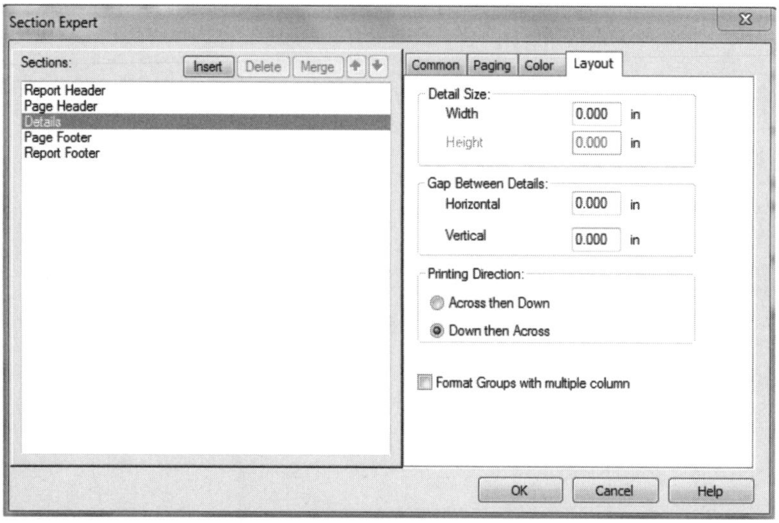

Figure 5.10
The Layout tab of the Section Expert.

The Layout tab has the following options:

- **Detail Size** – This option designates the size of each detail column.

- **Gap Between Details** – Use the Horizontal option to specify the gap between the columns printing across. Use the Vertical option to specify the gaps between the columns printing down.

- **Printing Direction** – The Across then Down option prints the details across the page in multiple columns. Good for a newsletter, for example. The Down then Across option prints the details down then across. Good for mailing labels.

- **Format Groups with Multiple Columns** – Use the Format Groups with Multiple Columns option to allow Crystal Reports to format the groups with multiple columns using the same settings specified in the detail size, gap width, and printing directions specified for the section.

INSERTING MULTIPLE SECTIONS

There are times when the business requirements of the report demand multiple sections of the same type of data. For example, you might want different page headers based on the customer or the type of invoice or statement.

You can insert multiple sections by right-clicking on the blue area of the section and choosing Insert Section Below, as shown in Figure 5.11. You can also access the Section Expert from the Report > Section Expert menu and then click the Insert button, as shown in Figure 5.12.

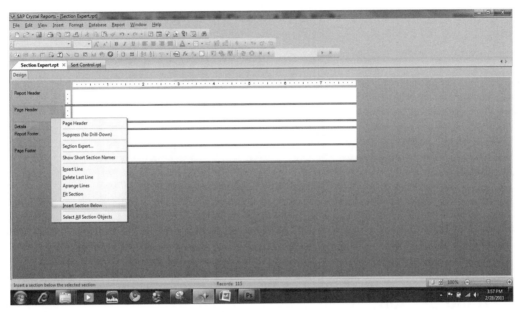

Figure 5.11
Inserting a new section.

You can insert a section by clicking the Insert button at the top of the Section Expert window. If you insert an additional Report Header section, the window should display as Report Header A and Report Header B. Two Report Header sections enable you to have a Title in Report Header A section and a chart or subreport in the Report Header B that is set to Underlay the Following Section to print side by side with the data in the report.

When inserting multiple sections, you can format each separately, suppressing one or both under certain conditions. In certain situations, for example, you might be charged with creating a very similar report, one for managers and another for staff users, with minor changes in data. Wouldn't it be better to have one report and have the correct data shown based on the level of the users? Well, the use of multiple sections and parameters allows you to minimize the number

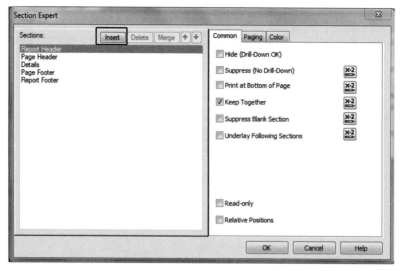

Figure 5.12
Using the Insert button in the Section Expert.

of reports that are to be maintained. I'll cover parameters in Chapter 7. Section orders can be changed using the up or down arrows in the Section Expert, which appear only after multiple sections are inserted.

Merging Sections

With multiple sections, you can merge the section directly from the Section Expert. Sections are merged upward, so if you have a Report Header A and Report Header B, Report Header B can be merged into Report Header A. The system will take whatever data is in the section and place it at the bottom of the section to be merged into. The Merge button will be enabled only for sections that have sections below it. Using the Merge option allows you to retain the information that is in the section. See Figure 5.13.

Deleting Sections

Often after inserting a section, you determine the section is not needed. You can delete the section, but be careful to first move any needed information out of the section prior to deleting it. You can delete a section from the Section Expert by selecting the Delete button that is enabled when multiple sections have been inserted or you can right-click the section in the Design window and choose Delete Section, as shown in Figure 5.14.

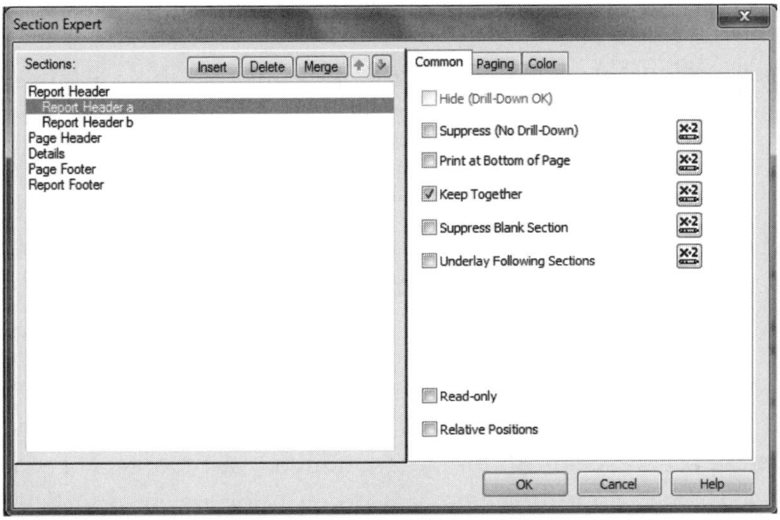

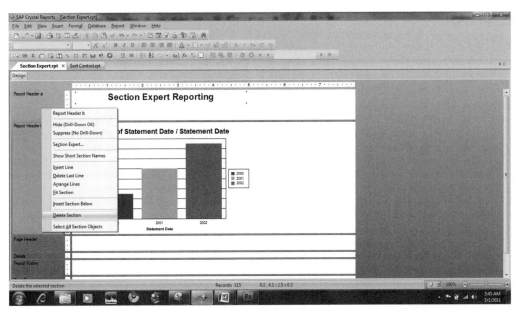

Figure 5.13
Merging sections in the Section Expert.

Figure 5.14
Deleting a section.

Splitting a Section

There are times when you might want to split a section into multiple sections based on the number of fields that are in the section or because you need additional formatting options. When you split a section, all existing formatting is retained. This is not true with the Insert Section option.

To split a section, place your cursor on the left border of the section; you will get a Section Splitting cursor. Drag up or down to split the section.

SUMMARY

Formatting your report with multiple sections and conditionally setting the options for the different sections can minimize the number of reports that you have to work with. A visually appealing report is going to be received well by your end users, so be sure to spend some time getting to know the features covered in this chapter.

EXERCISES

Exercise 1

You have created a report of last year's sales by country and included a graphical chart to correspond with the data. However, after previewing the report, you determined that the chart would look better next to the data instead of above it.

1. Open the Section Expert Summary report, located in the Chapter 5 sample files.

2. Preview the report. Notice the chart's location.

3. Switch back to Design view.

4. Insert another Report Header section. Right-click the blue Report Header section area and choose Insert Section Below. You should now have a Report Header A and Report Header B.

5. Drag and drop the chart from Report Header A into the right side of the Report Header B section. Make sure the chart is not over the Summary Field data.

Tip

When moving the chart into Report Header B, make sure the top of the chart is within the Report Header B section before releasing the mouse. Otherwise, the chart will not move.

6. Notice that the Report Header A section has too much whitespace now that the chart has been removed. To correct this easily, right-click the Report Header A section and choose Fit Section.

7. Preview the report.

8. Switch back to Design view and right-click the Report Header B section. Open the Section Expert. Select the Underlay Follow Section checkbox.

9. Save the report as **Section Expert Summary with Chart**.

10. Preview the report. Notice the chart is now next to the summary data. (Although you might have to resize the chart or move the summary fields to the left to ensure the complete chart is being displayed.) Figure 5.15 shows the end result.

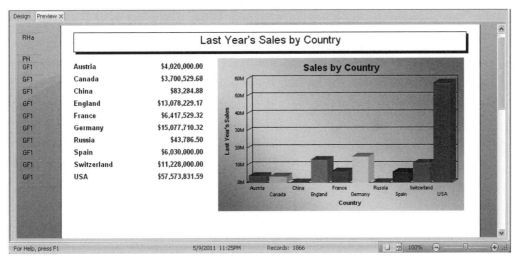

Figure 5.15
Report using the Underlay Following Section option.

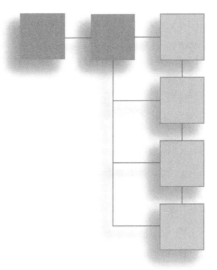

CHAPTER 6

FORMATTING FIELDS

The objectives of this chapter are to learn the following tasks:

- Formatting fields
- Setting global options

Formatting the fields on your report to make them user-friendly and meaningful is an important aspect of the design process. The formatting options available depend on the datatype of the field. The common datatypes are String, Number, Currency, Date and Time, Date, Time, Boolean, and BLOB (Binary Large Objects).

To format a field, select the field and access the Format Field dialog box from the Format > Format Field option or right-click the field and choose Format Field. The Format Editor dialog box will open. You can also change some of the formatting options by selecting the field and using the Formatting toolbar, shown in Figure 6.1.

With the field selected, you can quickly change the following from the Formatting toolbar:

- Font face
- Font size
- Increase font size (increments of one)

Figure 6.1
The Formatting toolbar.

- Decrease font size (increments of one)
- Set font style
- Font alignment
- Font color
- Add borders
- Suppress the field
- Lock format
- Lock position and size
- Format the field as currency
- Add/remove thousands separator
- Add percentage sign
- Increase decimals
- Decrease decimals

There are formatting options that are common with all datatypes and some that are dependent on the datatype. The following sections discuss Crystal Report's formatting options on a tab-by-tab basis.

THE COMMON TAB

The Common tab, shown in Figure 6.2, includes the following formatting options:

- **Object Name** – Use this option to give your field a descriptive name. Any database fields will have a default field name. This feature is helpful when looking for a field in the Report Explorer.

- **Tool Tip Text** – Use this option to add text to give the users an idea of what information the field stores. When the users hover the mouse pointer over the field, the tool tip will appear.

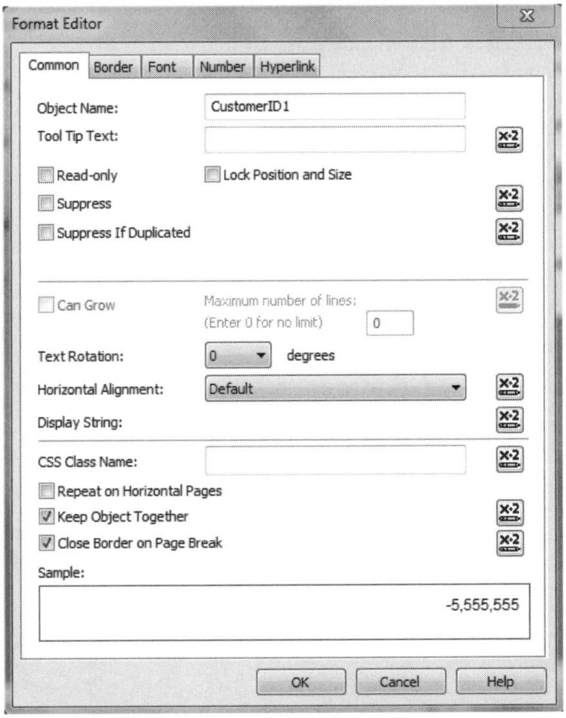

Figure 6.2
The Common tab in the Format Editor.

- **Read-Only** – Use this option to make the field read-only. No formatting can be done to the field with the exception of the Repeat on Horizontal Pages and the Lock Position and Size.

- **Lock Position and Size** – Use this option to lock the position and the width and height of the field. This option is valuable to protect your report formatting and in the case of variables where the location of the field is crucial in obtaining the correct value.

- **Suppress** – Use this option to permanently suppress the field when previewing and printing. This option is useful for variables that are needed on the report but are not printed or used as formulas, such as the `drilldown grouplevel`.

- **Suppress if Duplicated** – Use this option to hide any duplicate values when printing a report. This option can give the illusion of grouping in a detail report. See Figures 6.3 and 6.4.

Region	Customer ID	Customer Name	Last Year's Sales	Order Date
AL	61	Benny - The Spokes Person	$6,091.96	11/3/2004
AL	4	Psycho-Cycle	$52,809.11	3/2/2005
AL	61	Benny - The Spokes Person	$6,091.96	8/7/2004
AL	61	Benny - The Spokes Person	$6,091.96	8/5/2004
AL	61	Benny - The Spokes Person	$6,091.96	7/24/2004
AL	61	Benny - The Spokes Person	$6,091.96	7/3/2004
AL	61	Benny - The Spokes Person	$6,091.96	8/29/2004
AL	61	Benny - The Spokes Person	$6,091.96	4/30/2004
AL	61	Benny - The Spokes Person	$6,091.96	9/7/2004
AL	61	Benny - The Spokes Person	$6,091.96	3/15/2004
AL	61	Benny - The Spokes Person	$6,091.96	3/1/2004
AL	61	Benny - The Spokes Person	$6,091.96	2/19/2004
AL	61	Benny - The Spokes Person	$6,091.96	2/11/2004
AL	61	Benny - The Spokes Person	$6,091.96	12/12/2003
AL	4	Psycho-Cycle	$52,809.11	10/18/2004
AL	61	Benny - The Spokes Person	$6,091.96	5/23/2004
AL	61	Benny - The Spokes Person	$6,091.96	4/3/2005
AL	4	Psycho-Cycle	$52,809.11	10/20/2004
AL	4	Psycho-Cycle	$52,809.11	10/30/2004
AL	4	Psycho-Cycle	$52,809.11	11/23/2004
AL	4	Psycho-Cycle	$52,809.11	1/4/2005

Figure 6.3
With the Suppress if Duplicated option turned off.

Region	Customer ID	Customer Name	Last Year's Sales	Order Date
CA	5	Sporting Wheels Inc.	$85,642.56	3/2/2004
	62	Bike Shop from Mars	$25,873.25	3/11/2004
	5	Sporting Wheels Inc.	$85,642.56	6/11/2004
	62	Bike Shop from Mars	$25,873.25	6/5/2004
	62	Bike Shop from Mars	$25,873.25	6/27/2004
	5	Sporting Wheels Inc.	$85,642.56	2/19/2004
	5	Sporting Wheels Inc.	$85,642.56	2/16/2004
	5	Sporting Wheels Inc.	$85,642.56	4/18/2004
CO	114	Fred's Bikes	$7,874.25	5/21/2004
CT	115	Phil's Bikes	$27.00	5/21/2004
DC	116	Colin's Bikes	$40.50	5/21/2004
DE	117	Barry's Bikes	$33.90	5/21/2004
FL	25	Extreme Cycling	$69,819.10	1/19/2004
	20	Wheels and Stuff	$25,556.11	5/12/2004
	25	Extreme Cycling	$69,819.10	1/27/2004
	25	Extreme Cycling	$69,819.10	4/7/2004
	20	Wheels and Stuff	$25,556.11	6/13/2004
	25	Extreme Cycling	$69,819.10	2/2/2004
	20	Wheels and Stuff	$25,556.11	3/17/2004
	25	Extreme Cycling	$69,819.10	3/7/2004
	25	Extreme Cycling	$69,819.10	4/22/2004
	25	Extreme Cycling	$69,819.10	6/2/2004
	25	Extreme Cycling	$69,819.10	6/17/2004
	25	Extreme Cycling	$69,819.10	6/17/2004
	25	Extreme Cycling	$69,819.10	6/27/2004

Figure 6.4
With the Suppress if Duplicated option turned on.

- **Can Grow** – This option is the equivalent of wrap text. It allows string fields to grow vertically.

- **Max Number of Lines** – With the Can Grow option checked, you can specify how many lines the system is allowed to wrap the text. The default value is 0, which specifies no limit. The report will continue to wrap text until all of the data is shown. However, it is very useful when you want to print only the first number of lines, for example, the first five lines only.

- **Text Rotation** – This option allows you to rotate your text vertically.

- **Horizontal Alignment** – This option allows you to set your horizontal alignment (default, left, right, center, and justified).

- **Display String** – This option is set using the Conditional Formatting x+2 button. It allows you to set custom formats for the string, Boolean number, currency, date, time, and date and time datatypes. For example, you can display numbers as $1M.

- **CSS Class Name** – This option specifies a class name that can be used in a Cascading Style Sheet to consistently format the field in every report.

- **Repeat on Horizontal Pages** – This option is used for fields that span across page breaks horizontally such as text fields, charts, and crosstab charts. If your crosstab chart spans multiple pages, it's very helpful to have the row labels print on all pages so the users are not flipping to the previous page to see what row label the values correspond with.

- **Keep Object Together** – This option prevents an object from breaking across pages.

- **Close Border on Page Break** –This option prevents any field or object that has a border around it and spans multiple pages from printing partial borders. This option ensures that each page the field is printed on has a full border around all partial text.

The Border Tab

The Border tab is shown in Figure 6.5.

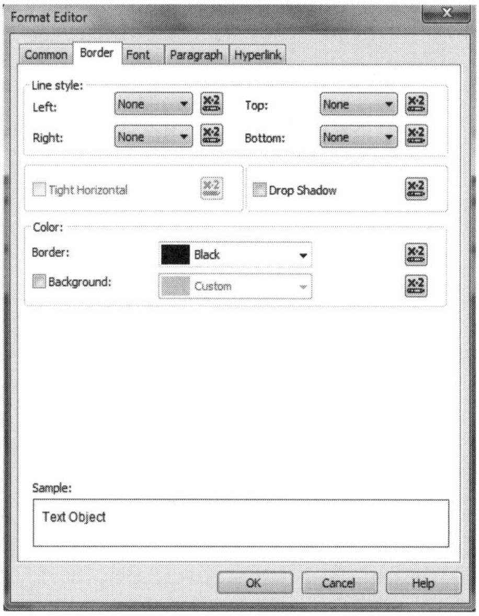

Figure 6.5
The Border tab of the Format Editor.

In the Line Style area of the Border tab, you'll find the following options:

- **Left** – Use this option to set a border on the left side of the field. This option can be conditionally set.

- **Right** – Use this option to set a border on the right side of the field. This option can be conditionally set.

- **Top** – Use this option to set a border on the top of the field. This option can be conditionally set.

Tip

The top border can be used as a total line indicator on a field instead of inserting a single line above the total field. The border line is the length of the field and stays with the field if exported.

- **Bottom** – Use this option to set the bottom border of the field. This option can be conditionally set.

Tip

The bottom border can be used as the double line at the end of a financial report instead of inserting a double line below the total field.

- **Tight Horizontal** – This option trims the space around the border. Use caution when using this option, because it will resize your fields. The borders will be tight around the length of the value in the field, not the original size of the field. Figures 6.6 and 6.7 show a report with this option off and on, respectively.

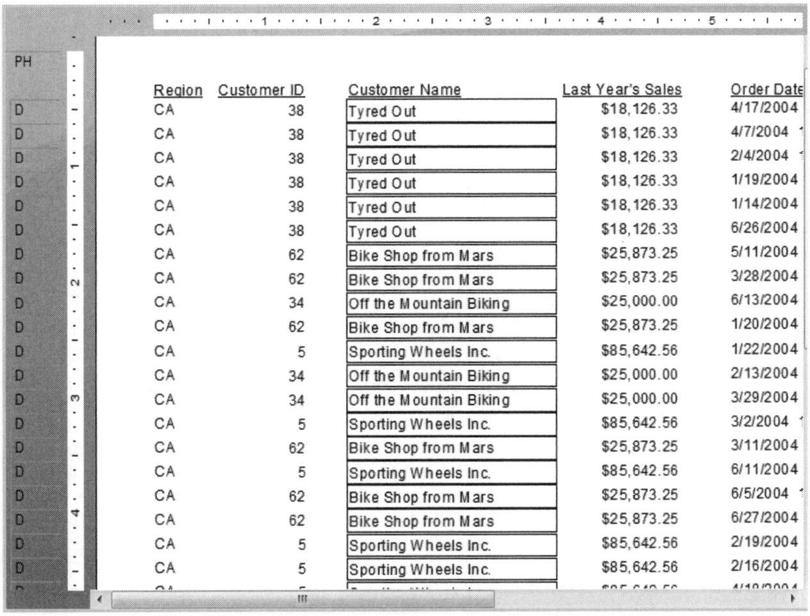

Figure 6.6
Field with full borders, with Tight Horizontal turned off.

- **Drop Shadow** – Use this option to print a drop shadow on the object. As shown in Figure 6.8, the drop shadow prints across the bottom and to the right of the object.

You can format the border color and fill color of the object by using the following options:

- **Border** – Use this option to set the border's line color. This option can be conditionally set.

- **Background** – Use this option to set the background color of the object. This option can be conditionally set.

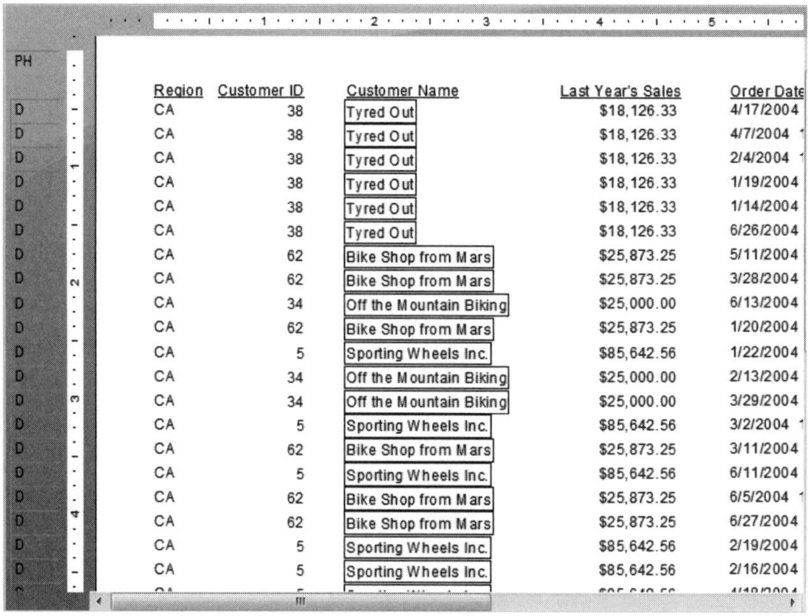

	Region	Customer ID	Customer Name	Last Year's Sales	Order Date
	CA	38	Tyred Out	$18,126.33	4/17/2004
	CA	38	Tyred Out	$18,126.33	4/7/2004
	CA	38	Tyred Out	$18,126.33	2/4/2004
	CA	38	Tyred Out	$18,126.33	1/19/2004
	CA	38	Tyred Out	$18,126.33	1/14/2004
	CA	38	Tyred Out	$18,126.33	6/26/2004
	CA	62	Bike Shop from Mars	$25,873.25	5/11/2004
	CA	62	Bike Shop from Mars	$25,873.25	3/28/2004
	CA	34	Off the Mountain Biking	$25,000.00	6/13/2004
	CA	62	Bike Shop from Mars	$25,873.25	1/20/2004
	CA	5	Sporting Wheels Inc.	$85,642.56	1/22/2004
	CA	34	Off the Mountain Biking	$25,000.00	2/13/2004
	CA	34	Off the Mountain Biking	$25,000.00	3/29/2004
	CA	5	Sporting Wheels Inc.	$85,642.56	3/2/2004
	CA	62	Bike Shop from Mars	$25,873.25	3/11/2004
	CA	5	Sporting Wheels Inc.	$85,642.56	6/11/2004
	CA	62	Bike Shop from Mars	$25,873.25	6/5/2004
	CA	62	Bike Shop from Mars	$25,873.25	6/27/2004
	CA	5	Sporting Wheels Inc.	$85,642.56	2/19/2004
	CA	5	Sporting Wheels Inc.	$85,642.56	2/16/2004

Figure 6.7
Field with full borders, with Tight Horizontal turned on.

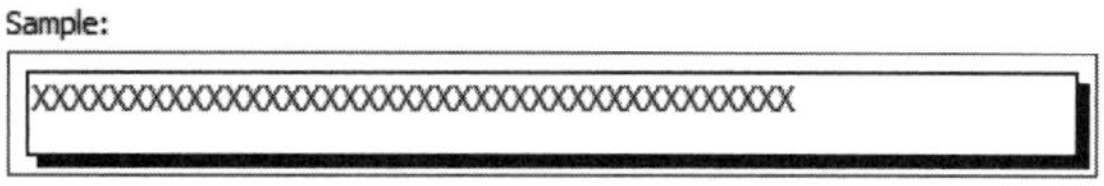

Sample:

XXXXXXXXXXXXXXXXXXXXXXXXXXXXXXXXXXXXXXXXXXX

Figure 6.8
Example of a drop shadow.

THE FONT TAB

The Font tab, shown in Figure 6.9, includes the following formatting options:

- **Font** – Use this option to set the font of the field. Crystal Reports default font face is Arial. If you want to use another default font, you must change it in the File > Options tab. This option can be conditionally set.

- **Style** – Use this option to set your organization's font style to Bold, Regular, Italic, or Bold Italic. This option can be conditionally set.

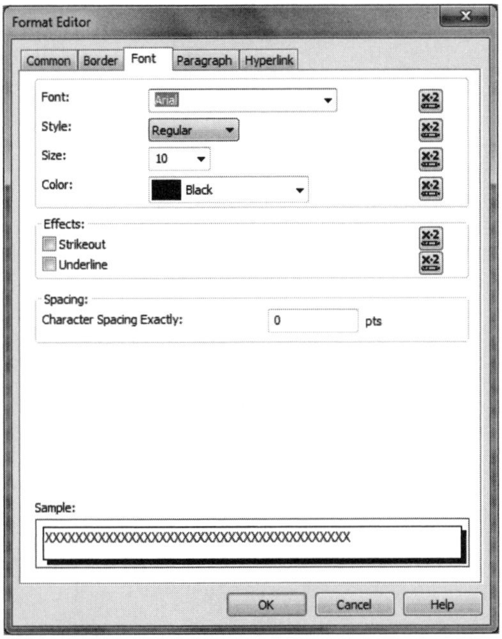

Figure 6.9
The Font tab of the Format Editor.

- **Size** – Use this option to set the font size. You can use this option to conditionally set the size based on the printer page orientation, the report audience, or the type of field (detail versus summary). This option can be conditionally set.

- **Color** – Use this option to set the color of the font. This option can be conditionally set.

- **Strikeout**– Use this option to enable the strikeout character. This option can be conditionally set.

- **Underline**– Use this option to underline the field. This option can be conditionally set.

- **Character Spacing Exactly** – Use this option to set the absolute character spacing between the characters.

THE PARAGRAPH TAB

The Paragraph tab is shown in Figure 6.10.

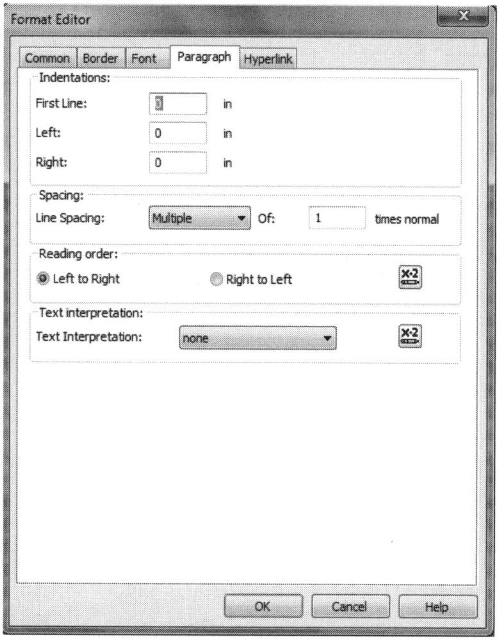

Figure 6.10
The Paragraph tab of the Format Editor.

You can format the Indentations of your fields based on the following options:

- **First Line** – Use this option to set the exact measurement in inches that the first line should be indented in a paragraph. If your report is measured in units, pixels, or centimeters, the measurement you enter here should match that.

- **Left** – Use this option to set the measurement for how far the paragraph should start from the left margin.

- **Right** – Use this option to set the measurement for how far the paragraph should start from the right margin.

When you want to control the spacing of the fields' data, you may use any of these formatting options:

- **Line Spacing** – Use this option to choose to set the exact line spacing or to set it as a multiple of your font size.

- **Of** – If you chose exact in the Line Spacing option, you need to enter the exact number. If you chose multiple, enter the multiple of the line spacing.

When there is a need to change the reading order of your data, you have the following options:

- **Left to Right** – Use this option to determine that the system reads the text from left to right.

- **Right to Left** – Use this option to determine that the system reads the text from right to left.

When the field requires the program to interpret the data in a particular text type, you can use the Text Interpretation option to select the type of preformatted text. You have the option to interpret the data as:

- **None** – The text is read as plain text.

- **RTF** – The text is read in Rich Text Format.

- **HTML** – The text is read as HTML data.

THE HYPERLINK TAB

The Hyperlink tab is shown in Figure 6.11.

The Hyperlink tab allows you to create a hyperlink to one of the following options:

- **No Hyperlink** – This is the default option. Select this option to not have the field displayed as a hyperlink.

- **A Website on the Internet** – Use this option to have the object point to a website address.

- **An Email Address** – Use this option to have the object point to an email address.

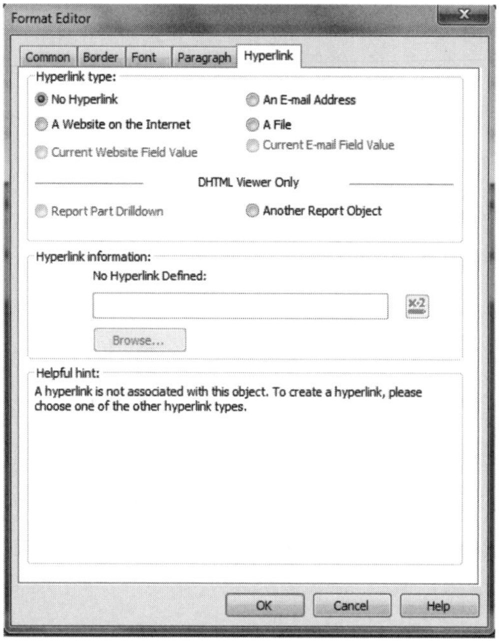

Figure 6.11
The Hyperlink tab of the Format Editor.

- **A File** – Use this option to point to a file that is accessible to the users of the report. It must be stored in a shared location.

- **Current Website Field Value** – Use this option to turn the current selected field into a website hyperlink. The field value must be formatted as a website in order for the option to be enabled.

- **Current Email Field Value** – Use this option to turn the current selected field into an email hyperlink. The field value must be formatted as an email in order for the option to be enabled.

The DHTML viewer options are as follows:

- **Report Part Drill-Down** – This option allows you to point to another part of the same report; similar to the drill-down capability.

- **Another Report Object** – This option allows you to link to another section in the same report or in another report. Use of the Enterprise Server is needed for another report option.

The options available in this section will depend on the option you selected in the Hyperlink Type section of this tab. Based on the settings, the options are:

- **No Hyperlink** – This option will be grayed out if the No Hyperlink option is chosen above.

- **Web Address** – Enter the website address for the hyperlink if the A Website on the Internet option is chosen above.

- **Email Address** – Enter the email address for the hyperlink if the An E-mail Address option is chosen above.

- **Filename** – Enter the path to the shared file if the A File option is chosen above.

FORMATTING OPTIONS SPECIFIC TO THE DATATYPE

Now that you've read about the formatting options that are common with all datatypes, it's time to learn about the formatting options that are dependent on the datatype. The following sections discuss Crystal Report's datatype-specific formatting options.

The Number Tab

The Number tab is shown in Figure 6.12.

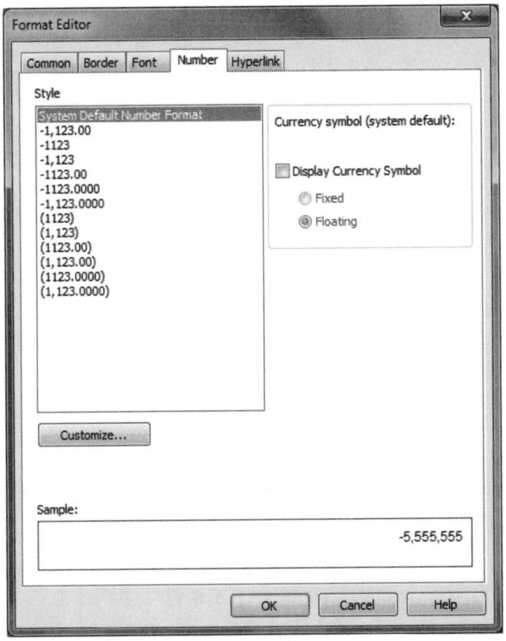

Figure 6.12
The Number tab of the Format Editor.

Currency Symbol (system default) options:

- **Display Currency Symbol** – This allows you to set the format of the number field to display the $ symbol.

- **Fixed** – The $ sign is displayed at the left edge of the field. All $ signs are aligned for the entire report for this field. This format presents a clean, professional appearance.

- **Floating** – The $ sign is displayed at the immediate left of the number field. The $ signs are not aligned consistently.

In the Style area of the Number tab, you can choose one of the preformatted styles for your numbers. If one of the preformatted styles does not fit your requirements, you can customize the number format. Click the Customize button. The Custom Style/Number tab, shown in Figure 6.13, will appear.

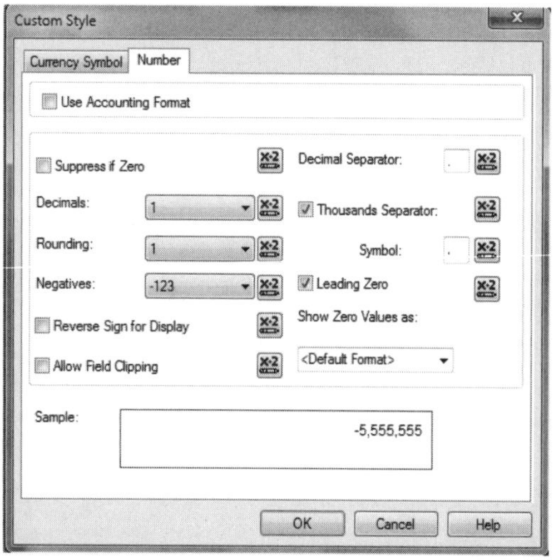

Figure 6.13
The Custom Style/Number dialog box.

The most frequently used options on the Custom Style/Number tab are as follows:

- **Use Accounting Format** – Selecting this option preformats the field to use the fixed currency symbol. The minus symbol will be determined by the Regional settings and the dash will be shown for zero values.

- **Suppress if Zero** – This option suppresses the values if zero.

- **Decimals** – Use this option to set the number of decimal places.

- **Rounding** – Use this option to set the rounding of the values.

- **Negatives** – Use this option to set the way you want the negative values to appear.

- **Reverse Sign for Display** – Use this option to reverse the signs for debits and credits in a financial report.

- **Allow Field Clipping** – This option is used to determine whether the number truncation sign is visible. If the field is not wide enough to show the whole number, the field will display on the report as ##########. If this option is chosen, it will show only the number of characters the field is wide enough to show, with no truncation indicators.

Caution

It is recommended that you not use this option because it could have severe undesired results. Numbers are by default right aligned; therefore, a field with the value of $1,231,567.89 that is wide enough to show only six characters will display as 567.89. If the field is left aligned it will display as $1,231. Either way, you can see the need for caution when using this option.

- **Show Zero Values As** – Allows you to set the value as a " – " or "0".

The options on the Custom Style/Currency Symbol tab, which is shown in Figure 6.14, are as follows:

- **Enable Currency Symbol** – This option enables the currency symbol to print on the field. You can conditionally set the currency symbol. The following example conditionally sets the $ symbol on the first record of each group.
  ```
  If {Customer.Region} <> Previous({Customer.Region})
  then crFixedCurrencySymbol else crNoCurrencySymbol
  ```

- **One Symbol Per Page** – Use this option to set one symbol per page.

- **Position** – Use this option to set the position of the symbol.

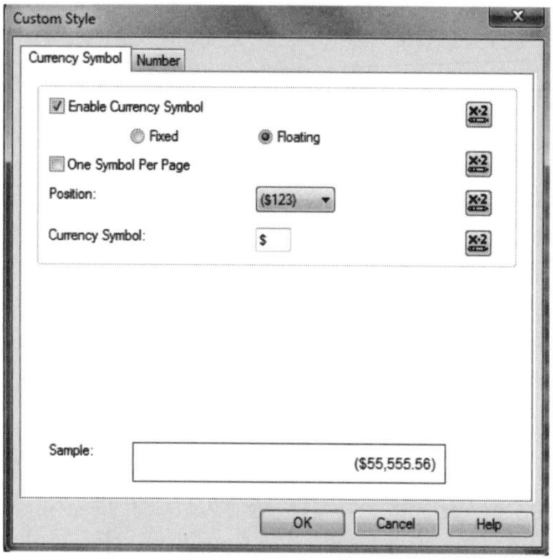

Figure 6.14
The Custom Style/Currency Symbol dialog box.

Tip

If you need to format a field to show the percentage sign, change the position to show the symbol on the right side of the field and change the Currency Symbol to a % symbol.

▪ **Currency Symbol** – Use this option to set the Currency Symbol. This option is used for foreign currencies or to show the percentage sign.

The Boolean Tab

The Boolean tab, shown in Figure 6.15, allows you to format Boolean fields as follows:

▪ True or False

▪ Y or N

▪ Yes or No

▪ 0 or 1

The Date and Time Tab

The Date and Time tab is shown in Figure 6.16.

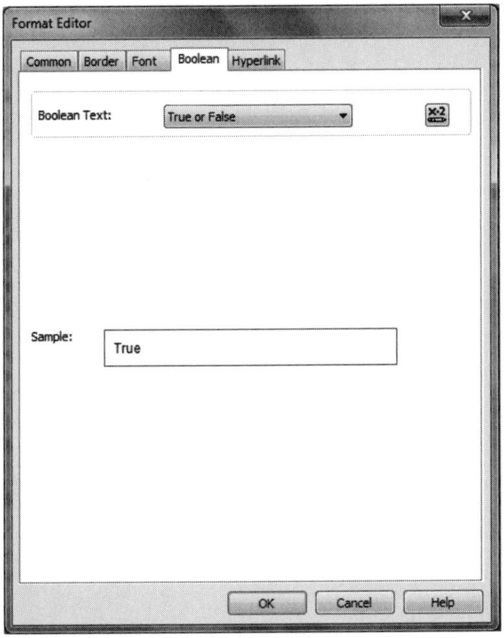

Figure 6.15
The Boolean tab of the Format Editor.

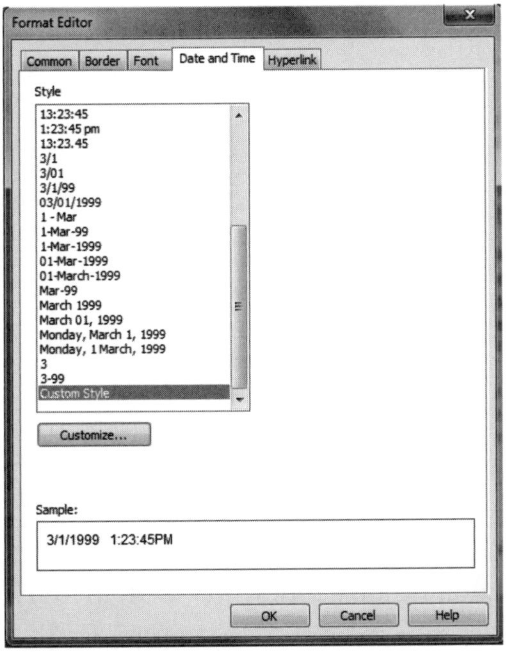

Figure 6.16
The Date and Time tab of the Format Editor.

From this tab, you choose one of the preformatted styles for your date or date and time fields. If one of the styles does not fit your desired format, you can click the Customize button to customize the format. The Custom Style dialog box, shown in Figure 6.17, will then appear.

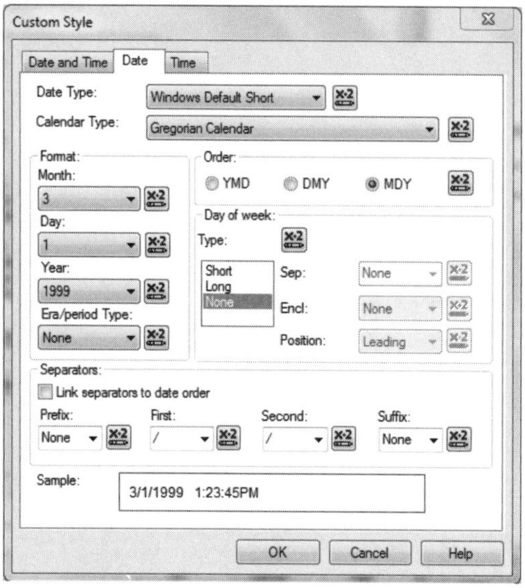

Figure 6.17
The Date Custom Style dialog box.

Follow these steps to create a custom date or time format:

1. Select the Date tab to format a Date field.

2. Format the date to your requirements.

3. To format the Time, select the Time tab.

4. Format the time to your requirements.

CREATING BARCODES

Crystal Reports 2008 introduced the option to format a number or text field as a barcode without requiring any additional fonts. Barcodes are used to track product information such as inventory sales and receipts. Crystal Reports 2011 includes the barcodes fonts for Code 39 and Code 39 Full ASCII. The integrated barcode fonts are from Azalea Software and, with the installation of Crystal Reports 2011, the Azalea Software UFL (User Function Library) is installed by default. The Code 39 barcode includes uppercase letters from A-Z and numbers from 0-9 and the following character symbols [$ % + - . /]. The Code 39 Full ASCII barcode includes the lower 128 ASCII characters. The codes are TrueType and Type 1 Postscript fonts.

Note

Barcode fields will be formatted with a font size of 24. Therefore, fields will be larger and may overlap. Proper formatting of the report after changing to a barcode may be necessary.

To insert a barcode format, follow these steps:

1. With the field selected, right-click the field and choose Change to Barcode.
2. Select the barcode font—Code 39 or Code 39 Full ASCII.
3. Click OK.

To remove a barcode format, follow these steps:

1. Right-click the field and choose Format Field.
2. On the Common tab, click on the x+2 next to the Display String option. (The x+2 button should appear in red to indicate conditional formatting.)
3. Delete the barcode text.
4. Change the font face from the Code39AzaleaWide2 to one of the regular fonts.
5. Change the font size to match the report font size.

Customizing Your System

Each of the field types can be formatted individually, but it is advisable for you to format your system to fit your environment. Global options are set to prevent you from having to format each field in every report. Any formatting options that you choose for the fields will be displayed for every new report.

Note

Changing your global options will not change any field formats for existing reports.

For example, if you know your organization rarely uses decimal places, you can format your number datatype to have zero decimal places. Another example is if you prefer the fixed currency symbol to the floating currency symbol on currency fields. To access the Global options, use the File > Options menu and select the Fields tab. See Figure 6.18.

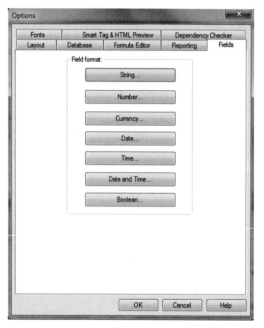

Figure 6.18
Formatting field types.

Select each one of the Field types to globally set the formatting options. The field types available are:

▪ **String** – Format your string fields with a specific font face and size.

▪ **Number** – Format your number fields to display no decimal places.

▪ **Currency** – Format your currency fields to display a fixed currency symbol.

- **Date** – Format the date as a two-digit month and day and a four-digit year.

- **Time** – Format your time fields to display in a 24-hour format.

- **Date and Time** – Format your Date and Time fields to display the date only.

- **Boolean** – Format your system to always display a Boolean field as Yes or No.

SUMMARY

Each field can be individually formatted but it's a more efficient use of your time to customize your Crystal Reports environment to fit your needs. It's best to set up your global options to format fields based on the norm, and then on a report-by-report basis, you can more quickly handle any report-specific formatting.

EXERCISES

Exercise 1

1. Open the Formatting Fields report, which is located in your sample files for Chapter 6. (These sample files can be downloaded from www.courseptr.com/downloads. Enter the book title, ISBN, or author's name to be linked to the sample files for the book.)

2. Right-click the {Last Year's Sales} field and choose Format Field.

3. Change the Currency Symbol from Floating to Fixed.

4. Click OK.

5. Right-click the {Order Date} field and choose Format Field.

6. Change the Date style to 03/01/1999.

7. Click OK. See Figure 6.19.

8. Right-click the {Shipped} field and choose Format Field.

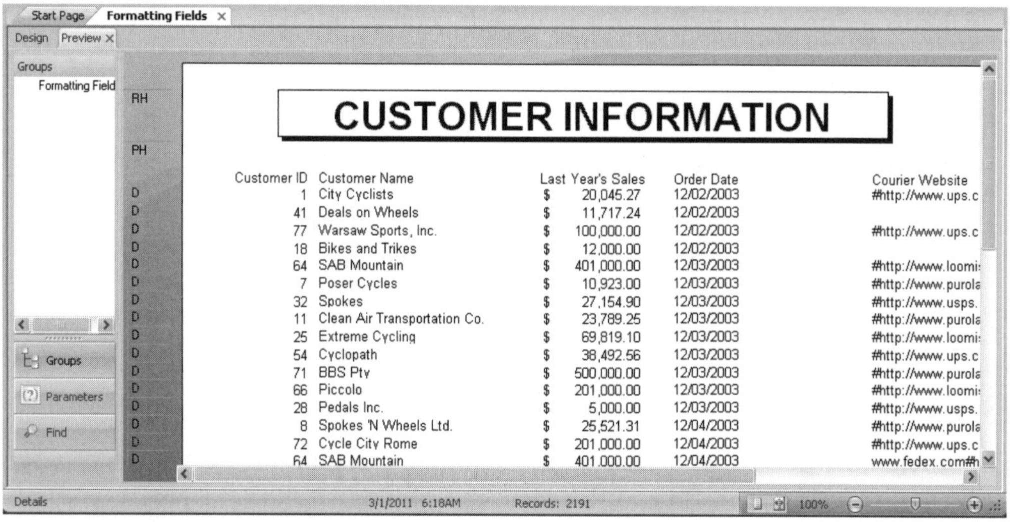

Figure 6.19
Preview of formatted fields.

9. From the Boolean tab, change the display option to Yes or No.

10. Click OK.

Your report should look similar to Figure 6.20.

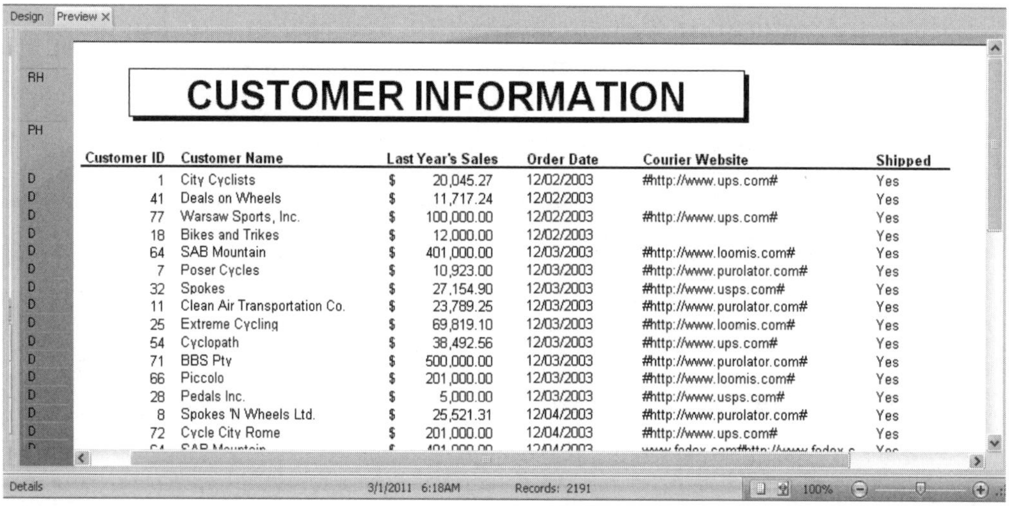

Figure 6.20
Report with formatted fields.

CHAPTER 7

FILTERING AND ANALYZING DATA

The objectives of this chapter are to learn the following tasks:

- Working with multiple tables
- Using the Select Expert
- Record selection
- Group selection
- Saved data selection
- Using Preview Sample
- Working with parameters
- Setting parameter order

WORKING WITH MULTIPLE TABLES

Most of the business requirements for the reports that you develop are going to involve the use of multiple database tables. It's important that you understand the dynamics of your database because you are responsible for pulling the correct data sources into the report to draw the correct information. Most relational DBMS databases have a data schema that detail the tables, fields, descriptions, indexes, relationships, views, stored procedures, packages, triggers, and other elements of the database. This schema is essential in determining the proper database tables and fields to use. After identifying the proper database tables and fields to use, you must determine how to link the tables together to retrieve the correct dataset.

There are performance issues for you to take into consideration when determining the fields to link the database tables. Most relational DBMS database tables have indexed fields. However, for some databases you may need to create your own indexed fields. Indexes allow faster retrieval of database records. Therefore, you should link on an indexed field whenever possible. The other point to consider is the use of a selection formula. Using a selection formula will limit the number of records that are read and retrieved from the database. Including an index field will increase the speed of record retrieval and require fewer records for the database to read. You'll learn about indexes in the next section of this chapter.

Figure 7.1 shows the Database Expert layout window after inserting multiple tables into a report.

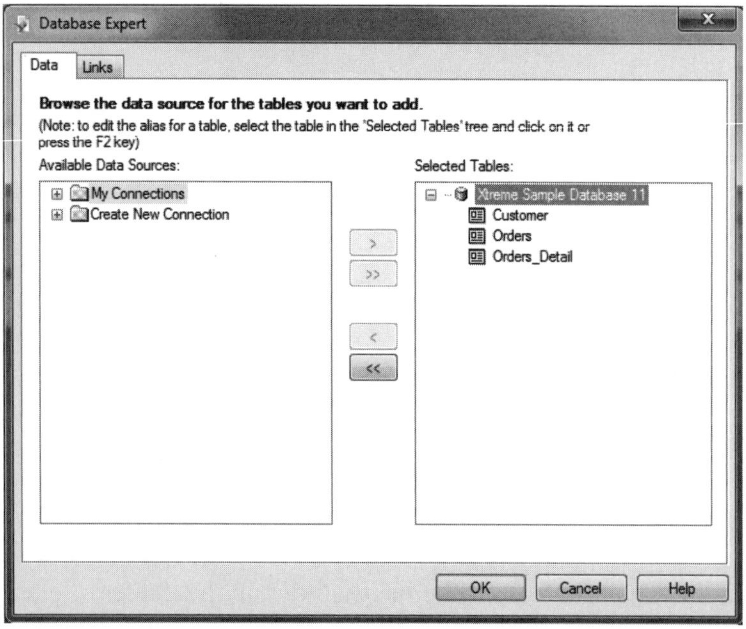

Figure 7.1
Adding multiple tables to a report.

Aliases

In certain situations you might need to retrieve different data from the same table. In order to achieve the desired results, you need to add the same table to the report twice. Crystal Reports allows you add the table as an *alias* table, as shown in Figures 7.2 and 7.3.

Figure 7.2
Message box when adding the same table multiple times.

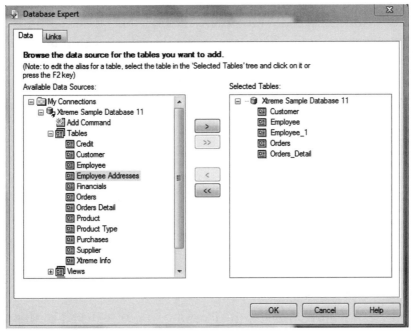

Figure 7.3
Same table displayed in data source table list.

Crystal Reports automatically adds an underscore and an incremental number to the table name. To make the table name more meaningful, you can rename it.

To rename a table, follow these steps:

1. From the Database Expert window, select the table to be renamed.

2. Press the F2 key.

3. Type the new table name.

4. Deselect the renamed table.

In the previous example, to retrieve both the employee names and the supervisor names, you needed to add the Employee table twice since the Supervisor ID is stored in the same table as the employee information.

When more than one table is inserted into the report, a Links tab is enabled on the Database Expert window, which you'll learn about more in the following sections.

Joins

Crystal Reports has a feature called Auto Smart Linking that is turned on by default. This feature automatically links the tables based on common field names, same datatypes, and length of fields. In order to understand how the tables are linked and the record dataset that is returned, you must understand the types of joins.

Tip

Turn the Auto Smart Linking off and link the tables yourself. File > Options > Database tab and uncheck the "Automatic Smart Linking" in the Advanced Options section.

There are four types of joins:

▪ **Inner Join** – This is the default join type. The recordset returned will only include records where there is a corresponding record with the field value that the tables are linked on.

In the example shown in Figure 7.4, the Customer table is linked to the Orders tables based on the customer ID field as an inner join. The resulting recordset will have only those customers who have placed an order. That's fine if that is the result that you are attempting to retrieve. What if your purpose was to pull all customers? Is it possible that a new customer has been set up in the system but an order has not been entered yet? When determining the proper join type of your links, you must take into account all possibilities.

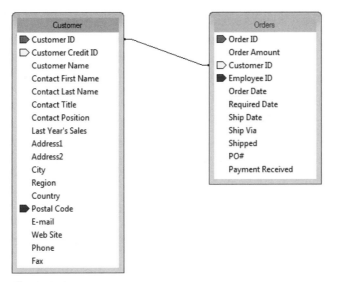

Figure 7.4
Linking two tables.

- **Left Outer Join** – A left outer join results in all records from the table on the left and only those records from the joining table that have a corresponding record based on the field that the table is linked on. When using an outer join, the placement of the tables in the Link window is important when selecting the join type.

  Using the previous example, if you used a left outer join, the resulting recordset will be a list of all customers regardless of whether they have placed an order along with the corresponding orders from the Orders table.

- **Right Outer Join** – A right outer join results in all records from the table on the right and only the records from the joining table that have a corresponding record based on the field that the table is linked on.

Again, with an outer join, the placement of the tables in the Link window is important.

Using the previous example, if you used a right outer join, the resulting recordset will be a list of orders and only those customers who have placed an order. This join type is commonly used to find orphan records. In this situation, it would find any orders where the customer's master record has been deleted.

▪ **Full Outer Join** – A full outer join results in all records from both tables regardless of whether there is a corresponding record in the join table. Your recordset will be larger than expected. A full outer join is not available for all databases in Crystal Reports.

Tip

Selecting the correct join type will ensure you retrieve the correct recordset. You should always have an idea of the number of records you should be retrieving from the dataset. It's recommended that you run the query in the query tool for the database you are working with. You will need the number of records you should be pulling from the database for your validation phase of your testing process.

As mentioned, Crystal Reports will automatically link all common fields between the tables. The system will link based on the field names, datatypes, and lengths of the fields. You do not want to allow Crystal Reports to continue to link the tables for you because it will significantly narrow your recordset. For example, if Crystal Reports finds 16 common fields between the two tables, it will create a link for all of them. However, based on your recordset needs, you may need only two fields linked to retrieve the desired dataset.

Using the Links Tab of the Database Expert Window

The Links tab of the Database Expert window, shown in Figure 7.5, has the following initial options:

▪ **Auto-Arrange** – This button can be used to strategically place the tables in the window.

▪ **Auto-Link** – This option will automatically link the tables.

By Name – This is the default option and Crystal Reports will link the fields based on the common field name, datatype, and field length.

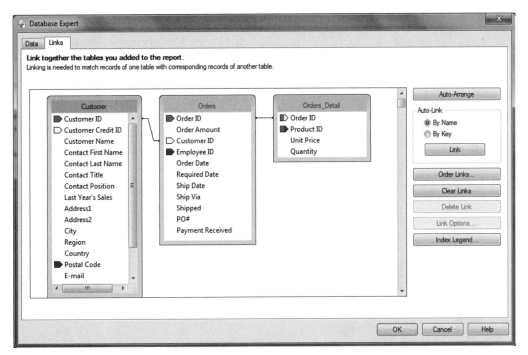

Figure 7.5
The Links tab of the Database Expert window.

By Key – This option will attempt to link the tables by the primary and foreign key. This option frequently fails and requests permission to link by name again, as shown in Figure 7.6. Often the database does not allow the tables' keys to be passed back to Crystal Reports or the tables do not include one or more keys.

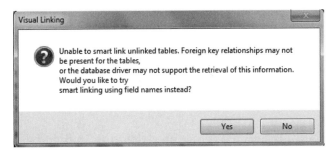

Figure 7.6
General error encountered using By Key Auto-Link option.

■ **Order Links** – This tab is enabled when more than two tables are included in the report. This option allows you to determine in what order Crystal Reports will read the links into the report. If you don't change the order, it will read the order based on the first link in the Link windows. The changes you make here can dramatically change your results set.

■ **Link Ordering is Enforced** – This option ensures the change in link order will be passed to the SQL query.

■ **Clear Links** – This option can be used to delete all links that currently exist in the link window. Often used to remove the links created by the Automatic Smart Linking.

■ **Index Legend** – This Index Legend, shown in Figure 7.7, shows the color index and the order that the indexes are read in the table.

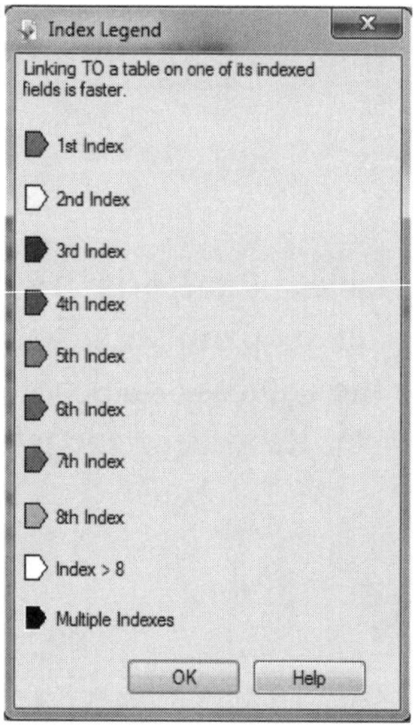

Figure 7.7
The Index Legend dialog box.

■ **Delete Link** – With the link selected, you can delete the individual link.

■ **Link Options** – With the link selected, this option will allow you to change the join type and join enforcement.

Link Options

With the link selected, click the Link Options button. (The options you set will only refer to the individual join line.) The dialog box shown in Figure 7.8 will appear.

Note

Click once on the join line. The link will turn blue when the link is selected. Double-click on the line or click the Link Options button.

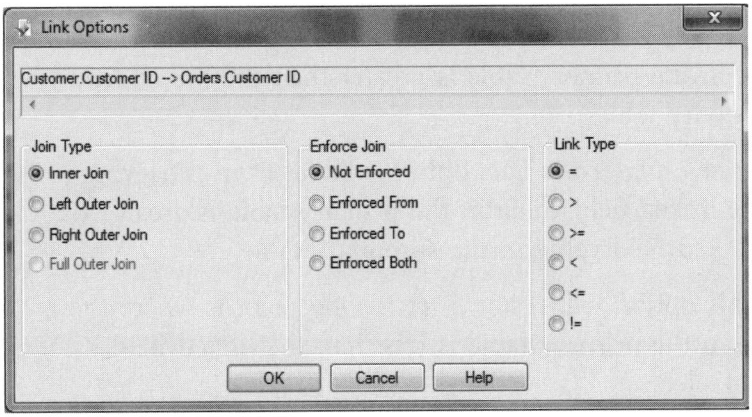

Figure 7.8
The Link Options dialog box.

You can change the following options by accessing the Link Options dialog box:

- **Join Type** – We discussed the join types earlier in the chapter. To change the join type, choose the desired join type.

- **Enforce Join**

  Not Enforced – This is the default option. The link is only used by the SELECT statement if it is required.

  Enforced From – This option ensures the primary table is included in the SELECT statement. If a field from the secondary table is used it is included in the report.

Enforced To – This option ensures the secondary table is included in the SELECT statement. If a field from the primary table is used it is also included in the SELECT statement.

Enforced Both – If a field from either table is used then the link is enforced and both tables will be included in the SELECT statement.

▪ **Link Type**

= *Equal To* – This option will result in retrieving records where the linked field value in the primary table is equal to the linked field value in the secondary table.

> *Greater Than* – This option will result in retrieving records where the linked field value in the primary table is greater than the linked field value in the secondary table.

>= *Greater Than or Equal To* – This option will result in retrieving records where the linked field value in the primary table is greater than or equal to the linked field value in the secondary table.

< *Less Than* – This option will result in retrieving records where the linked field value in the primary table is less than the linked field value in the secondary table.

<= *Less Than or Equal To* – This option will result in retrieving records where the linked field value in the primary table is less than or equal to the linked field value in the secondary table.

!= *Not Equal To* – This option will result in the retrieving records where the linked field value does not equal the field value in the secondary table.

SELECTING RECORDS USING THE SELECT EXPERT

When creating a report, rarely do you want to see every record that is in the table; this is particularly true with large databases. Crystal Reports allows you to choose the records you want to see using the Select Expert. The Select Expert filters your record selection based on the criteria that you select. It might be necessary to have multiple criteria to narrow your record selection to your report requirements. For example:

```
{State} in ["VA", "NC", "NY", "CA"] and {Date} in Calendar1stQtr
```

To access the Select Expert, click the Select Expert button on the Expert toolbar or choose the Report > Select Expert menu command.

With no field selected, you can select the Select Expert icon. The Choose Field dialog box, shown in Figure 7.9, will open. Select the field the record selection will be based on and choose OK.

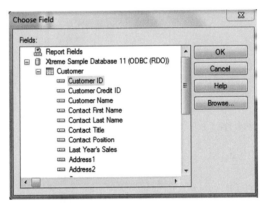

Figure 7.9
Choose a field for record selection.

The Select Expert dialog box, shown in Figure 7.10, will then open.

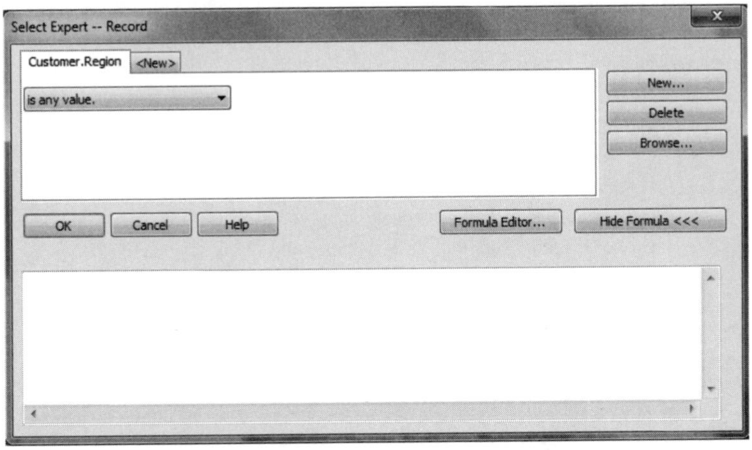

Figure 7.10
The Select Expert dialog box.

When the Select Expert dialog box first opens, the field you chose in the Choose Field dialog box will appear with the "is any value" operator which indicates at the time there is no filter on the field. There are many operators to choose from, depending on the datatype of the field that you are filtering and the desired result. For example, if you choose to exclude customers from foreign countries, you can use the Is equal to operator to specify that the customer's country must be equal to USA. Table 7.1 describes the list of operators.

Table 7.1 The Select Expert Operators

Operator	Description
Is any value	This is the default value. Indicates there is no filter and all records will be shown.
Is equal to	Allows you to specify one value the field value must equal. For example, {State} = "VA".
Is not equal to	Allows you to specify one value the field value must not equal. This option should be used to exclude a single value. For example, if I wanted to see all records except for those in the state of "VA", the record selection formula would be {State} <> "VA".
Is one of	Allows you to specify two or more values the field value could be within the list. For example, {State} in ["VA", "NC", "NY", "CA"].
Is not one of	Allows you to specify two or more values to exclude from the record selection. For example, not ({State} in ["VA", "NC","NY", "CA"]).
Is less than	Allows you to specify a value the field value must be less than. This operator works with dates and both numeric and alpha characters. For example, {LastName} < "J" will display all records with last names that are from "A" – "Izzz".
Is less than or equal to	This operator functions just as the "Is less than" except that it is inclusive of the value that you enter. This operator functions with dates and both numeric and alpha characters.
Is greater than	Allows you to specify a value the field value must be greater than. This operator works with dates and both numeric and alpha characters. For example, {LastName} > "J".
Is greater than or equal to	This operator functions just as the "Is greater than" except it is inclusive of the value that you enter. This operator functions with dates and both numeric and alpha characters.
Is between	Allows you to specify a range for dates, numbers, and alpha characters.
Is not between	Allows you to exclude a range.
Starts with	Allows you to retrieve records where the field value starts with the characters specified. Works with alphanumeric characters.
Does not start with	Allows you to retrieve records where the field value does not start with the characters specified.
Is like	Allows you to specify a pattern the field value could be. You can use the wildcards, * and ?, to assist in specifying the criteria.

Table 7.1 (Continued)

Operator	Description
Is not like	Allows you to specify a pattern the field value could not be. You can use the wildcards, * and ?, to assist in specifying the criteria.
Formula	Allows you to write your own Boolean formula to compare the field value to.
Is in the period	Allows you to filter your records based on the date being in certain timeframes, such as in "MonthtoDate", "YeartoDate", and many others. This option can be an alternative when you desire not to use the parameter.
Is not in the period	Allows you to filter your records based on the date not being in certain timeframes, such as in "MonthtoDate", "YeartoDate", and many others. This option can be an alternative when you desire not to use the parameter.
Is True	To be used with a Boolean field. You will pull only the records that are true.
Is False	To be used with a Boolean field. You will pull only the records that are false.

The operators that are available depend on the datatype of the field. Once you choose an operator, it's now time for you to specify the criteria that it must meet. You can type the value in or you can select the value from the drop-down list. See Figure 7.11.

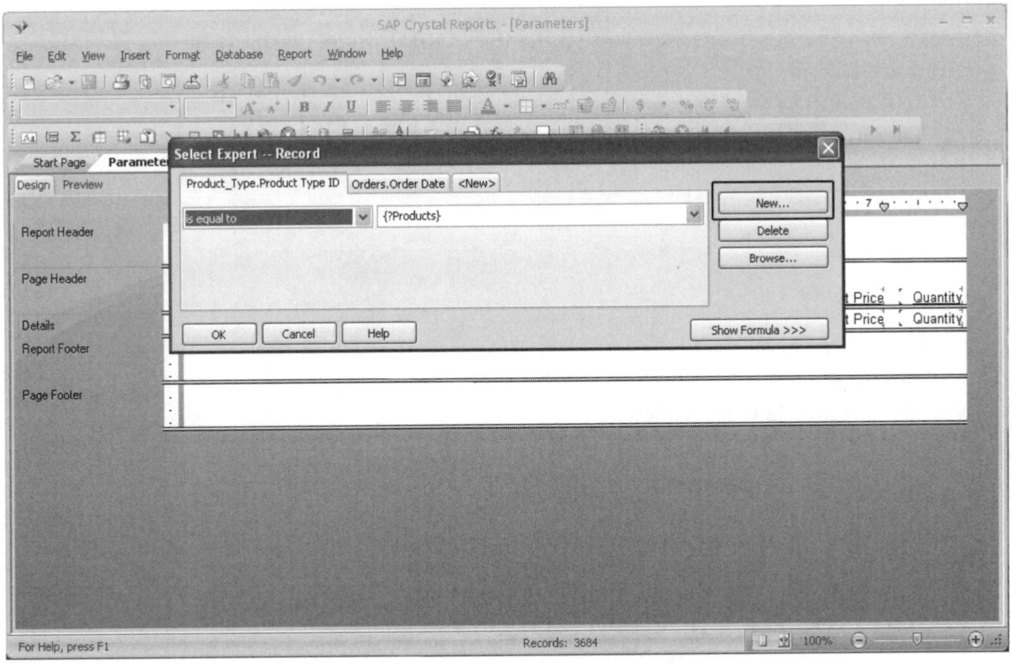

Figure 7.11
Selecting or entering database values.

Tip

You might not see all of the database values in the drop-down list because Crystal Reports is set by default to show only the first 500 unique values in the table. If you type the value in the entry field, you must make sure you type the value exactly as it is in the database; otherwise, it will not retrieve any values.

You can set multiple criteria for the record selection by clicking the New button on the right side of the Select Expert dialog box. Crystal Reports uses the and operator when reading multiple criteria. With multiple criteria, the records must meet all criteria set. If your criteria is to be considered an or situation, you must manually change the and to an or in the record selection formula.

To manually change the record selection formula, follow these steps:

1. Click the Show Formula button on the bottom of the Select Expert dialog box. See Figure 7.12.

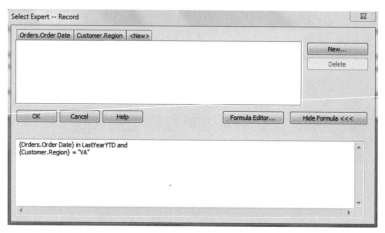

Figure 7.12
Record selection formula window.

2. Highlight the and operator and then type **or**.

3. Click OK.

Deleting Record Selection Criteria

If you inadvertently created a tab in the Select Expert, you can easily remove it by selecting the incorrect tab and clicking the Delete button on the right side of the Select Expert window or clicking the Show Formula button and manually deleting the criteria in the record selection formula.

Group Selection

Group selection is slightly different than record selection. Record selection filters the records from being retrieved from the database. Group selection displays the groups set in your group selection criteria after the records have been retrieved from the database. Group selection hides the groups that do not meet your criteria.

To enter group selection criteria, follow these steps:

1. Click the drop-down arrow next to the Select Expert icon, on the Expert toolbar.

2. Choose Group, as shown in Figure 7.13.

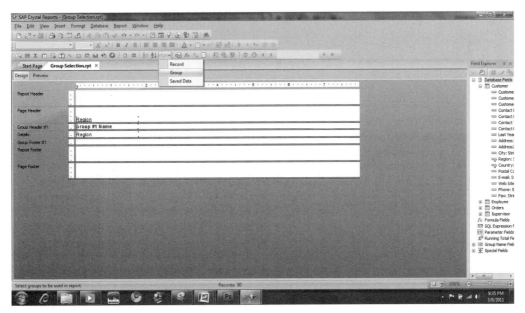

Figure 7.13
Using group selection.

3. Choose the field to filter the Group selection on.

4. Click OK.

5. Set the desired criteria.

Group Selection is slightly different than record selection so this is a good place to practice your Group Selection skills:

1. Open the Group Selection report located in the Chapter 7 sample files.

Note

The sample files can be downloaded from www.courseptr.com/downloads. Enter the book title, ISBN, or author's name to be linked to the sample files for this book.

2. Insert a summary field using the Count function as a grand total.

3. Notice the total count. (In sample database, the total count is 90.)

4. Click the Select Expert drop-down arrow and choose Group Selection.

5. Choose the Region field.

6. Click OK.

7. Set the following criteria: {Customer.Region} starts with "C".

8. Click OK.

The only groups that are displayed should be those starting with the character "C". Notice, however, that the total count is the same. The records are still there; the groups that didn't meet the criteria are just hidden.

Using Saved Data

Saving data with the report can allow users to quickly view the data without having to connect to the server; therefore minimizing the network traffic on the server. For those users who do not have a direct connection to the server, using saved data can be a valuable tool. However, use caution when using saved data with reports that contain sensitive information. Using the Saved Data option, all records are stored with the report file and can be updated on a scheduled basis if used with the Enterprise or Crystal Reports server. Records can also be updated on an as-needed basis by selecting the Refresh button on the Navigation toolbar.

Using saved data allows the end users to drill down on charts and groups, and change the parameter values. You'll read about parameters later in this chapter.

You have the ability to filter data based on the saved data using the Saved Data option under the drop-down arrow of the Select Expert.

1. Click the drop-down arrow next to the Select Expert.

2. Choose Saved Data.

3. Choose the field to filter the saved data.

4. Click OK.

5. Set the criteria for the field using the Saved Data.

Setting Indexes for Saved Data

As mentioned earlier, indexes allow faster retrieval of your records due to the fact that the database tables are optimized to search the field most widely used in search results. Crystal Reports allows you to set these indexes on saved data as well.

To set indexes on saved data, you choose the Report > Report Bursting Indexes menu.

Tip

You must determine the correct fields to index the saved data. Some of the considerations you should think about when deciding which fields to index are:

- Include the fields that are frequently used to filter the data.

- Include the fields that are in the report selection formula.

- You should not include all fields in the report. It just slows down the processing speed of your report.

- You should not include fields that only contain unique values.

You can allow Crystal Reports to determine the fields to include by choosing the Auto button on the Saved Data Indexes dialog box, shown in Figure 7.14.

You can manually choose the fields by selecting them from the left side of the dialog box and choosing the right pointing arrow to add them to the Indexed for Bursting section. When you're done adding indexed fields, click OK to close the dialog box.

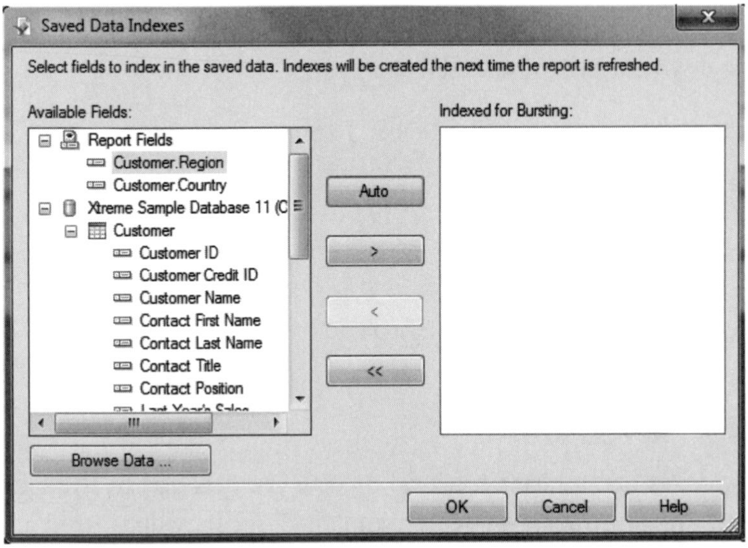

Figure 7.14
The Saved Data Indexes dialog box.

Previewing a Sample Dataset

During the development of the report, there are times when you may want to check the validity of a formula or formatting option. Crystal Reports allows you to connect to the database and retrieve only a small number of records that are necessary to validate your development. To preview just a sample, access the Preview Sample from the View > Preview Sample menu command. The Preview Sample dialog box will appear, as shown in Figure 7.15.

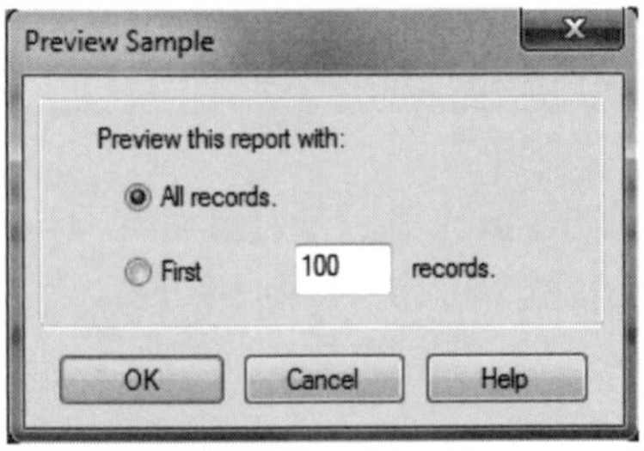

Figure 7.15
Using the Preview Sample feature.

You have the option to see all records or you can choose the option to view a specific number of records.

WORKING WITH PARAMETERS

During the report requirements gathering session that's conducted before the development of the report, you obtain the specific data the user is looking for, such as timeframe, a certain department or other criteria. Often, the user would like to be able to change the requirements on an ad-hoc basis. It is unrealistic for you as a developer to hard code the requirements and change them from the design window each time users want to make changes.

Crystal Reports allows the use of parameters to present to the user each time the user runs the report. Parameters are prompts that appear upon opening the report. It requests that the end user select the information he would like to see, such as a date range. The Parameter dialog box presents an interactive approach to changing the dynamics of the report on the fly. With the introduction of Crystal Reports 2008, the ability to use a parameter against the saved data without a refresh of the database was introduced in the Parameters panel. Prior to Crystal Reports 2008, if a parameter was created it was required that a value be entered in the parameter prompt or a default value had to be used. With the introduction of Crystal Reports 2008, an option was included to make the parameters optional.

Before creating a parameter, you should know the datatype of the field you intend to filter with the use of a parameter. You can verify the field type by right-clicking on the field and selecting Browse Data or by right-clicking a field in the Field Explorer and choosing Show Field Type, as shown in Figure 7.16. Using the Show Field Type option will display the field types for all fields in the table and will continuously display until you turn the option off.

Creating a Parameter

To create a parameter, right click Parameter Fields in the Field Explorer, or select Parameter Field and click the "New" button on the Field Explorer toolbar. The Create New Parameter dialog box will open, as shown in Figure 7.17.

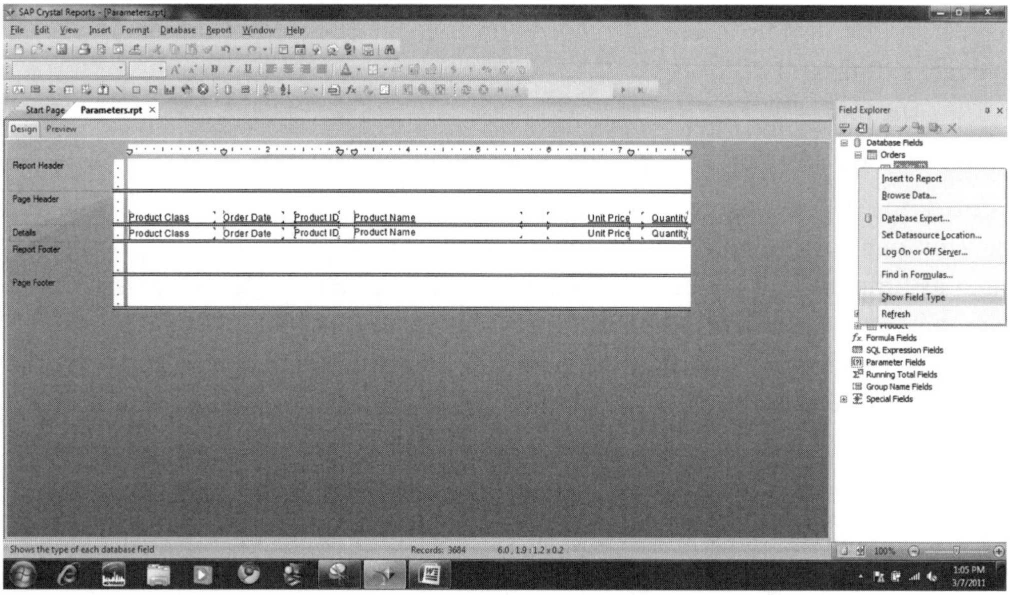

Figure 7.16
Showing the field type.

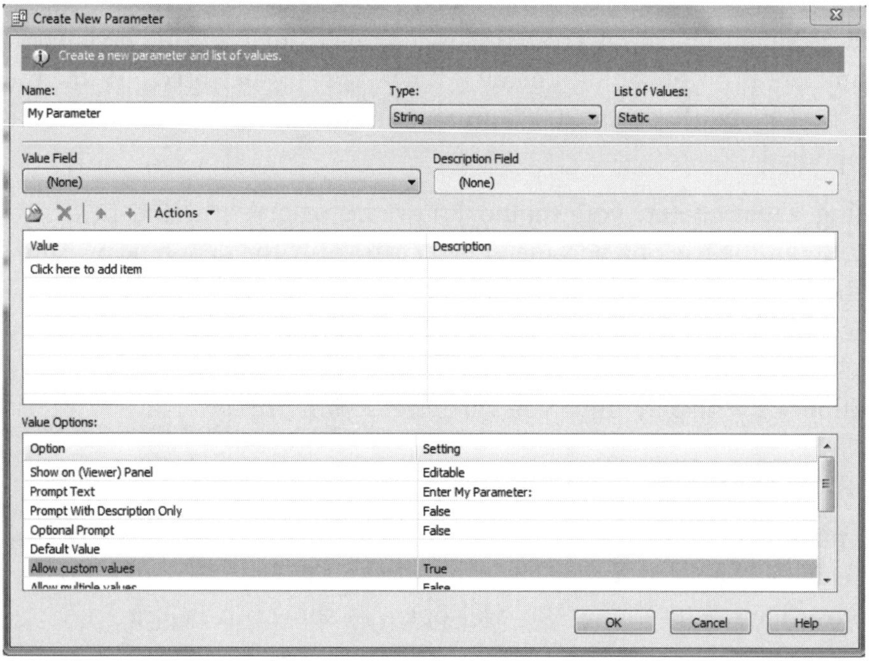

Figure 7.17
The Create New Parameter dialog box.

From the Create New Parameter dialog box, you have the following options:

- **Name** – Enter a name that is descriptive of the parameter.

- **Type** – Select the field type of the database field you will attach the parameter to. As mentioned, the datatype must be the same as the database field. If you choose the wrong datatype, the parameter will not be available to filter the records on the correct database field.

- **List of Values** – There are two types of parameter values, Static and Dynamic.

  Static – Static values are a list of values that do not change, such as a list of states or departments in your organization. You can import a list of values, and until you update the list, the list will remain the same.

Note

The disadvantage of using a static value list is that you have to maintain some type of list documenting where the parameters are used in order to keep the values updated as changes are made.

  Dynamic – Dynamic values are the most desired. A dynamic value list stays connected to the database, thereby reflecting any changes that are made, such as additions, updates, and deletions. This is the desired method; the values presented to the end user are always the most up-to-date information.

- **Value Field** – Select this option to display the database field that should be used as the value for the parameter, such as ProductID.

- **Description Field** – Select this option to display the database field that should be used as the description for the value field that you chose. In the case of the ProductID, you could use Product Name as the description.

Note

These values will be used to populate the drop-down list for the parameters.

With the values selected, you have the option to fill the parameter list with all of the unique values that exist in the current database or manually enter each entry in the Value and Description fields.

To automatically fill the list, choose the drop-down arrow next to the Actions button and choose from one of the following options, shown in Figure 7.18:

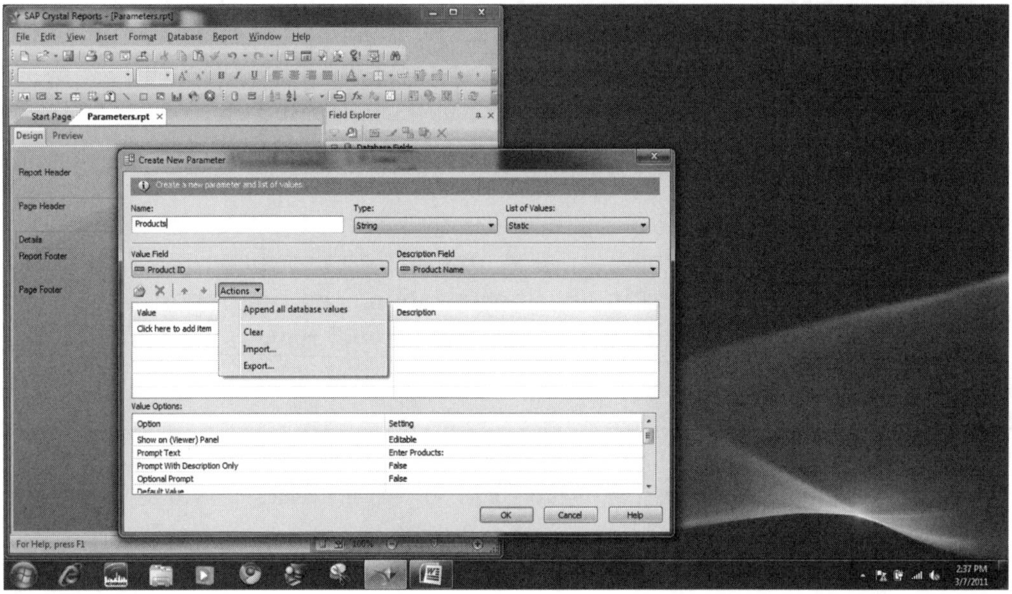

Figure 7.18
The Actions drop-down menu.

- **Append all database values** – Use this option to add all unique database values to the parameter list.

- **Clear** – Use this option to remove all values from the list and reimport values, append database values, or manually type the values.

- **Import** – Use this option to import values into the parameter list. If you have the values stored in Excel, a text file, or other database, you can populate the parameter list with those values without double entry.

- **Export** – If you want to use the values from this parameter in another report or application, you can export the list using this option.

Each parameter has options that allow you to control the data that is entered or selected from the Parameter drop-down list. The options may change depending on the datatype of the field.

Some of the options of the Create New Parameter dialog box that you can choose from are:

- **Show on (Viewer) Panel** – Use this option to determine whether the parameter will be available on the panel.

- **Editable** – With this option, the parameter values can be changed without refreshing the database.

- **Read Only** – The parameter values can be viewed but cannot be changed. In order to change the parameter values, use the Refresh button or press F5.

- **Do Not Show** – This option prevents the parameter from being displayed on the Parameters panel.

- **Prompt Text** – Use this option to enter the text you want the user to be prompted with when running the report. For example, "Select the region to view the report data."

- **Prompt with Description Only** – If you have entered a value and a description, this option gives you the ability to display only the description in the parameter. For example, say you have a customer ID and a customer name. If you set this option to true, the customer name will be the only value that appears in the parameter list.

- **Optional Prompt** – Use this option to set the parameter as optional. Use of this option gives the user the ability to bypass the parameter if desired.

- **Default Value** – Use this option to set a default value for the parameter. For example, if you are viewing data by state, you can set the default value to the most frequently viewed state.

- **Allow Custom Values** – Use this option to give the users the ability to enter values other than what you have populated the drop-down list with. This option should be used with static values to eliminate any restrictions for the users when you have not updated the parameter values with the database changes.

- **Allow Multiple Values** – Use this option to give the users the ability to choose more than one value in the parameter.

- **Allow Discrete Values** – Use this option to give the users the ability to select single values instead of a range.

- **Allow Range Values** – Use this option to allow the user to choose a start and ending range value.

- **Min Length** – Use this option to restrict the minimum number of characters that can be entered in the parameter value.

- **Max Length** – Use this option to restrict the maximum number of characters that can be entered in the parameter value.

- **Edit Mask** – Use this option to restrict the type of characters that can be entered in the parameter value field. See Table 7.2 for the character mapping descriptions.

- **Start** – Used with a date, time, or date time field. Use this option to enter a minimum starting point.

- **End** – Used with a date, time, or date time field. Use this option to enter a maximum ending point.

Table 7.2 The Edit Mask Characters

Character	Description
A	Alphanumeric character – non-required entry.
0	Numeric value [0-9] – required entry.
9	Numeric value [0-9] or a space – non-required entry.
#	Numeric value, a space or plus/minus sign – non-required entry.
L	Alpha character [A to Z] – required entry.
?	Alpha character [A to Z] – non-required entry.
&	Any character or space – required entry.
C	Any character or space – non-required entry.
.,:;-/	Separator characters. Use these masks to set up the format for the field value. Example, 000-000, this mask requires three numbers, a dash, and then three numbers.
>	Converts the parameter value to uppercase.
<	Converts the parameter value to lowercase.

Table 7.2 (Continued)

Character	Description
\	Use of this character displays the next character as a literal value.
Password	Use this option when you want to conceal the password being entered. Can be used for conditional formatting.

Once you save the parameter, it will be displayed in the Field Explorer under the Parameter Fields list. After you create a parameter, you must attach the parameter to the corresponding field through the Select Expert.

To attach a parameter to a field, follow these steps:

1. Select the Select Expert.

2. Choose the field the parameter will filter from in the Choose Field dialog box.

Tip

If you have a field selected, the Choose Field dialog box will not open.

3. Select the correct operator—is equal to or not equal to—based on the specifics of your parameter.

4. Select the value drop-down list. The parameter will be the first value in the list.

Note

All parameters start with a "?" and the name given to the parameter. If you do not see the parameter name in the list, it is an indication that the datatype chosen for the parameter is incorrect for the field you are attempting to attach the parameter to.

5. Click OK.

6. Preview the report. The Parameter dialog box will appear. Notice the prompting text, as shown in Figure 7.19.

7. Select a parameter value.

8. Click OK.

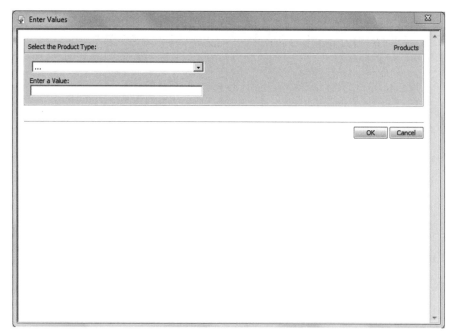

Figure 7.19
The parameter prompt dialog box.

Creating Dynamic Parameters

The use of dynamic parameters will ensure your parameter list is always up to date. To create a dynamic parameter, follow these steps:

1. Change the List of Values to Dynamic.

2. Select the Value field. Using the previous example, select the Product Type ID.

3. Select the Description. Using the previous example, select the Product Type Name field.

4. To create the parameter, click in the Parameter column of the value and description line.

5. Set up the parameter options as usual. Figure 7.20 shows the results.

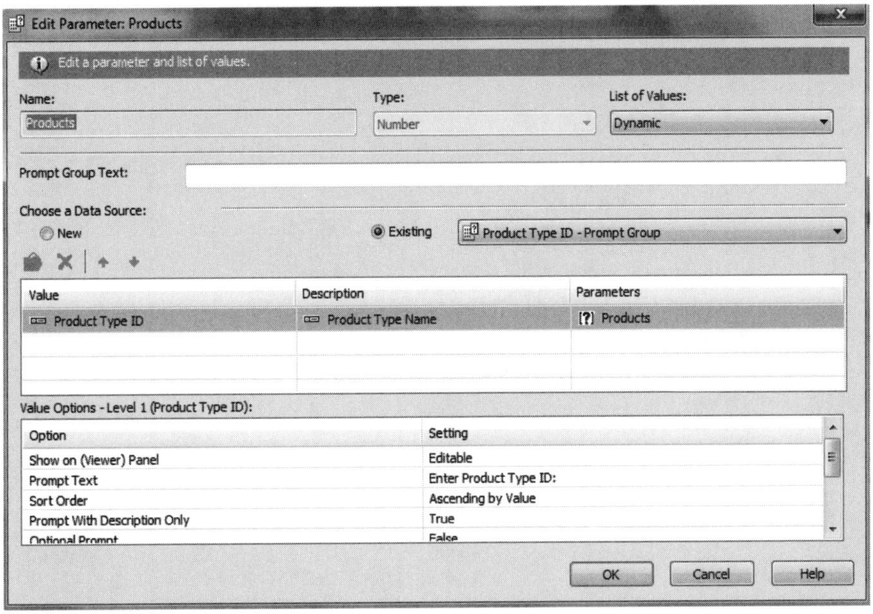

Figure 7.20
Using dynamic parameters.

Using Cascading Parameters

The use of cascading parameters was first introduced in Crystal Reports XI Professional version. Cascading parameters allow you to build a hierarchy of parameters, filtering the choices available as you step through the hierarchy. For example, consider the use of Country, Region, and City parameters. As you choose a country, only the regions that are available in the country are displayed. Then you choose a region, and only the cities located in the region you chose are displayed.

The cascading parameters (see Figure 7.21) are similar to the dynamic parameters, as they are always attached to the database. As you build the hierarchy, only create the parameter on the lowest level of the parameter hierarchy. The parameter should be attached to the same lowest level field in the Select Expert.

Based on the option you chose for the Viewer panel, if the parameter value is displayed in the Parameters panel of the Preview panel, as shown in Figure 7.22, it is editable or read-only.

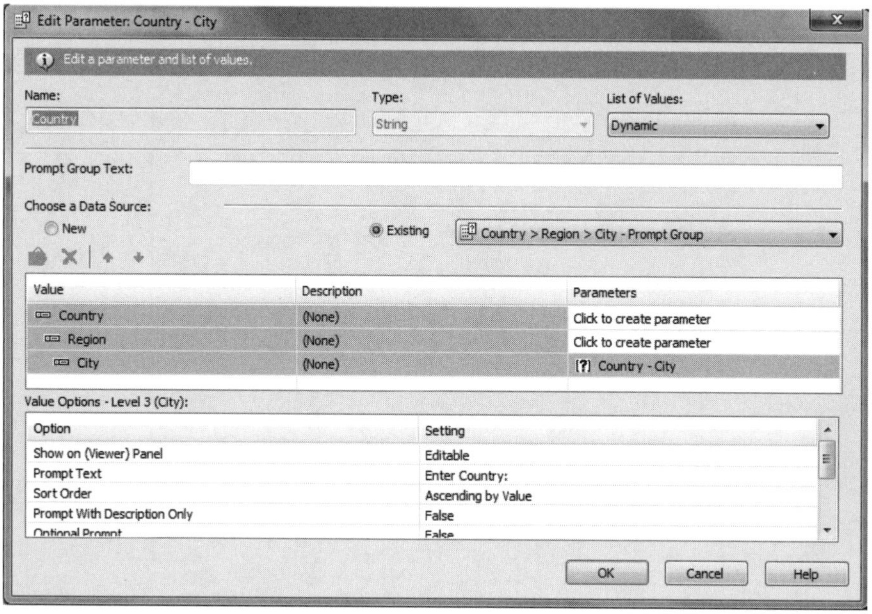

Figure 7.21
Cascading parameters.

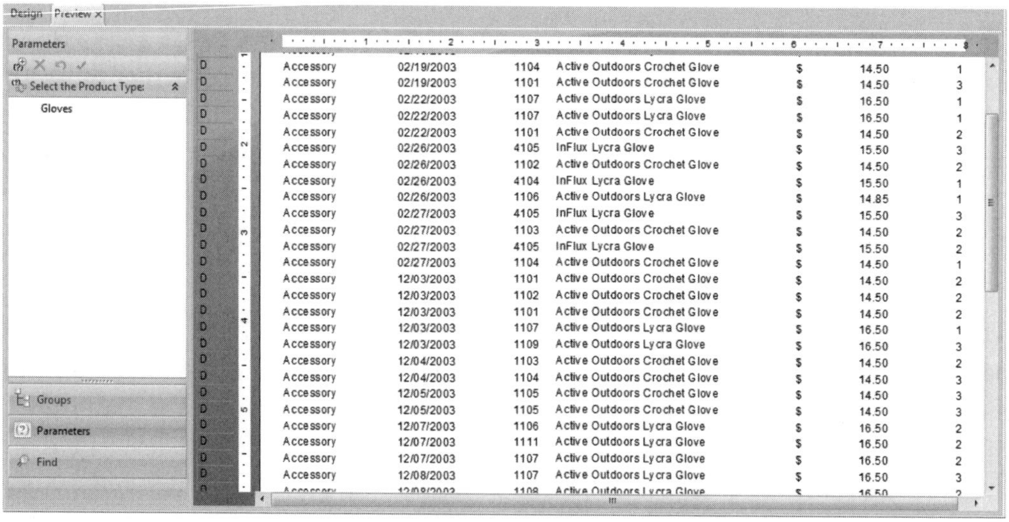

Figure 7.22
Parameters panel in the preview window.

The benefit of the Parameters panel is to allow the users to change the parameter values without accessing the database again or prompting for new parameter values. To change the parameter values, you select the parameter value and click the drop-down arrow, as shown in Figure 7.23. The Parameters panel is located on the Preview panel and only available in Preview. You can toggle the Parameters panel on and off by using the Toggle Preview Panel icon on the Standard toolbar.

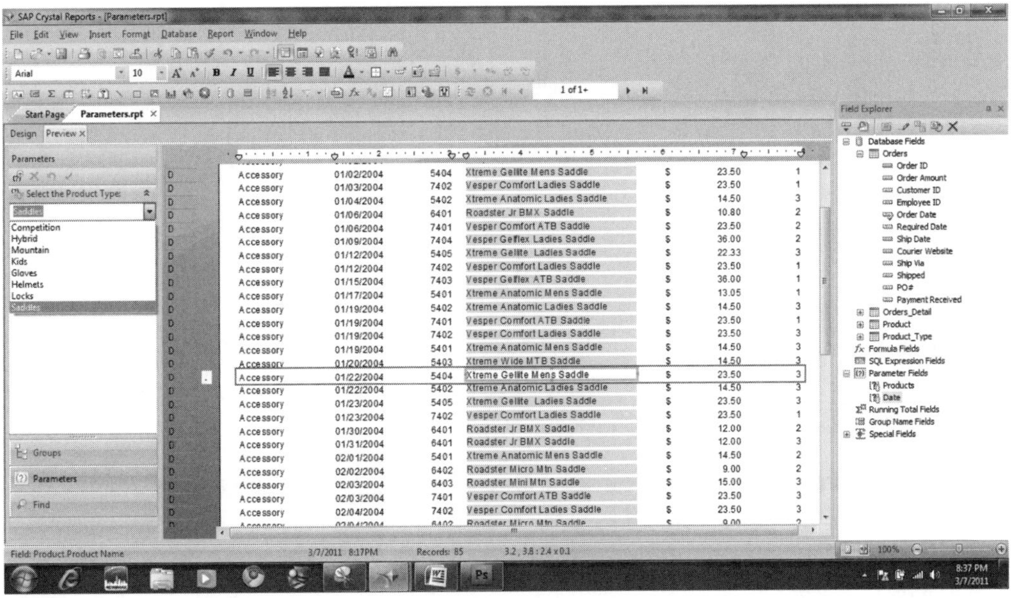

Figure 7.23
Changing the parameter values from Parameters panel.

After selecting the parameter values, you must click the Apply Changes check-mark on the Parameters panel toolbar, which is shown in Figure 7.24.

The report data will change based on the new parameter values.

Setting the Parameter Order

Often you create parameters in no specific order. However, when you run the report, the order the parameter values are entered can be confusing to the end users when you have multiple parameters. You can reorder the parameters by right-clicking on the Parameter Fields title in the Field Explorer or by clicking on one of the parameters and choosing Set Parameter Order, as shown in Figure 7.25.

Figure 7.24
Apply your changes from the Parameters panel.

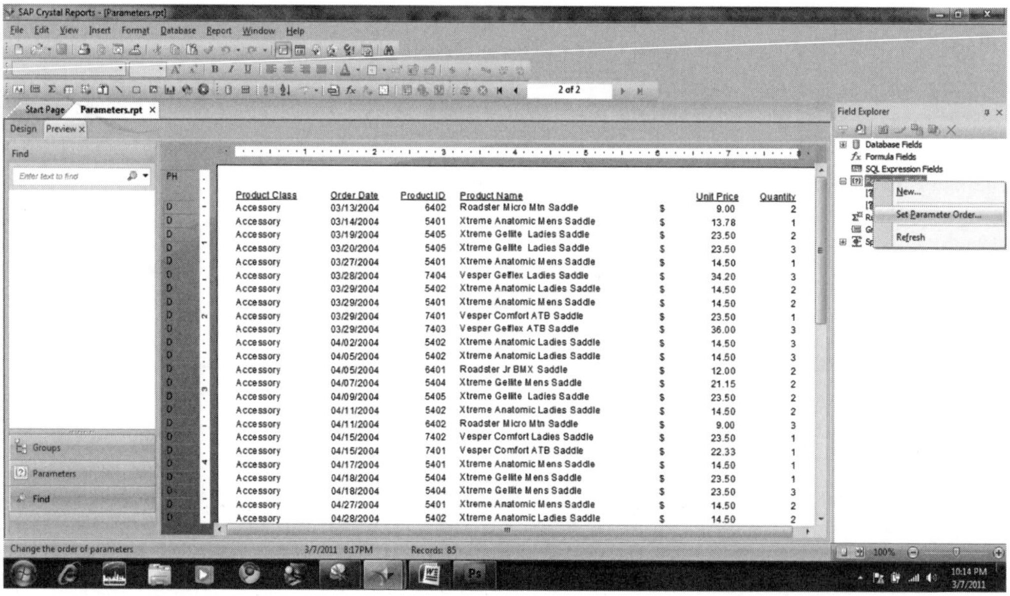

Figure 7.25
Setting the parameter order.

USING THE FIND PANEL

The Find panel, shown in Figure 7.26, allows you to search the report data for any word. The Find feature will locate every record that contains the value you entered. Once the search locates the records, you can double-click the record to have the cursor jump directly to it. The Find panel is located on the Preview panel. You can access it in Preview only and the Toggle Preview Panel option must be selected.

Figure 7.26
The Find panel.

SUMMARY

The majority of the reports that you develop are going to use multiple tables. Take careful consideration in linking tables efficiently using indexed fields. Linking on indexed fields will have a significant gain on the performance of the report and minimize the strain on the database when retrieving report data. The use of parameters is essential in allowing users to run reports on an ad-hoc basis.

Parameters can be used for grouping, conditional formatting, and sorting options. Parameters are very beneficial when dealing with large amounts of data.

EXERCISES
Exercise 1

1. Create a new blank report.

2. Add the Products, Orders, and Orders Detail tables to it.

3. Link the tables. The Products table links to the Orders Detail table and the Orders Detail links to the Orders table.

   Your report should look similar to Figure 7.27.

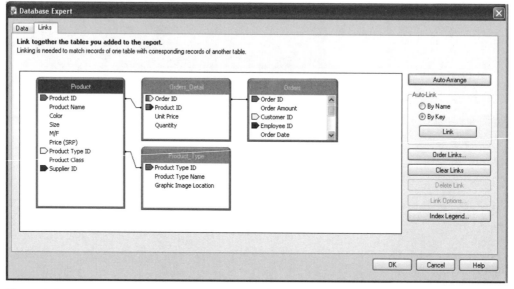

Figure 7.27
Preview of linked tables.

4. Insert the Product Class, Order Date, Product ID, Product Name, Unit Price, and Quantity fields into the Details section.

5. Format the fields as you desire.

6. Save the report as **Parameters**.

   Your report should look similar to Figure 7.28.

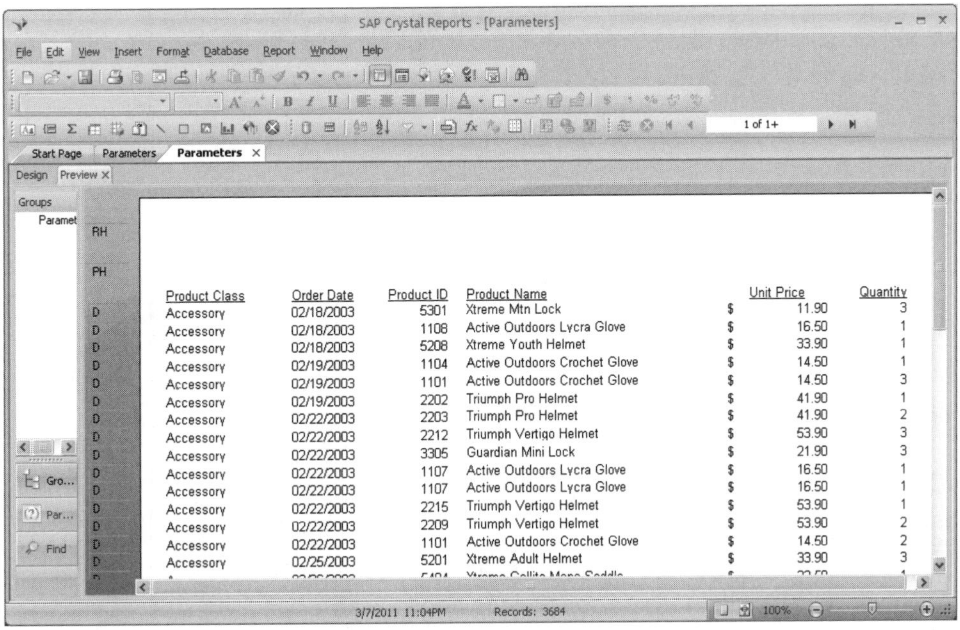

Figure 7.28
Preview of the Parameters report.

Exercise 2

1. Open the Parameters report you created in the previous exercise.

2. Create a static product parameter.

3. Set the Data Type as Number.

4. Choose the Value of Product Type ID.

5. Choose the Description of Product Type Name.

6. Choose Append Database Values from the Actions drop-down menu.

   Your report should look similar to Figure 7.29.

7. Leave the other options as the defaults.

8. Attach the product parameter to the Product Type ID field through the Select Expert.

9. Click OK.

10. Save the report.

11. Preview the report. Select a parameter value.

    Your report should look similar to Figure 7.30.

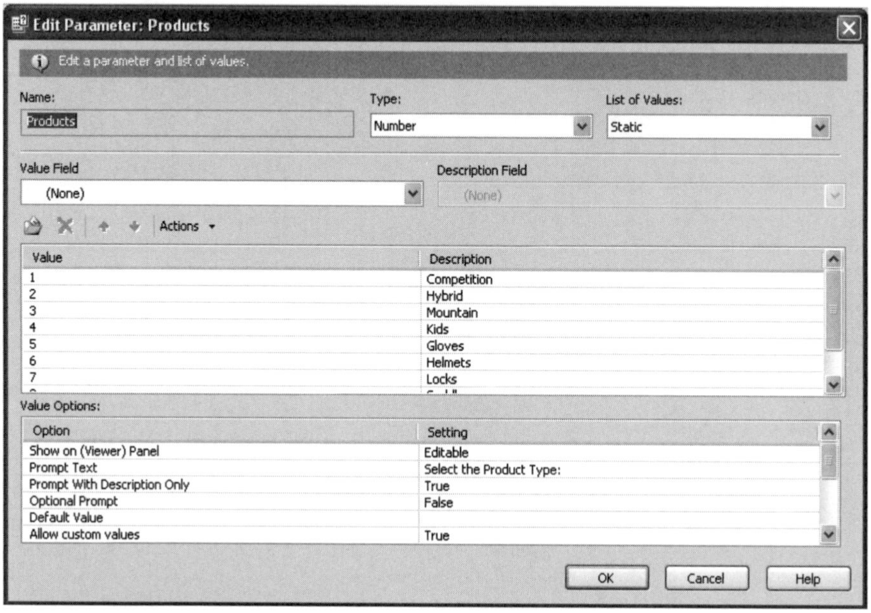

Figure 7.29
Creating a parameter.

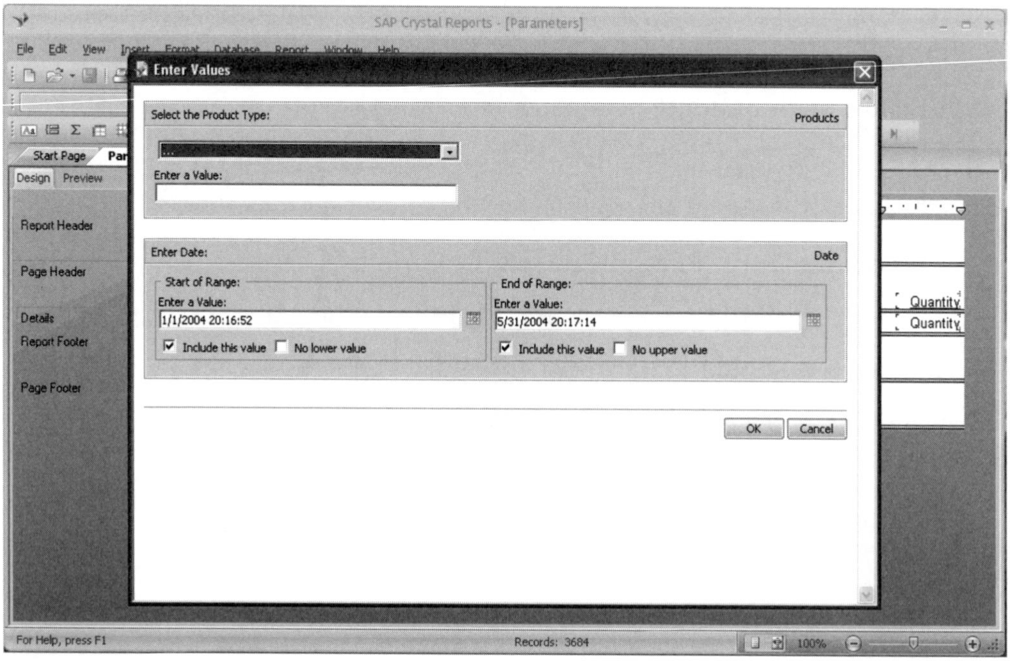

Figure 7.30
Preview of the final report.

CHAPTER 8

UNDERSTANDING FORMULAS, FUNCTIONS, AND EXPRESSIONS

The objectives of this chapter are to learn the following tasks:

- Understanding and creating formulas
- Using variables
- Working with SQL commands
- Working with custom functions
- Working with SQL expressions

Formulas are used in various ways throughout Crystal Reports. Simple list reports may not require any additional fields or formatting. However, the more complex your report gets, the more formulas are necessary. Formulas are needed to compile values that are not stored in the database, such as extended field values, costs, concatenating text fields, comparing data, and converting data-types. They are also used to format fields and sections conditionally.

In order to use formulas in a mathematical calculation, you need to understand how formulas are calculated. Knowing the basic rules of precedence is crucial to understanding the process. I think back to my pre-algebra school days and the many assignments involving the order of operations. Although Crystal Reports performs the calculations, it requires user intervention to set up the formula.

The order of operations is as follows:

Parentheses (x + y)

Exponentiation (^)

Negation (-)

Multiplication, Division and Percents (*, /, %)

Integer (\)

Modulus (Mod)

Addition and Subtraction (+, −)

Reading from left to right, the system will perform the calculation. However, in cases where you have two operations performed on the same level, you can control which operation is calculated first by using parentheses to force the evaluation.

Understanding Formulas

Most relational DBMS databases do not store all calculated values in the database for various reasons. As the developer during the report requirement gathering session, you will be responsible for determining the formulas for the report data.

Formulas are used for:

- Concatenation of data
- Datatype conversion
- Mathematical calculations
- Conditional formatting
- Value comparison

Simple formulas are created using basic static numbers and database fields. Crystal Reports formulas can be written in Basic or in the Crystal Reports language. Programmers familiar with writing code in Visual Basic may find that using the Basic language syntax is easier and more familiar. However, for users with little or no programming experience, the Crystal Reports language will be easier to learn. There are general syntax rules that apply to formulas in Crystal Reports, as follows:

Symbol	Description
{}	Database fields are enclosed in curly braces `{Orders.Order Date}`
@	Formulas begin with the @ symbol `{@ExtTotal}`
//	The slash is used for comments
"	Text fields must be enclosed in double quotation marks

The formula language in Crystal Reports is not case sensitive.

Tip

Typing the first characters of a function in the formula text area and using the Ctrl+Spacebar shortcut will produce the IntelliSense pop-up information showing all functions that begin with the characters that you typed. You can also use the Ctrl+Spacebar in the text area without typing any characters to get a full list of all functions available in Crystal Reports, as shown in Figure 8.1.

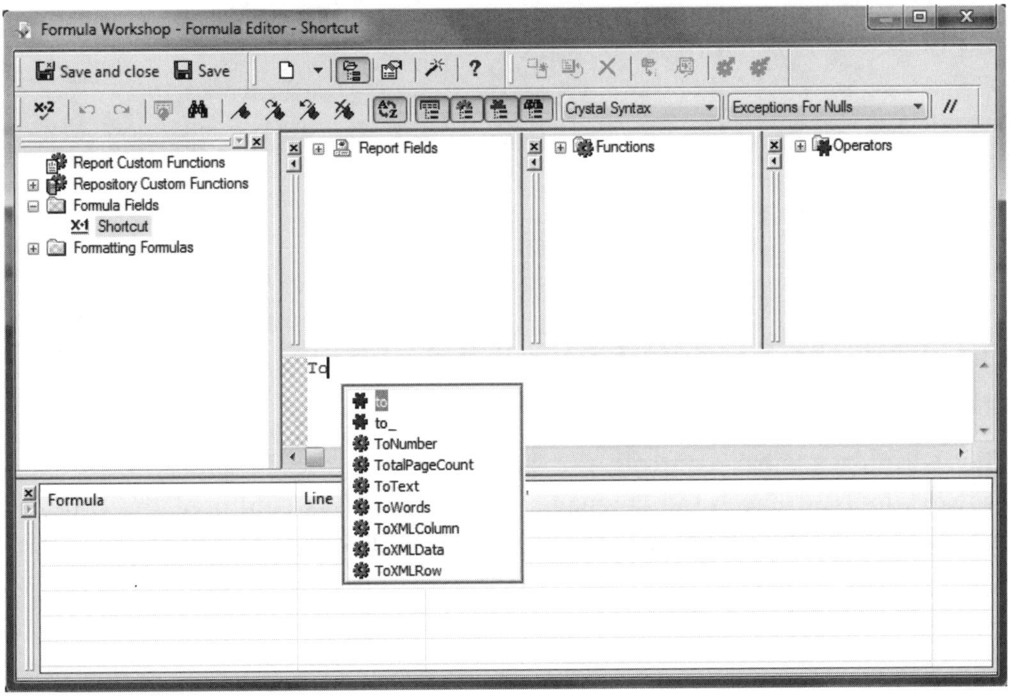

Figure 8.1
Using the Function shortcuts.

CREATING FORMULAS

To create a formula, right-click the category Formula Fields in the Field Explorer and choose New, as shown in Figure 8.2. Enter a name for the formula.

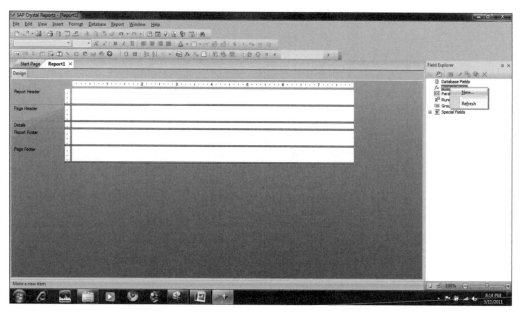

Figure 8.2
Creating a new formula.

Exploring the Formula Editor Window

The Formula Editor window appears in Figure 8.3.

The Formula toolbar controls the appearance of the Formula Editor and provides tools to check the language syntax as well as comment the code, as shown in Figure 8.4. Table 8.1 explores each of the options of the toolbar.

Field Tree   Function Tree   Operator Tree

Formula
Toolbar

Workshop
Tree

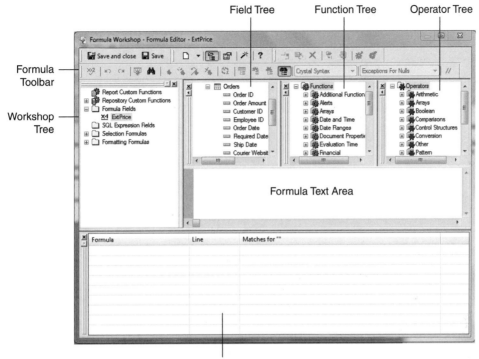

Find in Formula Pane

Figure 8.3
The Formula Editor window.

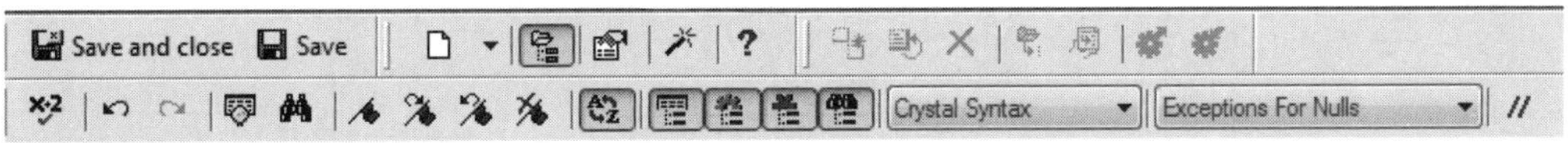

Figure 8.4
The Formatting toolbar.

Table 8.1 Formula Toolbar Options

Icon	Description
💾 Save and close 💾 Save	Save and Close (Ctrl+S) – Allows you to save the formula and close the Formula Editor. Save (Alt+S) – Allows you to save the formula and remain in the Formula Editor.
📄 ▾	New – Creates a new formula, custom function, SQL expression, record-selection formula, group selection formula, or saved data formula.
	Workshop Tree – Toggle button used to hide or show the workshop tree.
	Properties Window – Toggle button used to display the properties window of Custom Functions and Custom Properties.
	Use Expert/Editor (Alt+X) – Opens the Formula Expert, which is used to create custom functions. The Formula Expert is covered in more detail later in this chapter.
?	Help – Opens the context help guides.
	Copy/Duplicate Formula – Duplicates the selected formula.
	Rename – Allows you to rename the selected formula. You can also right-click the formula name in the Workshop tree or in the Field Explorer and choose Rename.
✕	Delete – Deletes the selected formula.
	Expand Node – Expands the list of the selected node in the Workshop tree.
	Show Formula Formatting Nodes Only – Toggle button used to show or hide report objects in the Formatting folders if the objects do not have a formula with it.
	Add to the Repository – Adds the custom function to the repository.
	Add to the Report – Adds the custom function in the repository to the report.
x·2	Check Syntax (Alt+C) – Checks the formula in the formula text area for syntax errors. If an error is found, a message will be displayed, as shown in Figure 8.5.
	Undo – Undoes the last action performed.
	Redo – Restores the last action performed using the Undo command. It restores the report to the way it looked prior to using the Undo command.

Table 8.1 (Continued)

Icon	Description
	Browse Data (Alt+B) – With a database field selected, you can browse the database for a list of values in the field. With the list displayed, you can use the Paste Data option to insert a specific value into the formula text area. Figure 8.6 shows an example of using the Browse Data command.
	Find/Replace (Ctrl+F) – Searches the formula workshop for the text entered. The feature allows for replacement of text with the Edit Text option selected in the Search area. Figure 8.7 shows the Find and Replace box.
	Bookmark (Ctrl+F2) – Toggle button that adds or removes a bookmark. Bookmarks are used to flag certain parts of the formula.
	Next Bookmark (Ctrl+Alt+F2) – Moves to the next bookmark in the formula.
	Previous Bookmark (Shift+F2) – Moves to the previous bookmark in the formula.
	Delete Bookmark (Ctrl+Shift+F2) – Deletes all bookmarks in the formula.
	Sort Trees (Alt+O) – Toggle button that sorts all of the trees (Report Fields, Function, and Operator) in alphabetical order.
	Field Tree (Alt+F) – Toggle button that hides/shows the Report Fields tree.
	Function Tree (Alt+U)– Toggle button that hides/shows the Function tree. The Function tree shows all available predefined functions; similar to Excel functions.
	Find Results (Alt+R) – Toggle button that hides/shows the results of the global formula search.
Crystal Syntax ▼	Syntax (Ctrl+T) – Allows you to select the Basic language syntax or Crystal Reports syntax language.
Exceptions For Nulls ▼	Handling of Null Values – Allows you to define how Crystal Reports will handle null values. You can use the Exception for Null (default) option: `If IsNull({Customer.Region}) then ""`. Or you can use the Default Values for Nulls option: `{Customer.Region} = ""`. See Figure 8.8.
//	Comment – Comments out the part of the formula immediately after the placement of the cursor.

Figure 8.5
A syntax error has been found.

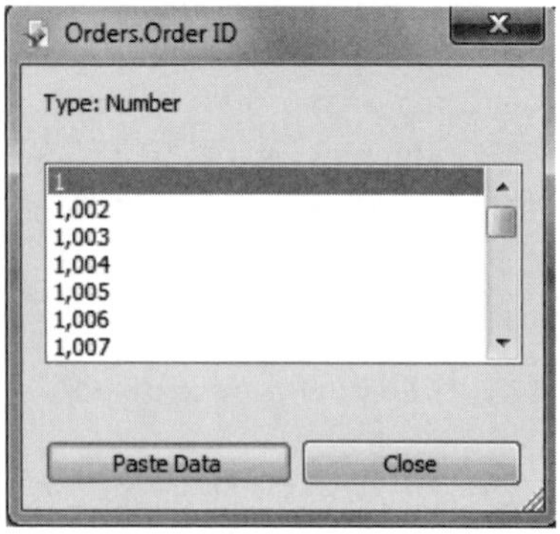

Figure 8.6
Sample of data using the Browse Data command.

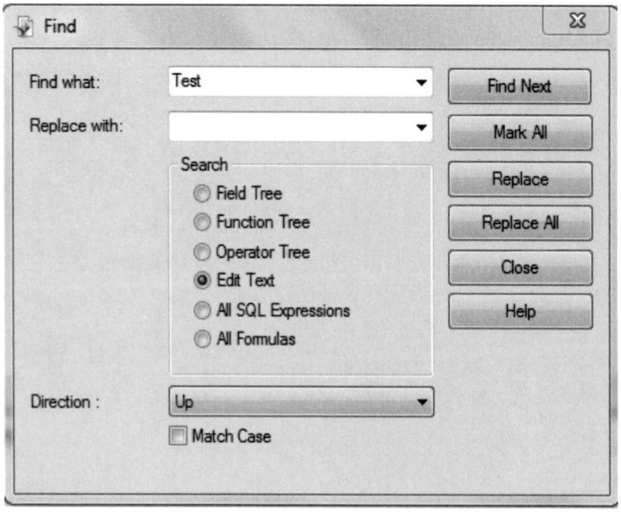

Figure 8.7
Find and Replace dialog box.

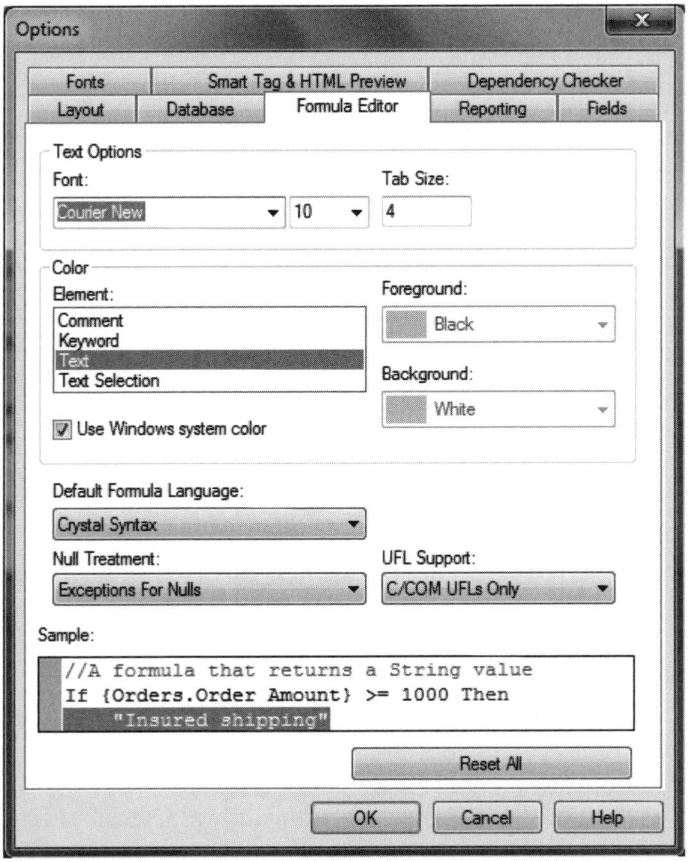

Figure 8.8
Setting default Null treatment options.

The default value presented is determined by the datatype of the formula, as follows:

Datatype	Default Value
String	" "
Number	0
Boolean	False
Currency	$0
DateTime	Null Date, Null Time
Date	Null Date
Time	Null Time

Tip

The default options can be changed by using the File > Options > Formula Editor tab > Null Treatment menu command.

Note

Using the Basic language, comments begin with Rem or with a single apostrophe.

Workshop Tree

The Workshop tree displays a complete list of the types of formulas that can be created in Crystal Reports, as well as SQL expressions and custom functions. You can use the Workshop tree to add a custom function to the repository or to the report depending on where the custom function currently resides. This tree displays any record selection, group selection, or saved data selection formulas that have been created in the Select Expert. All conditional formatting formulas are also displayed. You can add all types of formulas directly from this workshop by selecting the New drop-down button from the Formula workshop toolbar.

Fields Tree

The Report Fields tree, shown in Figure 8.9, displays all fields inserted in the report, including formulas, SQL expressions, running totals, parameters, and all the database fields in the Report Fields section. The field does not have to be used on the report to be included in a formula. Therefore, you also have access to all of the other fields that are included in data source but not placed on the report.

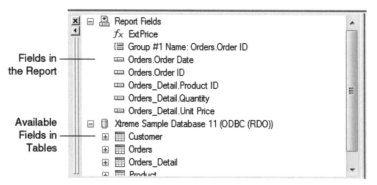

Figure 8.9
Available fields from the database.

Function Tree

The Function tree lists all predefined functions that Crystal Reports has, categorized by the type of field or operation that you are working with.

- **Additional Functions** – The additional functions will be based on the software on the computer.

- **Alerts** – Functions used to create formulas about results of report alerts.

- **Arrays** – Summary functions for elements of an array.

- **Date and Time** – Converts date to numbers and numbers to date, includes functions such as CurrentDate, Month(), and Datediff().

- **Date Ranges** – Predefined date intervals such as Calendar1stQtr, MonthToDate, and YearToDate.

- **Document Properties** – Presents attributes about a document such as creation date, author, and so on.

- **Evaluation Time** – Controls when a formula is going to be calculated and presented.

- **Financial** – Includes many functions that are used with Accounting systems such as functions to calculate accrued interest, present value, and other finance related calculations.

- **Math** – Used to calculate mathematical operations such as absolute value, explicit rounding using Ceiling or Floor functions.

- **Print State** – Report specific functions; shows values only known during the printing phase such as IsNull(), Previous().

- **Programming** – Alternatives to using control structures such as If Then Else.

- **Ranges** – Assist in determining the type of ranges you are working with.

- **Strings** – Used to evaluate, manipulate and convert text fields.

- **Summary** – Used to summarize field data.

- **Type Conversion** – Converting datatypes.

- **Xcelsius** – Used with Xcelsius SWF objects.

Operator Tree

The Operator tree defines the symbols needed to perform the calculation or evaluation of a formula. The tree is categorized by the type of operation that you are calculating, a list of which follows:

- Arithmetic
- Array
- Boolean
- Comparisons
- Control structures
- Conversion
- Other
- Pattern
- Ranges
- Scope
- Strings
- Variable declaration

Formula Text Area

The Formula Text Area, shown in Figure 8.10, of the Formula Editor window stores the actual compilation of the formula. To add fields, functions, and operators to the Formula Text Area, double-click the appropriate field from the corresponding trees.

Find Results Window

The Find Results window was a new addition with the release of Crystal Reports 2008. Many times, I have used a database field in a formula on a very complex report that contains suppressed fields and numerous formulas. Later, I may need to replace the field with another database field. However, without opening every formula, it's difficult to remember every formula the field was included.

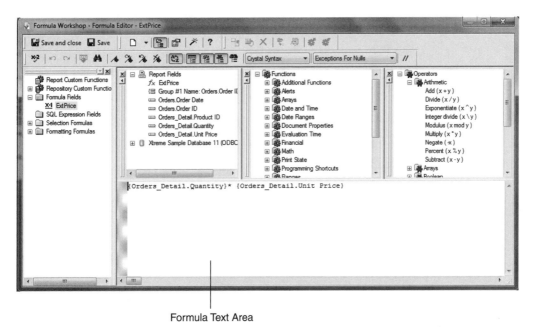

Formula Text Area

Figure 8.10
The Formula Text Area.

The Find in Formulas feature allows the system to search all formulas in the report and locate all formulas the field has been included in. The results are then displayed in the Find Results window, as shown in Figure 8.11.

CREATING A SIMPLE FORMULA

A simple formula consists of a static number or text and/or a database field. To create a new formula, follow these steps:

1. Right-click the Formula Fields category in the Field Explorer and choose New.

2. Give the formula a descriptive name. Formula names should easily identify the purpose of the formula.

3. Click OK. The Formula Editor window appears. Verify that the desired syntax language is being used. Double-click the database fields, functions, or operators to create the formula.

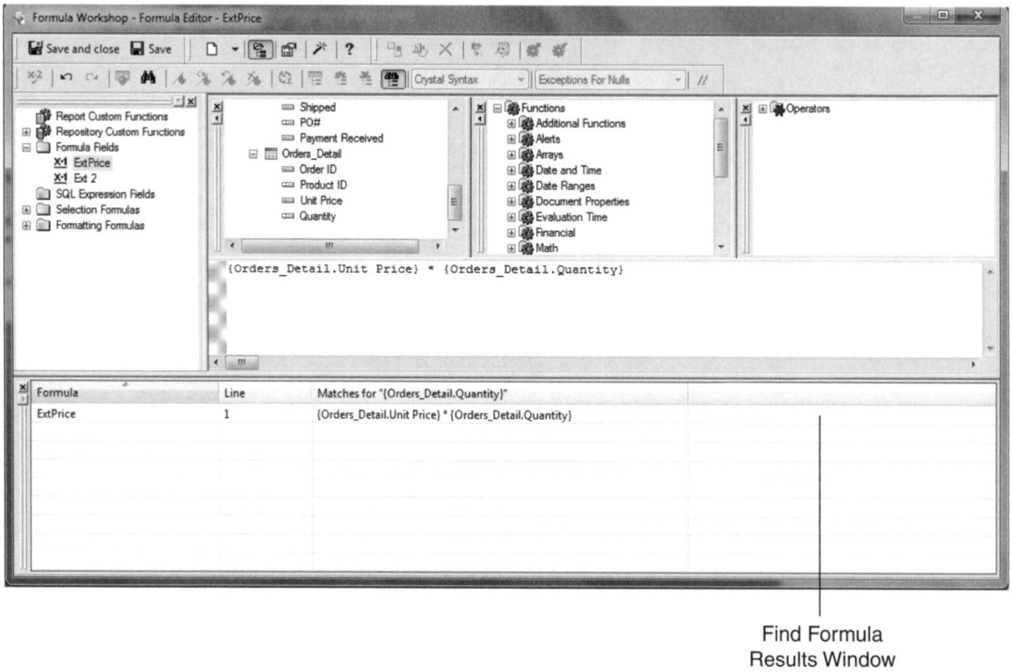

Find Formula
Results Window

Figure 8.11
The Find Results window.

For example, to create a formula to calculate the extended price, you would follow these steps:

1. Double click the database field, {Orders_Detail.Quantity}.

2. Expand the Arithmetic node in the Operator tree and double-click the Multiplication (*) sign.

3. Enter a space and double-click the {Orders_Detail.Unit Price} field in the Report Fields tree.

Tip

With the release of Crystal Reports 2008, the ability to add fields using the IntelliSense type option became available. In the Formula Text area, you simply type a curly brace { to view the list of available tables as shown in Figure 8.12.

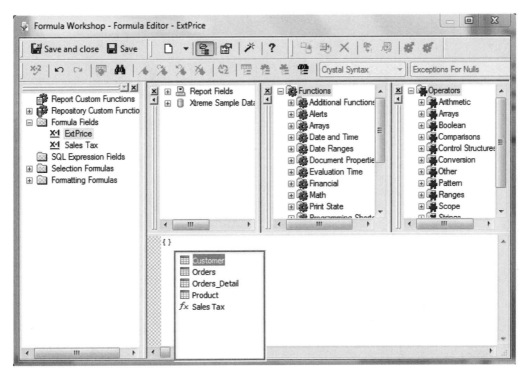

Figure 8.12
Using the IntelliSense option to select a field.

4. The fields in the selected table will appear in the list, as shown in Figure 8.13. Double-click the appropriate field.

5. Click the Check Syntax button (Alt+C), shown in Figure 8.14, on the formula workshop toolbar. If the syntax is validated, the No Errors Found message will appear, as shown in Figure 8.15.

6. If no errors are found, click the Save and Close button (Ctrl+S). The formula will be listed under the Formula Fields category in the Field Explorer.

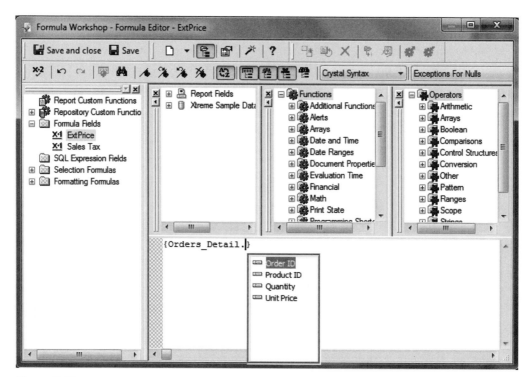

Figure 8.13
Selecting tables and fields.

Figure 8.14
The Check Syntax button.

Figure 8.15
Check syntax message.

Sizing Limitations

There are some basic sizing limitations you need to keep in mind when using the Basic and Crystal languages:

- 1,000 elements in an array
- 100,000 maximum loop condition evaluations per evaluation of a formula when using the `Do While` and `While Do` loops
- 1,000 limit of arguments in a function
- The maximum limit for a string value and result of a string array is 65,534

Number Formulas

Number formulas are common calculations that result in a numerical value. Use of a number formula requires the order of precedence mentioned earlier in the chapter. Formulas are calculated from left to right.

15 + 3 *10 = 45

(15 + 3) * 10 = 180

Notice in the first example, the multiplication piece of the formula is calculated first. To force the addition to be calculated prior to performing the multiplication, you must add parentheses to change the calculation order.

Numbers (Crystal Syntax):

```
{Order_Detail.UnitPrice} * 1.05
{Order_Detail.UnitPrice} * {Order_Detail.Quantity}
{Orders.ShipDate} - {Orders.OrderDate}
```

Basic Syntax:

```
Formula = {Order_Detail.UnitPrice} * 1.05
```

Using Operators in a Number Formula

Operators are symbols or words that are used to guide the system in performing an operation. Arithmetic operators are used in numerical formulas. The operators are shown in Table 8.2.

Table 8.2 Arithmetic Operators

Operator	Description
+	Addition
−	Subtraction
*	Multiplication
/	Division
%	Percent
\	Integer Division – Divides x\y
Mod	Modulus – Divides x by y and rounds the remainder to a whole number.
Negate [-()]	Multiples the value inside of the parentheses by −1
^	Exponentiation x^ y

String Formulas

String formulas are used to concatenate and join text fields as well as convert different datatypes to text fields. A prime example of needing to concatenate fields would be to display an employee's full name. Most relational databases store the first name in a separate field from the last name. But perhaps you need to combine the two fields into one field separated by a space. To accomplish that task in Crystal Reports, you need to create a string formula similar to the following one. This formula is created using Crystal syntax.

```
{Employee.FirstName} + " " + {Employee.LastName}
```

An ampersand (&) or a plus (+) sign operator can be used to join string fields together. Use of the plus (+) sign requires additional steps if you will include any datatype other than a text field. If the business requirements call for the customer number and the customer name to be displayed on the report, separated by a hyphen, you can concatenate the field using the ampersand or plus sign.

```
Customer Number = 123    Customer Name = ABC Company
{Customer.CustomerNumber} & " - " & {Customer.CustomerName}
```

Results in the following:

```
{123.00 - ABC Company}
```

Notice the two decimal places. When using the ampersand, the system automatically converts the different datatypes to a text field. However, it does not allow you to format the customer number field. To control the formatting of the converted field, you must use the ToText string function to set the format of the field.

Using Crystal syntax:

```
ToText({Customer.CustomerNumber}) & " - " & {Customer.CustomerName}
ToText({Customer.CustomerNumber}) + " - " + {Customer.CustomerName}
```

Using Basic syntax:

```
Formula = ToText({Customer.CustomerNumber}) + " - " + {Customer.CustomerName}
```

Often, you may find database users have entered data in all lowercase or all uppercase characters. However, when presenting the data in the report, you want the data to show in the proper case. In the past, database users were asked to correct the case of the data or accept the presentation of the data. Crystal Reports string functions include functions such as lowercase(), uppercase(), and propercase() to handle these types of issues.

```
Propercase({Customer.CustomerName}}
Uppercase({Customer.CustomerState})
```

The ToText function has multiple uses and multiple arguments available. You should carefully choose the function that corresponds with your datatype and the formatting required. The x argument is always required; the others are optional. However, you must populate all arguments prior to your last format. You cannot have any blank arguments between values. For example, to use the ToText(x,y,z) for a numerical value, the following would be an incorrect use of the function and will produce an error:

```
ToText({Customer.CustomerID},,""}
```

An error would be generated because the second argument has not been populated.

The correct use of the function will be:

```
ToText({Customer.CustomerID},0,""}
```

If the third argument is going to be used, argument 1 and 2 must also be populated.

The available ToText() functions are:

- ToText(x) – One argument required. The field that will be converted to text.

- ToText(x, y) - X argument is required; y is optional.

- ToText(x,y,z) - X argument is required; y and z are optional.

- ToText(x,y,z,w) – X argument is required; y, z, and w are optional.

- ToText(x,y,z,w,q) – X argument is required; y, z, w, and q are optional.

See the ToText function in the appendix for more information.

Join Function

The Join function of the Strings category is used to present an array of text values. This function is used frequently when displaying multi-value parameter text. For example, say you want to run the report for multiple states. On the State parameter you choose AL/AR/AZ/CA. If you were to place the parameter on the report now, you will only see the first value in the parameter. See Figure 8.16.

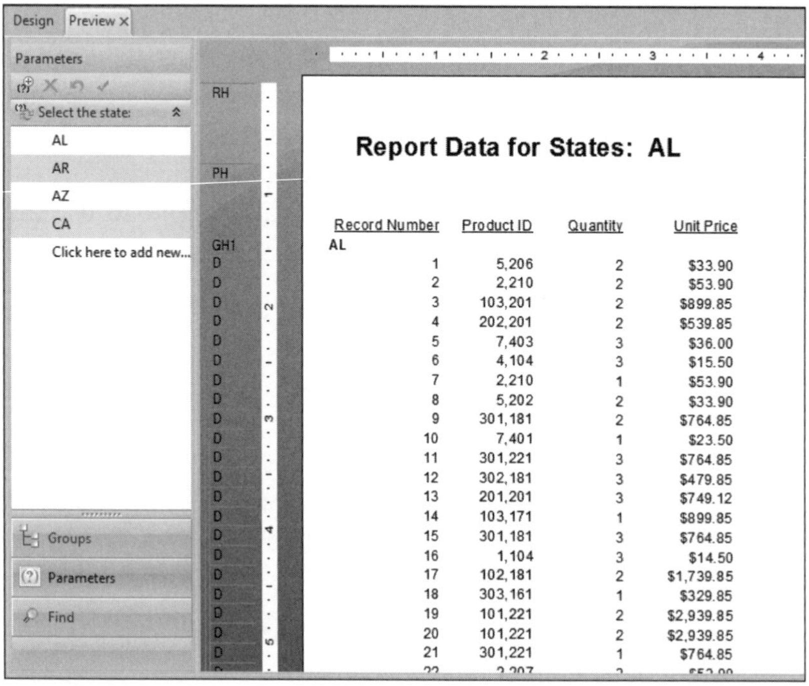

Figure 8.16
String array without the Join function.

Notice the report displays data for the groups AL, AR, AZ and CA. To account for all states in the array, use the Join function, as shown in Figure 8.17.

```
Join({?State},", ")
```

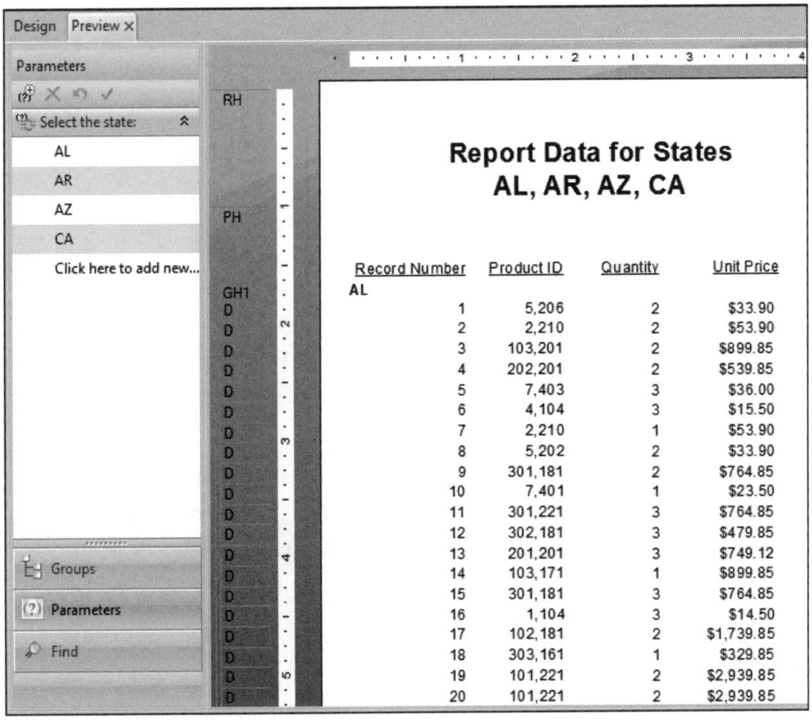

Figure 8.17
Using the Join function.

If Then Else Control Structure

The use of the If Then Else function provides a crucial benefit to testing a criterion against database values, results from formulas, expressions, and running totals while allowing you control of the final results. The If Then Else operator is located in the Operator tree under the Control Structures node.

```
If <criteria test> Then < result if true> Else < result if false>
```

Use of the criteria test requires use of the Comparison operators listed in the Operators tree of the Formula Workshop tree. See Figure 8.18.

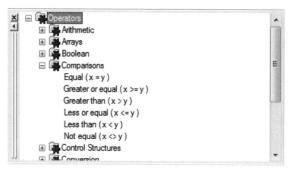

Figure 8.18
Comparison operators.

The Then part of the statement defines the results to be produced if the criterion is true. If you use the If statement, the Then part of the statement is required. The Else part of the statement defines what results are to be produced if the criterion is false. This is an optional argument. However, you want to be careful eliminating the Else part of the statement in certain situations, such as in a color-formatting scenario, because it may produce undesired results. Let's take a look at creating alternating background row colors for the report. The request is to have every other line's background to be silver. The formula to create the conditional background formatting color is as follows:

```
If recordnumber mod 2 = 0 Then crsilver
```

Notice the Else statement is missing from the statement. The results produced are displayed in Figure 8.19.

Due to the Else statement being missing, the background color defaulted to the default attribute. To correct the color formatting, it's important to specify what should happen when the criterion is false. See Figure 8.20.

```
If recordnumber mod 2 = 0 Then crsilver Else crNoColor
```

Specifying the result for the false statement presents the report data in a manner that can be read.

Using the If Then Else statement involves understanding the datatype requirements for the statement. The results that are produced if the criteria test is true must be the same datatype if the criteria test is false.

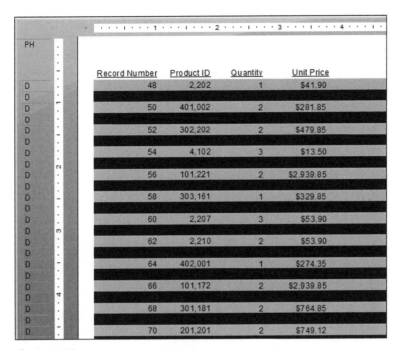

Record Number	Product ID	Quantity	Unit Price
48	2,202	1	$41.90
50	401,002	2	$281.85
52	302,202	2	$479.85
54	4,102	3	$13.50
56	101,221	2	$2,939.85
58	303,161	1	$329.85
60	2,207	3	$53.90
62	2,210	2	$53.90
64	402,001	1	$274.35
66	101,172	2	$2,939.85
68	301,181	2	$764.85
70	201,201	2	$749.12

Figure 8.19
The Else statement wasn't used here.

For example, you might use the following formula to display the word "International" when the customer is not located in the USA and to display 100 if the customer is located in the USA.

```
If {Customer.Country} <> "USA" then "International" else 100
```

This formula will generate an error message because the Then portion of the statement produces a "string" value and the Else statement produces a "number" value, as shown in Figure 8.21.

Notice the syntax checker highlights the Else portion of the statement and generates "A string is required" error message indicating that portion of the statement is producing the incorrect result. To correct the problem, you must convert the Else portion to a string by enclosing the 100 in quotation marks or apostrophes, as shown in Figure 8.22.

You can nest multiple If Then Else statements to accomplish your required goals. Let's take a look at a simple scenario.

Record Number	Product ID	Quantity	Unit Price
48	2,202	1	$41.90
49	101,181	3	$2,939.85
50	401,002	2	$281.85
51	101,171	3	$2,939.85
52	302,202	2	$479.85
53	2,201	3	$41.90
54	4,102	3	$13.50
55	301,161	1	$764.85
56	101,221	2	$2,939.85
57	102,181	2	$1,739.85
58	303,161	1	$329.85
59	101,221	2	$2,939.85
60	2,207	3	$53.90
61	301,221	1	$764.85
62	2,210	2	$53.90
63	201,201	3	$749.12
64	402,001	1	$274.35
65	103,171	1	$899.85
66	101,172	2	$2,939.85
67	3,301	1	$4.50
68	301,181	2	$764.85
69	5,206	3	$33.90
70	201,201	2	$749.12
71	5,205	2	$33.90
72	5,204	3	$33.90
73	4,103	1	$13.50
74	4,106	1	$15.50

Figure 8.20
The Else statement specifies what should happen when the criterion is false.

Suppose your database stores department codes and not the descriptions; however, when the report is printed you want to see the full name of the department.

- HR – Human Resources
- IT – Information Technology
- PR – Payroll
- FI – Finance

```
If {Employee.Dept} = "HR" then "Human Resources"
Else If {Employee.Dept} = "FI" then "Finance"
Else If {Employee.Dept} = "PR" then "Payroll"
Else If {Employee.Dept} = "IT" then "Information Technology"
Else {Employee.Dept}
```

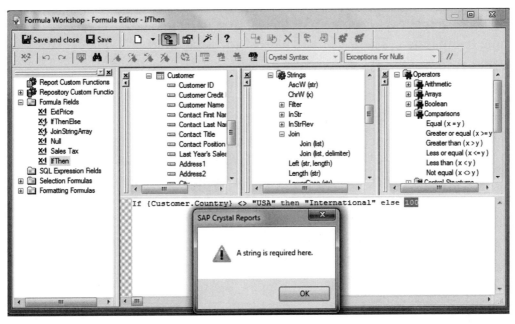

Figure 8.21
If Then Else error message.

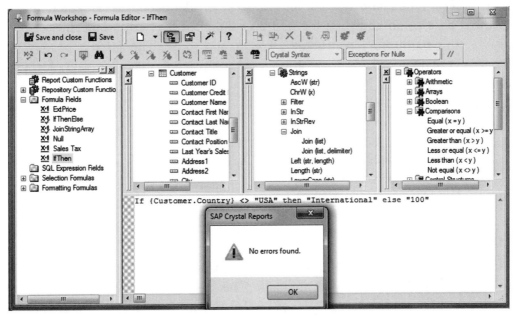

Figure 8.22
Proper use of the If Then Else statement.

This is a simple case of nested `If Then Else` statements; however, they can get quite complicated. There are alternatives to using nested `If Then Else` statements, such as the `Case` statement and the `Switch()` function.

Case Statements

`Select Case` statements are easier to read and manage than multiple nested `If Then Else` statements. Using the previous example with the nested `If` statement, the following `Case` statement provides a more user-friendly approach to managing the results.

```
Select {Database Field}
    Case <Criteria > : <Desired Results>
    Case <Criteria> : <Desired Results>
    Case <Criteria> : <Desired Results>
    Case <Criteria> : <Desired Results>
Default : <Desired Results if the criteria is not in the Case statement>
```

The syntax for the `Select Case` statement defines the field to compare the criteria against in the `Select` part of the statement.

Each criterion that you are looking for will be defined in a `Case` statement followed by a colon and then the desired results for that criterion. The desired results can be a number, a string, a formula, and so on. The `Default` portion of the `Select` statement is optional, but allows for you to establish a value for any criteria not specified.

```
Select {Employee.Dept}
    Case "HR: "Human Resources"
    Case "FI": "Finance"
    Case "PR": "Payroll"
    Case "IT": "Information Technology"
Default {Employee.Dept}
```

Switch Function

The `Switch` statement can replace the need for the `If Then Else` statement and is sometimes easier to read and manage. The `Switch` function involves using Boolean expressions and listing the value if the result is true. It is very similar to a `Case` statement, but uses arguments and values within the parentheses. Using the `Switch` function will allow you to manage results in your record-selection formula and still have them pushed to the database server for processing. You can have many expressions in a `Switch` function. Consider a case in which there are as many as 30 possibilities. You would not want to have to write 30 `If Then Else` statements to produce the desired results. You can add a `Switch` function in the Programming Shortcuts category of the Function tree instead.

```
Switch (expression 1, value1, expression 2, value 2, ...)
```

Let's take a look at a `Switch` function for the previous example:

```
Switch({Employee.Position} = "HR", "Human Resources",
    {Employee.Position}="FI", "Finance",
    {Employee.Position} = "PR", "Payroll",
    {Employee.Position} = "IT", "Information Technology",
        true, "Sales")
```

This code evaluates each expression from left to right and returns the value listed immediately after the expression argument. Note that if the records do not meet any of the specified criteria, the value will default to `"Sales"`.

Null Values

Null values in a formula will produce undesired results unless you stipulate in Crystal Reports how to handle them. Including a null value in a formula using the "Exceptions for Nulls" option requires you to indicate in the formula what should happen if the value is null and what should happen when it is not null. You must use the `If Then Else` statement in conjunction with the `Null` function to specify how to handle null values.

Crystal syntax:

```
If IsNull({Customer.Region}) then "" else {Customer.Region} +
                                       " " + {Customer.ZipCode}
```

Basic syntax:

```
If {Customer.Region} = "" then Formula = " " else Formula =
                      {Customer.Region} + ", " + {Customer.Postal Code}
```

Accounting for null values is so important when creating a formula because if the system locates a null value in your database and you have not specified how it should be handled, Crystal Reports will ignore the calculation for the record.

You may pull 1,000 records on your report and 999 of them show a result for the formula; however, one record does not and you cannot figure out why. Well, one of the likely causes would be the record has a null value for a field included in the formula. Let's look at a common scenario. You need to create a formula to concatenate the address information into one field. To create a formula to combine the address information, follow these steps:

1. Create a new formula called **Address**.

2. Enter the database fields and separators, as shown in Figure 8.23.

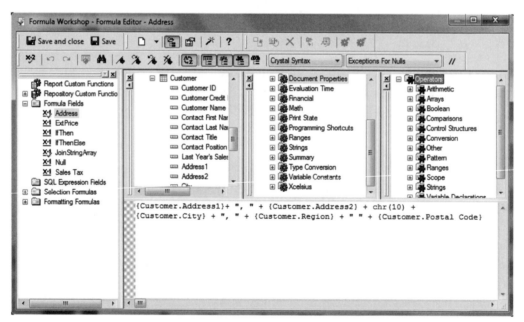

Figure 8.23
Concatenating address information.

3. Save and close the formula workshop.

4. Insert the Address formula into the Details section of the report.

5. Preview the report, as shown in Figure 8.24.

Customer ID	Customer Name	Address
1	City Cyclists	7464 South Kingsway, Suite 2006 Sterling Heights, MI 48358
2	Pathfinders	
3	Bike-A-Holics Anonymous	7429 Arbutus Boulevard, Suite 2017 Blacklick, OH 43005
4	Psycho-Cycle	
5	Sporting Wheels Inc.	480 Grant Way, Suite 1110 San Diego, CA 92150
6	Rockshocks for Jocks	
7	Poser Cycles	
8	Spokes 'N Wheels Ltd.	
9	Trail Blazer's Place	
10	Rowdy Rims Company	
11	Clean Air Transportation Co.	1867 Thurlow Lane, Suite 1304 Conshohocken, PA 19453
12	Hooked on Helmets	7655 Mayberry Crescent, Suite 209 Eden Prairie, MN 55327

Figure 8.24
Previewing your report.

Note

Notice that not all records have an address displayed, although every record has an Address1 value. One would assume at least the fields that are populated would be displayed on the report.

Due to the fact that the Address2 field is null on some records and it was not specified how Crystal Reports was to handle null values, Crystal Reports ignored the calculation of the record. Figure 8.25 shows how to correct the formula by denoting how the null values are to be handled.

Notice all of the addresses are now formulated in the Address formula. See Figure 8.26.

It's better to account for any possible abnormalities when developing your report versus waiting for a problem to occur to establish a solution for the exception.

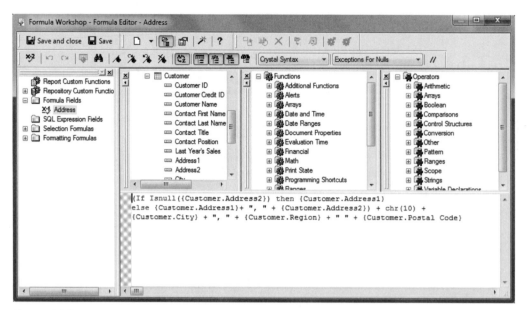

Figure 8.25
Using the IsNull function.

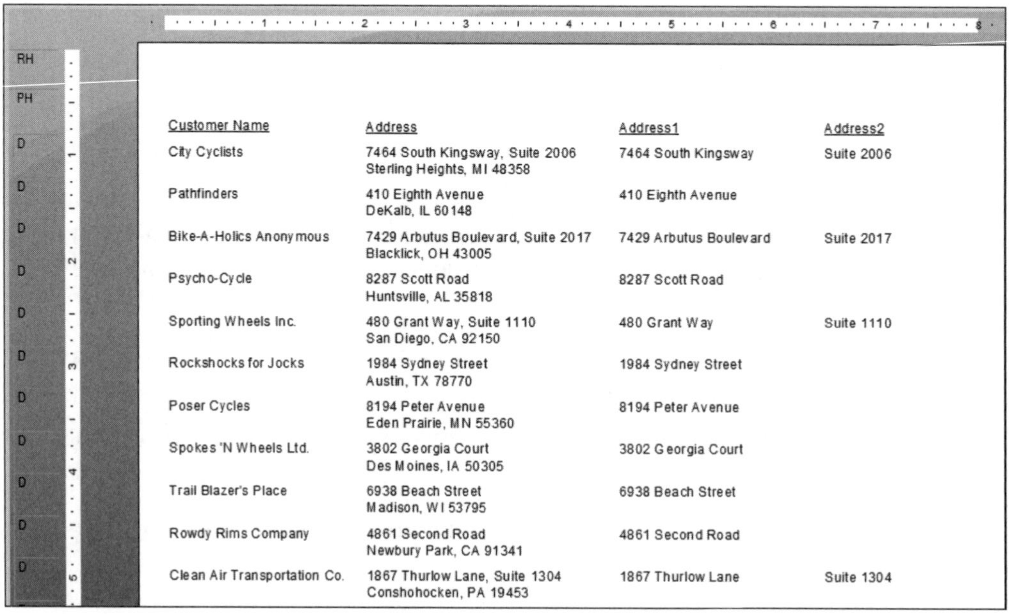

Figure 8.26
All data is displayed with the Null function.

The DateTime Functions

The DateTime functions, shown in Figure 8.27, are used to convert dates to numbers and numbers to dates. There are many predefined functions to assist you in obtaining numerical values from date, times, and date-time fields.

Figure 8.27
The DateTime functions.

A simple date calculation: How many days between the date the order was placed and the date it was shipped.

```
{Orders.Required Date} - {Orders.Ship Date}
```

This results in a whole number unless the field is a date-time field. If it is a date-time field, the result will be a whole number with a fractional value. For example, 4.27.

N o t e

You can use the `Truncate` function in Crystal syntax or the `Fix` function in the Basic syntax to remove the fraction from the number of days.

Many times, I am asked to create a report to display the number of minutes between two fields. For example, a call center needed to determine how many minutes it took to resolve a call once the support technician picked it up. As calls are escalated, the need becomes tracking the number of days and minutes to resolve. Using the `DateDiff` function allows you to calculate certain units between two dates. Take a look at the `DateDiff` function:

```
DateDiff(intervaltype, startDateTime, endDateTime)
DateDiff(intervaltype, startDateTime, endDateTime, firstDayofWeek)
```

Interval Type refers to the units that you want to calculate, as follows:

Interval Type	Description
d	Number of days
m	Number of months
yyyy	Number of years
q	Number of quarters
y	Day of year
n	Number of minutes
s	Number of seconds
h	Number of hours
w	Number of weeks
ww	Number of weeks based on the `FirstDayofWeek` constant. The first day of the week starts on Sunday in Crystal Reports. To change the first day of the week, use one of the following constants:

`crSunday`	1
`crMonday`	2
`crTuesday`	3
`crWednesday`	4
`crThursday`	5
`crFriday`	6
`crSaturday`	7

```
DateDiff ("n",{Orders.Order Date},{Orders.Ship Date})
DateDiff("d", {Orders.Order Date}, {Orders.Ship Date}, crMonday)
```

To calculate two different units such as hours and minutes, you need to use variables, which you'll read about later in this chapter. There are many other DateTime functions that are beneficial; see the functions in the appendix.

Evaluation Times

Crystal Reports processes reports in what is considered to be a multi-pass process. It consists of three processes. Each of those processes has an evaluation time associated with it that refers to the time Crystal Reports attempts to calculate the value of the formula. It is important to understand these processes and evaluation times in order to develop a report that will run as efficiently as possible.

The multi-pass process consists of the following steps:

1. **Prepass 1(BeforeReadingRecords)** – This pass does not connect to the database. It is collecting flat formula values only. Those are formulas that have static numbers and will not change from the detail records.

2. **Pass 1 (WhileReadingRecords)** – A connection to the database is made and the records are retrieved. If the record selection could not be processed on the server, it is processed locally at this pass. Recurring formulas are processed. Those are formulas that include a database field and will change for each detail record.

   Crosstabs, charts, and maps that include database fields and recurring formulas are read in this pass. However, it cannot include any summary fields or running totals. If it does, it will be processed in a later pass.

   Saved data is stored. The records that are retrieved using the report query will be stored with the report at this pass.

   Sorting of records and placement in the proper groups are processed in this pass. Grand totals and summaries are processed in this pass.

   With the addition of the Saved Data option in the Select Expert in version 2008 and later, the Saved Data Selection formula is processed in Pass 1.

3. **Prepass 2** – This pass is used to gather any Top N/Bottom N group data based on the data pulled in Pass 1.

4. **Pass 2 (WhilePrintingRecords)** – This pass is used to format the data to be printed on the report.

   Processes any Group Selection formulas.

   Processes running totals.

   Processes Print Time formulas. Those are formulas using the WhilePrintingRecords evaluation time including variables. These formulas include subtotals and summary fields.

   Processes crosstabs, charts, and maps that include running totals and summary fields or are based on a crosstab that was processed in Pass 1.

   Processes OLAP grids.

   Processes subreports.

   Generates pages on demand.

5. **Pass 3** – This pass is not required and will process only if you require a total page count or use the Page N of M field.

Tip

Unless the total page count or Page N of M is required, omit using them to eliminate the need for Crystal Reports to initiate the pass 3.

Now that you have an idea how the multi-pass process works, let's summarize the Evaluation Times. The Evaluation Times are used to control when the formulas are processed. As the developer, you can tell the system to calculate the formula at a certain pass. You cannot force the formula to process before its defined pass, but you can force it to calculate after the pass and even after a certain formula. Evaluation times are especially useful when formulating variables.

- **BeforeReadingRecords (Prepass 1)** – Specifies that the formula must be evaluated before making a connection to the database.

- **WhileReadingRecords (Pass 1)** – Specifies that the formula must be evaluated while the records are being read.

- **WhilePrintingRecords (Pass 2)** – Specifies that the formula must be evaluated while the records are being printed.

- **EvaluateAfter()** – The Evaluate After option allows you to force a formula to be calculated only after a specific formula is calculated. If the formula contains another formula, you want to make sure the first formula is calculated prior to trying to calculate the last formula. For example, sales tax cannot be properly calculated if the SubTotal formula has not been calculated. Therefore, you can use the EvaluateAfter function to force the correct processing time, as follows:

```
Sales Tax Formula
EvaluateAfter({@SubTotal})
{@SubTotal} * 1.05
```

To change or specify an evaluation time, the evaluation time must be the first line in the formula, as shown in Figure 8.28.

Figure 8.28
Using evaluation times.

UNDERSTANDING VARIABLES

Variables are used to store temporary values for later use in other formulas or to be shared between reports. A standard formula stores its value only long enough to present the value, whereas variables act as placeholders and allow the values to be stored in memory and can be assigned different values throughout the report. Often, you are unable to extract all information in one report, and therefore need a subreport. Variables are quite beneficial in this scenario as it may become necessary to summarize the data in the report footer section of the subreport.

Most programmers are familiar with variables and how to use them. In Crystal Reports, in order to use a variable, it must be declared, assigned a value, and then used in a formula.

Declaring a Variable

Declaring a variable involves specifying the variable datatype and giving the variable a name.

There are 28 variable types.

Crystal Syntax

StringVar	NumberVar Range	DateTime Array
BooleanVar	DateVar Range	StringVar Range Array
CurrencyVar	TimeVar Range	BooleanVar Range Array
NumberVar	DateTimeVar Range	CurrencyVar Range Array
DateVar	StringVar Array	NumberVar Range Array
TimeVar	BooleanVar Array	DateVar Range Array
DateTimeVar	CurrencyVar Array	TimeVar Range Array
StringVar Range	NumberVar Aray	DateTime Range Array
BooleanVar Range	DateVar Array	
CurrencyVar Range	TimeVar Array	

Basic Syntax

Dim x	Dim x As Currency Range	Dim x () As DateTime
Dim x ()	Dim x As Date Range	Dim x () As String
Dim x As Boolean	Dim x As Time Range	Dim x () As Number Range
Dim x As Number	Dim x As DateTime Range	Dim x () As Currency Range
Dim x As Currency	Dim x As String Range	Dim x () As Date Range
Dim x As Date	Dim x () As Boolean	Dim x () As Time Range
Dim x As Time	Dim x () As Number	Dim x () As DateTime Range
Dim x As DateTime	Dim x () As Currency	Dim x () As String Range
Dim x As String	Dim x () As Date	
Dim x As Number Range	Dim x () As Time	

Declaring a variable involves defining how long the variable will store the value in memory and determining where it can be accessed. You define the length through the use of scopes.

Syntax Scopes

There are four types of scopes, as follows:

- **Local** – A local scope allows the value to be used only in the formula in which it is declared. Local scope is the default for Basic syntax.

- **Shared** – A shared scope allows the value to be used in the entire report and passed back and forth between a main report and a subreport.

- **Global** – A global scope allows the values to be used anywhere in the main report. You cannot share variables between a main report and a subreport using the Global scope. Global scope is the default scope for Crystal syntax. If you do not define a scope, this scope is used.

- **Dim** – Only used in Basic syntax. A Dim scope can be used only in the formula in which it is declared. Same as the Local scope.

Crystal syntax:

```
Local stringvar MyTotal;
```

Basic syntax:

```
Local MyTotal as String;
```

Be sure to use the semicolon to end each statement.

Assigning a Value to a Variable

Variables are assigned values by using the assignment operators for the appropriate programming language. You can declare a statement and assign a value on the same line as shown here. It is not required that you declare the variable separately. If you do not assign a value to a variable, it defaults to the default value for the datatype. For example, if it is a numberVar, an unassigned variable would default to 0.

Crystal syntax:

```
Assignment character is ":="
Whileprintingrecords;
StringVar MyTotal := "The department s total is " & {Orders.OrderAmount}
```

Basic syntax:

```
Assignment character is "="
Whileprintingrecords;
Dim MyTotal As String
Formula =  MyTotal = "This department s total is " & {Orders.OrderAmount}
```

Using the Variable in a Formula

Once you have declared the variable and assigned a value to it, you can use it in a formula. Using it in a formula requires noting the evaluation time on the first line.

```
Whileprintingrecords;
Shared CurrencyVar MyTotal;
MyTotal:=Sum ({Orders.Order Amount})
```

In this example, a variable called MyTotal with a shared scope was declared. On the third line the variable MyTotal was assigned a value of the "sum of the Orders Amount" field. By declaring a shared scope, the variable can be shared anywhere on the report and between a main report and a subreport. When you're referencing a variable in another formula, whether on a main report or a subreport, it's crucial when you're calling the variable that you spell the variable name exactly as it was declared. Variable declarations are case-sensitive.

```
Shared CurrencyVar MyTotal <> Shared CurrencyVar Mytotal
```

Referencing the variable in another formula requires stipulating the evaluation time and calling the variable:

```
Whileprintingrecords;
Shared CurrencyVar MyTotal
```

Using a variable requires exact placement of the variable formula on the report in a section above the section you require the variable to be used. If you intend to use the variable in the Report Footer as part of a summary, the variable formula must be placed in a section prior to the Report Footer. Depending on the function of the variable, you must ensure that you are placing the variable in a section that is generating the correct result. For example, if you place the variable in group footer 2, the result will be different than if it is placed in group footer 1. The field and section cannot be suppressed on the main report in order for the value to be displayed. If you place the variable in an incorrect section, the value will be displayed as zero. You'll learn more about the placement in the "Manual Running Totals" section, next.

Manual Running Totals

Running totals are necessary when you need to control which fields are summarized. However, too many running totals can hurt your processing time. Manual running totals can minimize some of the performance issues. You will find it necessary to create a running total if you have any data suppressed as in a Top N or Bottom N report. You cannot create a running total on a formula that is evaluated in the WhilePrintingRecords pass. There are times when you might need to include the value of a running total within another running total. The system-generated running total feature will not allow you to summarize a running total or any Pass 2 formulas. To solve this dilemma, you replace the system running total with a manual running total.

Manual running totals consist of three formulas:

- A formula to summarize the appropriate field.

- A formula to reset the formula.
- A formula to display the value.

For example, to create a running total to count the number of products sold by Product Name, you would follow these steps:

1. Create a formula named **RunningTotalProduct**.

2. Enter the `WhilePrintingRecords` evaluation time. Don't forget the end of statement semicolon.
   `Whileprintingrecords;`

3. Declare the `numberVar` variable. Name the variable `TotalCount`.

4. Assign the value of `{OrdersDetail.Quantity} + TotalCount`. Your code should look similar to the code shown in Figure 8.29.

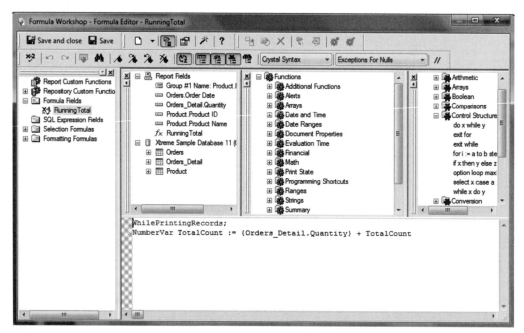

Figure 8.29
Assigning the variable a value.

5. Place the formula in the Details section.

Tip

Lock the position/size of the variable to prevent the field from being moved inadvertently. Moving the field from its intended section will result in an incorrect value.

Now you can create a Reset formula. Creating a Reset formula involves assigning the value of the variable to zero. Follow these steps:

1. Create a formula named **Reset**.

2. Enter the `WhilePrintingRecords` evaluation time.

3. Reference the variable name declared in the Summary formula, called `TotalCount`.

4. Assign the value 0 using the assignment operator. Your code should look similar to the code shown in Figure 8.30.

Figure 8.30
Creating a Reset formula.

Note

Be sure to put careful thought into the point at which the variable value should be reset. If you want the variable to reset before each new group starts, place the Reset variable in the Group Header or Group Footer.

Create a Display formula next. It will display the last value of the variable.

1. Create a formula named **Display**.

2. Enter the WhilePrintingRecords evaluation time.

3. Call the variable by redeclaring the variable type and type the variable name exactly as it was entered in the Summary formula, as shown in Figure 8.31.

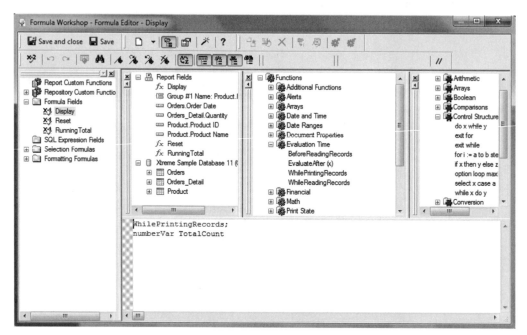

Figure 8.31
Creating a Display formula.

Place the Display variable in a section below the section where the summary variable is evaluated.

WORKING WITH SQL COMMANDS

Crystal Reports automatically creates a SQL query behind the scenes as the developer adds tables, views, and joins the tables together. The power of the SQL functionality enhances the performance of your report because the stress of the data retrieval is placed on the more powerful database server rather than on the client workstation. Although it is easy to insert tables and create joins for users with no SQL transact query experience, it is more powerful to use SQL statements. Most experienced developers and programmers will agree they are more comfortable controlling the SQL query by writing their own statements. In previous versions, Crystal Reports allowed you to modify the SQL query that the system generated automatically, but that feature was discontinued with the release of version 10. The feature was replaced with the ability to create your own ad hoc SQL statement. This feature is not available with all database drivers. It's important to note that using SQL commands puts your database at risk for SQL injection attacks.

Note

> *SQL injection attacks* are computer bugs or viruses that attack security vulnerabilities in a database or application at the business layer by passing invalid code data to the query that can destroy databases.

This feature was beneficial to those developers who did not have access or permission to create stored procedures in the application used to report data and had to rely on the IT department to create views and other security measures to allow them access to the correct data. The inclusion of the Add command option gives the users the ability to control their own SQL queries. This feature will not bypass any other security measures so if your permissions are limited in the SQL or Oracle database, writing your own ad hoc statement in Crystal Reports will not allow you to access any data beyond those permissions. This section is not intended to teach you how to write SQL statements, but discusses the power of the feature.

Tip

> To see the SQL query of an existing report, use the Database > Show SQL Query option. You can copy this query into the ad hoc SQL command option or into the querying tool for the database to test data results.

A SQL command is a series of statements written in the SQL language to retrieve the desired fields, join tables, group, and sort data. The SQL statement is passed to the database server for processing, which speeds up the performance of the report. The SQL command acts as virtual table for the database. The Add Command option is accessible from the Database Expert, as shown in Figure 8.32. Instead of inserting tables or views, choose the Add Command option from the Database Expert window.

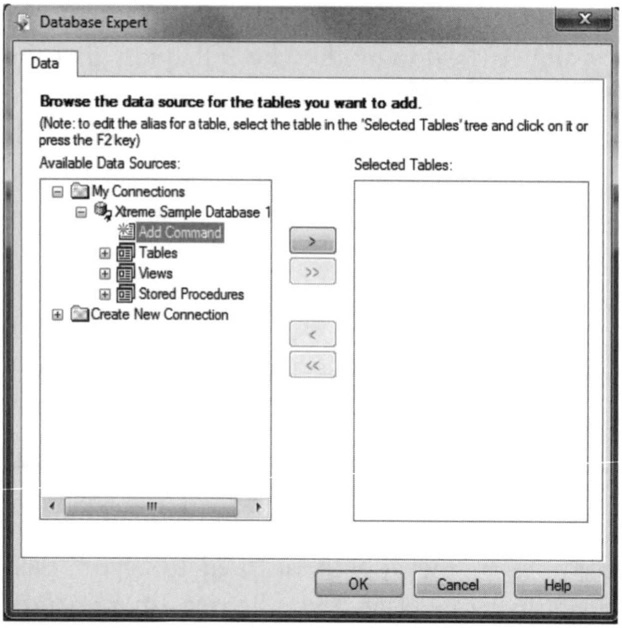

Figure 8.32
The Add Command option.

The Add Command to Report dialog box opens. Using the syntax for the reporting database, write the SQL statement to pull the desired fields. The example in Figure 8.33 selects all fields from the Orders table.

Tip

Use of the * as a wildcard is not recommended. You should list each field that you want on the report in the SELECT statement.

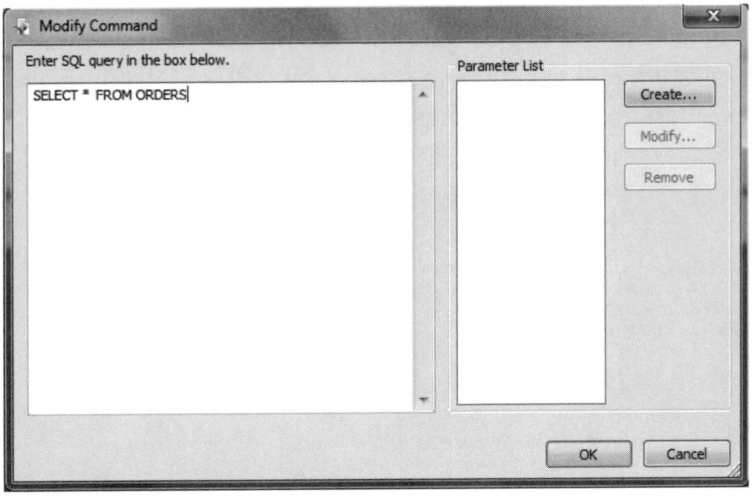

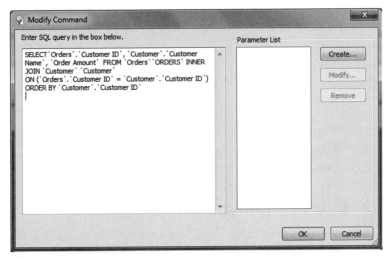

Figure 8.33
Selecting fields in the SQL Command window.

In the example shown in Figure 8.34, the Customer ID, Customer Name, and the Order Amount field have been selected from the Orders and Customer tables. The tables are joined on the Customer ID field in each table and sorted by the Customer ID field.

Figure 8.34
An ad hoc SQL command.

Accept the command by clicking the OK button. The syntax will be checked when clicking OK. The system will generate an error against the SQL command if it is unable to retrieve data from the database, as shown in Figure 8.35.

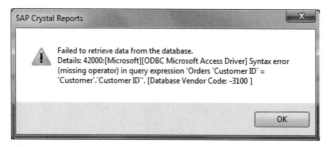

Figure 8.35
Unable to retrieve data.

If all syntax checks are validated, the command will be accepted and will appear in the Selected Tables pane of the Database Expert. The object appears as "Command" instead of a table name. It's best to rename the command to describe the query.

To rename the query, you follow these steps:

1. Select the "Command" object in the Database Expert.

2. Press the F2 key.

3. Rename the command. In the previous example, a suggested name for the Command may be CustomerSales.

Queries can be edited at any time by accessing the Database Expert window and right-clicking on the Command field > Edit Command. The Modify Command window will open; you then make the appropriate modifications to the query.

Adding Parameters to a SQL Command

You can add parameters to the SQL command. Adding parameters to your SQL command allows you to filter the information that you are retrieving from the database. From the Add Command to Report window, select the Create button on the right side of the Parameter List pane. Parameters created in this window will appear in the Parameter Field category in the Field Explorer. The setup of the parameters in the Add Command dialog box are minimal but can be modified from the Field Explorer. To modify additional options in a parameter created in the SQL command, you must edit the parameter from the Field Explorer. See Figure 8.36.

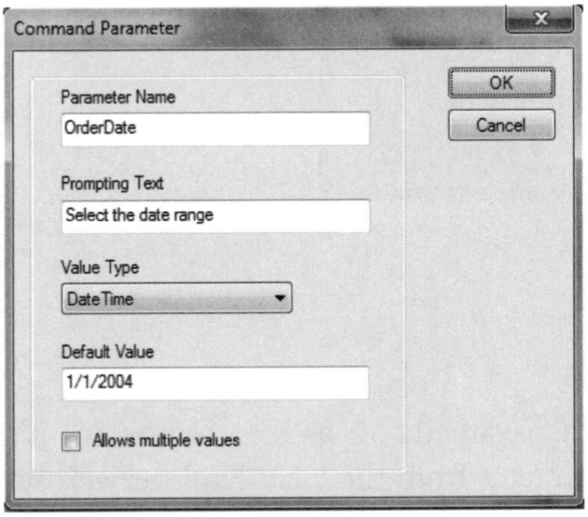

Figure 8.36
Creating a parameter in a SQL command.

To create a parameter in a SQL command, follow these steps:

1. Choose the Create button on the right side of the Add Command to Report dialog box.

2. Enter a parameter name.

3. Enter the prompting text. For example, `"Enter the date range"`.

4. In the Value Type drop-down list, select the datatype of the parameter field.

5. In the Default Value option, enter a default value if desired.

6. Select the Allow Multiple Values checkbox to allow users to choose more than one value in the parameter. See Figure 8.37.

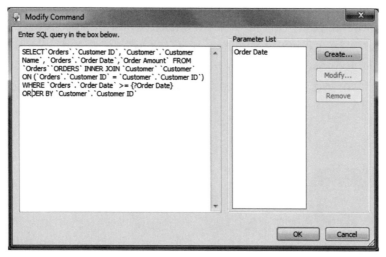

Figure 8.37
Parameters in the SQL command.

Due to the limited options of creating a parameter in a SQL command, it's important to note that you can edit a parameter from the Field Explorer and set the additional options for the parameter, such as import parameter values and set range values. You can also establish Parameters panel options, including making the parameter optional or setting edit masks.

To edit the parameters, follow these steps:

1. Right-click on the parameter name in the Parameter Fields category in the Field Explorer.

2. Select Edit.

3. Modify the desired options.

CREATING CUSTOM FUNCTIONS

Crystal Reports has many predefined functions; however, there are times when your report's business requirements might require a non-standard function. Crystal Reports allows you to create your own custom functions. SAP Business Objects also provided a library of custom functions called Web Elements that can be used in your own reports and then saved to the repository for sharing with other users. Custom functions allow you to write the logic for a formula for users who aren't comfortable writing formulas. They also allow you to include certain formula types in a function that you aren't able to include in a standard formula.

Custom functions require arguments that are very similar to writing Excel functions. Database fields cannot be referenced when creating a custom function. The function uses local variables and specific fields that give users the ability to use the function for multiple purposes. Custom functions cannot reference evaluation time formulas, summary fields, or shared or global variables.

Previously, I was asked to write a formula to display the job number at the top of the report. However, the job number was comprised of certain characters from multiple fields and was to be used by multiple users in many reports. The customer's personnel were very basic users and did not feel comfortable creating a complex formula. A custom function seemed to be ideal in this situation.

A custom function can be created using the Editor or the Formula Extractor, which will allow you to create a function from an existing formula.

To create a new function, follow these steps:

1. Click the *fx* button on the Expert toolbar.

2. Select the Report Custom Function and click the New button, as shown in Figure 8.38.

3. Give the function a descriptive name.

4. Select Use Editor. The Editor window is displayed, as shown in Figure 8.39.

5. Within the parentheses, declare a variable type and assign the variable a name.

Tip

You can have multiple variables in a custom function. It's best to give each variable a descriptive name that tells the users what value should be entered in that argument. See Figure 8.40.

6. Once the variable(s) have been declared, you must create the summary function to use the variables that you declared in the previous step.

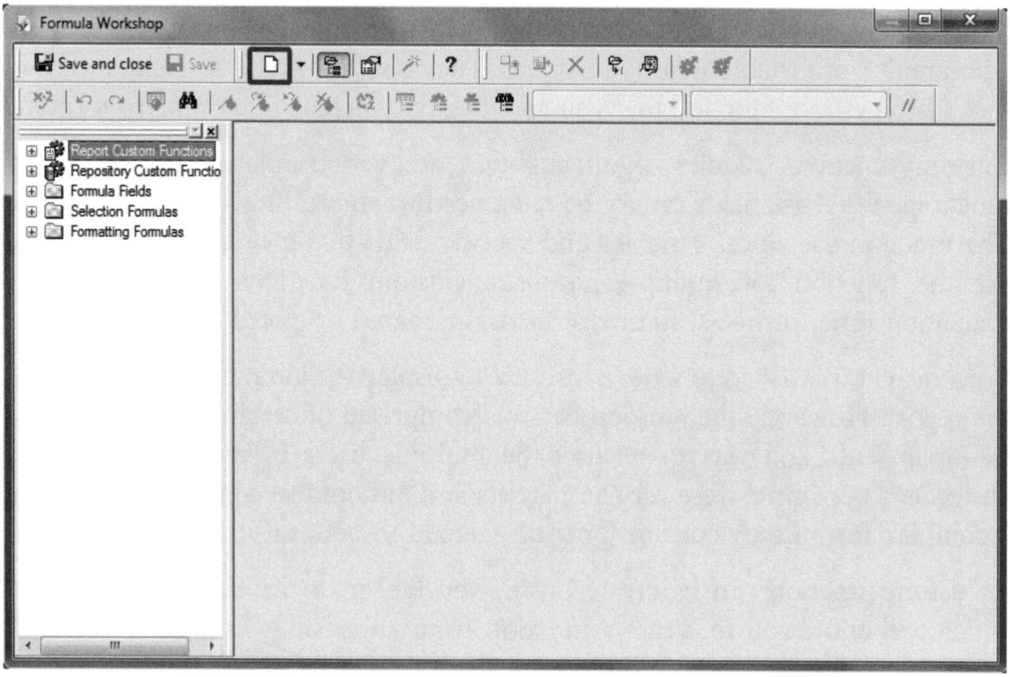

Figure 8.38
Creating a new function.

7. Verify the syntax.

8. Save and close.

Now that you have created the custom function, you can use it in a formula:

1. Start a new formula.

2. Expand the Custom Functions category in the Function tree. All of the custom functions previously created will appear in the list.

Tip

The categories displayed are context-sensitive and may change based on the feature being used.

3. Double-click the custom function you previously created, as shown in Figure 8.41.

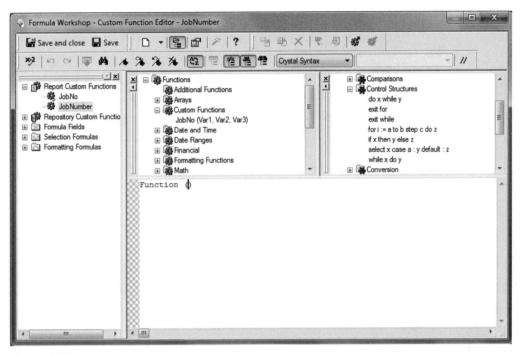

Figure 8.39
The Editor window.

Figure 8.40
Using the Custom function variables.

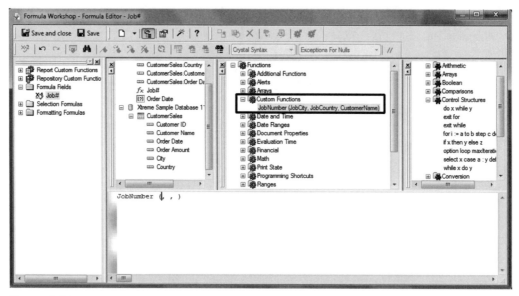

Figure 8.41
Using custom functions.

4. Select the appropriate database field or enter the value that corresponds to the variable. An example is shown in Figure 8.42.

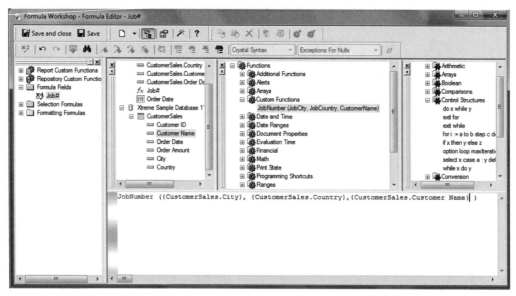

Figure 8.42
Using the function in a formula.

Note

Notice the variable names are descriptive enough to determine which database fields correspond to the variables.

When previewed, data will be displayed using the custom function, as shown in Figure 8.43.

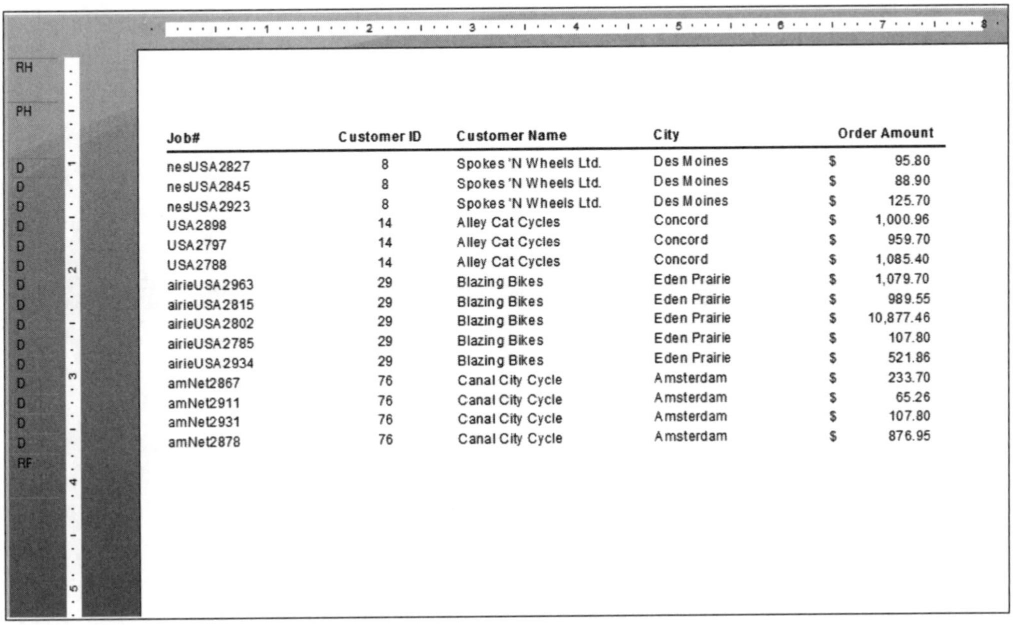

Job#	Customer ID	Customer Name	City	Order Amount
nesUSA2827	8	Spokes 'N Wheels Ltd.	Des Moines	$ 95.80
nesUSA2845	8	Spokes 'N Wheels Ltd.	Des Moines	$ 88.90
nesUSA2923	8	Spokes 'N Wheels Ltd.	Des Moines	$ 125.70
USA2898	14	Alley Cat Cycles	Concord	$ 1,000.96
USA2797	14	Alley Cat Cycles	Concord	$ 959.70
USA2788	14	Alley Cat Cycles	Concord	$ 1,085.40
airieUSA2963	29	Blazing Bikes	Eden Prairie	$ 1,079.70
airieUSA2815	29	Blazing Bikes	Eden Prairie	$ 989.55
airieUSA2802	29	Blazing Bikes	Eden Prairie	$ 10,877.46
airieUSA2785	29	Blazing Bikes	Eden Prairie	$ 107.80
airieUSA2934	29	Blazing Bikes	Eden Prairie	$ 521.86
amNet2867	76	Canal City Cycle	Amsterdam	$ 233.70
amNet2911	76	Canal City Cycle	Amsterdam	$ 65.26
amNet2931	76	Canal City Cycle	Amsterdam	$ 107.80
amNet2878	76	Canal City Cycle	Amsterdam	$ 876.95

Figure 8.43
Data displayed using the custom functions.

USING THE FORMULA EXTRACTOR TO CONVERT EXISTING FORMULAS

If you have existing formulas, it's easy to convert them to a custom function. Converting existing formulas will allow you to share them with others and use them repeatedly. To convert an existing formula to a function, follow these steps:

1. Right-click on the formula in the Field Explorer and select Edit.

2. Select the drop-down menu from the "New" icon on the Formula Editor toolbar and select Custom Function. See Figure 8.44.

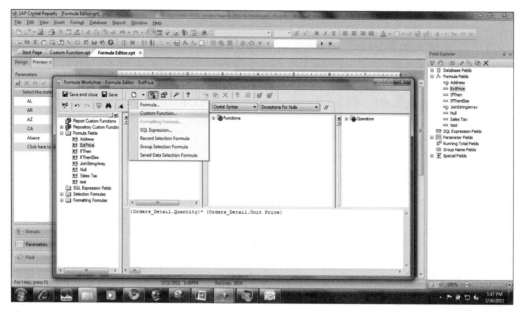

Figure 8.44
Creating a New Custom Function.

3. Enter a descriptive name for the function.

Tip

Give the function a name that describes the function it is performing.

4. Select Use Extractor. The Extract Custom Formula from Formula dialog box opens. See Figure 8.45.

Notice the arguments section. The database fields are shown with a replacement variable name of v1 and v2. Crystal Reports defaults the variable names to v1, v2, incrementally. You should rename the variables so that users can tell which fields should be used in the function, as shown in Figure 8.46.

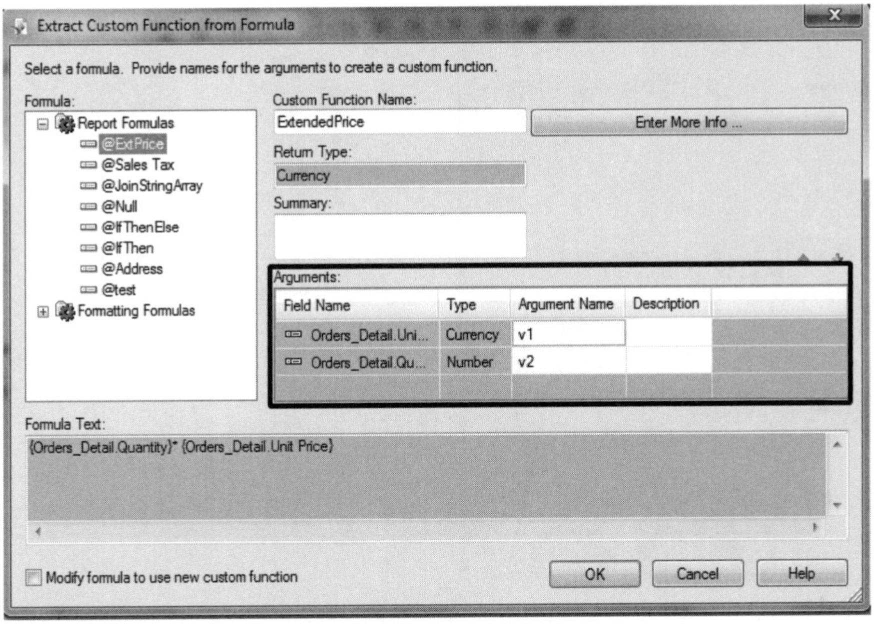

Figure 8.45
Using an existing formula to create a custom function.

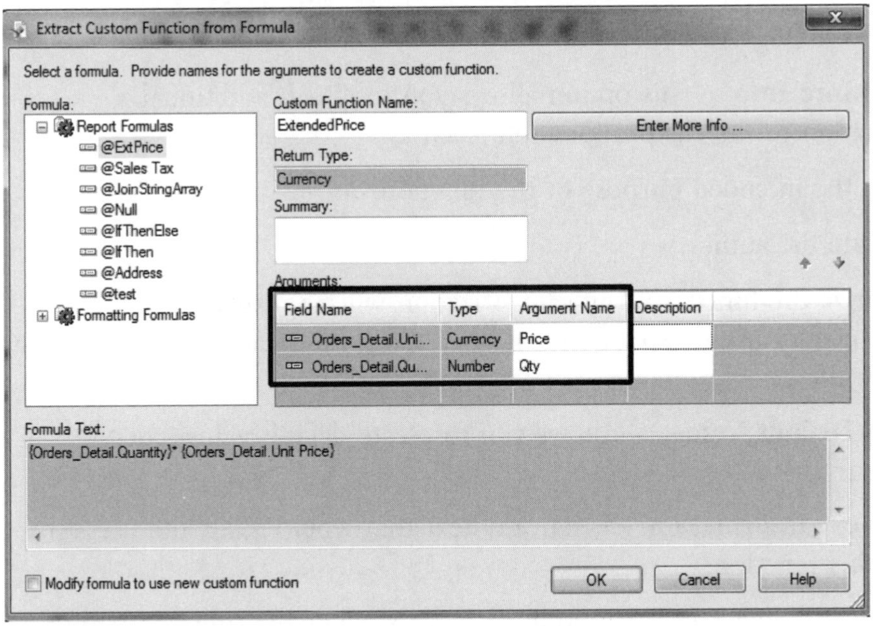

Figure 8.46
Renaming variables in a custom function.

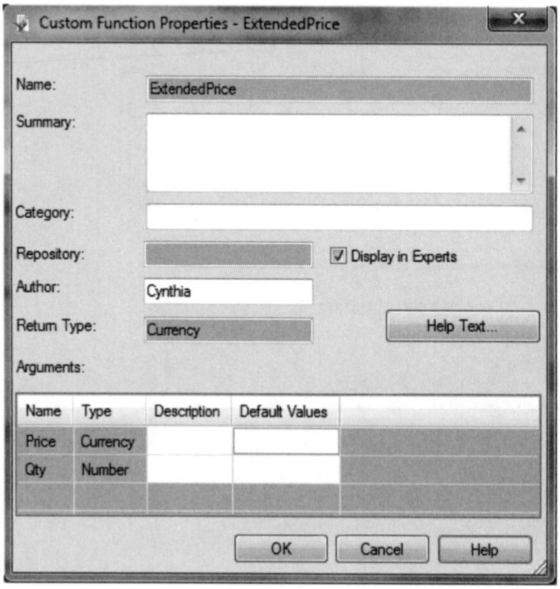

Figure 8.47
Additional options from the Custom Function window.

There are additional options that you can set in the Custom Function window, as shown in Figure 8.47:

- **Enter More Info** – This option allows you to attach additional information to the custom function, such as:

  Specify the intended purpose of the function in the Summary field.

  Designate the author.

  Categorize the function. Any categorization will be displayed as a sub-folder in the Custom Function Category. To create a subfolder, you must precede the category name with a forward slash.

- **Assign Default Values** – Allows you to create default values for the function.

- **Help Text Information** – Insert any text that would assist the users in using this function.

- **Display in Experts** – This option dictates whether the function will be displayed in the custom function logic in the Formula Expert.

There is one more important option on the Formula Extractor dialog box. You can modify the formula to use the Custom Function check box. This option will automatically turn the existing function into a custom function. See Figures 8.48 and 8.49.

Figure 8.48
Formula before creating a custom function.

Figure 8.49
Formula after converting to a custom function.

The formula has been converted to a function. Any changes made to the custom function will be updated in all formulas the function is used in.

Using Web Elements

SAP Business Objects released a library of custom functions called Web Elements that allow you to create drop-down lists, calculators, radio buttons, check boxes, date pickers, and many other useful control elements that can be embedded into your report. Ideally if you have the Crystal Reports Server or Business Objects Enterprise, the web elements will be saved to the repository. However, if you own only the standalone Crystal Reports version, you can still utilize these functions by saving these functions to a report that can be used as a function template. Visit the SAP website at http://www.sdn.sap.com/irj/boc/webelements for more information.

Using SQL Expressions

SQL expressions are comparable to formulas but written in Structured Query language. SQL expressions are used to enhance performance of a report due to the SQL language allowing the processing to be performed on the server whereas a lot of formulas require the formula to be executed on the local workstation. Certain formulas, such as any type of Date formula, will prevent the execution on the server. However, replacing the Date formula with a SQL expression will allow the processing to be performed on the server. SQL expressions are powerful and will enhance the performance, but you should not replace all of your formulas with them.

There are functions that a SQL expression cannot perform and instead you'll need the power of the Crystal Reports language. The SQL expression functions available will depend on the type of database that you are using. I remember one incident in which a client initiated a support call because she was unable to locate the IsNull function in the SQL expressions. However, she was reporting on a Microsoft Access database and the IsNull function is not accessible from an Access database. If you connect to a SQL database, though, the IFNull function is available under the System Function category. It's important to understand the SQL expression functionality depends on the type of database.

Creating a SQL Expression

Let's take a look at the effects of using a date formula on a record-selection formula. The objective here is to only show a dataset of orders from the year 2005. Using a normal formula, you will modify the record-selection formula to show only the desired data.

Open the SQL Expression report (located in the sample files of Chapter 8), and then follow these steps:

Note

The report is based on the Xtreme Sample database installed with Crystal Reports. You might have to set the data location to refresh the report.

1. From Report > Selection Formulas > Record, select the Year() function from the Date and Time Function category.

2. Enter an {Orders.Order Date} field in the Year() function.

3. Click outside of the ending parentheses and type = 2005, as shown in Figure 8.50.

4. Check the syntax.

5. Save and close the report.

6. Save and preview the report.

Now take a look at the statement being pushed to the server:

1. From the Database menu, choose Show SQL Query, as shown in Figure 8.51.

2. Notice the record selection that you enter to filter on records in the year 2005 is not in the Select statement; therefore all records will be pulled across the server and the filtering of 2005 records will be done on the local workstation.

Figure 8.50
Creating a Year() function.

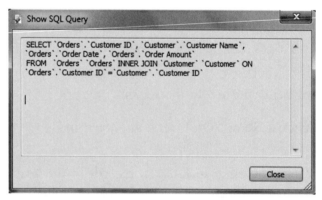

Figure 8.51
Choosing Show SQL Query.

Now you'll use the SQL expression to enhance the performance of the report:

1. Select SQL Expression from the Fields Explorer. Then right-click and select New.

2. Name the SQL expression **Year**.

3. The SQL Expression Editor dialog box will open. Notice the limited function categories.

4. Expand the Date/Time category in the Function Year and double-click on the Year() function. See Figure 8.52.

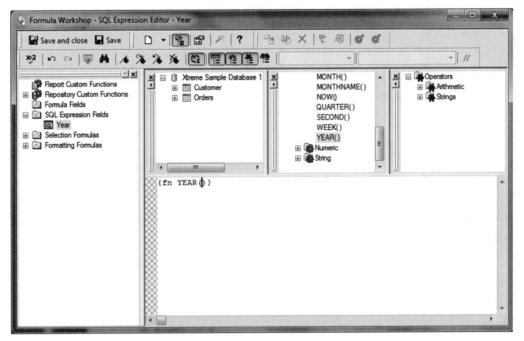

Figure 8.52
Using the Date function in a SQL expression.

Notice the function is referenced in the Formula Text area as {fn Year()}. All functions begin with fn in the SQL Expression Editor.

5. With the cursor inside of the parentheses of the Year() function, insert the {Orders.Order Date} field, and then type = **2005**. See Figure 8.53.

6. Check the syntax.

7. Save and close the expression.

8. Open the record-selection formula. (Choose Report > Selection Formula > Record.)

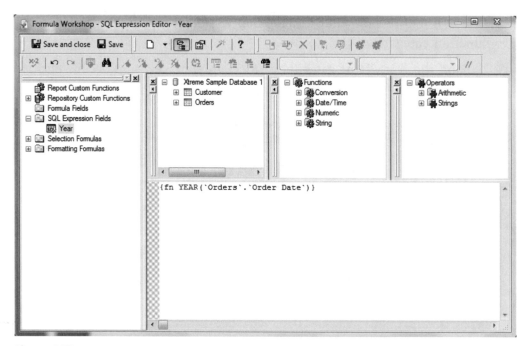

Figure 8.53
A SQL expression with Year().

9. Delete the current formula.

10. Expand the Report Fields tree and locate the Year SQL expression you just created. Double-click to add it, and then type **= 2005**. See Figure 8.54.

11. Save and close the record-selection formula.

12. Save and preview the report.

13. Take a look at the SQL Query now. Choose Database > Show SQL Query to do so. See Figure 8.55.

   Notice the Date condition is now passed to the database query. To enhance performance of your reports, consider options that will ensure that the majority of the processing is done on the server.

Figure 8.54
A SQL expression in the record-selection formula.

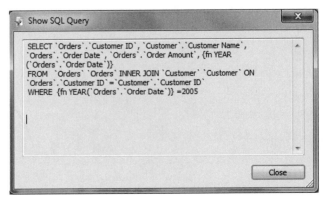

Figure 8.55
The SQL query with the SQL expression.

SUMMARY

Formulas are going to be required in most of the reports that you create for your organization. Understanding the predefined functions and the ability to create ad hoc SQL commands will greatly enhance your reports. As you start to become more familiar with formulas, you will identify easier ways to obtain the desired results. There are multiple ways to obtain any results, but take the additional time to compare the performance timing with the formulas in different manners. SQL expressions are going to be very useful in enhancing performance time, and will be necessary when using certain function types in the record-selection formula. You should spend the additional time understanding the predefined functions. It will pay off in the long run.

CHAPTER 9

CREATING COMPLEX REPORTS

The objectives of this chapter are to learn the following tasks:

- Using subreports
- Using crosstab charts
- Inserting charts
- Using report alerts

Many businesses require very sophisticated analytical reports in order to analyze their businesses. Many organizations spend a tremendous amount of time compiling spreadsheets, charts, and managerial reports manually because their system does not provide the level of information that they need to operate their business. Crystal Reports can accomplish most if not all of the necessary compilations with advanced features such as subreports, crosstab charts, and with types of charts such as trendline, bar, pie charts, and many others. Complex reports require charts, what-if type analysis, the representation of data in different ways, and complex formulas. Crystal Reports enables you to develop all of your business requirements with seamless integration with your reporting database.

USING SUBREPORTS

Most of the time when mentioning subreports, the first question I get is, what are they? Subreports are reports within reports. Subreports are created the same way a standard report is created. It can have the same record selection criteria or a totally different recordset; however, it is embedded within the main report. Subreports are created to show related data in a different manner, such as in a different dataset, or to display unrelated data in a report. Subreports can be a linked or unlinked report. Subreports allow you to combine reports and eliminate the need to run separate reports. For example, say management requires you to create a summary chart each month depicting sales for the current month and another report displaying the sales for the quarter broken down by employee. Currently, you are running each report separately and then copying and pasting the information into one report. With the help of subreports in Crystal Reports, one report can be run and both goals can be accomplished.

Subreports are used to link data that does not have a linkable field or when datatypes are not the same between two tables. For example, the Employee ID field in the Employee table is a number field but in the Employee Training table, the Employee ID field is a string field. Due to the different datatypes, you will not be able to link the two tables directly; therefore a subreport would be ideal to bring the information into one report.

Embedding a report within a report creates a subreport. The subreport becomes part of the main report, which means it no longer acts as a stand-alone report. You have two options for creating a subreport—you can use an existing report or you can create a new report.

Certain guidelines exist for creating a subreport:

- The subreport can be placed in any section in the main report.
- The subreport will not have a Page Header or Page Footer.
- The subreport is not a stand-alone report once embedded in the report.
- A subreport cannot contain a subreport. If you insert an existing report that has a subreport in it into a main report, the system will automatically drop the subreport within the report.

Note

Although subreports are extremely helpful in viewing data in different ways, the use of subreports comes with a performance hit. Therefore, the more subreports you include in your report, the slower the report is going to run.

When to Use Subreports

It's ideal to use subreports when you are:

- Sharing values between a main report and a subreport.

- Attempting to present the same data in different ways, as in a what-if analysis.

- Combining unrelated data, thus creating a dashboard type report. For example, you might have a chart or graph displaying accounts receivable information, another chart displaying accounts payable information, a chart displaying payroll information by department, and another chart displaying sales information. There is no direct link between these data results.

There are two types of subreports:

- **Unlinked subreport** — An unlinked subreport has no common field linked in the main report. The entire subreport will print in the section it was inserted in the main report. For example, if you wanted a list of all customers and vendors in one report and they are stored in two different tables, there is no way to link the two tables together. Therefore, you could create two reports—one report of customers and another report of vendors—and then insert the vendor report in the Report footer of the Customer report.

- **Linked subreport** — A linked subreport has a common field between the two reports. The data in the subreport will only print data that corresponds to the linked field. For example, you wanted to print a report that shows all active employees and all of the training and professional development expenses that have been incurred in the year 2010 by employee. You could create two reports—a main report with all active employees and a subreport based on the training tables with a criteria of only 2010 data—and then link the subreport to the main report based on the employee ID. Therefore, when the report runs, it will display the employee's information record with the employee training and professional development expenses immediately following the employee's name.

Subreports are very useful; however, if you can link the data tables instead of linking reports, it's better to do so. Linked tables have less of a performance effect on the report.

Unlinked Subreports

Let's take a look at how to create an unlinked subreport. An unlinked subreport is just a separate report that is inserted into a main report. When creating subreports, you have the option to insert an existing report into the report or to create a new report at the time you are inserting the subreport. As mentioned, an unlinked subreport is inserted into the section where you want it to print.

1. Open the main report in Design view.

2. Open the Sales by Month and Year.rpt file located in the sample files.

3. Before inserting a subreport, determine the best location for it. Normally, subreports are inserted in a separate section from the main report.

4. Insert an additional Report Header section in the Sales by Month and Year report. Move the new section up so that it becomes Report Header A.

5. Click in the blue area of the Report Header B section, and then drag and drop the area above Report Header A.

6. Select the Insert Subreport icon, shown in Figure 9.1, or choose Insert > Subreport from the menu.

Figure 9.1
The Insert Subreport icon.

The Insert Subreport dialog box, shown in Figure 9.2, has two tabs.

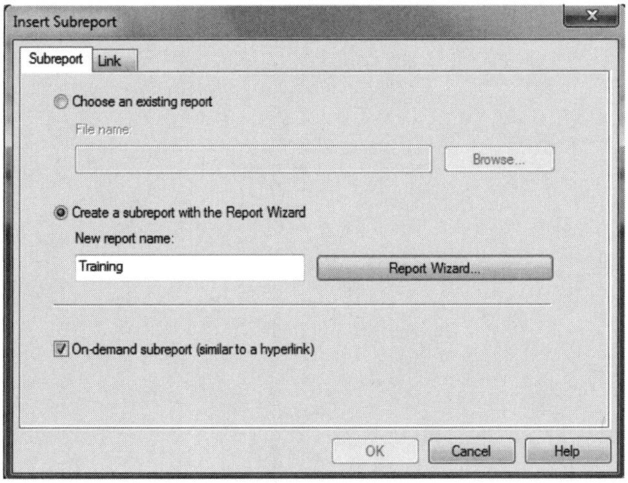

Figure 9.2
The Insert Subreport dialog box.

The Subreport Tab of the Insert Subreport Dialog Box

The Subreport tab is where you specify where the subreport will be derived from. It has the following options:

- **Choose an Existing Report** — If the report already exists, choose this option. Click the Browse button and locate the desired report.

- **Create a Subreport Using the Report Wizard** — If the report has not been created, this option enables you to create the report from this window. However, this option uses the Report Wizard, which in my opinion is undesirable. If you choose to use this option, enter the new report name in the name field and click Report Wizard. The Report Wizard, shown in Figure 9.3, will launch. Follow the steps through the wizard.

- **On-Demand Subreport (Similar to a Hyperlink)** — An on-demand subreport is a report that's not processed until a user clicks on the hyperlink to request the data. On-demand subreports are advantageous for performance reasons because the system does not have to process the additional records at the same time it is processing the main report. It is also beneficial to use when the report is very data intensive and includes lots of fields causing a real estate issue on the report.

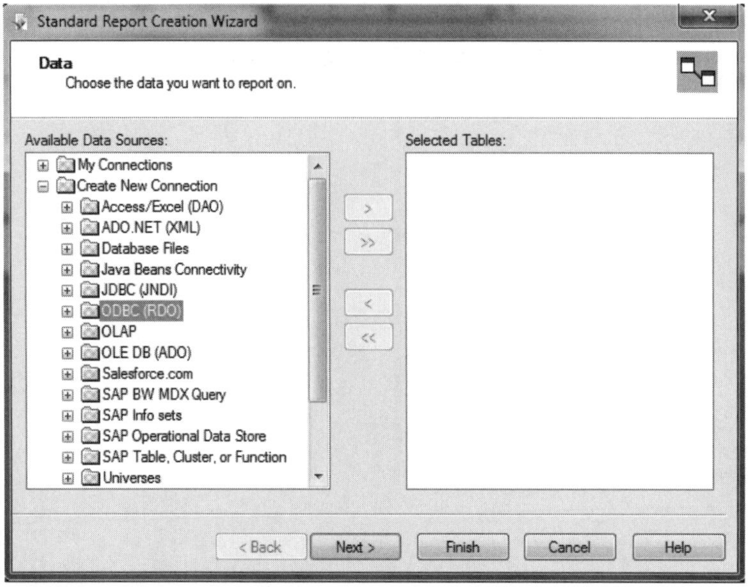

Figure 9.3
The Standard Report Creation Wizard.

You should select the option called Choose an Existing Report for this example. Then click Browse and locate the Accounts Payable.rpt in the Chapter 9 sample files. Click OK. The report will be attached to your mouse cursor. Click in the far-right side of the Report Header A section to insert the subreport.

Resize the subreport to be 5.30 inches wide.

Tip

Right-click on the subreport and then choose Size and Position.

Save the report as **Unlinked Report**. Preview the report. You may have to do some resizing and repositioning of the subreport. Notice the Accounts Payable Report prints before the Sales data. Let's correct that because you want the data to be side by side. Access the Section Expert for Report Header A and turn on Underlay Following Section on the Common tab of the Section Expert window. Finally, save and preview the report. Figure 9.4 shows the unlinked subreport.

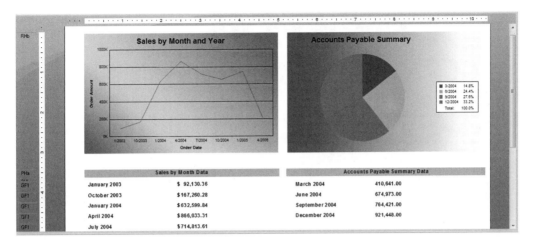

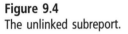

Figure 9.4
The unlinked subreport.

You have created an unlinked subreport. Notice there is no correlating field between the two datasets.

Linked Subreports

Next, you'll explore a linked subreport. In a linked subreport there is a correlation between the two reports. The data in the subreport is based on the data in the main report.

Open the main report in design view. Open the Employee Information.rpt located in the sample files. As stated in the unlinked subreport section, you should determine the best location for the subreport before inserting it into the main report. Insert an additional Detail section.

Select the Insert Subreport icon, shown in Figure 9.5, or choose Insert > Subreport from the menu. Figure 9.6 shows the Insert Subreport dialog box, which appears.

Figure 9.5
The Insert Subreport icon.

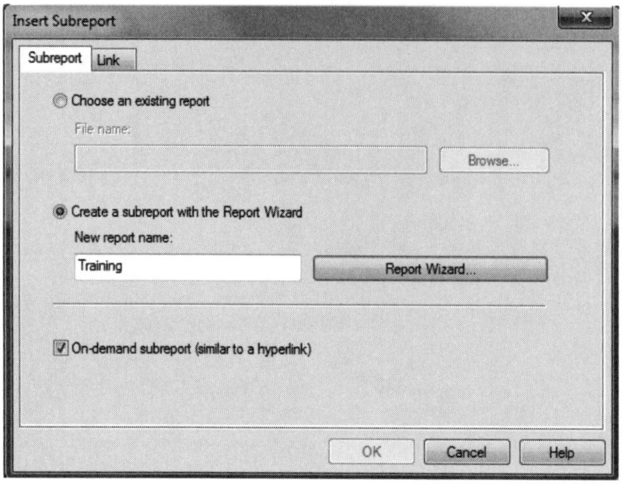

Figure 9.6
The Insert Subreport dialog box.

Select the Choose an Existing Report option. Click Browse, and then locate the Training.rpt in the Chapter 9 sample files. You want the training costs information directly below each Employee's name. In order to do that, you need to link the two reports.

Note

If you do not link the reports, the entire training report will print for every detail record in the Main report.

Click the Link tab in the Insert Subreport dialog box; you'll see the tab shown in Figure 9.7.

To link the two reports, there must be at least one common field between the two reports. You can have multiple links. In the Available Fields list are all of the fields in the report and in the data source attached to the report. The field does not have to be used on the report in order to link the two reports. The field(s) selected here will be passed to the subreport as parameter value(s). The system automatically creates the parameter once the field is selected.

Select {Employee.EmployeeID} and click the > arrow to add the field to the Field to Link to pane, as shown in Figure 9.8.

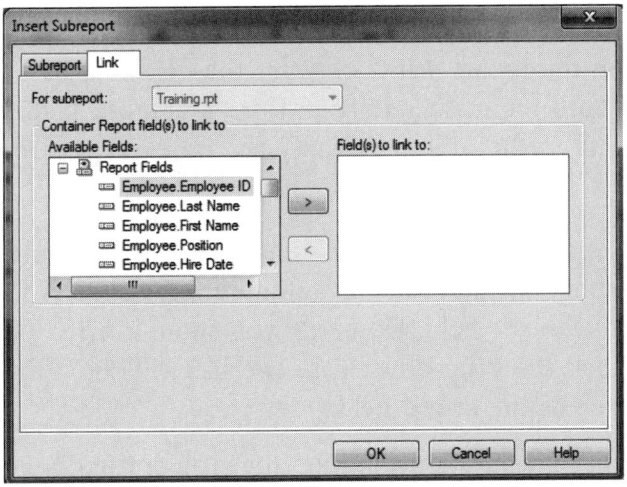

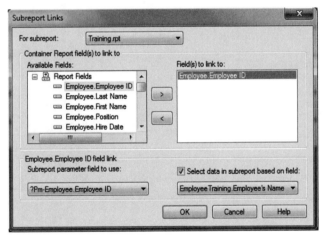

Figure 9.7
The Link Subreport tab.

Figure 9.8
Linking fields together.

With a field to link to selected, notice two new options are available:

- **Subreport parameter to use** — Crystal Reports automatically creates a parameter based on this field and passes the value to the subreport.

■ **Select data in the subreport based on field** — This option determines whether the data printed on the report prints only for the field that has a corresponding record in both the main report and the subreport. If this option is unchecked, the data in the subreport will print for every record in the main report.

The drop-down field below this option designates the subreport field that links with the linked field you chose above. Crystal Reports automatically attempts to locate the field that corresponds with the field. However, you should verify the field. If the field is incorrect, click the drop-down list. The list will show the fields only with the same datatype as the linked field.

Click OK. Insert the subreport into the additional section that you created. Save the report as **Employee Training Costs** and preview the report. It should look something like Figure 9.9.

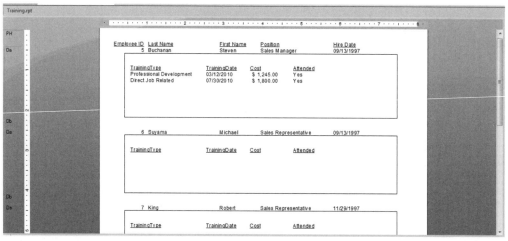

Figure 9.9
The final linked subreport.

Notice the training costs data is associated with the employee's record. If the employee does not have any training costs, the subreport is blank. The report is not formatted in an acceptable format at this point. You will learn about those options as you edit and format the subreport.

Modifying the Links

Subreport links can be changed at any time. From the Design view of the main report, you right-click the subreport and choose Change Subreport Links. Make the desired changes to the subreport links.

Editing a Subreport

There are times when you need to modify the subreport just as you would a main report. To edit a subreport, follow these steps:

1. Open the Design view of the main report, right-click on the subreport, and then choose the Edit Subreport option.

2. The Subreport tab opens. You should now have three tabs in the Design view—the Design view tab, Preview view tab, and the Subreport tab.

3. Edit the report as desired.

4. Suppress all blank sections in the subreport.

5. Return to the Design view of the main report, and then save and preview the report, as shown in Figure 9.10. Notice the effect that suppressing the blank sections has on the report.

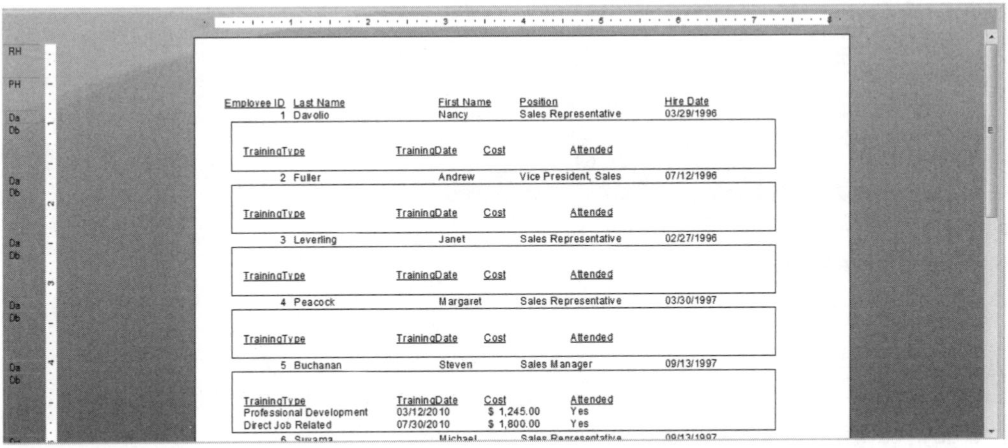

Figure 9.10
Preview of the edited subreport.

Formatting a Subreport

From the design view of the main report, right-click the subreport. Choose Format Subreport. The Format Subreport window will appear, as shown in Figure 9.11. Change the options as desired.

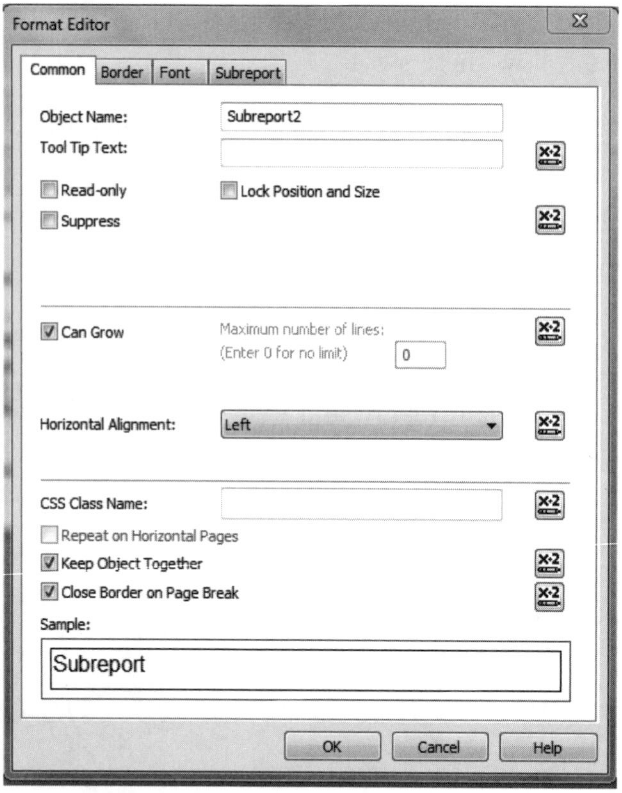

Figure 9.11
The Format Subreport window.

The Format Subreport window has options relating to borders, names, and preview captions as discussed here:

- **Border tab** — When inserting a subreport, a single line border on all four sides is used by default.

Change the borders to None. Having no borders allows the subreport to blend easier with the main report.

■ **Subreport tab** — Shown in Figure 9.12, this tab contains all of the options relating to a subreport.

Figure 9.12
The Subreport tab.

- *Subreport Name* — Allows you to rename the subreport title that appears on the main report in Design view.

- *On-Demand Subreport* — Allows the subreport to be displayed as a hyperlink and not display the entire report when printing.

Tip

Creating on-demand subreports will enhance the performance of the main report. The subreport is not processed unless a user clicks on the hyperlink.

- *On-Demand Subreport Caption* — By default, the filename of the report will appear as a hyperlink if you make the report an on-demand subreport. Most of the time, the filename is not the text the user wants to display. Use this option to enter appropriate text for the hyperlink, such as "Click Here for 2010 Sales Data".

- *Subreport Preview Tab Caption* — Use this option to change the title of the Design and Preview tab from the default filename.

- *Reimport when Opening* — This option should be carefully considered. When a subreport is embedded in a main report, it loses its link to the original report. Therefore, any changes made to the original report will not be reflected in the report you inserted into the subreport. This option will allow you to update the subreport each time the report is open with any changes that have been made to the original report.

Caution

Any sizing and positioning changes you make to the report when the subreport is inserted will be overwritten each time the report is opened.

- *Suppress Blank Report* — If no data is printed on the subreport, this option allows you to suppress the report.

CREATING CROSSTAB CHARTS

Crosstab charts display data in rows and columns with a summarized field. If you are familiar with a crosstab chart in Excel, the crosstab in Crystal Reports functions the same way except only the summarized field is required to create a crosstab in Crystal Reports. Crosstab charts allow you to easily compare data in a side-by-side view. For example, crosstabs are good when you want to analyze sales by product or product line month by month or year by year.

In the crosstab chart shown in Figure 9.13, the chart displays sales data for each product type by month giving the users a full view of what trends have occurred month by month.

	Total	1/2004	2/2004	3/2004	4/2004	5/2004	6/2004
Total	$ 2,867,085.18	$ 211,265.10	$ 240,366.85	$ 180,967.89	$ 202,186.19	$ 217,648.93	$ 446,198.19
Competition	$ 1,976,005.07	$ 150,183.92	$ 199,405.43	$ 94,572.06	$ 139,192.77	$ 152,594.03	$ 333,990.80
Gloves	$ 12,165.95	$ 1,003.93	$ 590.50	$ 442.21	$ 1,184.00	$ 909.00	$ 1,694.76
Helmets	$ 49,985.03	$ 4,462.82	$ 1,733.77	$ 1,634.82	$ 5,680.12	$ 4,292.24	$ 6,057.11
Hybrid	$ 265,532.90	$ 20,895.34	$ 18,304.47	$ 15,799.35	$ 5,778.96	$ 23,961.08	$ 24,119.29
Kids	$ 51,696.12	$ 1,661.10	$ 5,008.53	$ 5,020.80	$ 2,716.06	$ 2,491.65	$ 8,049.99
Locks	$ 5,953.97	$ 697.71	$ 155.99	$ 366.83	$ 228.66	$ 824.60	$ 1,197.46
Mountain	$ 495,540.07	$ 31,461.14	$ 14,223.81	$ 62,599.69	$ 46,936.99	$ 32,201.83	$ 69,568.87
Saddles	$ 10,206.07	$ 899.14	$ 944.35	$ 532.13	$ 468.63	$ 374.50	$ 1,519.91

Figure 9.13
A sample crosstab chart.

Crosstab charts can be placed in the Report header/footer or the Group header/ footer. You can have as many crosstab charts in the report as you need. If you insert the chart in the Report header or footer, the crosstab will depict data for the entire report. If it is inserted in the Group header or footer, there will be a crosstab chart for every group, which could be very useful in many scenarios such as charting data by geographic region. For example, you need to chart data for an international company that has multiple sales people per region by region and salesperson. You can have multiple dimensions in a crosstab—rows, columns, and multiple summarized fields.

Tip

If you need to chart multiple dimensions, creating a manual crosstab chart may be more user-friendly for the end user. The presentation using the Cross-Tab Expert can be somewhat confusing to users with too many dimensions.

Give careful attention to the business needs for the crosstab chart; determine the fields that are going to be included in the chart prior to starting the Cross-Tab Expert. You can include summary fields, running totals, print time formulas, and group sorts (Top N or Bottom N) in the crosstab.

Inserting a Crosstab Chart

Select the Insert Crosstab icon, shown in Figure 9.14, or choose Insert > Cross-Tab from the drop-down menu.

Figure 9.14
The Insert Crosstab icon.

Insert the crosstab in the Report header or footer or the Group header or footer, as shown in Figure 9.15.

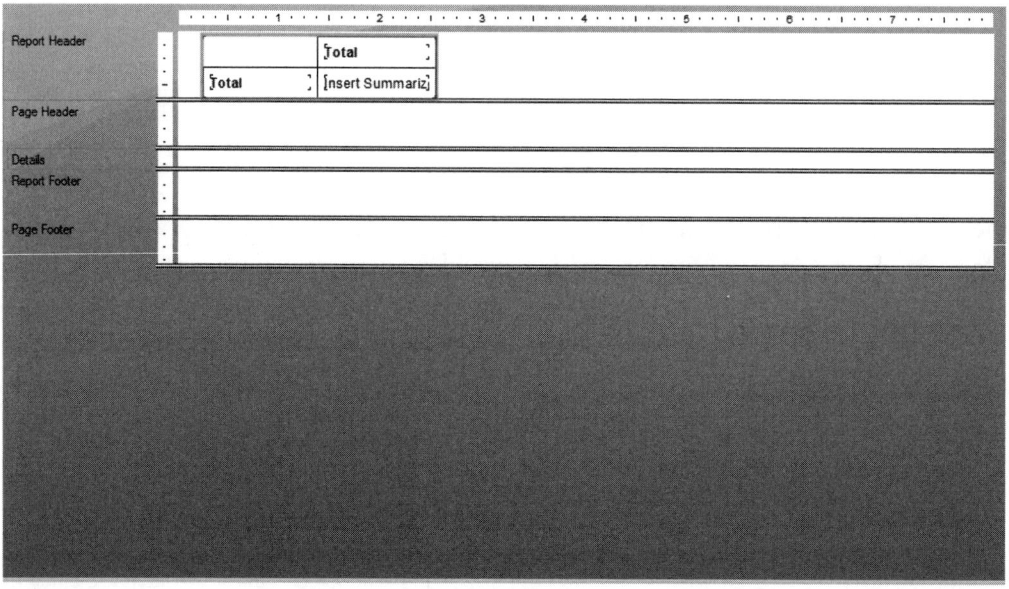

Figure 9.15
Inserting a crosstab.

To specify data for the chart, right-click the blank cell in the upper-left corner of the crosstab and choose Cross-Tab Expert. Once you've chosen your data, which is covered next, click OK. Then you can save the report and preview the crosstab.

The Cross-Tab Expert is comprised of three tabs: the Cross-Tab tab, the Style tab, and the Customize Style tab. Each one allows you to control the data and customize the appearance of the crosstab chart, as shown in Figure 9.16.

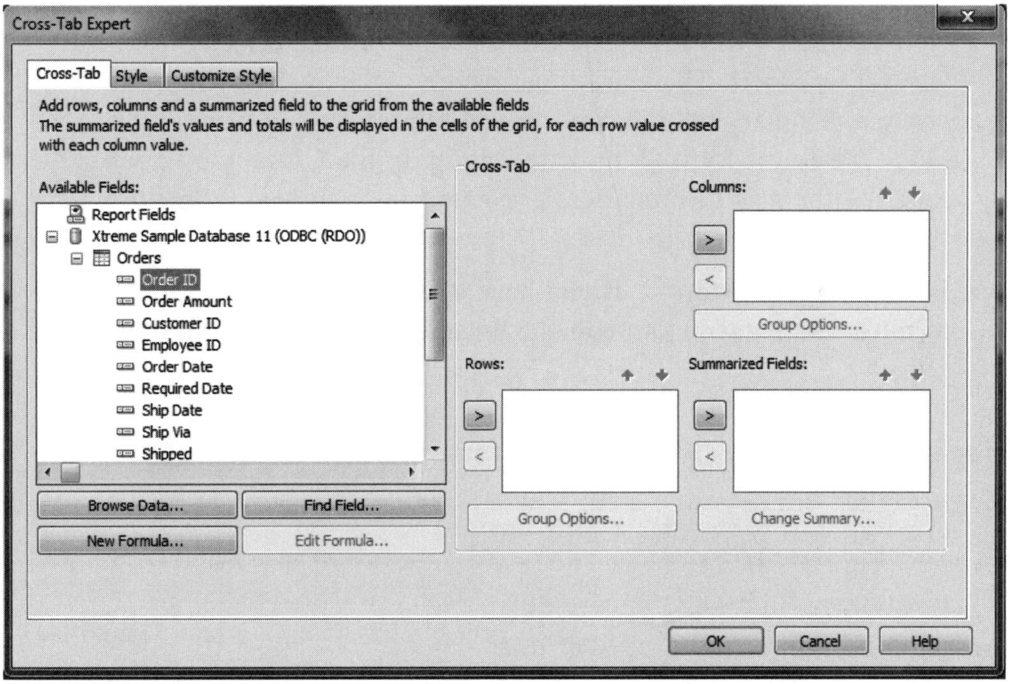

Figure 9.16
The Cross-Tab Expert window.

The Cross-Tab Tab

You can use the Cross-Tab tab in the Cross-Tab Expert to choose the fields that are to be displayed as rows, columns, and the summarized field(s). The tab is comprised of multiple sections to help you build a crosstab chart with ease. The sections are as follows:

- **Available Fields** — The Available Fields pane displays the fields that are on the report in the Report Fields node and all fields that are in the data source attached to the report. You do not have to have fields on the report to insert a crosstab. The report can be a crosstab chart only. With a field selected, you can browse data using the button located below the Available Fields list.

- **Find Field button** — If you have a large list of fields, you can use the Find Field button to quickly locate the field if you know its name.

- **New Formula button** — You can create a formula directly from the Cross-Tab Expert. There are times where you may find you need to create a summary field in order to get the results you need and you didn't create the formula prior to setting up the Cross-Tab Expert. Entering the new formula here prevents you from having to close out the Expert.

- **Edit Formula button** — If you have a formula in the report, with the formula selected, you can edit the formula directly from the Cross-Tab Expert.

Tip

You can edit formulas using the Edit Formula button regardless of when they were created, whether outside of the Cross-Tab Expert or within.

Cross-Tab Section of the Cross-Tab Tab

This section is the crux of the crosstab chart. You will add the dimensions of your crosstab chart in this section using the row, column, and summarized field(s) options.

Based on your charting needs, you should determine whether you need to break the data down by row, by column, or both. You do not have to have a row or a column; you can display a summarized field only if you wanted to, although I have rarely seen a crosstab used in that manner. See Figure 9.17.

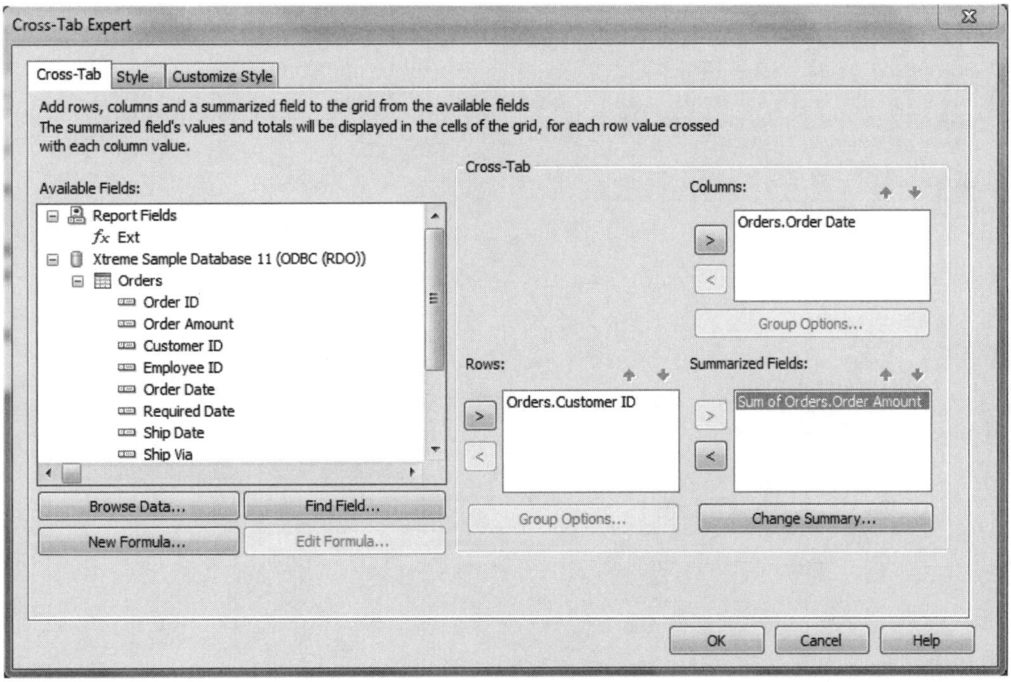

Figure 9.17
Crosstab options.

Note

In Crystal Reports, the only required field in a crosstab is a summarized field.

Modifying a Crosstab Chart

From Design view, right-click in the blank cell in the upper-left corner of the crosstab and choose Cross-Tab Expert.

You can make any necessary changes to your crosstab. Row and Column dimensions automatically create a grouping for the chart. Each Row and Column field has its own Group Options that you can modify.

Select the field you want to change and choose the Group Options button located below the Row pane of the Cross-Tab Expert, as shown in Figure 9.18. The Cross-Tab Group Options dialog box, shown in Figure 9.19, will appear.

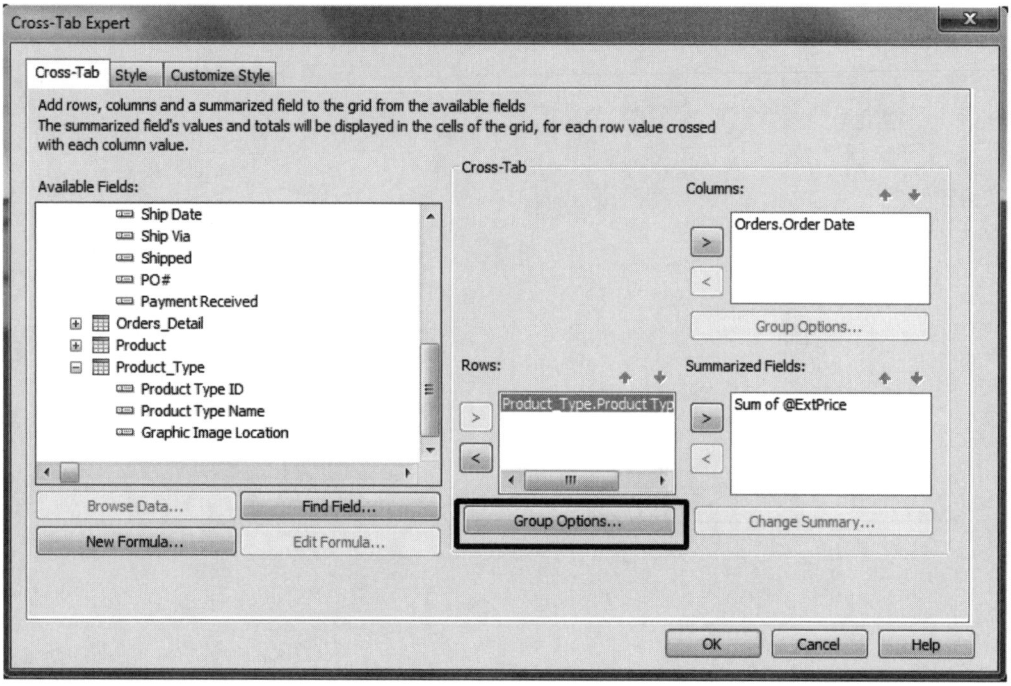

Figure 9.18
The Group Options button.

Figure 9.19
The Cross-Tab Group Options dialog box.

The crosstab group options are the same ones you encountered when creating a group in Chapter 4. You should modify the options to fit your business needs.

Changing Summarized Fields

You might find that you have a need for multiple summarized fields. For example, you want to include a summary amount and a percentage value of the total in a crosstab. By default, all numerical fields' summary type is SUM. Naturally, this does not always fit your needs.

To modify the summarized fields' summary operation, follow these steps:

1. From the Cross-Tab Expert, select the summarized field.

2. Select the Change Summary button, located below the Summary Fields pane in the Cross-Tab Expert. The Edit Summary window, shown in Figure 9.20, will appear.

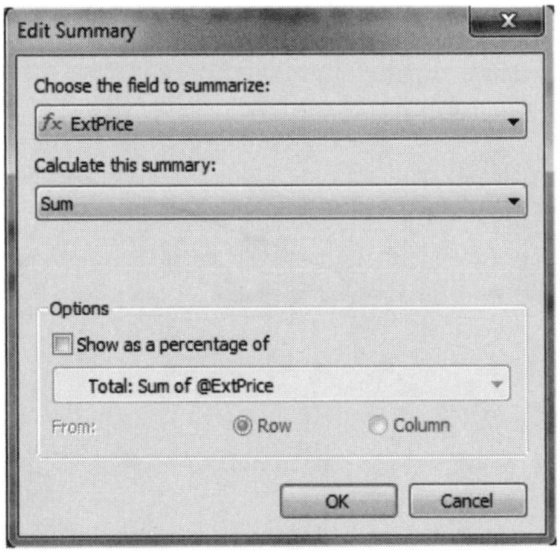

Figure 9.20
The Edit Summary window.

3. Change the summary operation to meet your business requirements and click OK.

The Style Tab of the Cross-Tab Expert

The Style tab, shown in Figure 9.21, enables you to use formatted attributes for the crosstab, such as font size, totals, and grid style options. You simply select any formatted style and the style that's applied to your chart will be displayed.

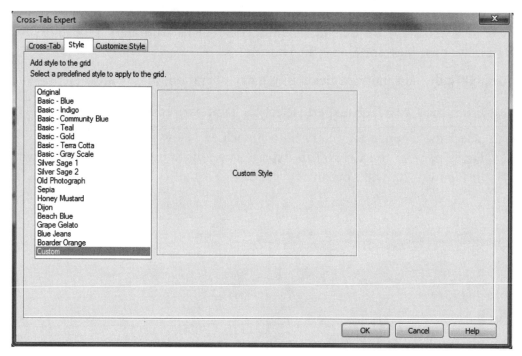

Figure 9.21
The Style tab.

The Customize Style Tab of the Cross-Tab Expert

The Customize Style tab, shown in Figure 9.22, enables you to format the grid's background, cell margins, and gridlines. You can customize the data you want to display in the report such as suppressing grand totals, suppressing empty columns, and removing the Grand Total from the left column.

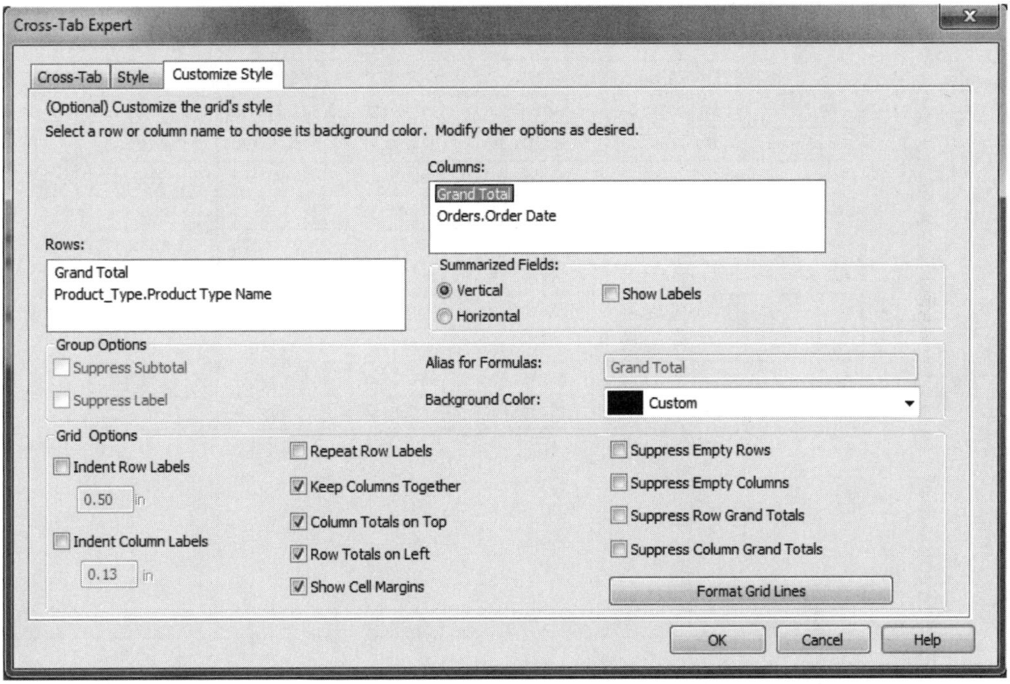

Figure 9.22
The Customize Style tab.

Additional Crosstab Options

Additional options are available for crosstab charts. They can be accessed from the submenu by right-clicking on the crosstab chart. They are as follows:

- **Pivot Cross-Tab** — Right-click on the crosstab and choose Pivot Cross-Tab from the shortcut menu. This option quickly turns the column data to row data and row data to column data, as shown in Figures 9.23 and 9.24. This is a toggle option.

- **Summarize Field Labels** — You can change the orientation of the field labels horizontally or vertically and display the labels of the summarized field. Right-click the crosstab and select Summarize Field Labels, and then choose the option you want. See Figure 9.25.

	Total	2/2003	12/2003	1/2004	2/2004
Total	$4,083,665.34	$92,130.36	$167,260.28	$211,265.10	$240,366.85
Competition	$2,800,861.53	$51,434.16	$95,671.97	$150,183.92	$199,405.43
Gloves	$17,402.71	$363.35	$1,251.39	$1,003.93	$590.50
Difference	$2,783,458.82	$51,070.81	$94,420.58	$149,179.99	$198,814.93
Helmets	$70,251.84	$1,074.89	$5,081.83	$4,462.82	$1,733.77
Hybrid	$385,733.36	$17,006.25	$15,581.25	$20,895.34	$18,304.47
Kids	$76,390.15	$2,226.62	$7,604.97	$1,661.10	$5,008.53
Locks	$8,721.53	$101.40	$476.20	$697.71	$155.99
Mountain	$710,623.36	$19,728.69	$41,036.83	$31,461.14	$14,223.81
Saddles	$13,680.86	$195.00	$555.84	$899.14	$944.35

Figure 9.23
Unpivoted crosstab table.

	Total	Competition	Gloves	Helmets	Hybrid
Total	$4,083,665.34	$2,800,861.53	$17,402.71	$70,251.84	$385,733.36
2/2003	$92,130.36	$51,434.16	$363.35	$1,074.89	$17,006.25
12/2003	$167,260.28	$95,671.97	$1,251.39	$5,081.83	$15,581.25
1/2004	$211,265.10	$150,183.92	$1,003.93	$4,462.82	$20,895.34
2/2004	$240,366.85	$199,405.43	$590.50	$1,733.77	$18,304.47
3/2004	$180,967.89	$94,572.06	$442.21	$1,634.82	$15,799.35
4/2004	$202,186.19	$139,192.77	$1,184.00	$5,680.12	$5,778.96
5/2004	$217,648.93	$152,594.03	$909.00	$4,292.24	$23,961.08
6/2004	$446,198.19	$333,990.80	$1,694.76	$6,057.11	$24,119.29
7/2004	$313,481.73	$219,601.57	$966.47	$3,626.03	$32,658.38
8/2004	$219,437.06	$135,550.04	$1,098.77	$4,885.29	$18,828.00
9/2004	$181,894.82	$123,130.30	$866.05	$4,727.85	$29,007.73
10/2004	$255,488.79	$188,668.64	$978.98	$3,452.16	$30,291.46
11/2004	$241,880.36	$125,365.92	$923.44	$4,099.19	$34,033.74
12/2004	$156,269.27	$113,749.59	$1,507.84	$5,333.63	$11,855.10

Figure 9.24
Pivoted crosstab table.

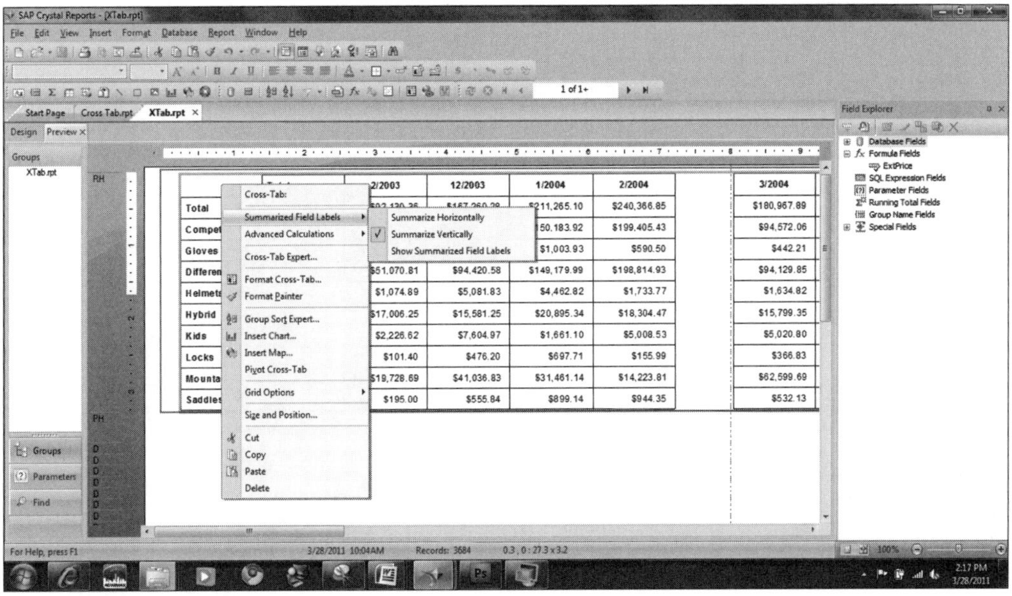

Figure 9.25
Summarized Field Labels options

■ **Advanced Calculations** — This advanced feature allows you to include additional calculations in the crosstab such as the difference between two groups (Helmet sales — Gloves sales), product of two group values, and growth and trend data.

To access this feature, right-click the crosstab and choose Advanced Calculations from the shortcut menu, as shown in Figure 9.26. Then choose the appropriate option.

The Calculated Member window will open, as shown in Figure 9.27. You can use this window to create custom calculations.

INSERTING A CHART

Creating a chart from a crosstab is a quick and easy option. Follow these steps:

1. Select the crosstab.

2. Right-click and choose Insert Chart from the shortcut menu. The chart is automatically created and inserted into a separate section on the report, as shown in Figure 9.28.

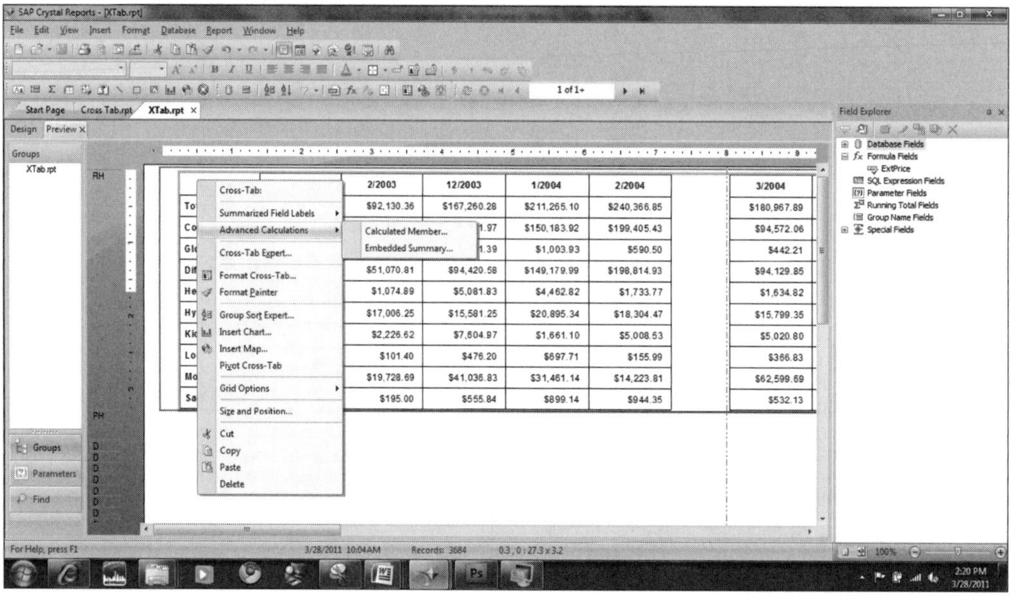

Figure 9.26
Advanced calculations in a crosstab.

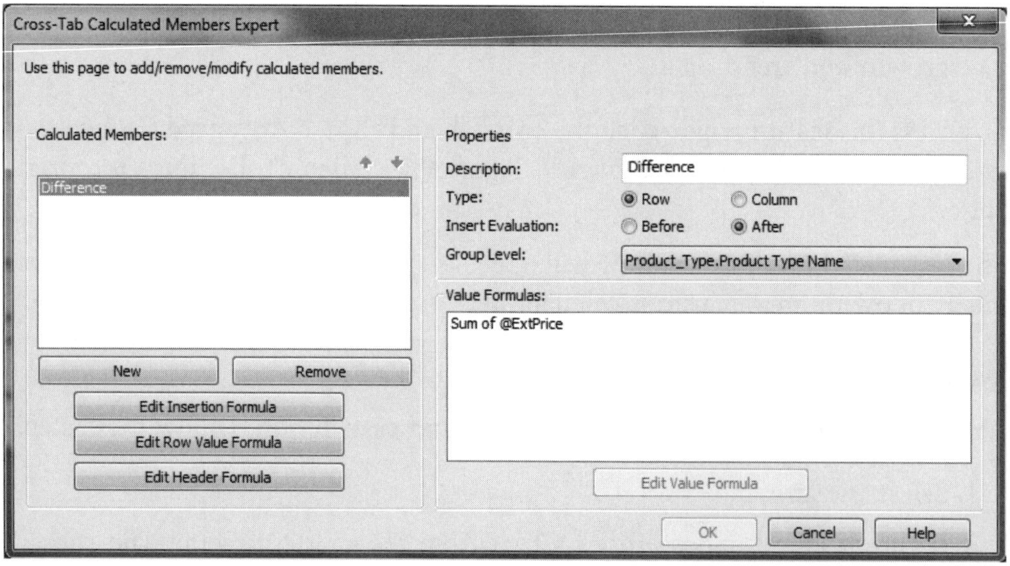

Figure 9.27
Calculated members.

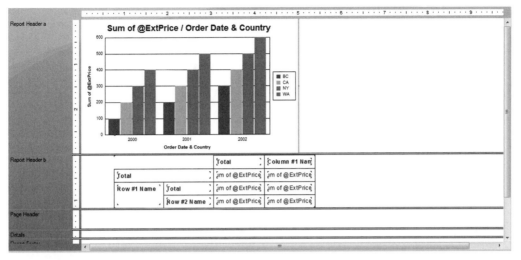

Figure 9.28
Inserting a chart.

The location of the chart will depend on the crosstab's location. If the crosstab is located in the Report Header, the graphical chart will be placed in an additional Report Header.

You can modify the chart options at any time. I will discuss working with charts in the next section.

WORKING WITH CHARTS

Charts present your data visually. A large number of users prefer to see data visually and some prefer to see it in both formats. Crystal Reports allows you to design very sophisticated and meaningful charts. Crystal Reports allows you to create a variety of types of charts such as bar charts, trendlines, pie charts, and many others, as shown in Figure 9.29. During the report requirements-gathering discussion, you should determine whether a chart is needed and if so, what type of chart is appropriate for the type of data presented. Charts are normally based on grouped information but in Crystal Reports you also have the option to chart based on advanced data, OLAP grids, and crosstabs. You learned how to insert a crosstab chart in the previous section.

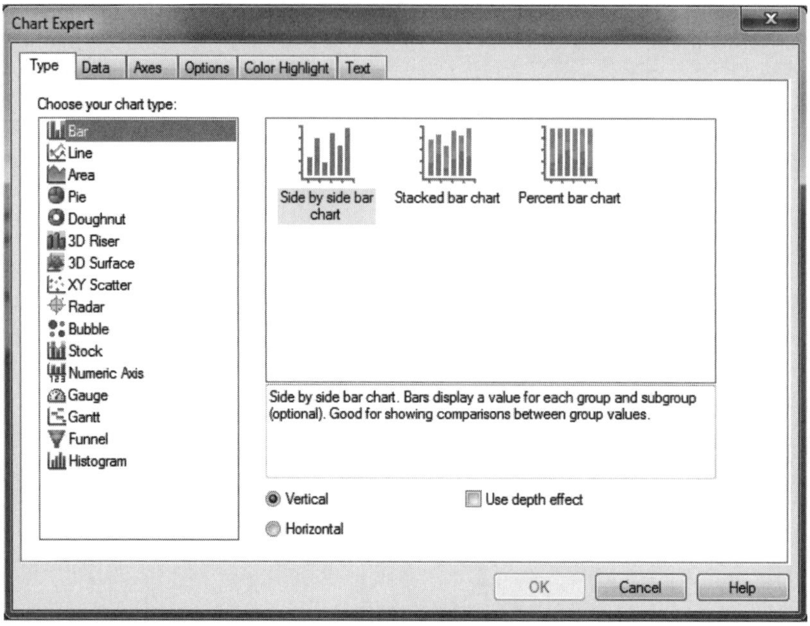

Figure 9.29
Chart types available in Crystal Reports.

Each chart type has subtypes. For example, within the Bar type, there is the side-by-side bar chart, the stacked bar chart, and the percent bar chart. It is important to choose the correct chart that will display your data in a meaningful way.

Tip

See chart types under "Charting Concepts" in the Crystal Reports Help guide for more information on chart uses.

The chart types available in Crystal Reports are:

- **Bar charts** — These are used to compare multiple groups of data. You can choose from the side-by-side bar chart and the stacked bar chart.

- **Line chart** — These are used to show data for numerous groups over a period of time.

- **Area chart** — These are used for a small number of groups to show data mappings. An Area chart displays the group as an area filled with the color or a pattern of your choice.

- **Pie chart** — One of the most commonly used chart types. Displays your data in a pie shape with each group of data represented as a slice of the pie.

  Multiple pie chart — Each pie depicts a group and shows the distribution to the group's totals.

  Proportional multiple pie chart — Same as the Multiple Pie chart but the size of each pie is relative to the overall total.

- **Doughnut chart** — Similar to a pie chart but shows the data as a section of a circle. Displays the grand total in the center of the doughnut.

- **3D riser chart** — Displays series data in a 3D plane. This chart type depicts the extremes in your data.

- **3D surface chart** — Displays data in a 3D plane and should be used when you need to show relation and the extremes of your data.

- **XY scatter chart** — Used to consider large sets of data with multiple considerations to determine trends. For example, to determine why some items sell better than others.

- **Radar chart** — Use to determine how specific group data relates to the overall group of data.

- **Bubble chart** — Displays data as a series of proportional size bubbles based on the amount of data. Useful when displaying quantity numbers.

- **Stock chart** — Used to monitor financial or sales activities. Show high and low data values.

- **Numeric axis chart** — Used to display a true numeric or date-time X axis.

- **Gauge chart** — Used to show one group of data. For example, on-time delivery or returns for a vendor.

- **Gantt chart** — Used to display a graphical view of a schedule in a horizontal bar style view.

- **Funnel chart** — Used to show pipeline data for the sales process.

- **Histogram chart** — Statistical chart used to show how measurements vary from the mean.

Often, you have to change the chart type to determine which type best depicts the data. Crystal Reports allows you to change the chart type quickly and seamlessly with the click of another selection.

Determining Chart Layout on the Data Tab

It's important to understand the chart layout because this is the critical point where you determine what data is going to be included in the chart. The section where the chart is going to be placed also determines what data is going to be charted. Charts can be placed in the Report Header or Footer or the Group Header or Footer. You cannot place a chart in a Detail section nor would you want to. Charts are memory intensive. Therefore, the more charts you have in a report the more processing power it needs. A chart in a Detail section could bring the server down to its knees. A chart placed in the Report Header or Footer will depict data for the overall report whereas a chart in the Group Header or Footer will depict data for each group. Therefore, you will have multiple charts in a report.

Figure 9.30 shows the Data tab of the Chart Expert, where you determine the kind of layout you want for your charts.

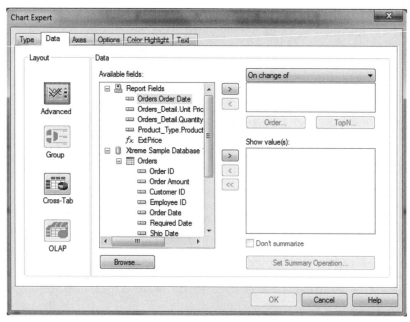

Figure 9.30
Data tab of the Chart Expert.

The following sections cover the Layout types available from the Data tab of the Chart Expert.

Advanced Layout

The Advanced layout is always available and should be used when you want complete control over what is charted and when it is displayed. If you do not have any grouping in your report, you must use the Advanced option to create any type of chart other than a crosstab chart. To build the chart using the Advanced options, you must populate the following options:

■ **Available fields** — From the Available Field list, you should select the fields to be included on the x and y axes. All of the fields that are available in the data source can be used in the chart. The field does not have to be on the report in order to be charted.

■ **The x-axis** — You can control the data on the x axis. The options are:

● *On Change of* — When the value of the field changes, a new bar or entity type based on the chart type will be generated. This option allows a maximum of two levels. With one of the fields selected, you can change the sort order for the field. If the field is a date field, you should specify the sort order and the interval type (by month, quarter, year, and so on) by selecting the field and then selecting the Order button below the section. See Figure 9.31.

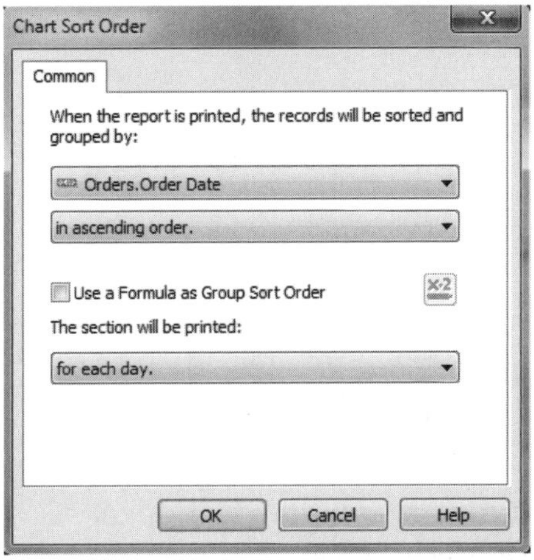

Figure 9.31
Sort Order and Interval Type of Date fields.

- *For each record* — A new entity type will be generated for every record in the database. Don't use this option unless you have a very small table or are using a very small subset of data in the report.

- *For all records* — This option generates a grand total type situation and you will have only one entity for the chart.

- With a field selected in the On Change of option, you can create a Top N chart as well, by selecting the Top N button. This option is available in the Advanced layout even without a group. Crystal Reports creates a group in the background. The Group Sort Expert dialog box opens, as shown in Figure 9.32.

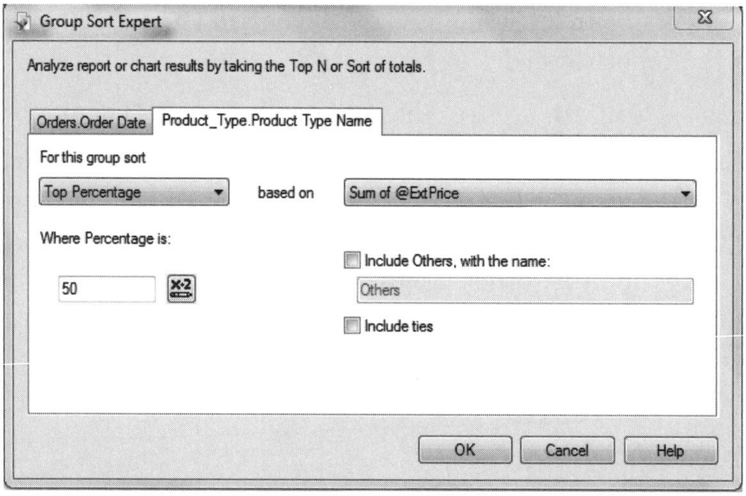

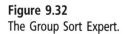

Figure 9.32
The Group Sort Expert.

- **Show Value of** — This option allows you to control the summary values to be displayed in the chart. By default, all numerical values default to the SUM operation. You can change the option at any time by selecting the field and clicking the Set Summary Operation button at the bottom of the Show Value(s) section. The Edit Summary window will open, as shown in Figure 9.33, where you can set the options.

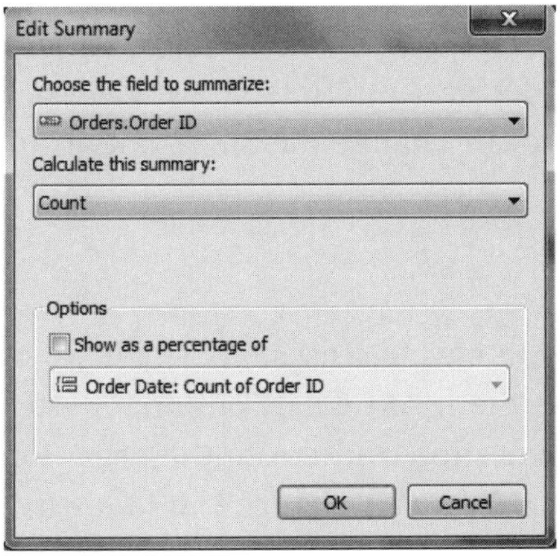

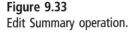

Figure 9.33
Edit Summary operation.

- **Don't Summarize** — You can include formulas and running totals in the Show Value(s) section. Often the formulas have generated the values you are expecting; therefore, you do not require Crystal Reports to treat it as a standard number and perform an additional SUM function on the formula. You can control that additional summation by checking the Don't Summarize option. This option is available only if a formula is in the Show Value(s) box.

Tip

If you have two On Change of fields, you can only have one Show Value field.

Group Layout

To enable the Group layout option, you must have at least one group and one summary field in the report.

Tip

If you have more than one group and you want to chart by group, the chart must be placed in Group 1. If you insert the chart into group 2, the Group option will be disabled.

Crystal Reports populates the On Change of and Show values automatically based on the organization of your report. If you have multiple Show Value(s), such as a SUM amount and a percentage, you can change the Show option to your desired result.

Cross-Tab Layout

The Cross-Tab Layout is available only when you have a crosstab object in your report. With the crosstab selected, you can use the Insert Chart option. Crystal Reports will automatically insert an additional section and create the chart for you based on the dimensions in your crosstab. You can change the following options, as shown in Figure 9.34:

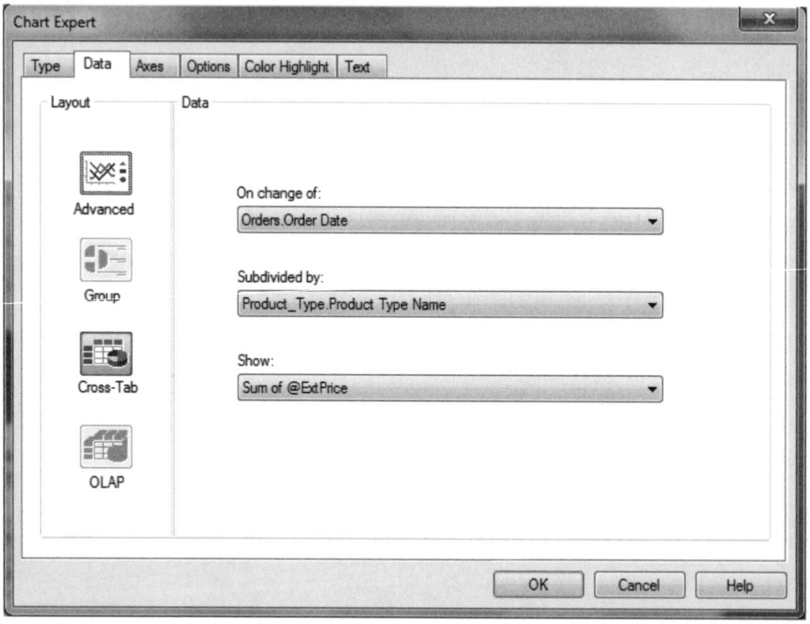

Figure 9.34
The Cross-Tab Layout option.

- **On Change of** — Allows you to choose the On Change of field. If you have multiple groups, you can change this option.

- **Subdivided by** — If you have multiple level grouping, you can choose the second group level.

- **Show** — Displays the summary values. If you have multiple summary fields, you can change the option to reflect the desired values.

Tip

If you have multiple crosstabs in your report, be sure to select the one you want to chart before selecting the Insert Chart option.

OLAP Layout

The OLAP option is available only when you have an OLAP grid in the report. You can change the following options:

- **Chart off entire grid** — Enables you to create the chart based on the overall grid.

- **On Change of** — You can choose the field or dimension to chart from.

- **Subdivided by** — If your grid allows secondary grouping, this option can be used.

The Axes Tab of the Chart Expert

The Axes tab, shown in Figure 9.35, is available on charts that have an X and Y axis. The pie, doughnut, Gantt, and funnel charts do not display data in an X, Y axis format, therefore the Axes tab is not available with these charts. This tab allows you to control the formatting of the axes in the chart.

You can modify the following settings from the Axes tab:

- **Show gridlines** — Allows you to specify where the gridlines will fall on the chart.

- **Data values** — Gives you control of the number ranges that are displayed on the chart.

- **Auto scale** — Adjusts the labels along the data axis so it is a clear presentation.

- **Auto range** — Uses a default range of numbers on the Y axis.

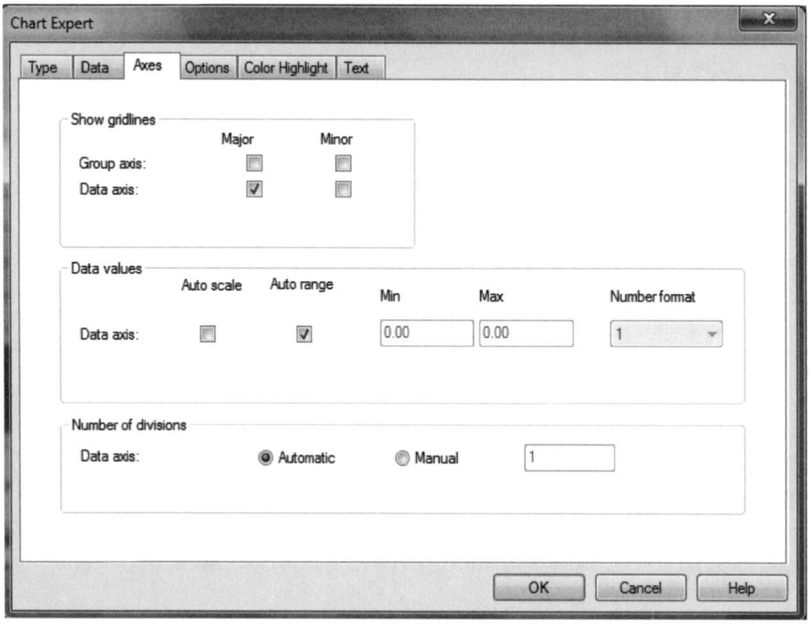

Figure 9.35
The Axes tab.

- **Minimum** — Allows you to specify the minimum number to display on the Y axis. The Auto-Range option must be unchecked to use this option.

- **Max** — Allows you to specify the maximum number to display on the Y axis. The Auto-Range option must be unchecked to use this option.

- **Number format** — Allows you to specify the number format, for example $1K. It is used in conjunction with the Min and Max options.

- **Number of divisions** — Allows you to determine the specific number of divisions to have on the X axis.

- **Automatic** — Makes the system determine the appropriate number of divisions.

- **Manual** — Allows you to enter the number of divisions to display on the chart.

The Options Tab of the Chart Expert

The Options tab, shown in Figure 9.36, allows you to specify attributes of the chart such as color, labels, and values and even the size of the markers. The options here will change based on the type of chart that you have selected.

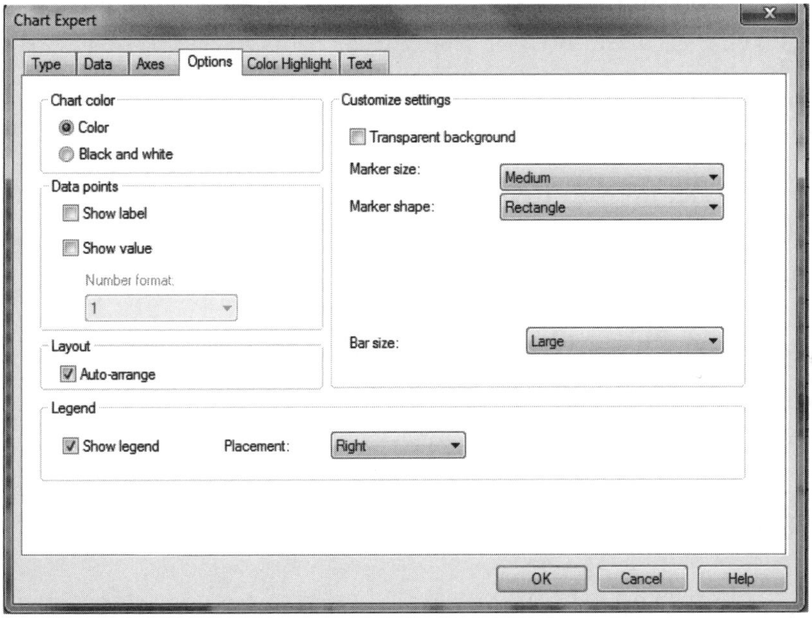

Figure 9.36
The Options tab.

You can modify the following settings from the Options tab:

- **Chart color** — Choose to display the chart in color or black and white.

- **Data points** — Choose to display the labels and or values on the chart. If you show values, you can choose the number format such as $1K. The Labels and Values are turned off by default.

- **Layout** — Auto-arrange (turned on by default).

- **Legend** — Choose to display the legend or not and the location of the legend on the report in relation to the chart.

- **Customize settings** — Customize specific attributes of the chart:

  Transparent background — Makes the background of the chart transparent. Any objects behind the chart will be visible.

  Marker size — Determines the size of the markers. Medium is the default.

  Marker shape — Determines the shape of the marker; you can choose from rectangle, circles, diamonds, or triangles.

  Bar size — Determines the size of the bar. This option name changes based on the chart type. For example in a pie chart, it will be Pie Size.

  Detach pie slice — Allows you to detach the smallest or largest piece of a pie chart from the whole pie. (Available only if you're using a pie or doughnut chart.)

The Color Highlight Tab of the Chart Expert

This tab, shown in Figure 9.37, allows you to color-code your chart. You are conditionally setting the colors.

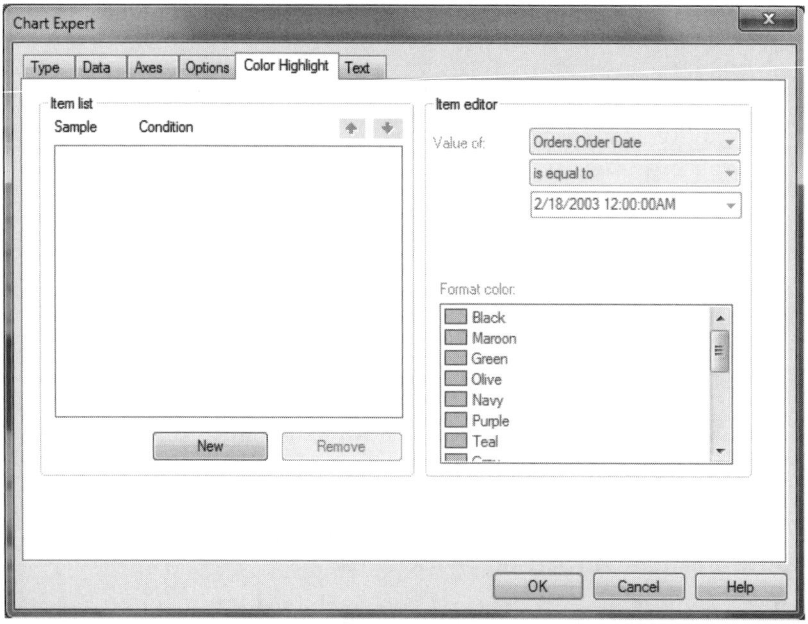

Figure 9.37
Color highlighting.

This color-highlighting tab is the same as the Highlighting Expert option. There are only two exceptions that you must take into consideration when you need to color-code your chart:

- With a line chart, the chart must have data markers.

- An area chart must have two On Change of values.

The Text Tab of the Chart Expert

The Text tab allows you to specify the title, subtitles, footnotes, group title, and data title for your chart. It has the following options:

- **Titles** — The system automatically creates the title, group title, and data title based on the data in the chart. To manually define these titles, uncheck the Auto-Text option and type the desired titles.

- **Format** — You can set the font face, size, and style for all of the titles mentioned here.

Creating a Chart

The objective of this section is to practice creating a chart. You'll create a chart displaying the total sales by month. Follow these steps to do so:

1. Open the Chart.rpt report located in the Chapter 9 sample files.

2. From Design view, select the Insert Chart icon on the Insert toolbar or choose Insert > Chart from the drop-down menu.

3. Insert the chart in the report header section.

4. Notice the chart template in the Design view. This is only the template. Your data will not be displayed in Design view. You must preview your report to view the actual data.

5. Right-click the chart and select Chart Expert.

6. Choose the Bar (side by side) chart type.

7. Turn on the Use Depth Effect option for a 3D view.

8. Select the Data tab and verify that On Change of is set to Order Date. Also make sure that the Show option reflects the Sum of Order Amount.

9. Select the Text tab. Uncheck Auto-Text for Title and change the title to **Quarterly Sales.**

10. Delete the group and the data titles.

11. Click OK.

12. Save the report and preview it. It should look similar to the chart shown in Figure 9.38.

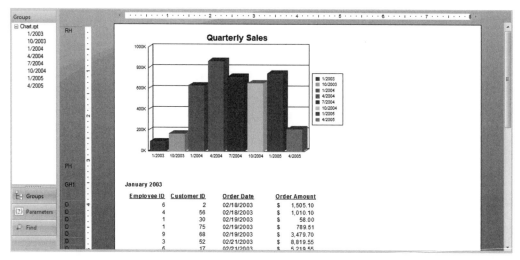

Figure 9.38
The Preview Chart report.

Formatting a Chart

The appearance of the chart can be modified outside of the Chart Expert using the Chart Options and Format Background options. From Design view, right-click on the chart and select Chart Options in order to access the Chart Options window, as shown in Figure 9.39.

The Appearance tab of the Chart Options window has the following options:

- **Overlap** — Use this option to choose the overlap space between the risers.

- **Gap Width** — Use this option to choose the distance between each riser.

- **Use Depth** — Use this option to increase or decrease the depth of each riser.

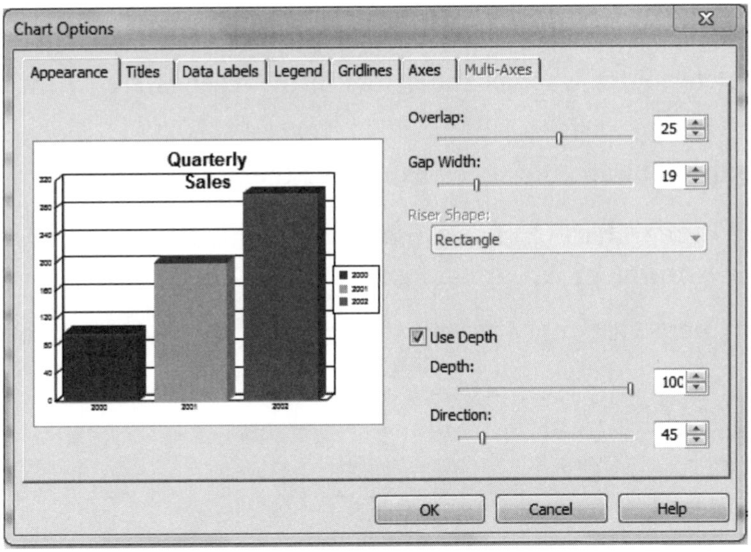

Figure 9.39
The Chart Options window.

- **Use Direction** — Use this option to change the direction of the bars.

The Titles tab of the Chart Options window allows you to change the titles for the chart. This option is also available from the Chart Expert.

The Data tab of the Chart Options window has the following options:

- **Show Data Labels** — Select this box to show or hide data labels.
- **Label Location** — Specify where the labels will be displayed in relation to its riser.
- **Label Format** — Specify whether the value, the series label, or both the series label and value are displayed on the riser.

The Legends tab of the Chart Options window formats the legend box and has the following options:

- **Show Legend** — Turns the legend on or off.
- **Layout** — Determines the location of the legend.
- **Markers and Text** — Determines the location of the markers.

- **Box Style** — Determines the style of the box around the legend.

- **Color Mode** — Determines whether the colors in the legends are by the group or series.

- **Swap Series/Group** — Swaps the series names for the group names.

From the Gridlines tab of the Chart Options window, you can choose to display major or minor gridlines in the group or data axis.

The Axes tab of the Chart Options window, shown in Figure 9.40, has the following options:

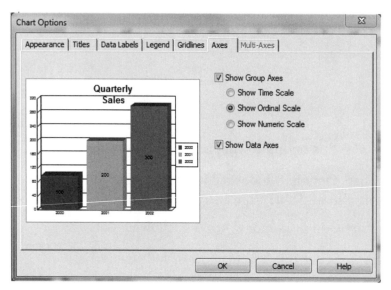

Figure 9.40
The Axes tab.

- **Show Group Axes** — Turns on or off the group axes on the X axis.

- **Show Data Axes** — Turns on or off the data axes on the Y axis.

- **Show Dual Axes** — Used to display two numeric axes in a chart. If the Show Dual Axes option is selected, the Multi-Axes tab will be enabled. The Multi-Axes tab allows you to specify which entities will be displayed on which axes, as shown in Figure 9.41.

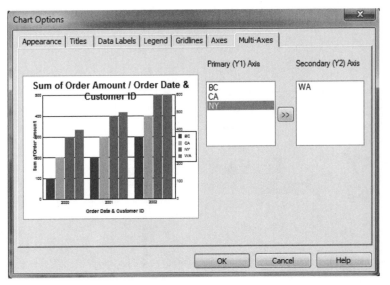

Figure 9.41
The Multi-Axes tab.

Formatting Your Chart's Background

Formatting a chart with background, patterns, and textures can present a sophisticated and graphically appealing chart, particularly with reports that have multiple charts. The ability to present each chart in a different format is very appealing. From Design view, you right-click the chart and select Format Background to access the Format background window shown in Figure 9.42.

You'll find the following options in the Format Background window:

- **Foreground Color** — Select any color for the foreground. When you choose Transparent, Crystal Reports makes the background transparent so that objects behind the chart are visible.

- **Pattern** — Select this button to choose a pattern.

- **Texture** — Select this button to choose textures such as granite, gray, marble, mixed dark, mixed light, and so on.

- **Picture** — Select any clipart from the Microsoft Office library.

- **Gradient** — Select this button to apply a gradient to the chart.

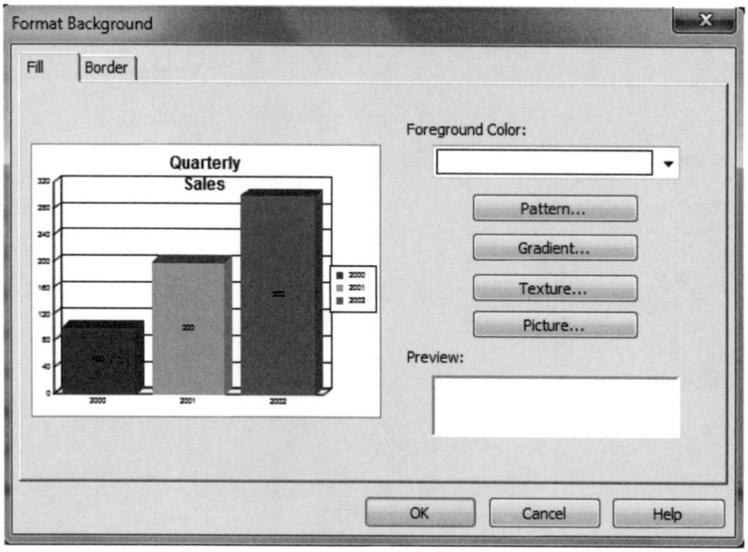

Figure 9.42
The Format Background window.

LOADING A TEMPLATE

Formatting a chart can be time consuming; therefore, if you have a standard format for charts in your organization, it is beneficial to save your chart as a template and apply that template to each of your charts. Crystal Reports has pre-defined chart templates that can be applied to your charts and modified as well.

To load a template, you right-click the chart and select Load Template from the menu. The window shown in Figure 9.43 will appear.

There are multiple templates within each category; choose a template that fits your needs. Click OK when you find the template you want.

Saving Your Chart as a Template

Saving your chart as a template is quick and easy. Just follow these steps to do so:

1. Format your chart as desired.

2. Right-click the chart and select Save as Template.

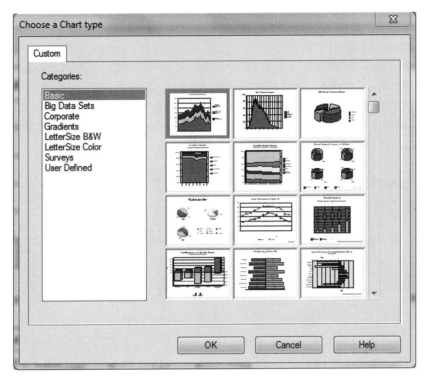

Figure 9.43
Choose a Chart Type template.

3. Save the chart in the Templates/User Defined directory for the Crystal Reports 2011 program.

   Note that the template of the chart must be saved in the User Defined directory of the Templates directory in order for it to show in the Templates directory of the chart.

4. Right-click the chart and choose Load Template.

5. Select the User Defined category and locate your saved template.

USING REPORT ALERTS

Report Alerts are custom messages used to alert the users that a certain condition has occurred in the report data. Financial users find great use of this feature when monitoring budgets versus actual numbers. In this economic time, when managers are monitoring overtime hours closely, imagine a company that sets up an alert to notify managers when employees are nearing the maximum 40 hours before the end of the work week. Report Alerts can eliminate the need for multiple reports pulling from the same tables. When you have multiple reports pulling from the same tables, it is helpful to be able to create one report and add alerts to query the desired dataset in the same report instead of creating separate reports.

Creating a Report Alert

To create an alert, follow these steps:

1. Identify the condition that needs to be monitored and the message that you want to be notified with.

2. Choose Reports > Alerts > Create or Modify Alerts. Figure 9.44 appears.

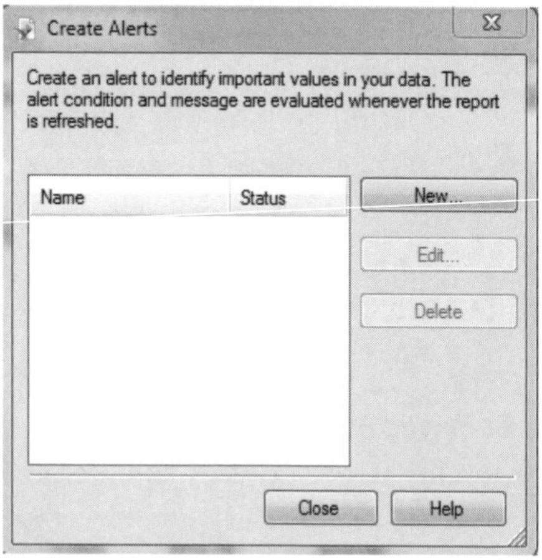

Figure 9.44
Create or modify an alert.

3. Click the New button to create an alert. The Create Alert window, shown in Figure 9.45, appears.

4. Give the alert a name.

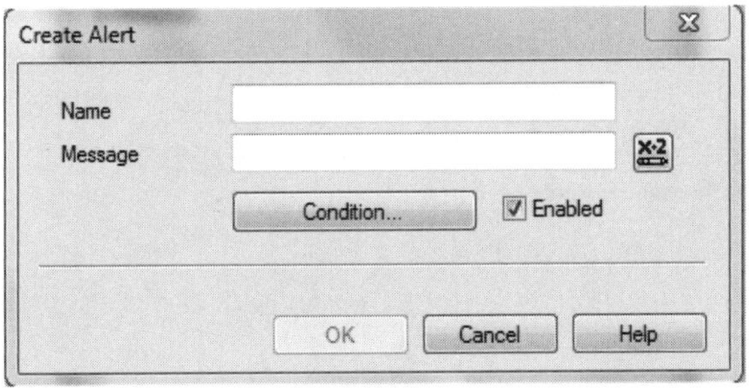

Figure 9.45
The Create Alert window.

5. Designate the message that is to appear when the alert is triggered. For example, "Employees are nearing overtime hours. You must send them home." Use the Condition button to create the formula that defines the condition that you are monitoring:

```
Sum ({Payroll.HoursWorked},{Employee.EmployeeID}) > 32
```

6. Save and close the formula when you've added all the data.

7. Click OK.

8. Click Close to close the Create Alerts dialog box.

9. Save the report.

10. Preview or refresh the report.

Figure 9.46 shows what you'll see when a Report Alert has been triggered. This Alert box will pop up when the report is run or refreshed. When an alert is triggered, it creates its own report that displays just the records that have met the criteria that was set in the alert.

To view the records, click the View Records button on the Report Alerts dialog box. An additional tab will open with the triggered records. Click Close to close the Report Alerts dialog box.

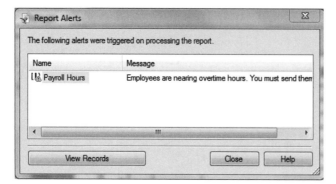

Figure 9.46
The Report Alerts message.

Tip

If you close the Report Alerts dialog box, you can reopen the window to view the triggered records again by choosing Reports > Alerts > Triggered Alerts.

SUMMARY

The use of subreports can give you the functionality needed to create complex reports and share values between reports. You should attempt to link tables to gather the data needed before choosing to use subreports. The presentation of data in crosstab charts gives the users an easier view of data because it's shown in a familiar row and columnar format. The use of Report Alerts will eliminate the need to manually review your data.

CHAPTER 10

SETTING REPORT OPTIONS AND EXPORTING REPORTS

The objectives of this chapter are to learn the following tasks:

- Setting reporting options
- Evaluating performance information
- Setting the print date and time
- Exporting options and settings

Delivering an effective and efficient report is a key factor of report development. Understanding the options and performance consideration statistics will assist you in designing an effective report. It's important to develop a report, but it's useless if you can't get the report to other users without a lot of manual manipulation. It's important that you understand the report distribution options before you start to design your report.

SETTING REPORTING OPTIONS

Report options are specific to the report that you are currently developing. You should use Global options to set the default options for all reports and the Report options to establish exceptions. For example, your relational database is case-insensitive; therefore, customer ABC is the same as customer abc. However, for the report that you are developing, you want to see the differences in character case so you want to make the report case-sensitive. You can change the report to be case-sensitive using the Report options. To access the Report options, select

File > Report Options from the drop-down menu. You'll access the Report Options dialog box, as shown in Figure 10.1. Most of the report options are also available on the Database and Reporting tabs of the Global Options window. However, there are a few options that are accessible only through Report Options. You will learn more about them in the following section.

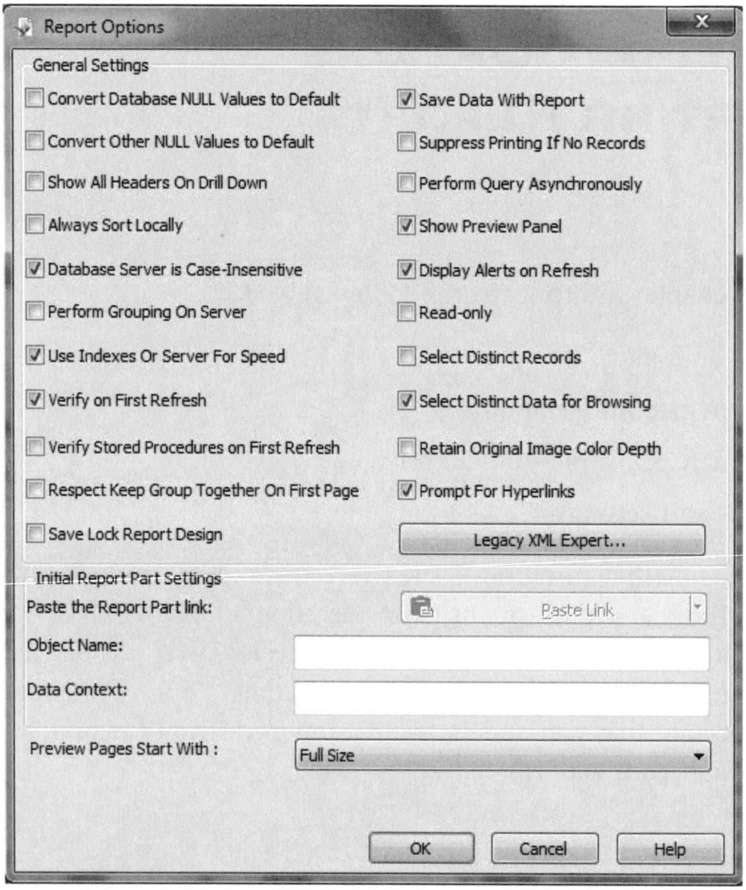

Figure 10.1
The Report Options dialog box.

Options may be different based on the database driver being used.

The Save Lock Report Design check box gives you the ability to set up a username and password required to make changes, as shown in Figure 10.2. Use this option when you don't want the user to make any changes to the report. This option requires the user to perform a "save as" and save the report as another filename in order to make any changes. This feature protects you from having to troubleshoot any unauthorized changes in the event the report crashes or there are issues with the dataset.

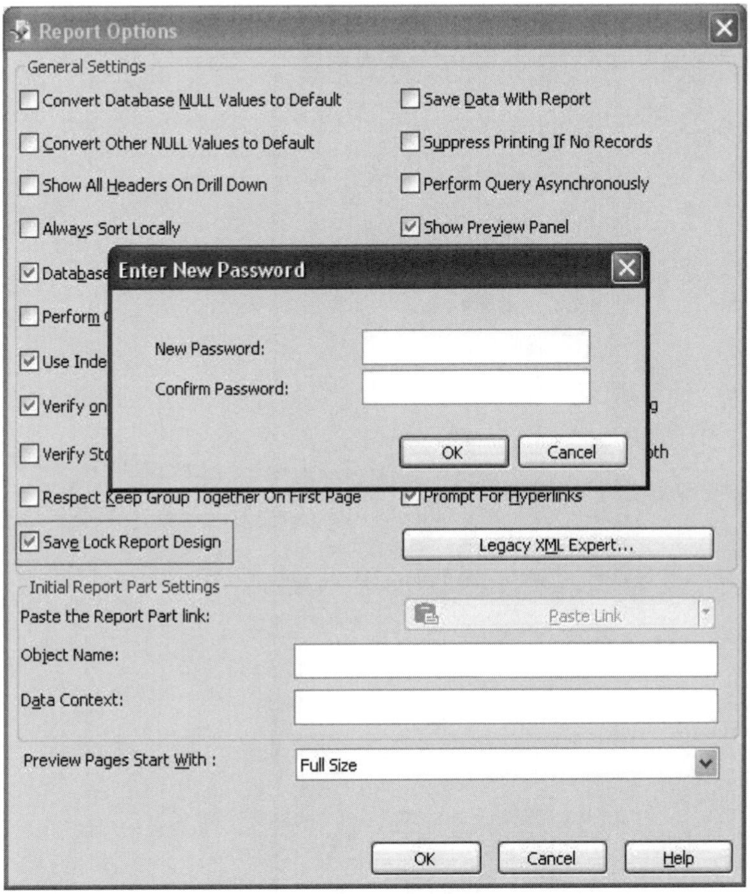

Figure 10.2
Locking the report design.

The Limit Size of Result Set To feature allows you to set the maximum number of records Crystal Reports can display on the report. This option allows you to predict the speed and performance of the report.

Tip

Depending on the database driver you have selected for the report, this option may not be available.

The Show Preview Panel check box, highlighted in Figure 10.3, was first introduced in Crystal Reports 2008.

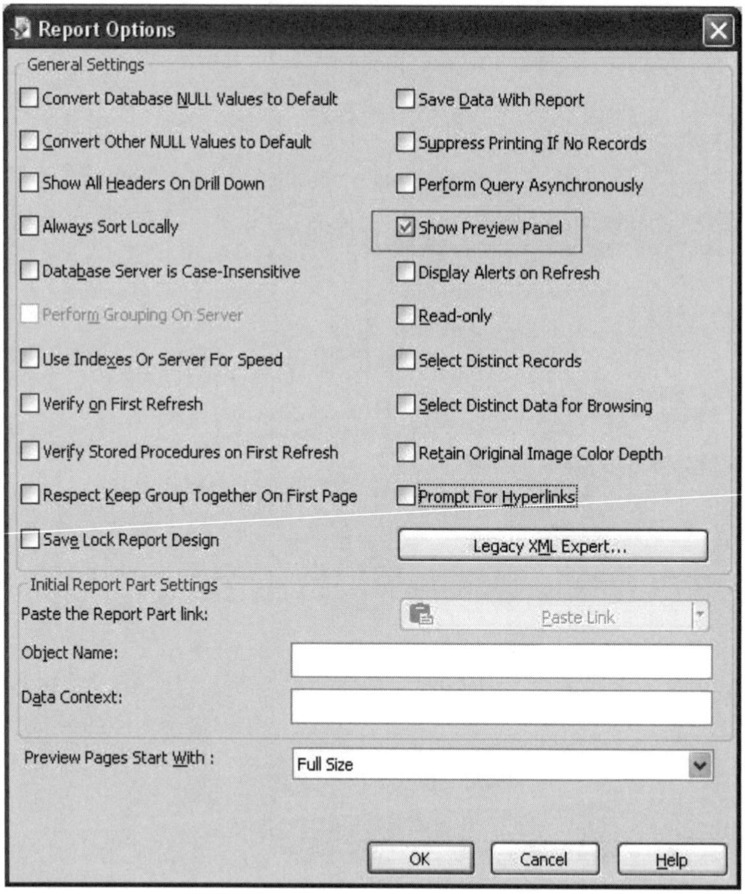

Figure 10.3
The Show Preview Panel check box.

With this option selected, a Preview panel is displayed in the Preview tab. The Group Tree, Find, and Parameter options are available in the Preview panel.

This option allows you to access parameters values without connecting to the database again, view groups, and use the Find feature to locate certain text.

EVALUATING PERFORMANCE INFORMATION

Ensuring the report performs efficiently is a very important part of report development. Understanding why your report is performing as it is, is crucial to producing a solid report. In the final stage of developing a report, you will be validating the entire dataset expected. There may be times when you press the Refresh button and experience a much more extensive wait time than previously encountered. You will need to look at different pieces of the report such as the grouping, selection export, formulas, and so on, to determine whether there is anything that would cause the report to run slowly. Crystal Report's Performance Information dialog box can be a valuable tool in determining where the problem areas are. You access the Performance Information dialog box by choosing the Report > Performance Information drop-down menu, as shown in Figure 10.4.

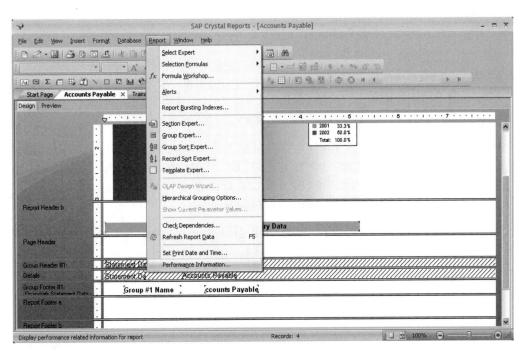

Figure 10.4
Accessing the Performance Information dialog box.

The components of the Performance Information dialog box, shown in Figure 10.5, are outlined in the following list.

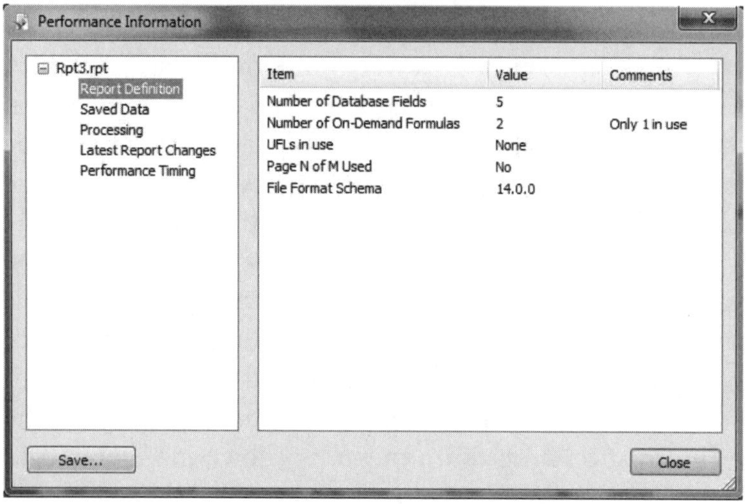

Figure 10.5
The Performance Information dialog box.

- **Report Definition**—Defines the content of the report such as the number of fields, formulas, user-defined functions, the use of Page N of M, and the Report Format version.

- **Saved Data**—Defines information about the data in the report such as number of data sources in the report, use of saved data option, total number of records, number of selected records, size of saved records, recurring formula information, and so on.

  All of this statistical information will give you information to determine if your SQL Query is developed and processing effectively.

- **Processing**—Based on the development of the report, this option will show you how the data will be processed.
  - Grouping done on the server
  - Sorting done on the server
  - Recording selection done on the server
  - Require two passes

- Require the total page count
- Size of saved group tree
- Number of nodes in group tree
- Number of summary values
- Build the group tree in progress

- **Latest Report Changes**—This option lists the latest changes made to the report, such as database linking, print time formulas, and so on.

- **Performance Timing**—This option details the processing time for different stages of the report. This information is important to check when experiencing a slow report.
  - Open document
  - Run query
  - Read database records
  - Average time to format page

All of these options will give you the necessary information needed to fine-tune the performance of your report.

REPORT DESIGN AND PERFORMANCE CONSIDERATIONS

The ideal report will be designed to perform as much of the work on the server as possible, which will eliminate pulling large number of records across the network and processed on the local workstation. In order to ensure most of the work is done on the server, there are some performance considerations that you want to consider when designing a report.

- **Use Indexes or Server for Speed**—Ensure this option is checked. You want the database to use the server and indexed fields whenever possible.

- **Perform Grouping on Server**—You must enable this option in order for the grouping to be processed on the server. Choose Database > Perform Grouping on Server or enable the option in the Global Options section.

- **Grouping**—You must have at least one group in the report. The group cannot be sorted in the In Specified Order sort order. If you have multiple groups, take note of the Group By clause in the query. Suppression of group sections will affect the Group By portion of the statement.

- **Top N or Bottom N**—You cannot use a Top N or Bottom N Group sort.

- **Details Section**—The Details section must be hidden in order to process the groups on the server.

- **Grouping on Formulas**—Do not group on formula fields. Convert the formulas to SQL expressions and group on the SQL expression instead.

- **Summaries**—You cannot include any formulas that are based on summary fields.

- **Summary Operations**—In order for grouping to be performed on the server, you cannot use any other function besides Sum, Minimum, Maximum, and Count.

- **Record Selection**—Do not use formulas in the record selection. Convert the formulas to SQL expressions and replace the formula in the record selection with a SQL expression.

SETTING THE PRINT DATE AND TIME

The Set Print Date and Time option is a beneficial feature. Reports that are based on a print date can be modified to print information based on any date you specify. For example, I have a report that prints records for the next 60 days based on the current date, but it's important that I run the report from the first of the month; otherwise, I will not get the full month. Therefore, when I want to run the report ahead of time, I can set the date to the first of the month using the Set Print Date and Time option and generate the expected results. You can access the Set Print Date and Time option from the Report > Set Print Date and Time drop-down menu, as shown in Figure 10.6. Figure 10.7 shows the Set Print Date and Time dialog box.

EXPORTING OPTIONS AND SETTINGS

Exporting a report is an important means of distribution. During the report requirements gathering process, you should have determined how the report will be distributed to the end users. Many reports are exported to PDFs, Excel sheets, and other formats. The exporting options and settings will be determined based on how the recipient needs to view the data. There are two export formats—

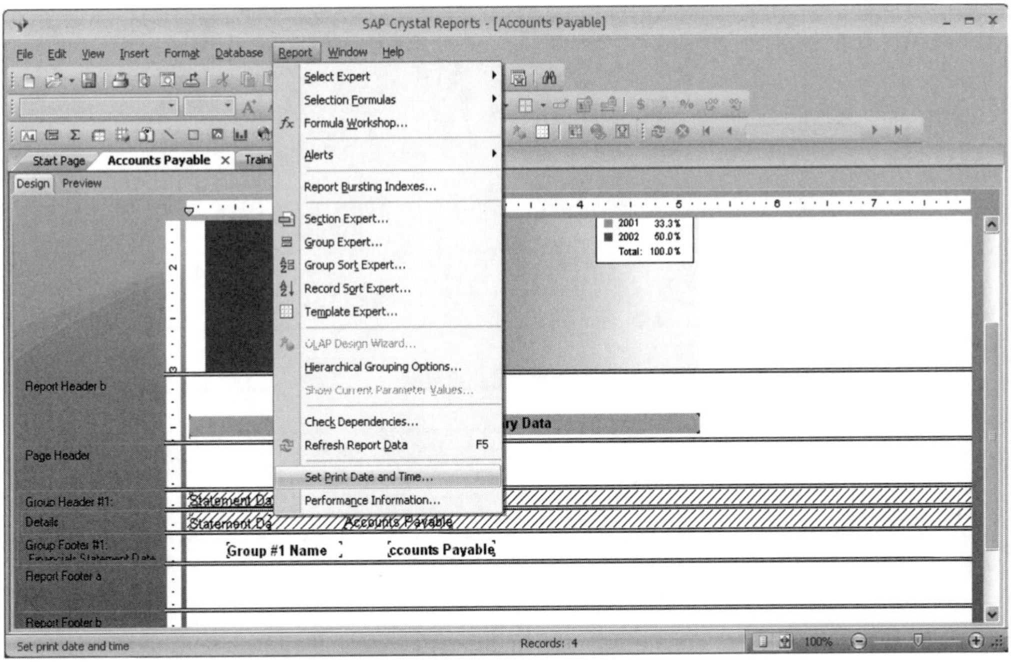

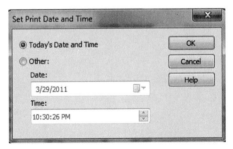

Figure 10.6
Accessing the Set Print Date and Time option.

Figure 10.7
The Set Print Date and Time dialog box.

page-based formats and record-based formats. Page-based formats are geared toward layout and formatting. Formatting refers to font, text color, and alignment, and layout refers to object size and position. Data is the main focus in record-based formats. You access the Export option by choosing File > Export or by choosing the Export icon from the Standard toolbar, as shown in Figure 10.8.

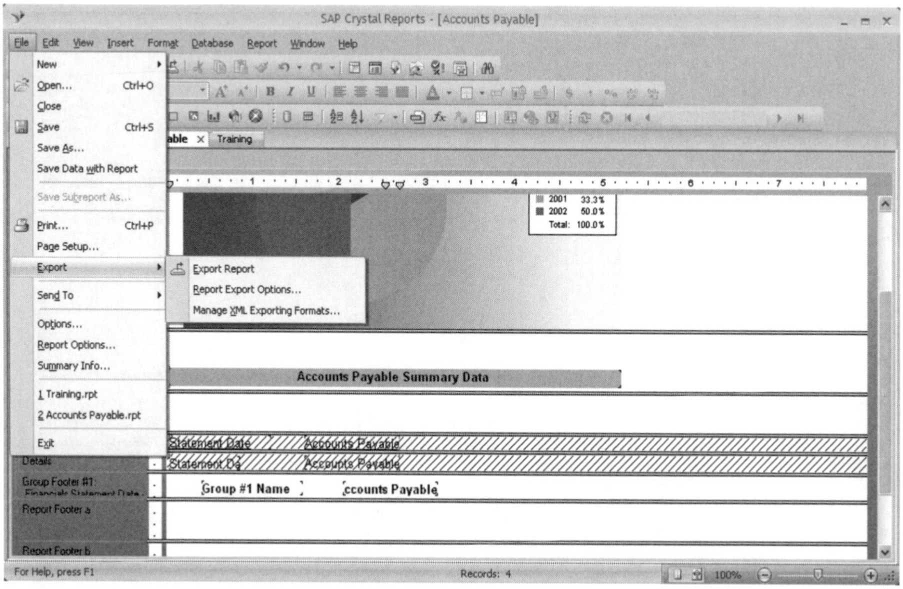

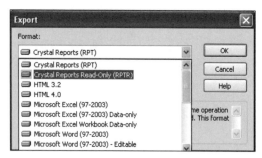

Figure 10.8
Access the Export option from the menu or by using the Export icon from the Standard toolbar.

Export Formats

The Export formats you can choose from are shown in Figure 10.9 and described are as follows:

Figure 10.9
Crystal Reports has many Export formats to choose from.

- **Crystal Report (RPT)**—Use this option if the users have Crystal Reports or the Crystal Reports Viewer installed on their computers. It will export as an .rpt and will save the report with the existing data. Exporting as an .rpt is the same as if you were doing a "save as".

- **Crystal Report Read-Only (RPTR)**—This is a new Crystal Reports 2011 feature that allows you to save the original data in the report in a read-only format, which can be viewed with a report viewer application but cannot be opened in the Crystal Reports designer. The report is protected from any modification and provides a level of protecting intellectual property contained in the designing of the report.

- **HTML 3.2**—Use this option for all browsers that do not support HTML 4.0. Unlike HTML 4.0, this option does not retain the report's layout.

- **HTML 4.0**—DHTML is used to keep the formatting and layout of the report. This is a page-based format.

- **Microsoft Excel (97-2003)**—This is a page-based format that exports data into Excel. There is a limit of 256 columns in Excel and anything beyond that is not exported. Most formatting is preserved, but line objects are not exported. The export will merge cells when an object extends across more than one cell.

- **Microsoft Excel (97-2003) Data Only**—This is a record-based format. Cells are not merged as with Microsoft Excel (97-2003). Summaries such as SUM, Average, Count, and so on can be exported. Most of the formatting is not maintained while exporting.

- **Microsoft Excel Workbook Data Only**—This option is new in Crystal 2011. Using this option allows you to export using the .xlsx format. It does not merge cells, so each object from Crystal Reports is exported to one cell.

- **Microsoft Word (97-2003)**—This is a page-based format that creates an RTF file with drawing and text object. All formatting is retained. In this format, text objects cannot be outside the left edge of the page. If the object is before the left edge it will be pushed right.

- **Microsoft Excel (97-2003) — Editable**—Although this is a page-based format, not all layout and formatting is kept during export. All report object contents are converted to text lines. Page Number and Page N of M do not work with this option. The option to insert page breaks at the end of each page is available; however, it may not be compatible with the page breaks created by Microsoft Word.

- **ODBC**—This is a record-based option with a data exchange format. Using this option allows you to export to any ODBC-compatible database.

- **PDF**—Exported documents are intended for printing and distribution. All formatting and layout is exported as what is displayed on the Preview tab.

- **Record Style — Columns With Spaces**—Data is exported as text. Only one line is exported at a time, per each record in the data. All data is exported with spaces between the columns.

- **Record Style — Columns Without Spaces**—Exports report data as text. Exports only group and detail data.

- **Record Definition**—Details the report's design information, including tables, fields, formulas, grouping, and record selection of the report. The report is exported as a text file. Most users forget to document their reports. This option, although generic, can act as basic report documentation.

- **Rich Text Format (RTF)**—This is a page-based format. Exports an RTF format similar to Microsoft Word.

- **Separated Values (CSV)**—This is a record-based format. The report is exported using separators and delimiters. A record in this format has all the fields that are displayed in the Design view. This option cannot be used with OLAP or reports with subreports in the page header or page footer. Microsoft Excel users use this option a lot.

- **Tab Separated Text (TTX)**—This option is very similar to Text format. Multi-line objects are exported in a single line and data is surrounded by double quotes and separated by tab characters.

- **Text**—This is a record-based format. The output is plain text.

- **XML**—Crystal XML Schema is used in this record-based format. This option's primary use is for data exchange.

- **XML Legacy**—Used primarily for data exchange and is in the Crystal Reports XML Schema.

- **MHTML**—Used to send HTML files via email. Also used to save web pages with all their contents—pictures, applets, and so on—in MHTML format.

Export Destinations

Choose the export format and then select the destination. The destination refers to where the export file is to be saved or viewed.

- **Application**—This option opens the application associated with the Export type. For example, if you export in a PDF format, it will export the report and open it in Adobe Reader for you to view.
- **Disk File**—This option will require you to save the exported file to a disk, local hard drive, or network.
- **Exchange Folder**—This option allows you to export the file to an Exchange folder.
- **Lotus Domino**—Exports to Lotus Domino.
- **Lotus Mail**—Exports to Lotus Mail.
- **MAPI**—Exports to a MAPI client.

Report Export Options

Exporting Options can be saved with the individual report as a default export option. Choose File > Export > Report Export Options to access this window, as shown in Figure 10.10. Any options set here will be saved as opposed to setting them every time the report is exported. This setting is not a global setting, but pertains to the report that you are working on.

Tip

I often hear reports are exported because users do not have access to Crystal Reports. Crystal Reports provides a free viewer that can be downloaded and distributed to as many users as necessary. This eliminates the need to export to Excel in some cases. With the Viewer installed, users are able to read the report in the Crystal Reports format without having the full version of Crystal Reports installed. You can download the Crystal Reports viewer from the bottom of the Start page or from http://www.businessobjects.com/forms/crystalreports/viewer/.

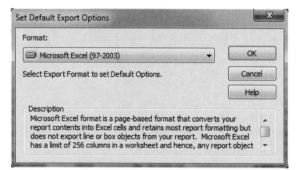

Figure 10.10
Set Default Export Options window.

Summary

Presentation is a major part of submitting a report once you're done with it. The report options and settings discussed in this chapter will allow you to deliver a well-formatted and efficient report. Options and settings can make all the difference when creating reports. Remember, it is not just the data that makes report creation a success; it's also the performance and presentation that add to it.

CHAPTER 11

CRYSTAL REPORTS .NET VISUAL STUDIO 2010 INTRODUCTION

The objectives of this chapter are as follows:

- Installing Crystal Reports .Net for Visual Studio
- Working with the viewers
- Learning the API enhancements
- Integrating Crystal Reports into a Windows application
- Integrating Crystal Reports into a web application

Crystal Reports has been included in Microsoft's development applications since Visual Basic 3. As Microsoft Visual Studio was released in 1997, Crystal Reports was merged into this application. With the release of Microsoft Visual Studio 2010, Crystal Reports .Net still a very important reporting tool was removed as an out-of-the-box installation. The Crystal Reports for Visual Studio 2010 must be downloaded from the SAP BusinessObjects website at http://www.sap.com/crystalreports/vs2010.

In this particular version, several of the needed files for Crystal Reports .Net are not installed by default, such as the Help files and the Update Service. You have to manually install the Help files and the Update Service. I will go into more detail about this installation process later in this chapter.

Crystal Reports can be included in both Windows and web applications. This chapter focuses on using the WPF viewer in a WPF application as well as the new features included in Crystal Reports .Net for 2010. It is not intended to teach you how to develop applications in Visual Studio, but how to incorporate Crystal Reports into the applications. The .Net Framework 4.0 is being used in Visual Studio .Net for 2010. The exercises in this chapter assume you have Microsoft Visual Studio 2010 and Crystal Reports for Visual Studio 2010, as well as the Crystal Reports for Visual Studio 2010 Service Pack 1 installed.

PREPARING TO INSTALL CRYSTAL REPORTS .NET VISUAL STUDIO

Crystal Reports .Net for Visual Studio is supported in the following Visual Studio versions:

- Visual Studio 2010 Professional
- Visual Studio 2010 Premium
- Visual Studio 2010 Ultimate

Note

🏃 Crystal Reports .Net for Visual Studio is not supported in the Visual Studio 2010 free Express versions.

In SAP, Crystal Reports for Visual Studio 2010 x64 (AMD64) 64-bit architecture is supported. However, IA64 (Itanium) architecture is not currently supported.

Supported Operating Systems (Design and Runtime)

Crystal Reports for Visual Studio 2010 is supported on the following 32-bit and 64-bit operating systems.

- Windows XP SP3 Professional
- Windows Server 2003 SP2
- Windows Server 2003 R2
- Windows Server 2008 R2
- Windows Vista SP2
- Windows 7

64-Bit Limitations

Although Crystal Reports .Net for Visual Studio does support 64-bit platforms, there are limitations that you should consider. The 64-bit Itanium processor is not supported. The following features are also limited when using Crystal Reports .Net in a 64-bit environment.

- Dynamic cascading prompts may not work because they use managed command tables as part of their architecture
- SAP BusinessObjects Enterprise integration
- Exporting reports to HTML format
- Geographic mapping components
- Azalea barcode font components

Supported Assemblies

Each version of Crystal Reports .Net has its own compatible version of runtime assemblies that must be installed in order to deploy your application correctly. The assemblies for Crystal Reports .Net for Visual Studio 2010 can be downloaded from the website https://websmp130.sap-ag.de/sap(bD1lbiZjPTAwMQ==)/bc/bsp/spn/bobj_download/main.htm.

The .msi and .msm files are available for download in 32-bit and 64-bit formats. If you are working with a 64-bit application, note the assemblies are available only in the .msi format.

It is recommended that you choose the .msi file over the .msm file. Installing the .msi file allows you to install the required files directly on the end user's computer and support many applications without having to embed the assemblies in each application. Also, using the .msm file will require you to rebuild and redeploy your application each time a Crystal Reports fix is applied to the application. As the developer, you should weigh the advantages and disadvantages of each type of file.

The current assemblies compatible with Crystal Reports .Net for Visual Studio 2010 are as follows:

- CRRuntime_32bit_13_0.msi

- CRRuntime_64bit_13_0.msi

- CRRuntime_13_0.msm

Supported Frameworks

Framework version 2.0, 3.0, 3.5, and 4.0 are all supported. Visual Studio also includes .Net Framework 4 Client Profile; however, SAP BusinessObjects does not support the use of this client framework.

Tip

You need to modify the app.config file to enable backwards (mixed-mode) .Net Framework compatibility. It defaults to .Net Framework 4 Client Profile. Legacy applications may not run properly without the modification to the configuration file. You must add the line, `useLega cyV2RuntimeActivationPolicy="true"`, to the startup section of the app.config file.

INSTALLING CRYSTAL REPORTS .NET

Visual Studio 2010 must be installed prior to installing Crystal Reports .Net. Download Crystal Reports .Net from www.sdn.sap.com/irj/sdn/crystalreports-dotnet, located in the Knowledge Center area under the section titled Download Crystal Reports for Visual Studio 2010. I suggest you download the Complete Package.exe, which includes Crystal Reports and all of the necessary assemblies or merge module files that will be needed to deploy your application on other computers.

1. Double-click the CRforVS_13_0_1.exe and follow the installation wizard.

2. Ensure you have installed Crystal Reports for Visual Studio service pack 1. If not, after the installation is complete, download the Service Pack 1 from the http://wiki.sdn.sap.com/wiki/display/BOBJ/CRVS2010+-+Service+Pack+1+-+Fixed+Issues website. Follow the installation instructions.

Installing the Help Files

Follow these steps to install the Help files:

1. Open Visual Studio 2010 and select Help > Manage Help Settings, as shown in Figure 11.1.

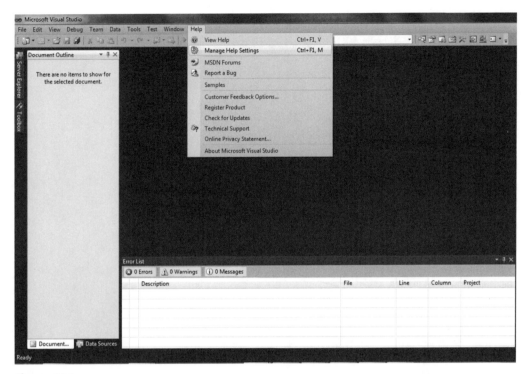

Figure 11.1
Installing the Help files.

2. From the Help Library Manager shown in Figure 11.2, select the option called Choose Online or Local Help. Choose the desired option. I chose to use local help.

3. Click OK.

4. Verify the path to the local media containing the Help files, as shown in Figure 11.3.

Note

This path may not be exactly the same as yours because my installation is on a 64-bit operating system.

5. Click Next.

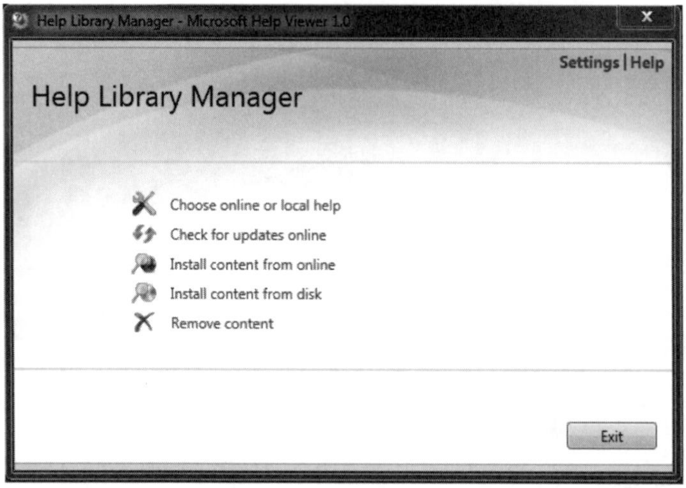

Figure 11.2
The Help Library Manager.

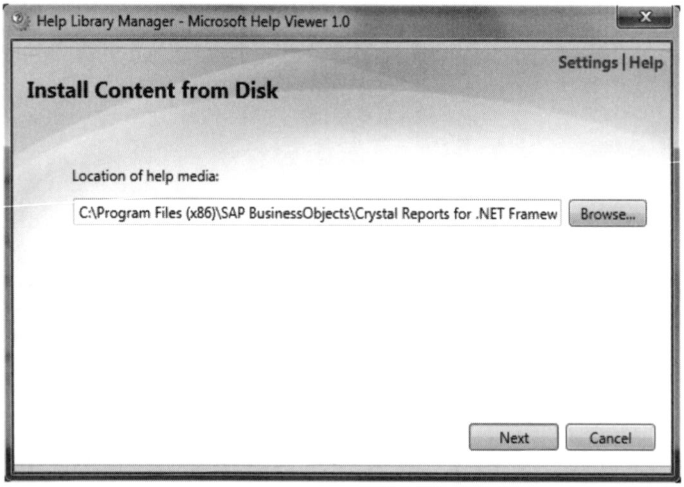

Figure 11.3
Installation path to local Help files.

6. Click the Add link next to the Crystal Reports for Visual Studio Help Files on the Install Content from Disk window, as shown Figure 11.4.

7. Click Update.

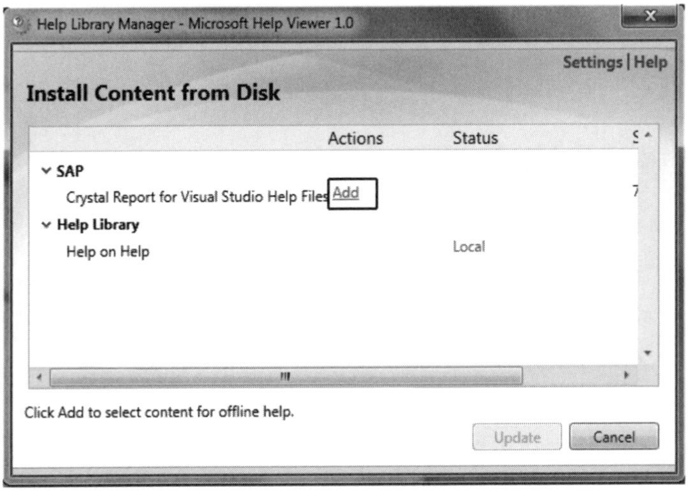

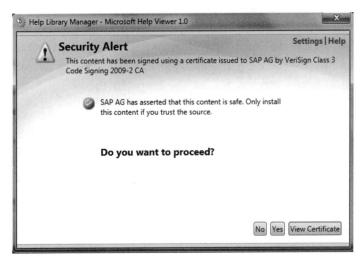

Figure 11.4
Install the Crystal Report for Visual Studio Help files.

8. Click Yes when you're notified that the certificate has been signed by the SAP AG by VeriSign Class 3 Code Signing 2009-2 CA. This appears on the Security Alert window shown in Figure 11.5.

Figure 11.5
Accept the Security Certificate Notification.

9. Click Finish when you're notified that the process has completed, as shown in Figure 11.6.

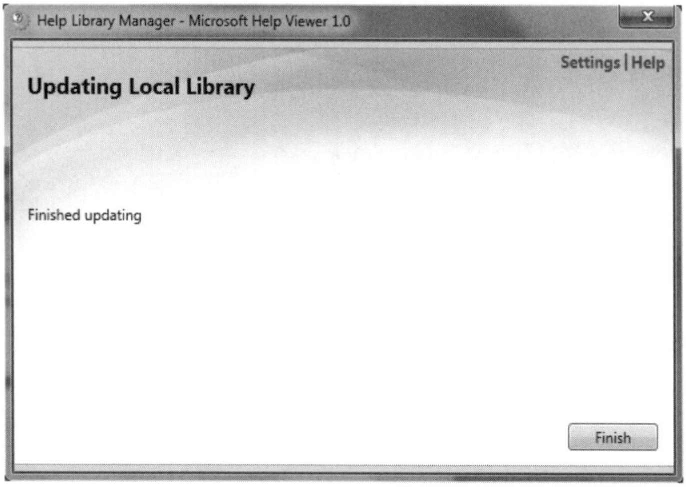

Figure 11.6
Complete the Help File Installation Process.

Installing the Update Service

You need to install the Update Service in order to ensure your system is always updated with the latest hot fixes, patches, and service packs. As mentioned earlier, this update service is not part of the Crystal Reports .Net installer, as you might expect. To install the Update Service, follow the steps in this section.

After you have installed Crystal Reports for Visual Studio, create a new website or Windows project and insert a new Crystal Report to check for the Update Service. The language that you choose is not important. For the purposes of this book, I will use C#.

To insert a new Crystal Report into your project, follow these steps:

1. From the Solution Explorer, right-click the project name and choose Add > New Item, as shown in Figure 11.7.

2. Scroll down the Installed Templates list, locate the Reporting category, and select Crystal Reports.

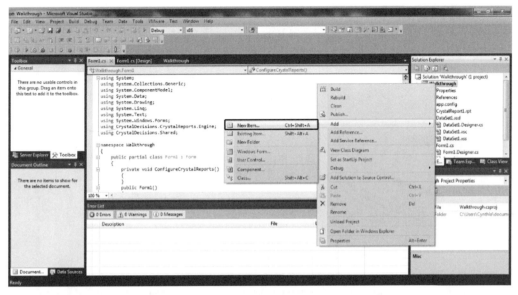

Figure 11.7
Inserting a new item.

3. Enter a name for the Crystal Reports. For this example, enter **Update.rpt,** as shown in Figure 11.8.

4. Click Add. The Crystal Reports Gallery window will open.

5. Choose to create a report using the wizard or from a blank report. See Figure 11.9.

Tip

A blank report is recommended. It's always best to design the report from scratch instead of allowing the Crystal Reports wizard to walk you through the process.

6. Click OK. The embedded Report Designer window will open, as shown in Figure 11.10.

Now you're ready to check for updates:

1. From the Design window menu, choose Crystal Reports > Check for Updates, as shown in Figure 11.11.

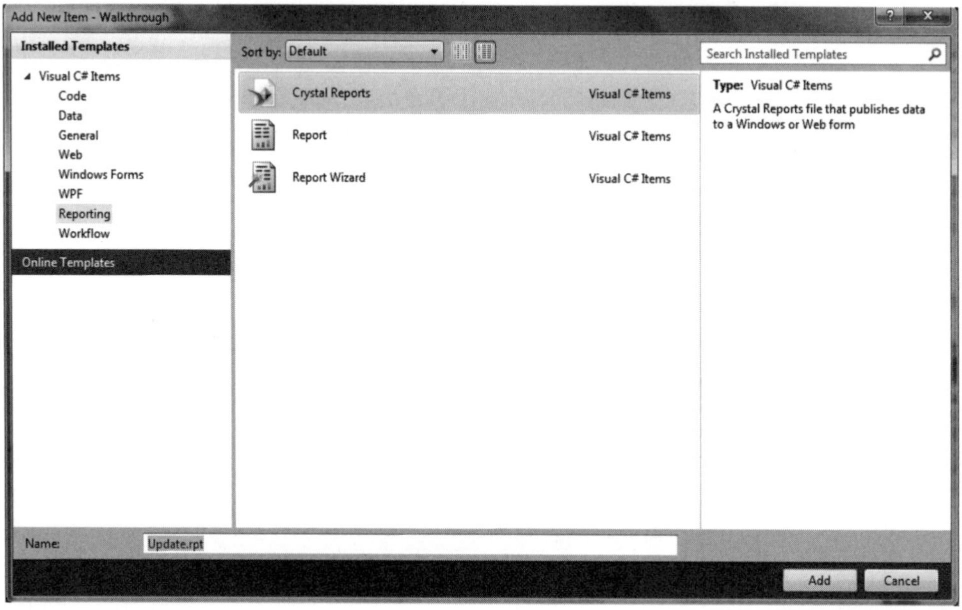

Figure 11.8
Selecting Crystal Reports.

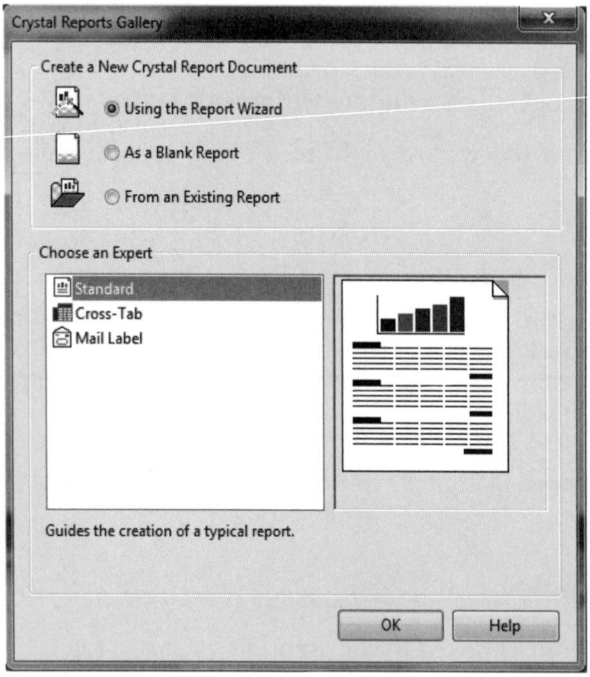

Figure 11.9
Creating a report using the blank report template.

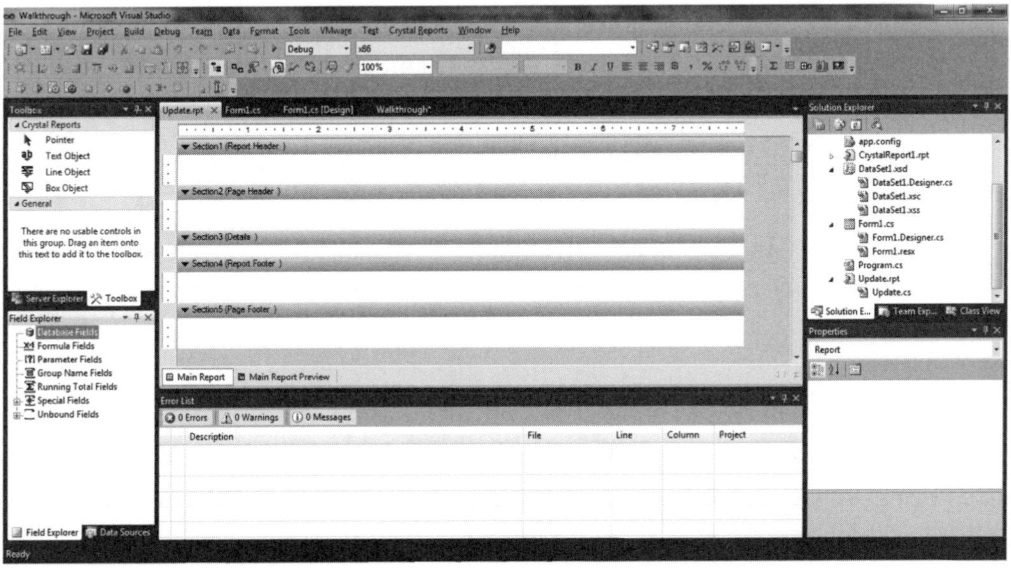

Figure 11.10
The Report Designer window.

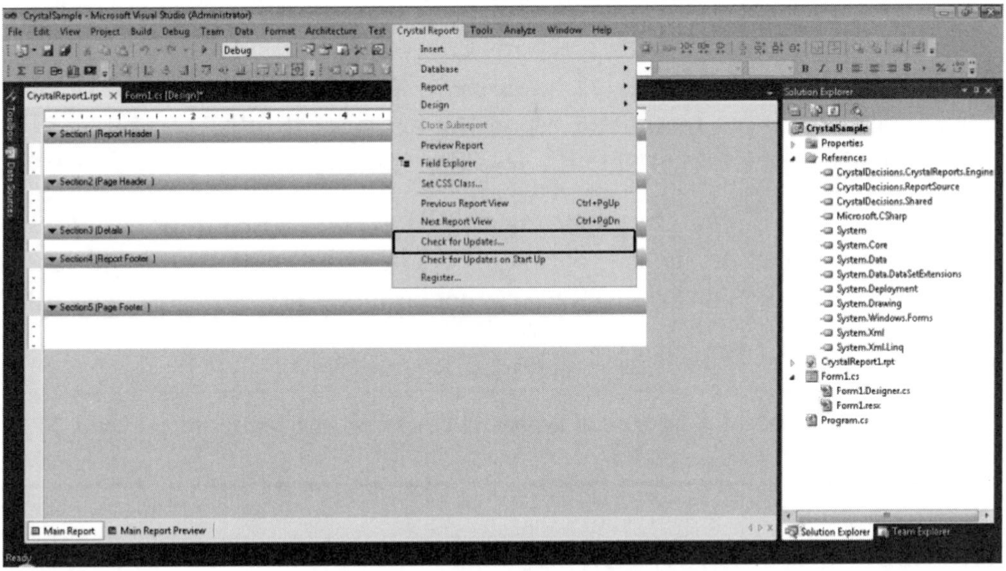

Figure 11.11
Selecting Check for Updates in Crystal Reports.

2. The Update Service launches, and then checks for updates. You can choose to install the updates or delete them. If the Update Service has not been installed, you will be asked if you want to install it.

3. Click Yes. You will be forwarded to the SAP Crystal Reports Update Service website where you can download and install the service.

4. Once the installation is complete, launch Visual Studio again and open the previously used project and report and follow Steps 1 and 2.

REVIEWING CRYSTAL REPORTS .NET'S NEW FEATURES

The version of Crystal Reports .Net for Visual Studio 2010 includes several new features, which are covered in the following sections.

SAP Crystal Reports Read-Only (RPTR) Format

SAP Crystal Reports Read-Only (RPTR) format lets you share Crystal Reports while protecting your intellectual property. An RPTR file can be refreshed at runtime but the report definition cannot be modified or exported.

RPTR files can be viewed using a report viewer control. For security purposes, an RPTR file cannot be converted to an RPT. An RPTR file cannot be opened with a designer that can modify the report, for example, the SAP Crystal Reports 2011 Designer or the Visual Studio embedded designer.

You create an RPTR report by exporting an RPT report to RPTR format. If a file that includes a subreport file is exported to RPTR, both the subreport and report will be exported as RPTR. An RPTR file cannot be added as a subreport to an RPT.

Note

Only reports created with SAP Crystal Reports 2011 can be exported to the read-only (RPTR) format.

Microsoft Excel (xlsx) Format

Crystal Reports .Net for Visual Studio now allows you to export your report into Excel 2007 utilizing the .xlsx format. This format supports the increased number of exportable rows and columns that were introduced in Microsoft Excel 2007. This feature allows for up to 16,385 columns and 1,048,576 rows in a single workbook.

Choosing an Object Model

Determining which report object model to integrate into your application is essential to ensuring your application meets your business requirements. The options include the `CrystalReportsViewer` object, the `ReportDocument` object model, and the new WPF viewer. Each viewer has its own set of advantages, including different export capabilities. Therefore, it's important to take into account the need to export the data and build the application with the appropriate viewer.

The `CrystalReportsViewer` object allows you to set properties and methods that control how the report is displayed. It also has a limited number of methods and properties that interact with reports bound to the control.

The `ReportDocument` object model is more extensive and gives you better control than the `CrystalReportsViewer`. SAP recommends for most binding tasks that you use the `ReportDocument` model because use of the `CrystalReportsViewer` can distort the separation between the presentation layer and the business layer in your code. The `CrystalReportsViewer` has limited interaction with reports and sometimes has model conflict. SAP's guidelines encourage you to use the `ReportDocument` model if you are not going to use the SAP Crystal Reports Server or SAP BusinessObjects Enterprise.

N o t e

> Model conflict occurs when the developer integrates multiple object models in the same application. For example, this can happen when using the `CrystalReportsViewer` object and the `ReportDocument` models in the same application.

As you move through this chapter, you will become familiar with each viewer and its capabilities. The `CrystalReportsViewer` object is now accessible in WPF applications in Crystal Reports for Visual Studio. The new WPF viewer has improved graphics and performance benefits.

EMBEDDED VS. NON-EMBEDDED REPORTS

You can integrate embedded reports or non-embedded reports into your application. There are considerations you should take into account before deciding which one to choose. Crystal Reports imports or creates embedded reports directly in the project. On the other hand, a non-embedded report is saved in an external location and referenced through a location path or through a link in the project.

When a report is embedded into the application, it automatically creates the wrapper class that represents the report. Therefore, all future references to the report will be referenced by the class and not the report itself. When the project is compiled, the report and the wrapper class will be added to the assembly of the project. The wrapper class extends from the ReportDocument class.

Another consideration is the size of your embedded reports. All .Net Frameworks have limitations on the size of DLL files. If your embedded reports are large including using the saved data option, your project may not compile due to the size limitations. Therefore, you may need to turn off saved data or consider using non-embedded reports in the application.

A non-embedded report is referenced from a file location stored on a hard drive. The report is not included as part of the project and is never imported into the project. The report is accessed at runtime through the ReportDocument model using the ReportDocument.Load() method or through the CrystalReportsViewer model using the CrystalReportsViewer.ReportSource property.

A non-embedded report can be exposed as a web service. An embedded report is simpler because all of your files are in one place when the application is compiled; however, in some cases it is better to use non-embedded files anyway, such as when your reports are large or when there will be frequent changes to the reports. In an application with embedded reports, any changes to the reports require the application be recompiled. Consequently, you must weigh the pros and cons and use the method that best fits your business's requirements.

Example: Visual C#

Embedded report:

```
MyParameters Prpt = new MyParameters();
crystalReportsViewer1.ViewerCore.ReportSource = Prpt;
```

Non-embedded report:

```
MyParameters Prpt = new MyParameters();
crystalReportsViewer1.ViewerCore.ReportSource =
                        "(C:\\Sample\\MyParameters.rpt)"
```

TOURING THE CRYSTAL REPORTS USER INTERFACE

The embedded Crystal Reports design window is used to create and modify reports. The Designer does not include all of the features that are encapsulated in the standalone Crystal Reports version. Although it does not include all features, it does allow you to create powerful reports and applications.

New API enhancements were added with the `SAPBusinessObjects.WPF.Viewer` namespace. This addition gives the developer the use of the `CrystalReports-Viewer` or the `ViewerCore` class. It also allows easier migration between COM components and .NET applications.

`SAPBusinessObjects.WPF.Viewer`

Note

This example uses the SAPBusinessObjects.WPF.Viewer.dll.

The `ViewerCore` class allows you to control how the CrystalReportView control will appear and function.

There are many properties that can be set for this control. Table 11.1 lists the properties that control the buttons that are displayed on the CrystalReports-Viewer toolbar.

ViewerCore Class

The `ViewerCore` class is the base class of the `CrystalReportsViewer` control. `ViewerCore` will allow you to open the members of the class to be used in the `CrystalReportsViewer` control. The members are described in Table 11.2.

The `ViewerCore` class includes the methods shown in Table 11.3.

Table 11.1 ViewerCore Properties

Properties	Description
EnableToolTips	Sets the option to display tooltips in the viewer. This refers to the `CrystalReportsViewer` only, not the toolbar.
MatchCase	Determines whether the search variables in the viewer are case sensitive.
MatchWholeWord	Determines whether searches return partial matches in the viewer.
Owner	Gets the name of the owner of the displayed document.
ShowCopyButton	Hides or shows the copy button on the CrystalReportsViewer toolbar.
ShowExportButton	Hides or shows the export button on the CrystalReportsViewer toolbar.
ShowGoToPageButton	Determines whether the Goto Page number button will appear on the CrystalReportsViewer toolbar.
ShowLogo	Sets the property to display or hide the SAP BusinessObjects logo.
ShowNextPageButton	Sets the visible property for the next page button on the CrystalReportsViewer toolbar.
ShowOpenFileButton	Sets the visible property of the Open File button on the CrystalReportsViewer toolbar.
ShowPrevPageButton	Sets the visible property of the Previous Page button on the CrystalReportsViewer toolbar.
ShowPrintButton	Sets the visible property to display the Print button on the CrystalReportsViewer toolbar.
ShowRefreshButton	Sets the visible property to display the Refresh button on the CrystalReportsViewer toolbar.
ShowSearchTextButton	Sets the visible property to display the Search textbox on the CrystalReportsViewer toolbar.
ShowStatusbar	Sets the visible property to display the Status bar.
ShowToggleSidePanelButton	Determines whether the toggle button to display the side panel is hidden or visible.
ShowToolbar	Determines whether the main toolbar is displayed.
ViewerCore	Determines whether the ViewerCore is associated with the `CrystalReportsViewer` class.

Note

The properties and methods listed in Tables 11.1 through 11.3 assume you are familiar with the .Net programming language and understand the usage of the previous properties.

Table 11.2 ViewerCore Class Properties

Properties	Description
ActiveViewIndex	Gets or sets the index of the active view of the CrystalReport Viewer.
AllowedExportFormats	Allows you to specify the export formats allowed for the current report.
BackgroundBrush	Gets or sets the Brush used on the background.
CurrentPageNumber	Gets the current page number.
DisplayBackgroundEdge	Determines whether the report is offset from the edge of its view window.
EnableDrillDown	Determines whether drilling down to a page/chart/summary is enabled.
EnableRefresh	Determines whether the user can refresh the report.
EnterpriseLogon	Gets or sets the logon information for an Enterprise report.
LogOnInfo	Gets or sets the TableLogOnInfos collection.
Owner	Gets the owner name of the displayed document.
ParameterFieldInfo	Gets or sets the TableLogOnInfos collection object.
ProductLocale	Gets or sets the product locale of the current report.
ReportSource	Sets the report to bind to the `CrystalReportsViewer` control.
ReuseParameterWhenRefresh	Determines whether saved parameter values are reused when the report is refreshed, or whether the user will be prompted to select values.
SelectionFormula	Gets or sets the record selection formula of the report.
SelectionMode	Gets or sets the record selection mode in the current viewer.
ToggleGroupTree	Determines whether the group tree view is displayed.
ToggleParameterPanel	Determines whether the Parameters panel is displayed.
ToggleSidePanel	Determines whether the side panel is displayed.
TotalPageNumber	Gets the total number of pages for the current report.
ViewContextItems	Gets or sets the ViewContext items associated with this viewer.
ViewCount	Gets the number of times the currently displayed document has been viewed.
ViewTimeSelectionFormula	Determines whether the current browse locale is used to display the report.
ZoomFactor	Gets or sets the zoom level of the report.

Table 11.3 ViewerCore Methods

Methods	Description
CloseView	Closes a view tab in the `CrystalReportsViewer` control.
CopySelectedObjectsContentToClipboard	Copies the content of the selected object to the clipboard for later retrieval.
Dispose	Disposes of the viewer.
DrillDownOnGroup	Drills down on a group.

Table 11.3 ViewerCore Methods (*Continued*)

Methods	Description
ExportReport	Exports the report displayed in the `CrystalReportsViewer` control.
GetCurrentPageNumber	Gets the current page number of the report.
GetLastPageNumber	Gets the last page number for the report.
GetSelectedObjects	Gets the selected objects.
InitializeComponent	Initializes a viewer with default values.
PrintReport	Prints the report displayed in the `CrystalReportsViewer` control.
RefreshReport	Refreshes the report displayed in the `CrystalReportsViewer` control.
SearchForText	Searches for the specified text within the document.
ShowFirstPage	Shows the first page of the report in the `CrystalReportsViewer`.
ShowLastPage	Shows the last page of the report in the `CrystalReportsViewer`.
ShowNextPage	Moves to the next page in the report.
ShowPreviousPage	Moves to the previous page in the report.
Zoom	Changes the magnification level of the `CrystalReportsViewer` control.

WORKING WITH CRYSTAL REPORTS .NET FOR VISUAL STUDIO 2010

Reports created in Visual Studio are either embedded as the reporting source for the custom application or developed as a single reporting application.

Note

As mentioned, this chapter is based on Visual Studio 2010 and Crystal Reports .Net 2010 with Service Pack 1 installed.

Using the WPF Viewer

The new WPF viewer can be used in a Windows Form application or the new Crystal Reports WPF application. Let's explore using the WPF viewer in a Windows form application. The release of Crystal Reports for Visual Studio 2010 service pack 1 does not allow you to bind a report to the WPF viewer using the binding drop-down element that is available when using the CrystalReportsViewer, as shown in Figure 11.12.

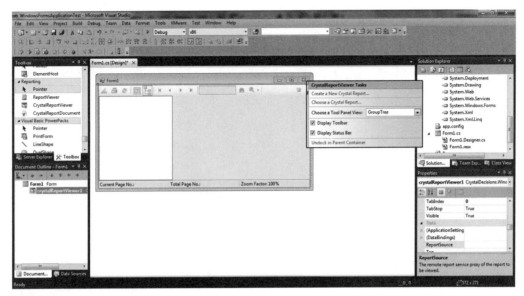

Figure 11.12
Binding a report in WPF CrystalReportsViewer.

You must write code to bind a report using the WPF viewer. The WPF viewer for Crystal Reports may not be visible in the toolbox by default. You have to prepare the environment for its use. Let's take a moment and walk through the steps necessary to prepare your environment.

Start Visual Studio by following these steps:

1. Choose File > New Project.

2. Select the language category, such as Visual C#. Then select the Windows node > Windows Form Application as shown in Figure 11.13.

3. Enter a name for the project.

4. Enter the path to save the project. It will default to the document/Visual Studio/Projects directory for the user.

5. Choose to Create a New Solution or Add to a Solution in the Solution property as shown in the bottom section of Figure 11.13.

6. Enter a new name for the solution or accept the default.

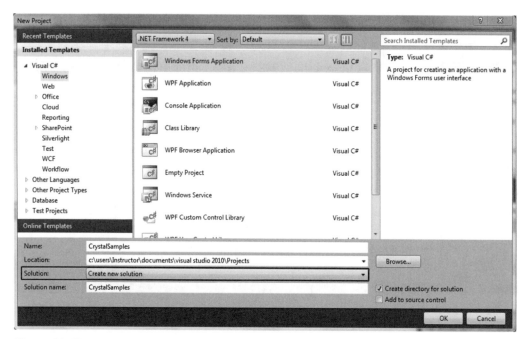

Figure 11.13
Creating a new project.

7. Click OK. The Visual Studio Form1 design window will open as shown in Figure 11.14.

Now you're ready to prepare your environment to work with the WPF viewer for Crystal Reports.

The .Net Framework for Visual Studio 2010 defaults to .Net Framework 4.0 Client Profile. However, to enable all of the features in Crystal Reports for Visual Studio, you must change the framework to .Net Framework 4.0.

To change the framework, follow these steps:

1. Access the project's properties from the Project menu by choosing Project > [Project Name] Properties, as shown in Figure 11.15.

2. Locate the Target Framework property and change the drop-down option from the .Net Framework 4 Client Profile to .Net Framework 4.0, as shown in Figure 11.16.

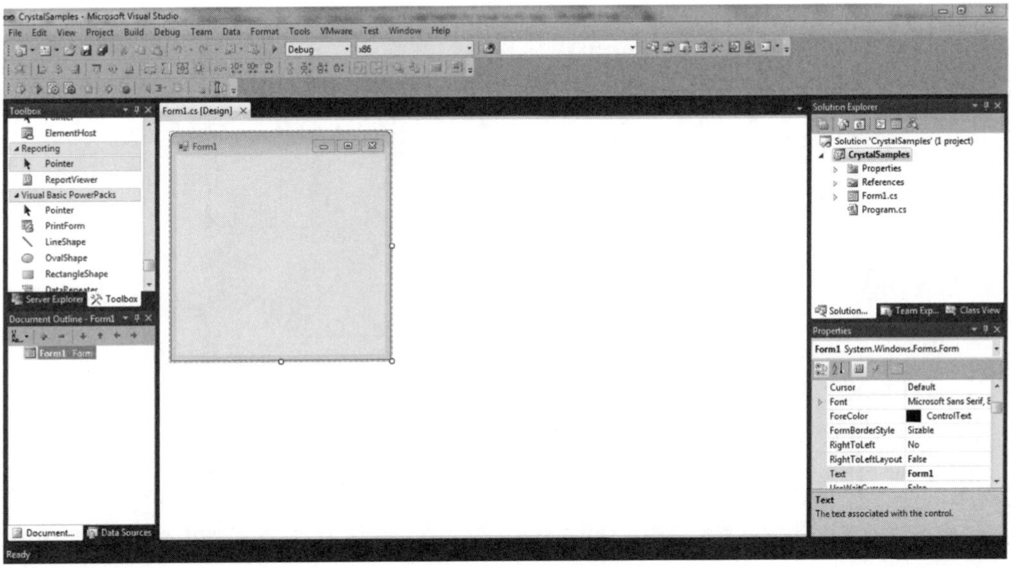

Figure 11.14
Visual Studio Windows Application.

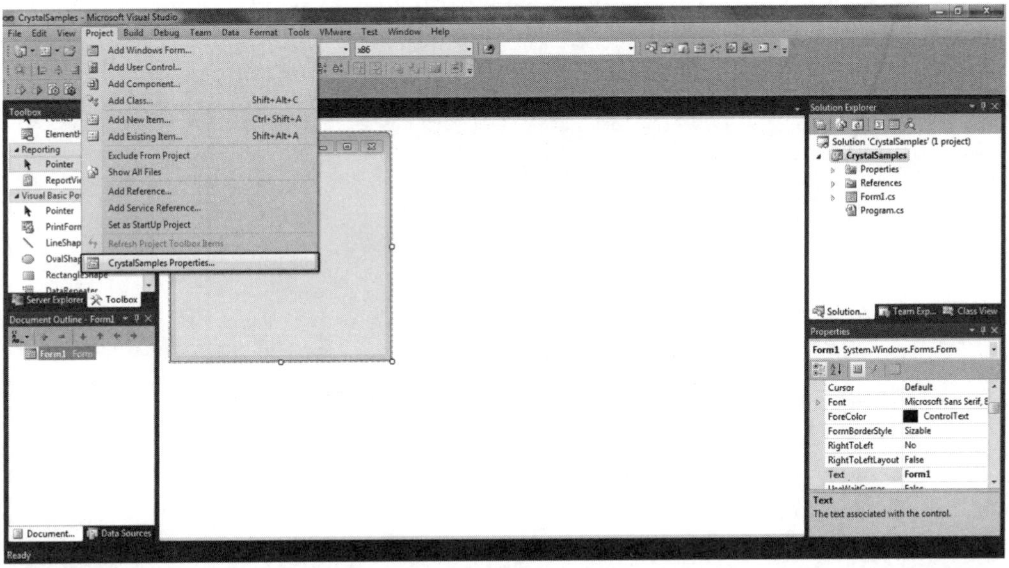

Figure 11.15
Accessing the Project's properties.

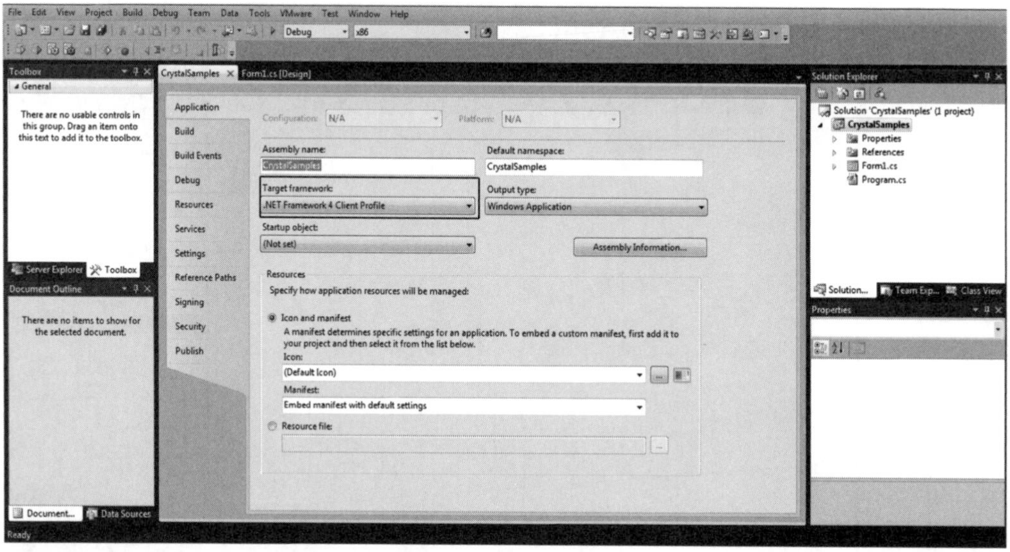

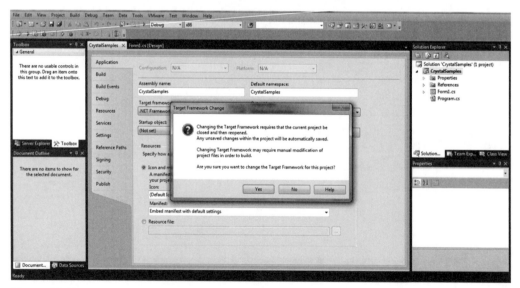

Figure 11.16
Changing the target framework.

3. Changing the framework requires the program be shut down and restarted. When the message box appears, click Yes to confirm the change of the target framework, as shown in Figure 11.17.

Figure 11.17
Accepting the change of framework.

The project will reopen with a blank window.

Now you are ready to use the WPF viewer. Follow these steps to add it:

1. You must add a WPF user control to the project. Access the Add New Item control from Project > Add New Item or by right-clicking on the project name in the Solution Explorer and choosing Add > New Item, as shown in Figure 11.18.

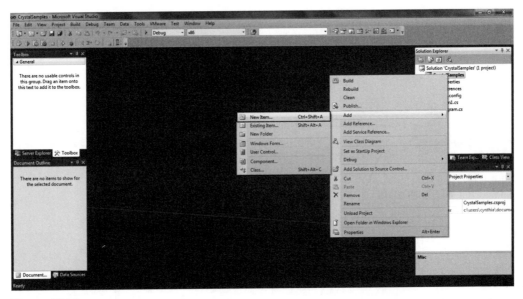

Figure 11.18
Adding a new item.

2. Select the WPF node in the Installed Templates section.

3. Select the User Control (WPF) option.

4. Enter a name for the user control, as shown in Figure 11.19.

5. Click Add. The .xaml page will be displayed, as shown in Figure 11.20.

The WPF user control object is visible. Now is a good time to resize the element to fit your report size. This will prevent only a small excerpt of your report from being visible at bind time. The CrystalReportsViewer may not be listed in your toolbox.

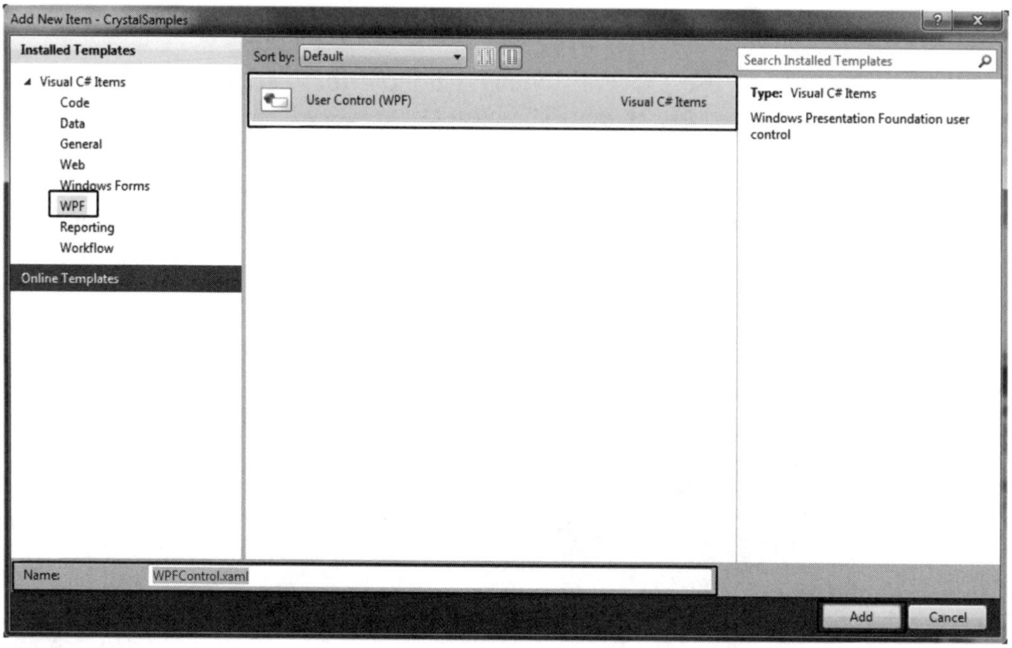

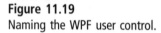

Figure 11.19
Naming the WPF user control.

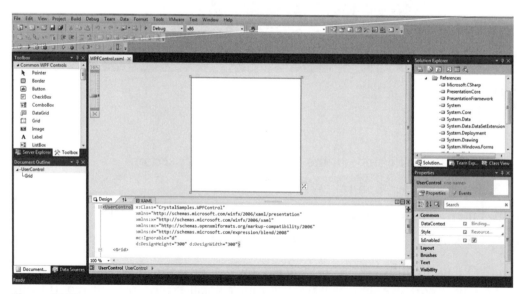

Figure 11.20
Using the WPF user control.

To add the CrystalReportsViewer, follow these steps:

1. Right-click a white area of the WPF control area in the toolbox and select Choose Items, as shown in Figure 11.21.

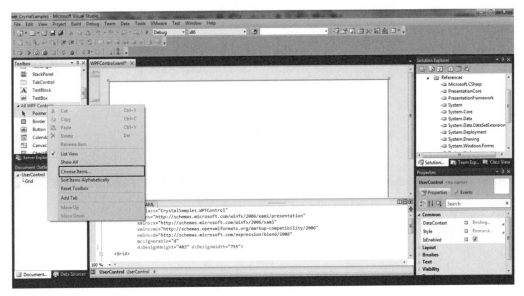

Figure 11.21
Adding items to the toolbox

2. On the WPF Components tab, scroll down and select the checkbox next to the CrystalReportsViewer item, as shown in Figure 11.22.

3. Click OK. The CrystalReportsViewer will now be listed in the All WPF controls section of the toolbox, as shown Figure 11.23.

4. Drag the CrystalReportsViewer from the toolbox onto the .xaml window for the WPF user control that was created previously, as shown in Figure 11.24.

Tip

If you don't see the CrystalReportsViewer in the toolbox after adding it from Step 3, check to make sure the Target Framework has been set to .Net Framework 4.

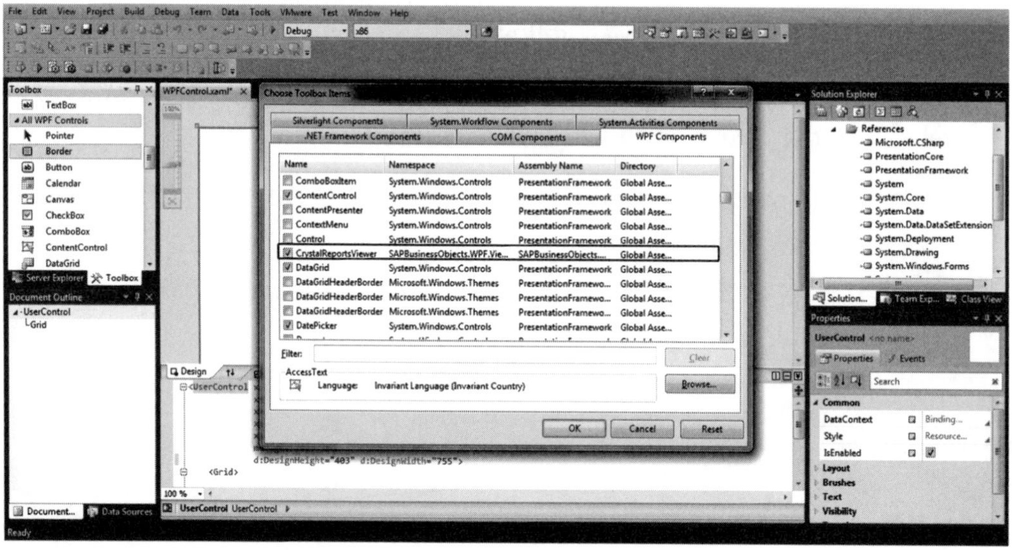

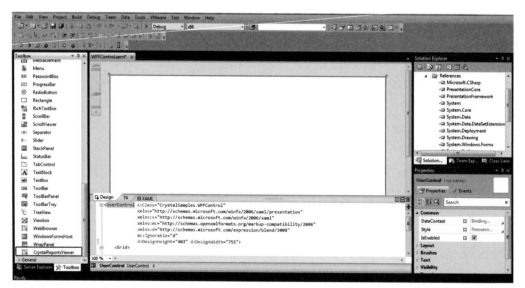

Figure 11.22
Making the CrystalReportsViewer accessible.

Figure 11.23
The CrystalReportsViewer in the toolbox.

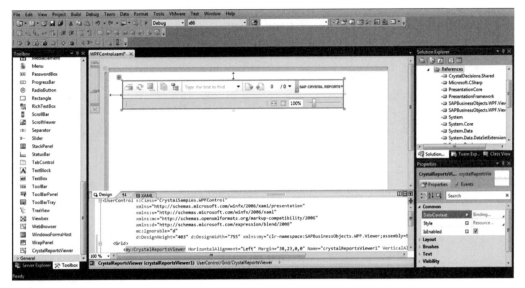

Figure 11.24
The WPF CrystalReportsViewer.

Tip

You may need to resize the `CrystalReportsViewer` object.

You are now ready to bind the report to the CrystalReportsViewer. You can bind the report programmatically or give the user more control of the report to access by enabling the Open Report option. I'll discuss the Open Report option in the next section.

To bind the report programmatically, follow these steps:

1. Access the code of the WPF user control by right-clicking the .xaml control and choosing View Code.

2. Add the following namespaces to the code.

   Example using Visual C:

   ```
   #using SAPBusinessObjects.WPF.Viewer;
   using CrystalDecisions.CrystalReports.Engine;
   using CrystalDecisions.Shared;
   ```

3. Click in the public `WPFControl()` area of the code and add the following code after the `InitializeComponent()` line, seen in Figure 11.25. This

code assumes you have an existing Crystal Report embedded in the report saved as **Formatting Fields**. Replace the report name with the name of your report.

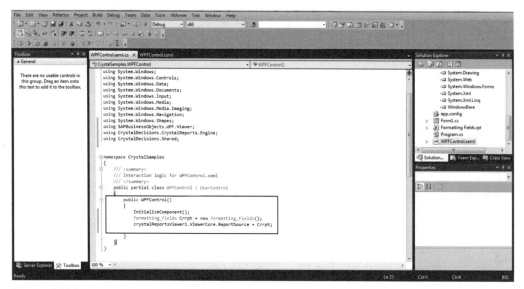

Figure 11.25
Programmatically binding a report to the viewer.

4. Build the solution from the Build menu or by pressing F6.

Tip

If you encounter an error referencing the `System.Window.Markup.IQueryAmbient` or stating the `IComponentConnector` assembly is not found, you might need to add the reference. Right-click the Solution Explorer and choose Add Reference. Select the .Net tab and locate the System.Xaml reference. Click OK. Rebuild the project.

5. Switch to the form where the viewer should be placed.

6. From the toolbox in the WPF Interoperability category, drag the Element Host to the form.

7. Select the Element Host task arrow at the top-right corner of the box and select the WPF user control created earlier, as shown in Figure 11.26.

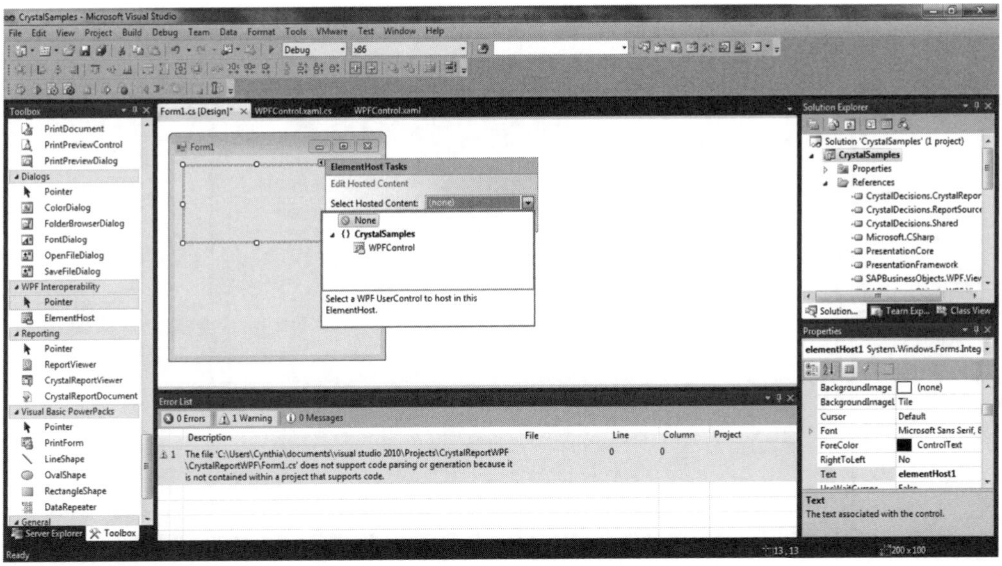

Figure 11.26
Selecting the WPF user control.

Tip
_____

If the WPF user control does not appear in the drop-down list, rebuild the solution. If that still does not work, go back and verify that the SAP BusinessObjects CrystalReportsViewer item is checked on the WPF Components tab of the item list. If it is not, check the option again and rebuild the solution. The user control should be available now.
_____

You may need to resize the user control. You can select the option called Dock to Parent Container when you select the user control from the Element Host task window.

1. If you have configured the report and viewer correctly, you should be able to see the report in the preview window on the control, as shown in Figure 11.27.

2. Click F5 or Debug > Start Debugging to launch the form in Debug mode. The form will be displayed as it will be seen in the application, similar to Figure 11.28.

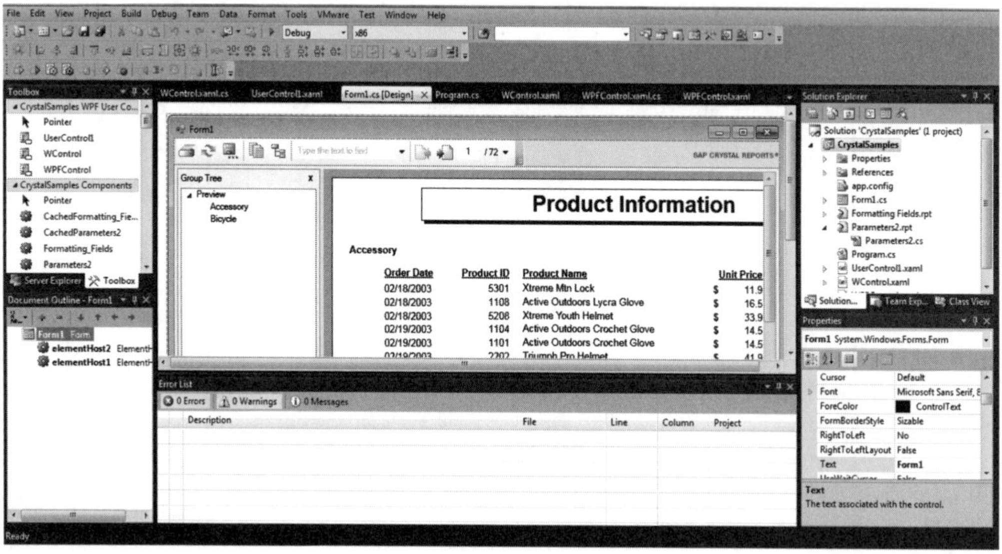

Figure 11.27
Preview of report in WPF viewer in Design mode.

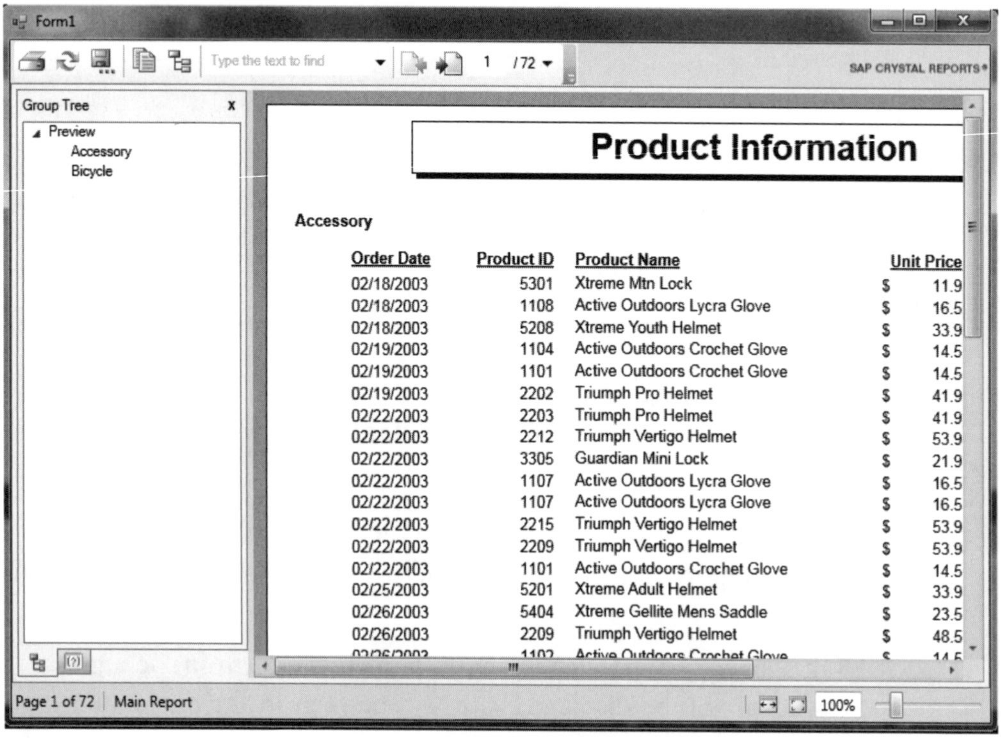

Figure 11.28
WPF Viewer in Debug mode.

The WPF CrystalReportsViewer toolbar is slightly different than the standard CrystalReportsViewer, as shown in Figure 11.29. It is discussed in detail in Table 11.4.

Figure 11.29
The WPF viewer toolbar.

Icons	Description
Table 11.4 WPF Viewer Toolbar Options	
Icons	Description
	Print – Launches the Print dialog box.
	Refresh – Refreshes the data in the report.
	Export – Opens the Export Report window. You can export the report in many formats, such as .RPTR, Excel, Word, PDF, ODBC, and .csv.
	Copy – Copies the selected object to the clipboard to paste in another application. For example, select the Employee's name in the report, and then click the copy button. The name is copied to the clipboard; you will be able to paste the name into another application such as Microsoft Word.
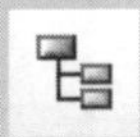	Group Tree – This toggle button hides or shows the Side Panel as shown in Figures 11.30 and 11.31.
	Search – Enter text to search for in the report.
	Page Navigators – Click the left- or right-pointing arrows to move to the next or previous pages of the report.
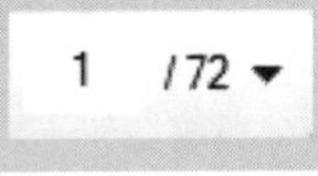	Go to Page – Allows you to jump to another page in the report quickly by entering the page number in the box.

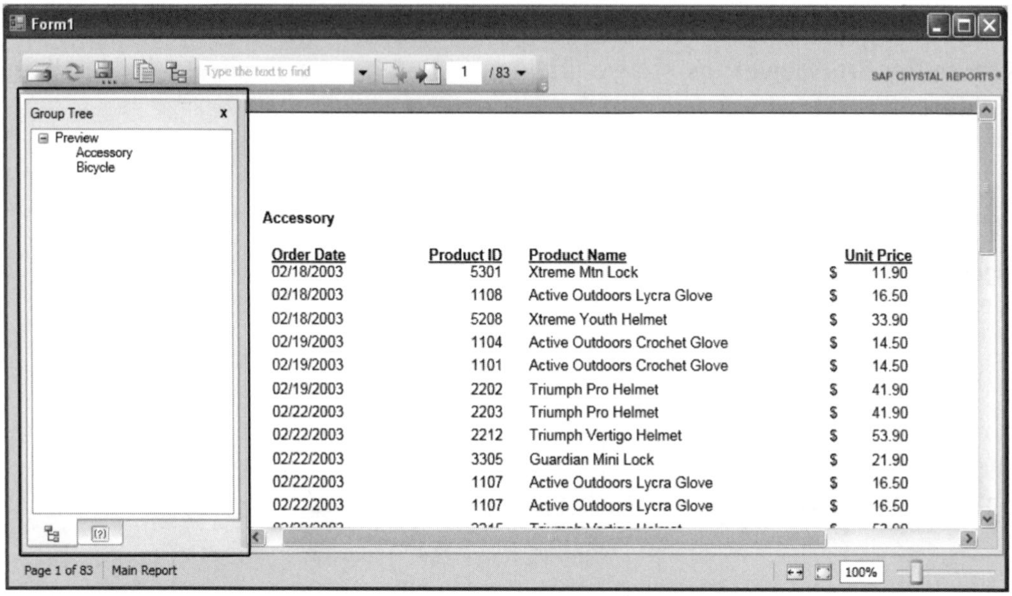

Figure 11.30
The side panel is visible.

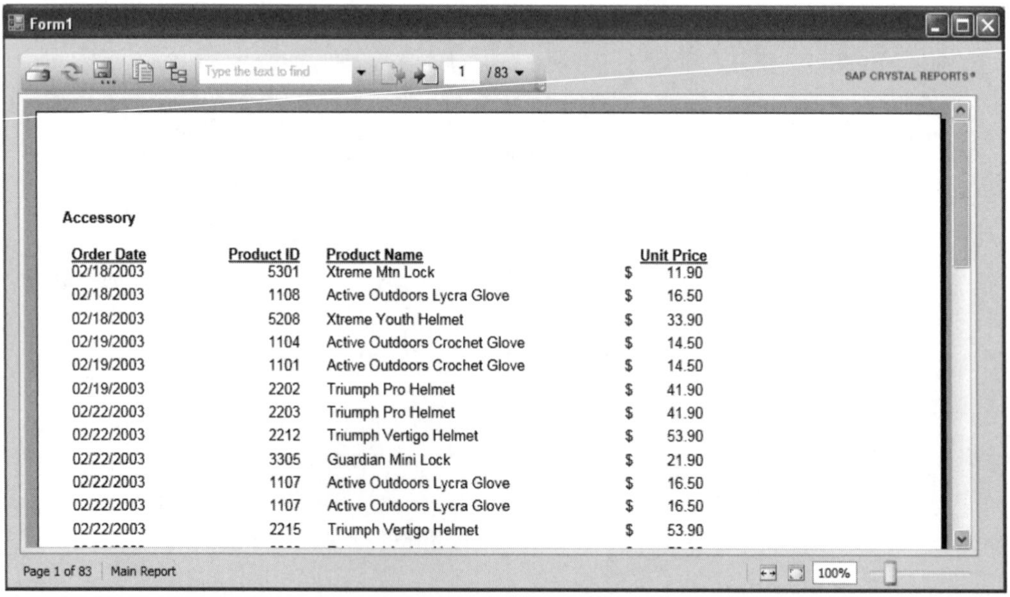

Figure 11.31
The side panel is hidden.

In the previous section, the report was embedded in the application programmatically. If you want to give users a little more control over the report that is viewed, you can enable the Open File feature from within the WPF viewer. The option is disabled by default. To enable the feature, follow these steps:

1. You must add a WPF user control to the project. Access the Add New Item control from Project > Add New Item or by right-clicking on the project name in the Solution Explorer and choosing Add > New Item.

2. Select the WPF node in the Installed Templates section.

3. Select the User Control (WPF) option.

4. Enter a name for the user control.

5. Click Add.

The WPF user control object will now be visible. Now is a good time to resize the element to fit your report size. This will prevent only a small excerpt of your report from being visible at bind time. The CrystalReportsViewer may not be listed in your toolbox.

To add the CrystalReportsViewer to the WPF user control, follow these steps:

1. Right-click a white area of the WPF Control area in the toolbox and select Choose Items.

2. On the WPF Components tab, scroll down and select the checkbox next to the CrystalReportsViewer item.

3. Click OK. The CrystalReportsViewer will now be listed in the All WPF controls section of the toolbox.

4. Drag the CrystalReportsViewer from the toolbox onto the .xaml window for the WPF user control that you created previously. You might need to resize the CrystalReportsViewer.

5. With the CrystalReportsViewer selected on the .xaml window, open the Properties window.

6. Expand the Other category of the Properties window, as shown in Figure 11.32, and then click the checkbox next to the ShowOpenFileButton property, as shown in Figure 11.33. The Open File button will be enabled.

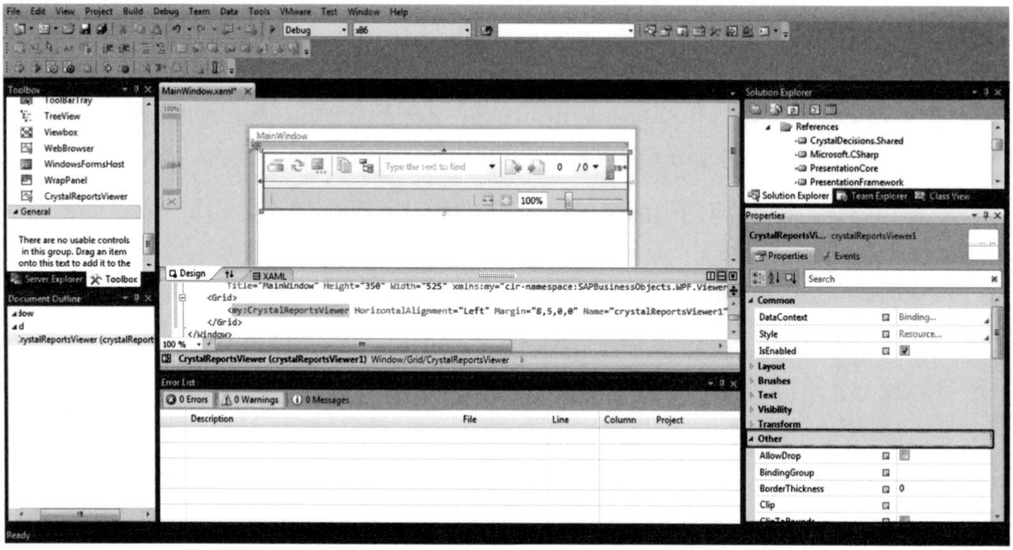

Figure 11.32
Expanding the Other property category.

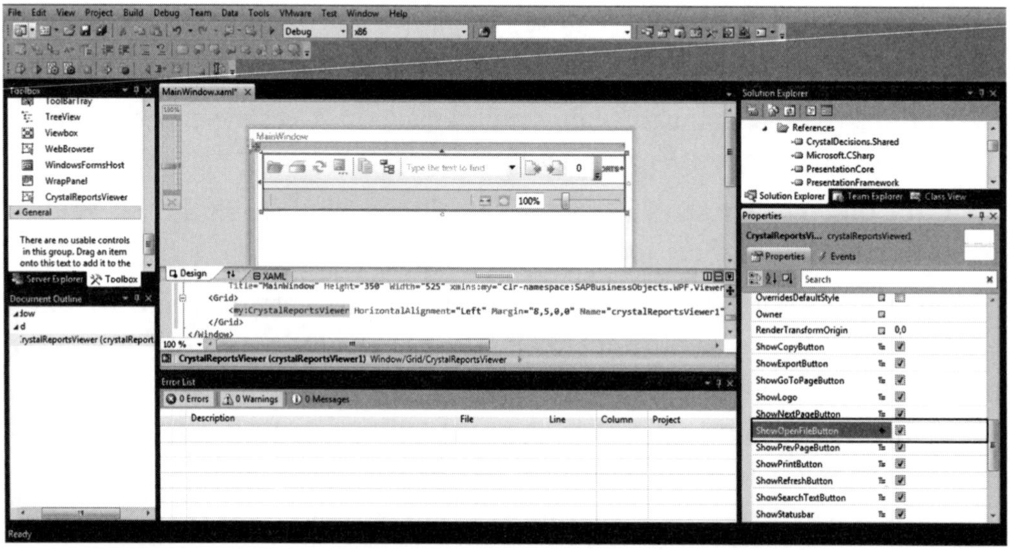

Figure 11.33
Selecting the ShowOpenFileButton property.

7. From the Debug menu, select Debug > Start Debugging option. You can also use F5 to do this. Click the Open File button and select a report, as shown in Figures 11.34 and 11.35. The selected report will open in the CrystalReportsViewer, similar to Figure 11.36.

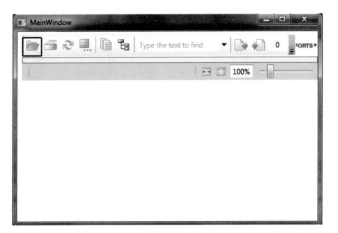

Figure 11.34
Use the Open File button.

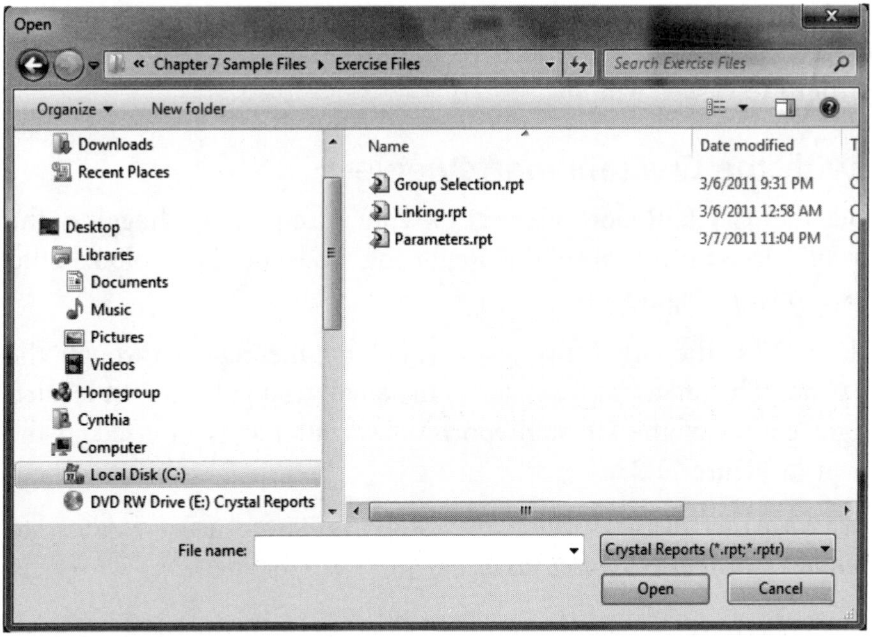

Figure 11.35
Selecting a report.

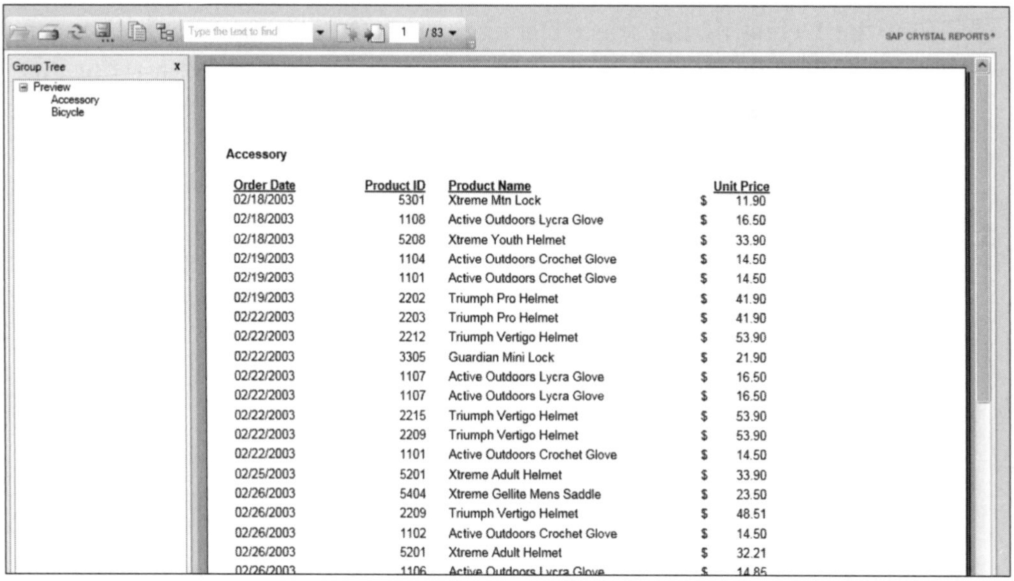

Figure 11.36
Previewing a report from the Open File button.

The user can now view additional reports by just selecting the Open File button at any time from the viewer window.

Working with the CrystalReportsViewer

You can add the CrystalReportsViewer to your project by dragging the CrystalReportsViewer control from the Reporting node of the toolbox onto your form, as shown in Figure 11.37.

In the standard CrystalReportsViewer, you can bind the report through the Smart Tasks panel. The Smart Tasks panel is the small triangular object located in the top-right corner of the CrystalReportsViewer after it is inserted in the form, as shown in Figure 11.38.

The Smart Tasks panel displays the CrystalReportsViewer tasks window to enable you to perform the following tasks:

■ **Create a new report** — You can create a new report from within Visual Studio using the embedded Report Designer. See Figure 11.39.

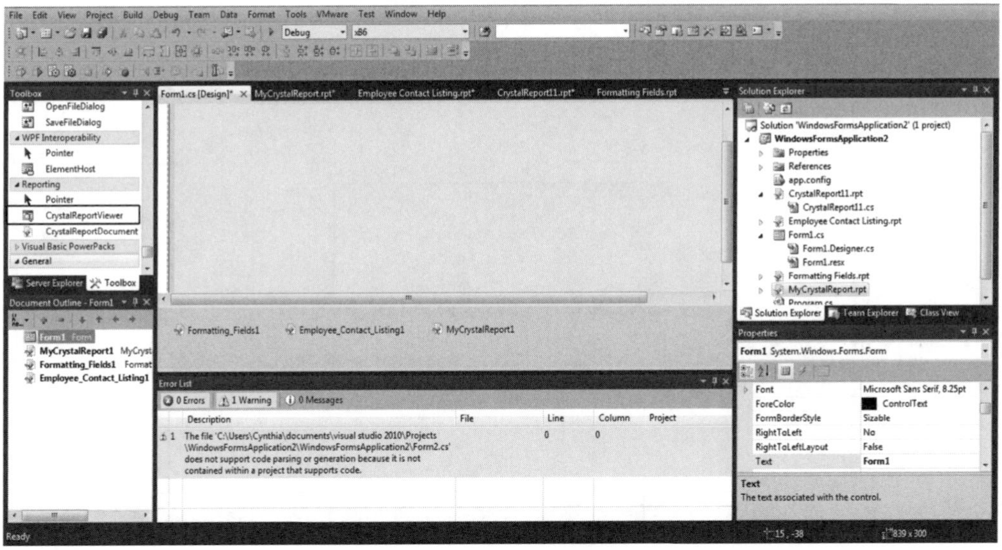

Figure 11.37
Standard CrystalReportsViewer.

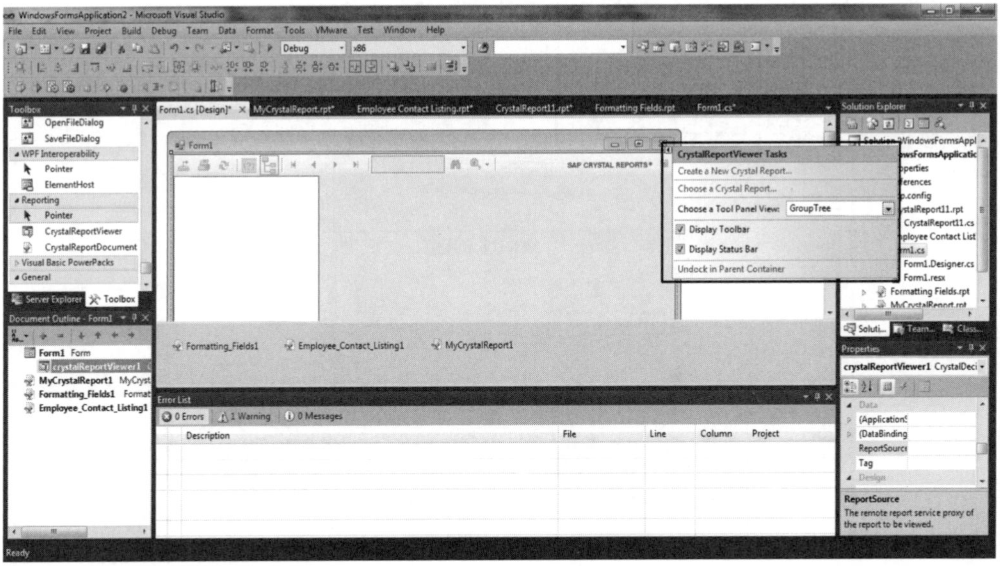

Figure 11.38
Launching the Smart Tasks panel.

Figure 11.39
Creating a new report from the Smart Tasks panel.

■ **Select a report** — You can select an existing report and integrate it into the project. You have the option to add the report to the project or reference it as an external report, as shown in Figure 11.40.

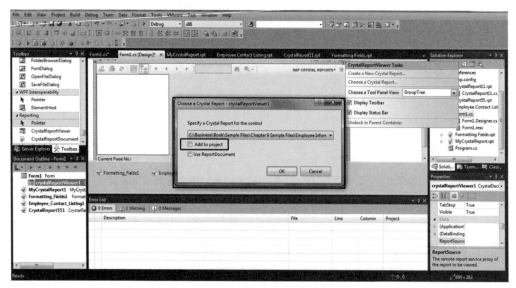

Figure 11.40
Integrating an existing report.

- **Choose a Tool Panel view** — You can specify which panel view will be the active panel when the report is viewed. The options are Group Tree panel, Parameters panel, or None.

- **Display toolbar** — You can specify whether the CrystalReportsViewer toolbar will be visible when the report is previewed.

- **Display status bar** — You can specify whether the status bar will be displayed at the bottom of the report viewer window.

- **Undock in parent container** — Undocks the CrystalReportsViewer from the size of the form that the viewer was inserted into. The viewer is docked by default.

You can programmatically bind the report through code (rather than using the Smart Tasks panel), which gives you better control over how the viewer and report are displayed. To program the code, follow these steps:

1. Right-click the Form and choose View Code or access the code from View > Code.

2. Set the `ReportSource` property to the file location of the report.

   Example: Visual C
   ```
   #CrystalReportsViewer.ReportSource = "C:\\Sample\\MyReport";
   ```

   Example: VB.Net
   ```
   CrystalReportsViewer.ViewerCore.ReportSource = "C:\Sample\MyReport"
   ```

CREATING A REPORT

You can create a report in Visual Studio using the Crystal Reports Designer for Visual Studio or you can create the report in the standalone version of Crystal Reports. The designer for Visual Studio does not have all of the functionalities of the full version. However, it still remains a powerful tool.

From the Solution Explorer, follow these steps:

1. Right-click the project-name and choose Add > New Item as shown in Figure 11.41.

2. Locate the Reporting node of the Installed Templates and select Crystal Reports.

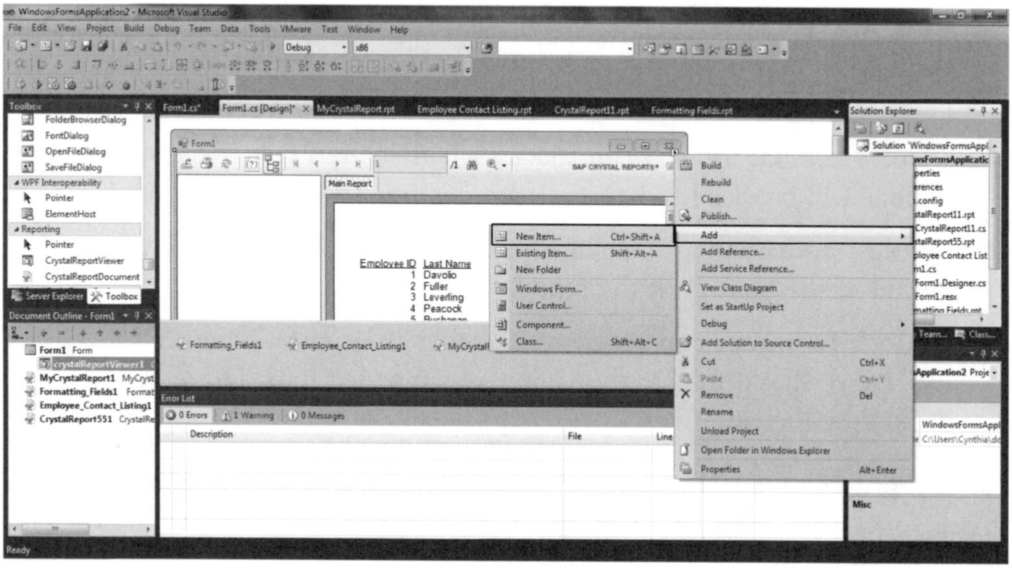

Figure 11.41
Inserting a new item.

3. Enter a name for the report, as shown in Figure 11.42.

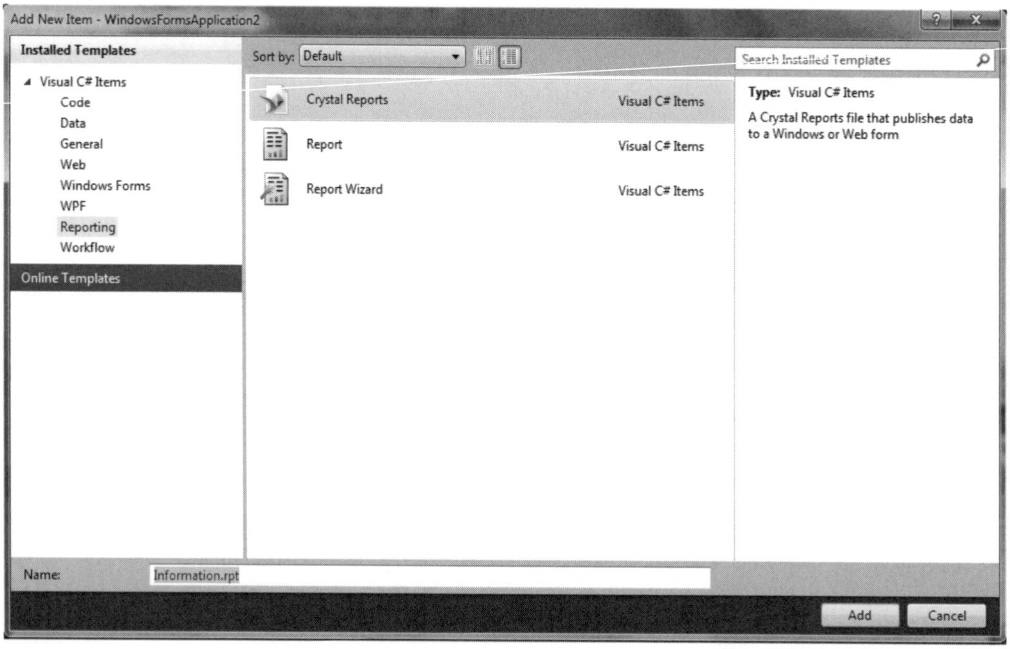

Figure 11.42
Creating a Crystal Report.

4. Click Add.

5. You can create the report using the Report Wizard, as a blank report, or from an existing report. For the book's purpose, select the blank report. See Figure 11.43.

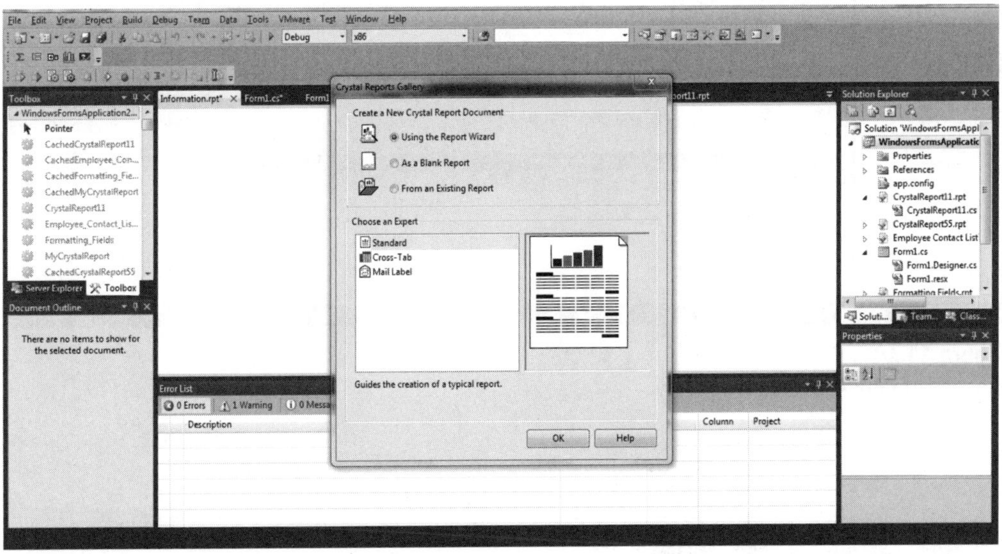

Figure 11.43
Report creation options.

6. Click OK. The Report Designer window opens, as shown in Figure 11.44.

7. Connect to a data source by accessing the Database Expert from the Crystal Reports > Database Expert menu or by selecting the icon from the toolbar as shown in Figure 11.45.

   As mentioned, the embedded designer in Visual Studio does not have all of the functionalities of the standalone version.

8. Design the report using the normal design procedures.

WORKING WITH PARAMETERS

You can use parameters to set the value of a field at runtime or to format fields based on the value of the parameter. Parameters can also be passed into the

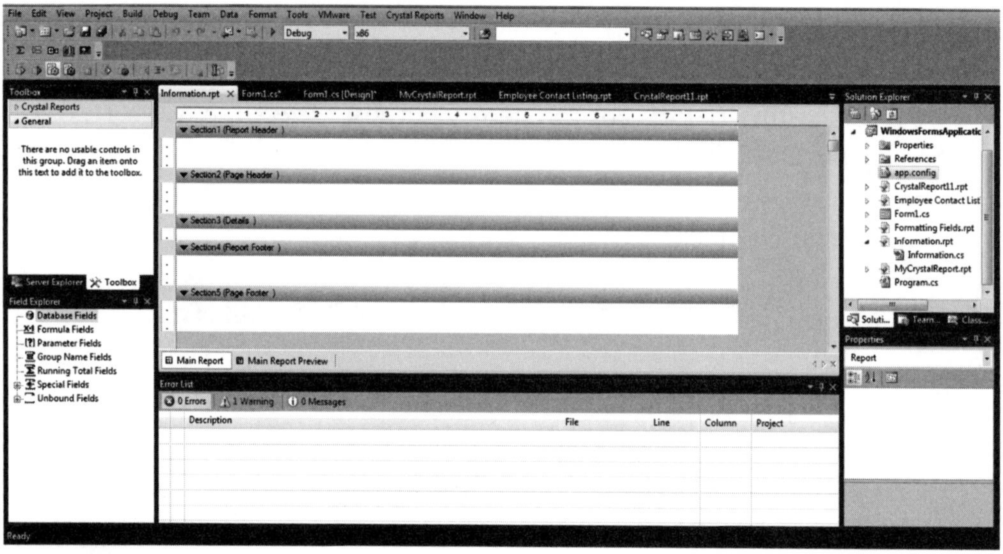

Figure 11.44
Embedded Report Designer window.

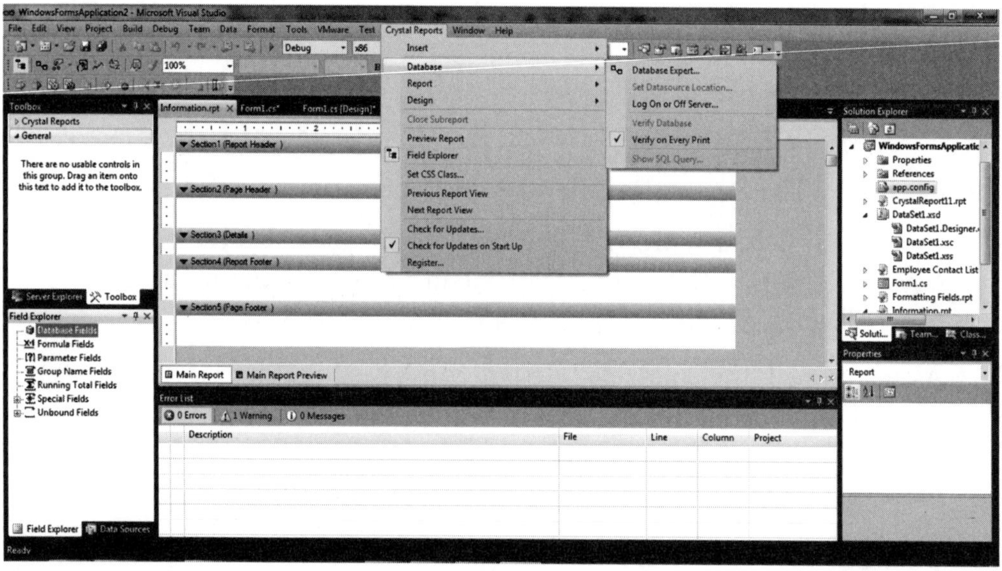

Figure 11.45
Crystal Reports toolbar.

main report and the subreport. Parameters are programmatically set using the `ParameterField` class. When you are working with parameters in a .Net application, you should follow some of the same guidelines when creating a parameter in the full version of Crystal Reports 2011. Table 11.5 shows the `ParameterField` class properties.

Table 11.5 ParameterField Class Properties

Property	Description
AllowCustomValues	Determines whether the default values can be edited.
CurrentValues	Gets or sets the current values.
DefaultValueDisplayType	Gets or sets the default value display type of the parameter field.
DefaultValues	Gets or sets the default values through the ParameterValues collection.
DefaultValueSortMethod	Sets the method in which the default values are sorted.
DefaultValueSortOrder	Specifies the order in which the default values are sorted.
DiscreteOrRangeKind	Determines whether the parameter field contains discrete or range values or both.
EditMask	Gets or sets an edit mask that restricts what can be entered for string parameters.
EnableAllowEditingDefaultValues	Gets or sets the option to allow editing of default values.
EnableAllowMultipleValue	Gets or sets the option to allow multiple values in the parameter.
EnableNullValue	Gets or sets the "allow null value" option for stored procedure parameters.
HasCurrentValue	Determines whether the parameter has a current value.
MaximumValue	Gets or sets the maximum value.
Minimum Value	Gets or sets the minimum value.
Name	Gets or sets the name of the parameter field.
ParameterFieldName	Gets or sets the name of the parameter field.
ParameterType	Gets or sets the type of the parameter value.
ParameterValueKind	Gets the type of the parameter value.
ParameterValueType	Gets or sets the type of the parameter.
PromptingType	Determines whether the parameter field contains discrete values, range values, or both.
PromptText	Gets or sets the parameter field prompting string.
ReportName	Gets or sets the report name the parameter field is in. No name will be returned if it is the main report.
ReportParameterType	Gets or sets the type of the parameter.

You should:

- Ensure the parameter value is the same datatype as the parameter.

- Ensure the upper bound value is higher than the lower bound.

- Set the bound type on a range value before adding it to the parameter.

- Identify whether the parameter is discrete or ranged.

The Parameters panel and Print button are displayed by default in the viewer toolbar, as shown in Figure 11.46. To programmatically set the Parameters Panel property and hide the Print button, you would use the code similar to what is shown in Figure 11.47. The Parameters Panel and Print button will be hidden, as shown in Figure 11.48.

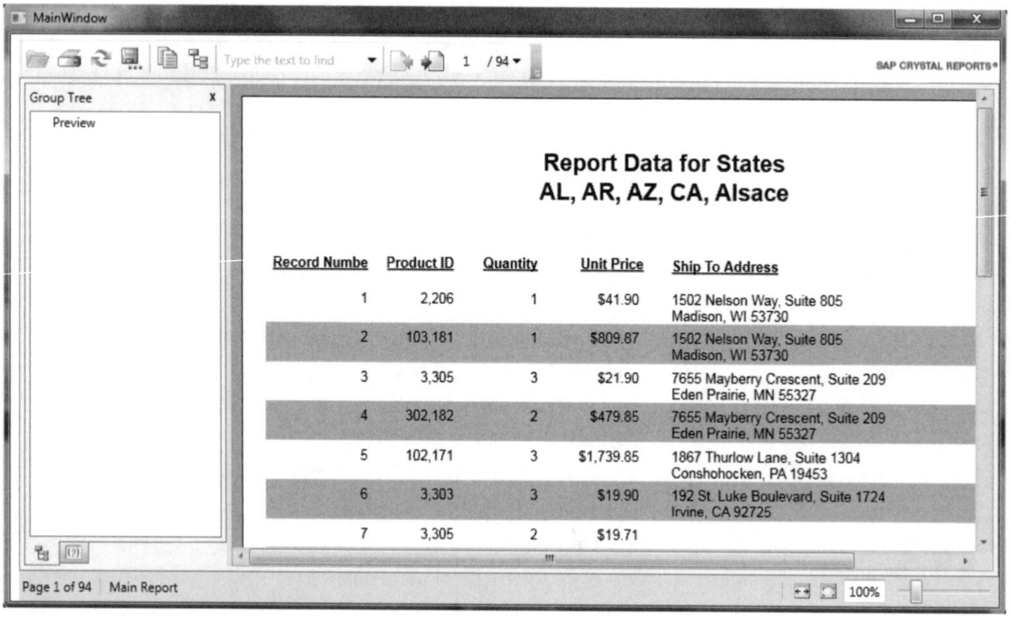

Figure 11.46
Parameter side panel.

Using the methods and properties of the `ParameterField` class will give you extensive control over the display and execution of the parameter.

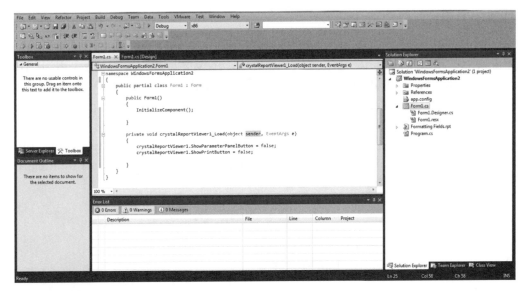

Figure 11.47
Report in standard viewer.

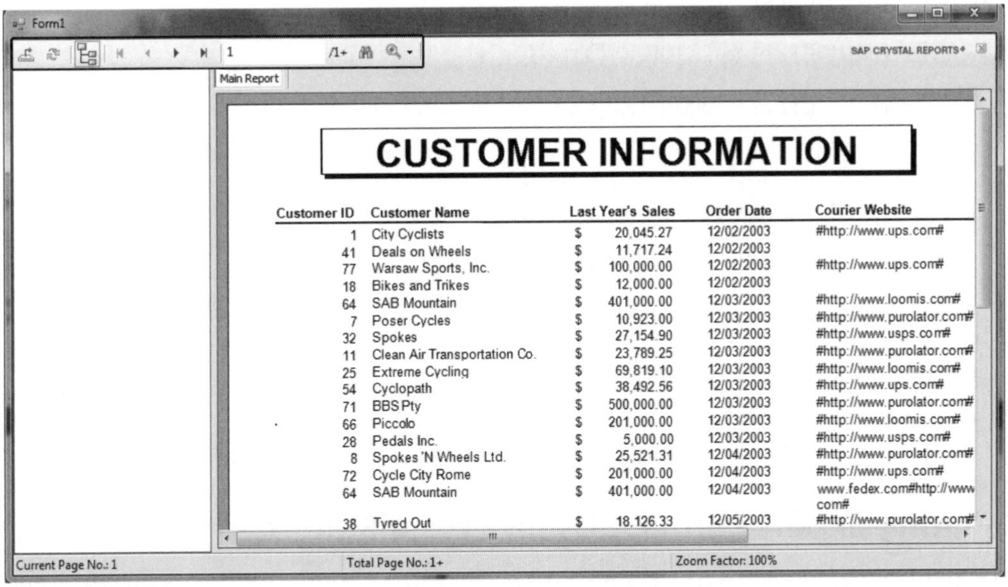

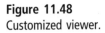

Figure 11.48
Customized viewer.

Exporting a Report

Often you want to give your users the ability to export the report in formats other than the Crystal Reports format. Each viewer allows a minimum of 10 export format types, but there are many export formats that are only available in certain viewers. The standard CrystalReportsViewer has the best export options. As a developer, you can limit the formats that are available in the application. For example, you might want the users to be able to export in Excel or text file formats only, which are two common formats, and you can programmatically impose those limitations.

Crystal Reports for Visual Studio export format types are:

- Crystal Reports (RPT)
- Crystal Reports Read-Only (RPTR)
- PDF
- Rich Text Format (RTF)
- Microsoft Word (97-2003)
- Microsoft Excel (97-2003)
- Microsoft Excel (97-2003) Data-Only
- Microsoft Excel (2007) Data-Only
- HTML 4.0
- Separated Values (CSV)
- Microsoft Word – Editable (RTF)
- Tab Separated Text (TTX)
- Text
- XML

Limiting Export Formats Using CrystalReportsViewer

As mentioned, CrystalReportsViewer has the most export options. You can limit the export options programmatically in a Windows application by adding the following namespace:

Example: Visual C#

```
Using CrystalDecisions.Windows.Forms
```

The namespace opens the properties to specify the available formats. For example, you have a report that you want to export to a PDF or Excel format only. To accomplish this task, you would write code similar to the following:

```
private void MyAllowedExportFormats()
        {
            int exportFormats =
(int)(CrystalDecisions.Shared.ViewerExportFormats.ExcelRecordFormat |
CrystalDecisions.Shared.ViewerExportFormats.PdfFormat |
CrystalDecisions.Shared.ViewerExportFormats.RptFormat);
            crystalReportsViewer1.AllowedExportFormats = exportFormats;
        }
```

This code uses the `CrystalReportsViewer` class.

Using the `ReportDocument` class allows you to expand on the Export options and specify the parameters and capabilities accessible to the users in the application. For example, you might limit the formats users can export and include the date or other custom text in the filename of the file to be exported. You can specify all of these options using the `ReportDocument.Export` methods in the `ExportOptions` class.

The `ExportOptions` class properties include those listed in Table 11.6.

Table 11.6 Customizing the Export Options

Property	Description
ExportDestinationType	Determines how to export the report, such as to a disk file, exchange folder, Microsoft Mail, or no destination.
ExportDestinationOptions	Sets the location and name of the file. The `ExportDestinationOptions` are going to depend on the `ExportDestinationType` selected.
ExportFormatOptions	Sets output-specific outputting formats.
ExportFormatType	Sets the destination file type.

As mentioned, not all of the export options are available in every viewer. Table 11.7 lists the viewers and the available export formats for each.

Table 11.7 Viewer Export Capabilities

Format	CrystalReports Viewer	SAP Crystal Reports .Net SDK	SAP Crystal Reports Designer
SAP Crystal Reports (RPT)	X	x	x
SAP Crystal Reports Read-Only (RPTR)	X	x	x
HTML 4.0		x	x
Microsoft Excel (97-2003)	X	x	x
Microsoft Excel (97-2003) Data Only	X	x	x
Microsoft Excel 2007 (XLSX) Data Only	X	x	x
Microsoft Word (97-2003)	X	x	x
Microsoft Word (97-2003) - Editable	X	x	x
ODBC		x	x
PDF	X	x	x
Record Style – Column with Spaces			x
Record Style – Columns without Spaces			x
Report Definition			x
Rich Text Format (RTF)	X	x	x
Separated Values (CSV)		x	x
Tab Separated Text (TTX)		x	x
Text		x	x
XML	X	x	x

Setting the export options programmatically requires you to use the following namespace:

Example: Visual C#:

```
using CrystalDecisions.CrystalReports.Engine;
using CrystalDecisions.Shared;
```

To limit the export formats you would use code similar to this:

```
Private void MyAllowedExportFormats (string AllowedExport)
```

```
{
ExportOptions AllowedExport = new ExportOptions();
AllowedExport.ExportFormatType = ExportFormatType.ExcelRecords;
}
```

The methods and properties available give the developers a tremendous amount of control over the application. I encourage you to spend more time becoming familiar with them.

Summary

Integrating Crystal Reports into your Visual Studio application can be a powerful step. Understanding the limitations of each available viewer and the business requirements of the users will help you make an educated decision as to which one holds the best functionality for your application. WPF's new graphical enhancements add a flavor to your report with such a smooth transition between pages. Combining the new viewer enhancements with the ability to export to the new read-only (RPTR) format and the Excel 2007 (XLSX) format will improve your users' experience.

CHAPTER 12

INTRODUCTION TO CRYSTAL REPORTS FOR ECLIPSE

The objectives of this chapter are as follows:

- Getting to know the new SDKs
- Creating a new Java application
- Embedding Crystal Reports
- Working with the Crystal Reports for Eclipse interface

Crystal Reports for Eclipse has been developed to integrate Crystal Reports functionality into Eclipse applications using Java runtime function libraries. Crystal Reports for Eclipse adds the following features to Eclipse:

- Embedded Report Designer.
- Crystal reports viewers for viewing reports in Java applications and over the web.
- Use of the SDKs to programmatically modify reports.
- Project wizards, views, and perspectives for reporting.
- Sample reports, sample database connections, and helper code.

This chapter is intended to give you a brief introduction into using Crystal Reports for Eclipse and not intended to teach you how to develop in Eclipse. It is based on Crystal Reports for Eclipse 3.06.

New Features of Eclipse

Eclipse has several integration enhancements, including a new Crystal Reports Java project wizard. The Crystal Reports project wizard automatically creates a connection to the sample database.

Eclipse also has new extension points that allow you to customize the Crystal Reports designer, such as:

- Creating custom report wizards.

- Adding pages to the Crystal Reports designer.

- Providing a custom data source to a report.

- Opening and saving reports from a custom location.

- Customizing drag-and-drop functionality.

Eclipse also has several viewer enhancements. It provides an enhanced DHTML viewer for web-based application. The DHTML viewer supports rendering the new Crystal Reports 2008 features such as interactive sorting, Flash integration, Calculated Crosstab Members, Optional parameters, Interactive parameters, and the Parameters panel.

Other enhancements include:

- The SDK encompasses access to most report objects that are available in the Crystal Reports Designer.

- Support for Excel (data only) export format and an improved PDF export format.

- Improved support for Plain Old Java Objects (POJO) data sources and for building reports based on custom SQL (using Eclipse SQL files).

- Dynamic image location: you can define the location of a dynamic image using a conditional formula.

New SDKs in Crystal Reports for Eclipse

There are several new SDKs included with this version of Crystal Reports for Eclipse. It continues to support SDKs from previous versions.

Crystal Reports Java SDK (12.0)

The Crystal Reports Java SDK (12.0) is the latest SDK included for report modification. This SDK contains APIs for modifying Crystal Reports. This is the recommended version of the Crystal Reports Java SDK (12.0).

The Crystal Reports Java SDK (12.0) includes the following packages:

```
com.crystaldecisions.sdk.occa.report.application
com.crystaldecisions.sdk.occa.report.data
com.crystaldecisions.sdk.occa.report.definition
com.crystaldecisions.sdk.occa.report.document
com.crystaldecisions.sdk.occa.report.exportoptions.
com.crystaldecisions.sdk.occa.report.lib
```

This SDK allows you to programmatically create, view, and modify Crystal Reports files.

Viewers.Java.SDK (12.0)

The Viewers Java SDK (12.0) contains APIs for the viewers and includes the following packages:

```
com.crystaldecisions.report.web
com.crystaldecisions.report.web.jsf
com.crystaldecisions.report.web.viewer
com.crystaldecisions.ReportViewer
com.crystaldecisions.sdk.occa.report.partdefinition
```

These properties allow you to customize actions such as displaying buttons, group trees, pages, or toolbars. It also supports event handling, exporting, printing, displaying multiple viewers in the same page, and handling database and parameter information.

Crystal Reports Designer Extension Points SDK (12.0)

The Crystal Reports Designer Extension Points SDK (12.0) contains APIs for enhancing the Crystal Reports designer integration with Eclipse. It includes the following packages:

```
com.businessobjects.crystalreports.designer.sdk
com.businessobjects.crystalreports.designer.sdk.input
com.businessobjects.crystalreports.designer.sdk.util
com.businessobjects.crystalreports.designer.sdk.wizard
```

The Extension Points SDK allows you to extend the Crystal Reports functionality in the following ways:

- Create report wizards that produce customized reports.

- Extend the drag-and-drop functionality to convert custom objects to report objects and add them to a report.

- Add pages to the Report Designer that provide custom views of the report.

- Open reports from a custom location, or save reports to a custom location.

- Populate the report with data from a custom data source.

- Enhanced capabilities for open and close events.

Java Reporting Component SDK (11.8)

The Java Reporting Component SDK (11.8) was included in previous versions and is still supported for legacy systems. However, new applications should include the Crystal Reports Java SDK (12.0). It includes the following packages:

```
com.crystaldecisions.reports.sdk
com.crystaldecisions.reports.reportengineinterface
```

Java Reporting Component SDK (11.5)

The Java Reporting Component SDK (11.5) was also included in previous versions and is still supported for legacy systems. However, new applications should include the Crystal Reports Java SDK (12.0). It includes the following packages:

```
com.crystaldecisions.reports.reportengine.interface
com.crystaldecisions.reports.sdk
com.crystaldecisions.sdk.occa.report.application
com.crystaldecisions.sdk.occa.report.data
com.crystaldecisions.sdk.occa.document
com.crystaldecisions.sdk.occa.exportoptions
com.crystaldecisions.sdk.occa.report.lib
com.crystaldecisions.sdk.occa.report.reportsource
```

The JRC SDK allows the developer to control the process of viewing and exporting reports.

TOURING THE ECLIPSE REPORT DESIGNER WINDOW

The Report Designer window in Eclipse has a number of useful tools for developers. The interface, shown in Figure 12.1, is similar to the Visual Studio application.

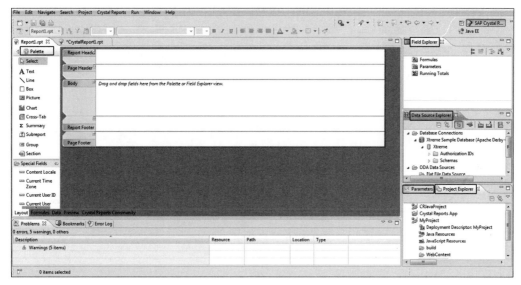

Figure 12.1
The Eclipse User Design window.

The user interface includes the following Explorers and task panes:

- **Field Explorer**—Use the task pane to create formulas, parameters, and running totals. Choose Window > Show View > Field Explorer to access it.

- **Data Source Explorer**—This explorer is used to connect the report to the data source. Choose Window > Show View > Data Source Explorer to access it.

- **Project Explorer**—Lists all Eclipse projects and their contents. Choose Window > Show View > Other > General > Project Explorer to access it.

- **Parameters**—Use this task pane to refresh and modify parameters. Choose Window > Show View > Parameters to access it.

- **Palette**—Contains Crystal Reports objects and special fields to be used in the report. Objects include items such as Text, Lines, Groups, Sections, and Special Fields. Choose Window > Show View > Other > General > Palette to access it.

- **Layout tab**—The Design window is used to create the layout of your report.

- **Formulas tab**—This is used to create formulas, as shown in Figure 12.2.

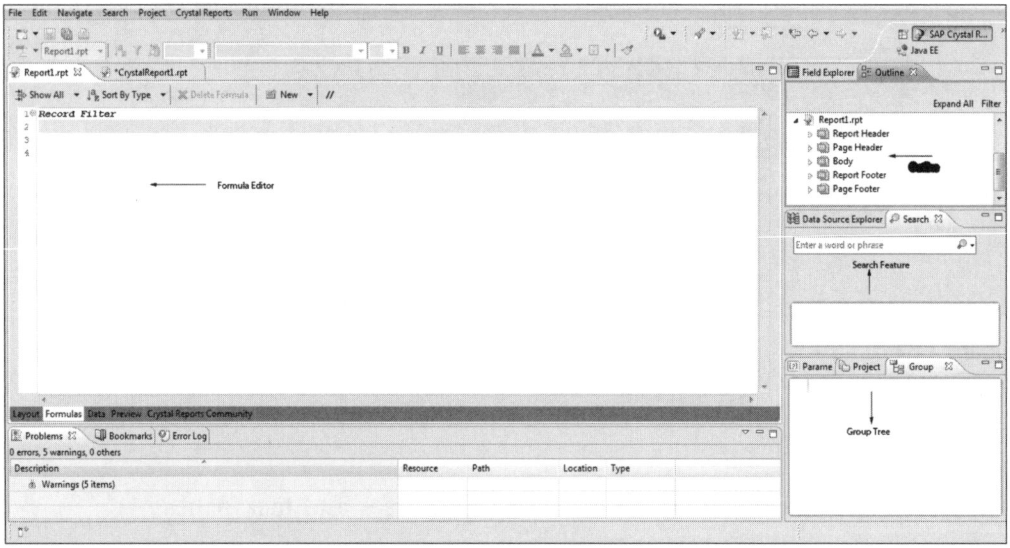

Figure 12.2
Formula Editor window of the user interface.

- **Data tab**—This is used to add tables and joins to the report as the data source, as shown in Figure 12.3.

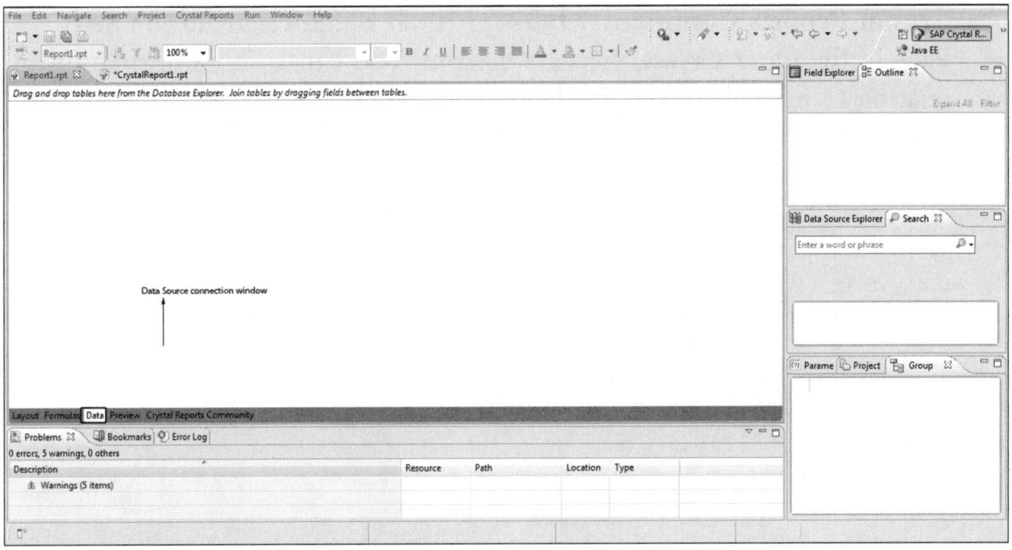

Figure 12.3
Data Connection window of the user interface.

■ **Preview**—This is used to render the data and display how the report will look. You can edit the report from this view as shown in Figure 12.4.

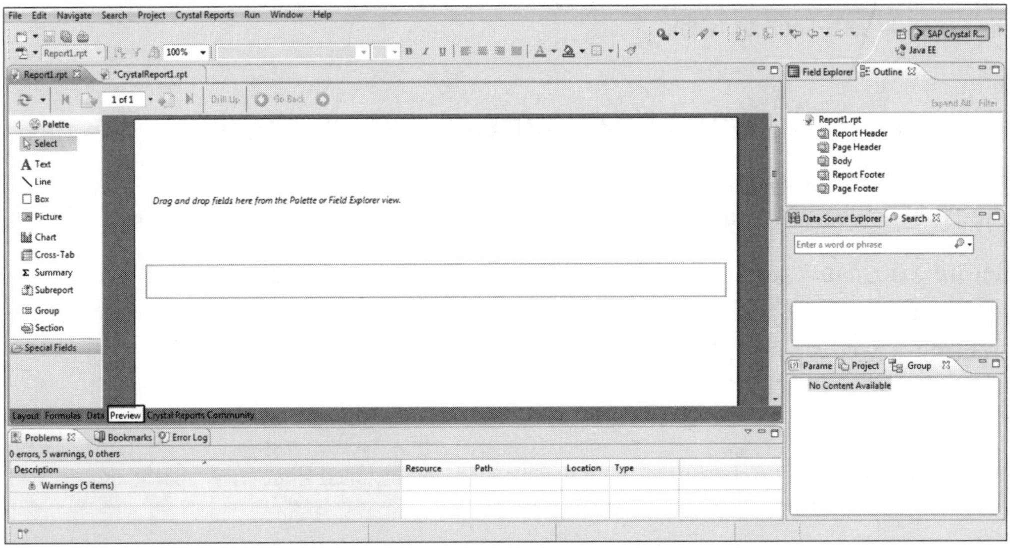

Figure 12.4
Preview mode of the user interface.

■ **Crystal Reports Community tab**—This tab is equivalent to the Start Page in the other Crystal Reports version. You can access information relating to upgrades, downloadable tools, patches, and support from this tab, as shown in Figure 12.5.

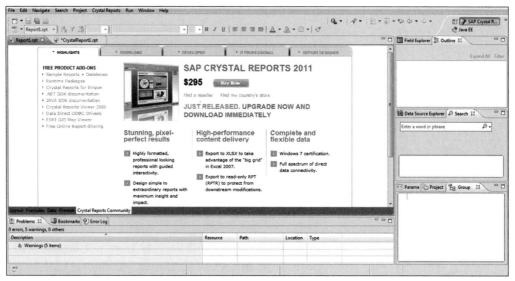

Figure 12.5
The Crystal Reports Community tab.

CREATING A NEW JAVA WEB APPLICATION

Many developers create web applications that are used to distribute reporting needs. This section walks through creating a Crystal Reports web application.

Before you can create a web application, you must install and set up a web server. You must configure the runtime environment and define a server before creating a web project.

Tip

The Apache Tomcat web server can be downloaded and installed from www.apache.org.

Once you have completed the Apache Tomcat setup, you can begin to create the web project.

To create a web application:

1. From the menu, choose File > New > Project, as shown in Figure 12.6.

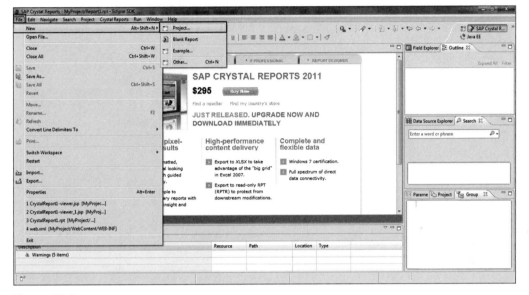

Figure 12.6
Creating a new project.

2. Select the Crystal Reports web project from the Crystal Reports node, as shown in Figure 12.7.

3. Click Next. The Dynamic web settings page appears, as shown in Figure 12.8.

4. Enter the Dynamic web settings:

   Enter a name for the project.

   Change the project location path or select the checkbox to use the default location path.

   Verify the Target runtime refers to the web server created prior to starting this project. The path must point to the directory where the Tomcat server is installed.

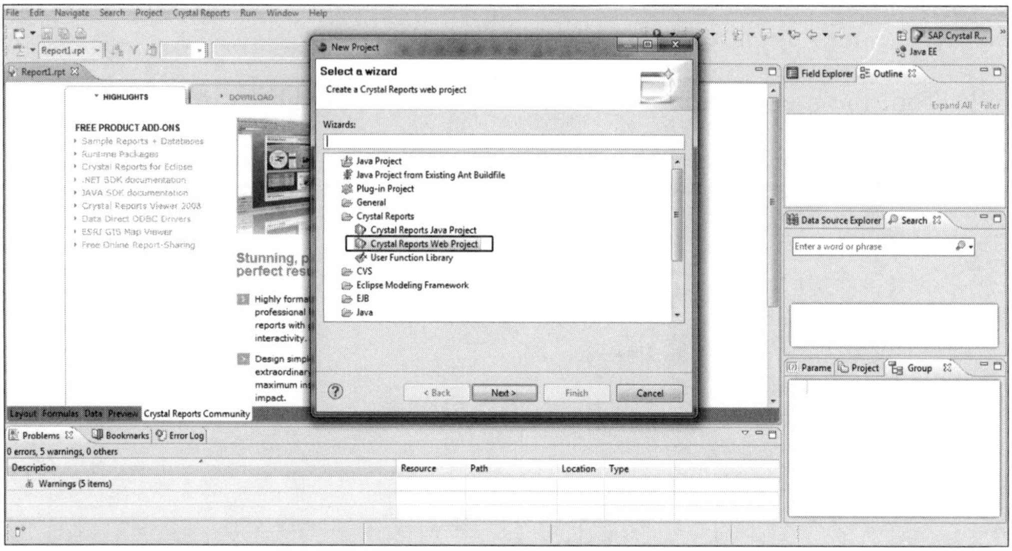

Figure 12.7
Web Project Wizard.

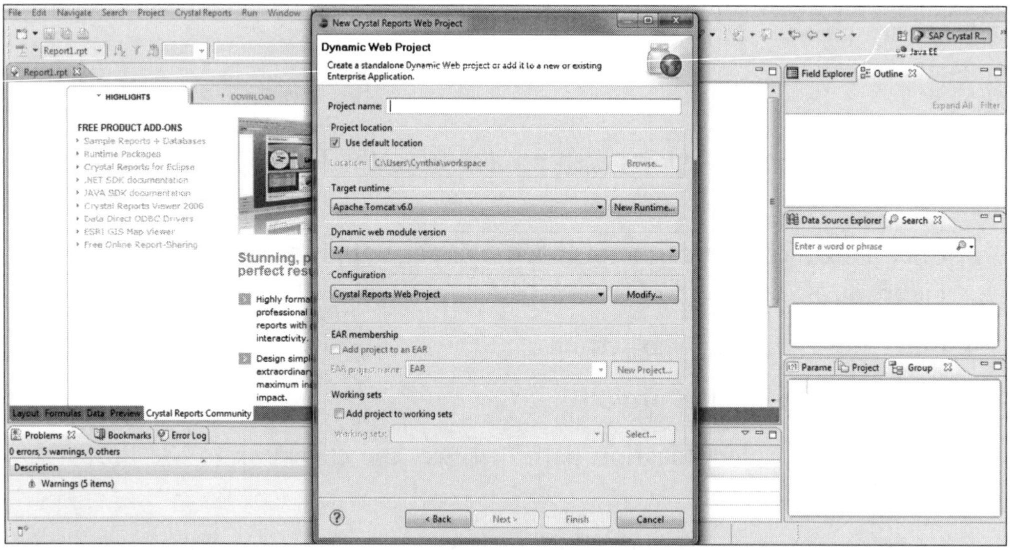

Figure 12.8
Naming the web application.

5. Click Next.

6. Add other Java source folders to the web application or accept the default on the Java settings page as shown in Figure 12.9.

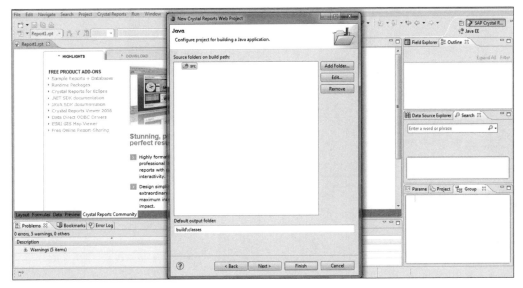

Figure 12.9
Setting the Java folder properties.

7. Click Next.

8. Set any configuration settings for the web module, as shown in Figure 12.10.

9. Click Next.

10. Check or uncheck the options to install sample reports and a new Crystal Report, as shown in Figure 12.11.

11. Click Finish.

12. Click Yes to open the corresponding perspective, as shown in Figure 12.12.

13. Your project should now be visible from the Project Explorer, as shown in Figure 12.13.

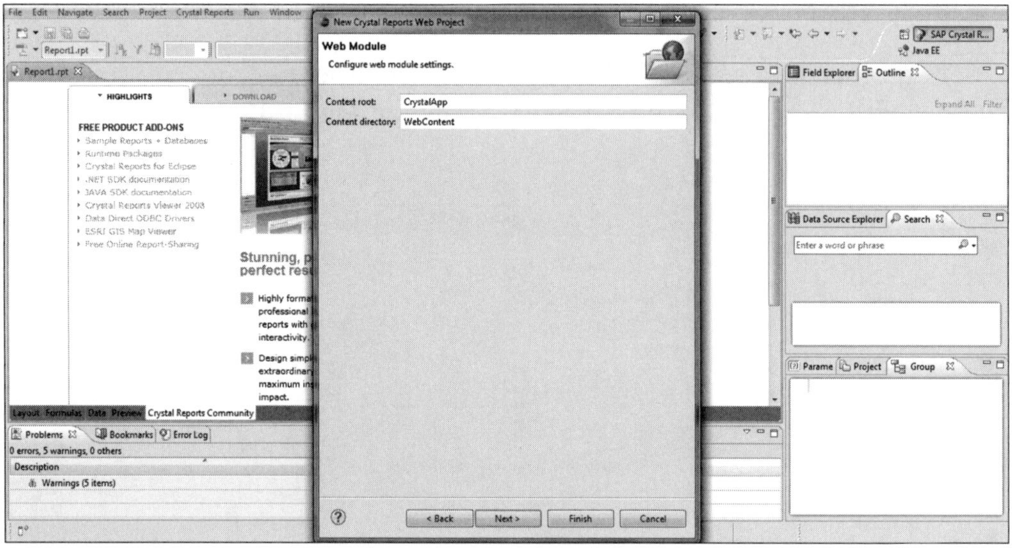

Figure 12.10
Configure Web Module Settings.

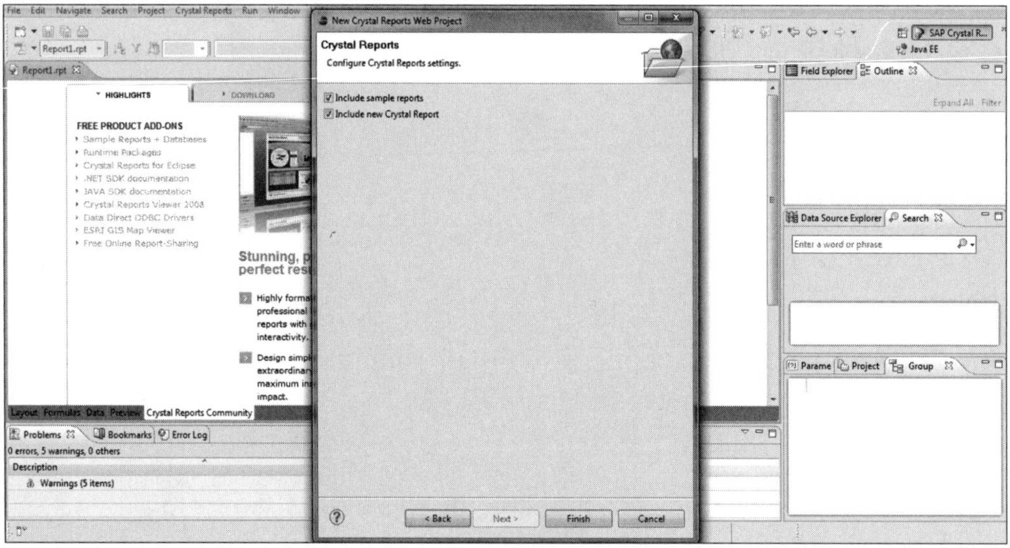

Figure 12.11
Install sample applications and reports.

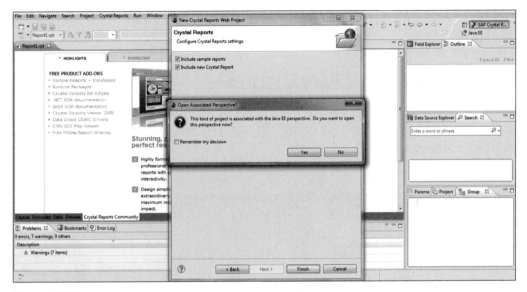

Figure 12.12
Open Perspective.

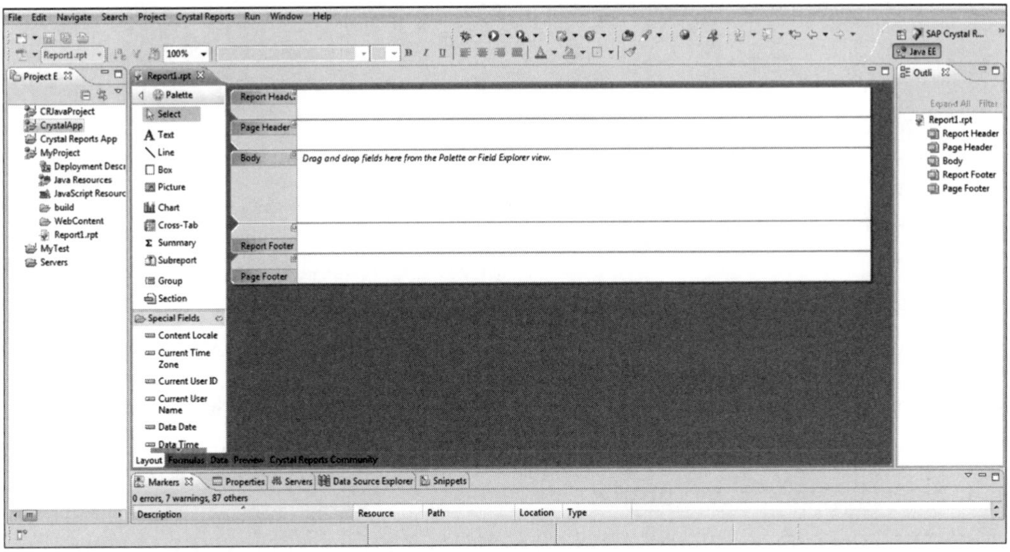

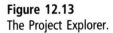

Figure 12.13
The Project Explorer.

The Layout window will be displayed if you chose the option to include a new Crystal Report during the project wizard.

CONNECTING TO A DATA SOURCE

Select the data source to use in your current report. Open the Data Source Explorer if it is not already open by choosing Window > Show View > Data Source Explorer, as shown in Figure 12.14.

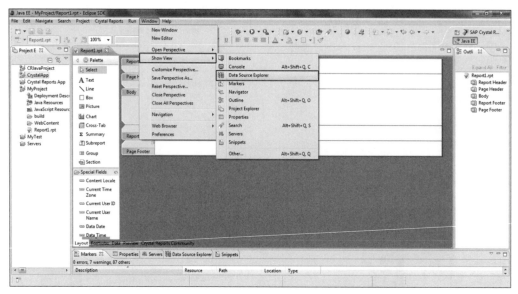

Figure 12.14
Opening the Data Source Explorer.

1. Right-click Data Source connections or one of the ODA Data Sources as shown in Figure 12.15 and select a new or existing data connection.

2. Select the type of data connection profile. For the purpose of this exercise, choose Derby, as shown in Figure 12.16.

3. Enter a name for the profile.

4. Click Next. Depending on the type of data connection profile selected the next options will be different. For the Derby connection profile, the options are as shown in Figure 12.17.

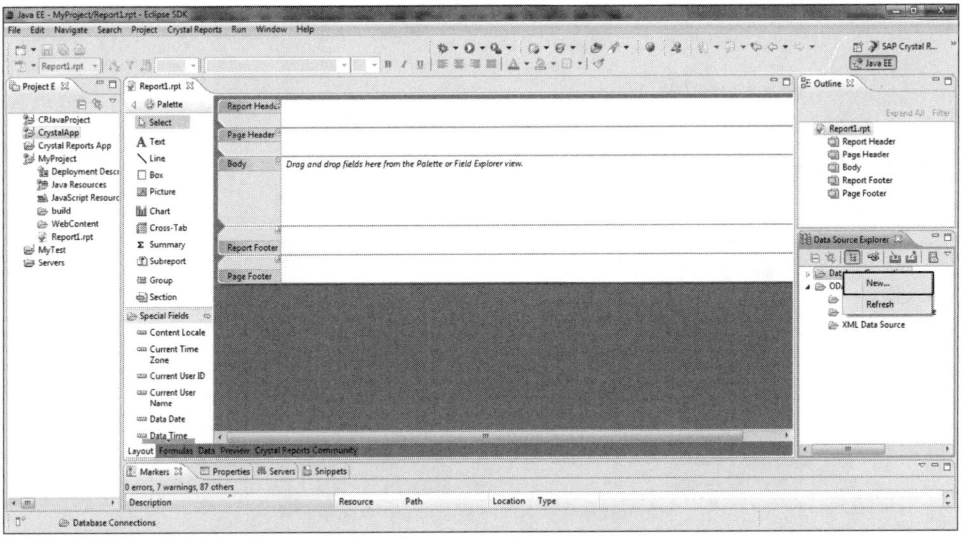

Figure 12.15
Creating a new connection.

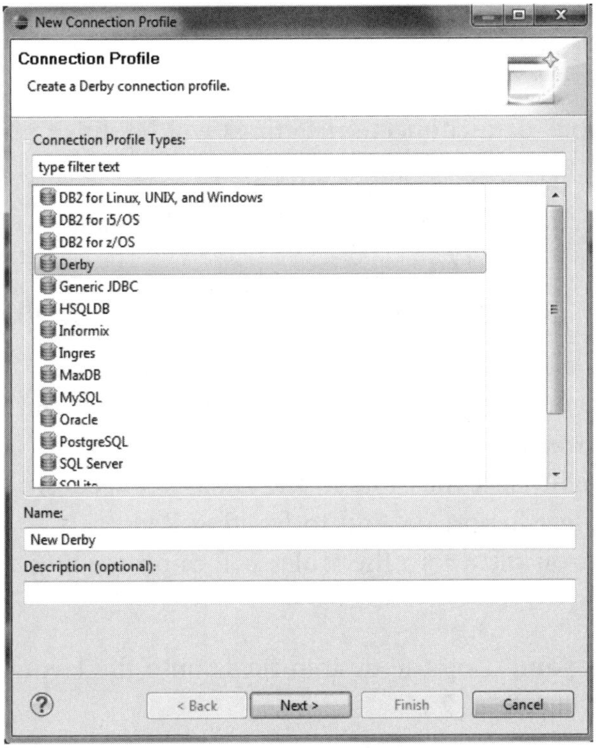

Figure 12.16
Selecting a connection profile.

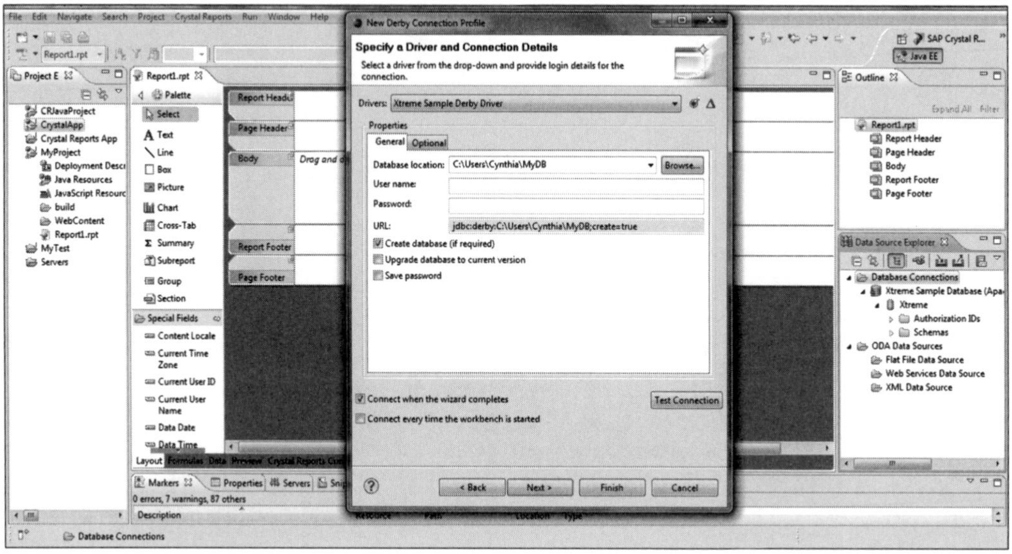

Figure 12.17
Data connection settings.

5. Enter the appropriate settings.

6. Click Next. A summary of your data connection settings will be displayed, as shown in Figure 12.18.

7. Click Finish. The data connection should now be visible in the Data Source Explorer, as shown in Figure 12.19.

8. Select the Data tab from the Interface window, as shown in Figure 12.20.

9. Expand the Connection in the Data Connection Explorer window and locate the appropriate data source, such as views, stored procedures, and tables. Drag the appropriate source to the Data tab area as shown in Figure 12.21. You can also right-click the table in the Data Connection Explorer and select Add to New Report or Add to Existing Report. If you're using multiple tables, you must join the tables before proceeding.

10. Change to the Layout view.

11. From the Field Explorer, drag and drop the desired fields onto the layout design window, as shown in Figure 12.22.

12. Click the Preview tab as shown in Figure 12.23.

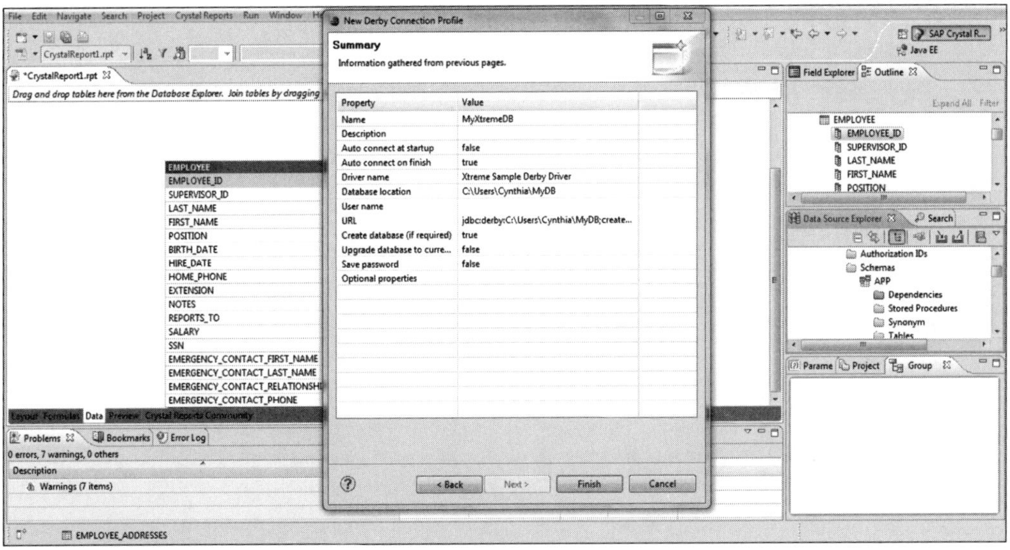

Figure 12.18
Verify your settings.

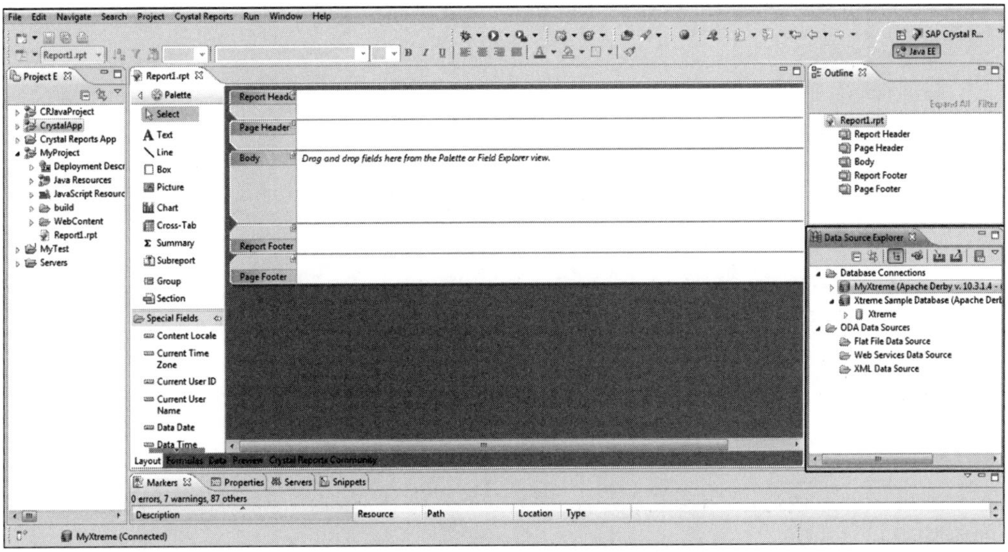

Figure 12.19
New Database connections are shown in the Data Source Explorer.

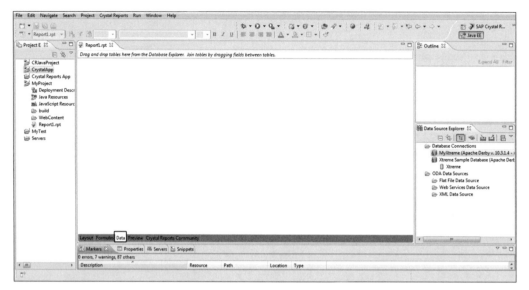

Figure 12.20
Choose the Data tab.

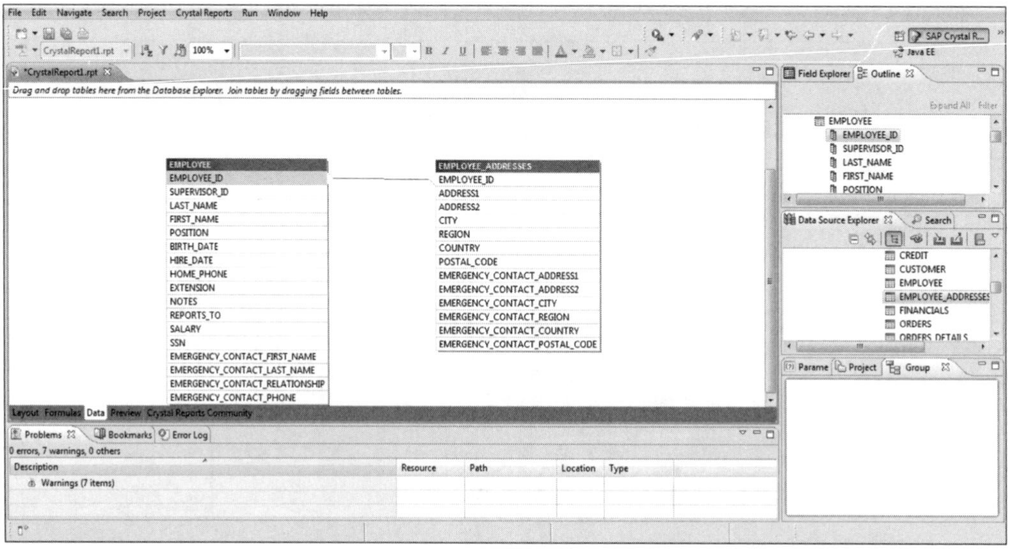

Figure 12.21
Selecting tables.

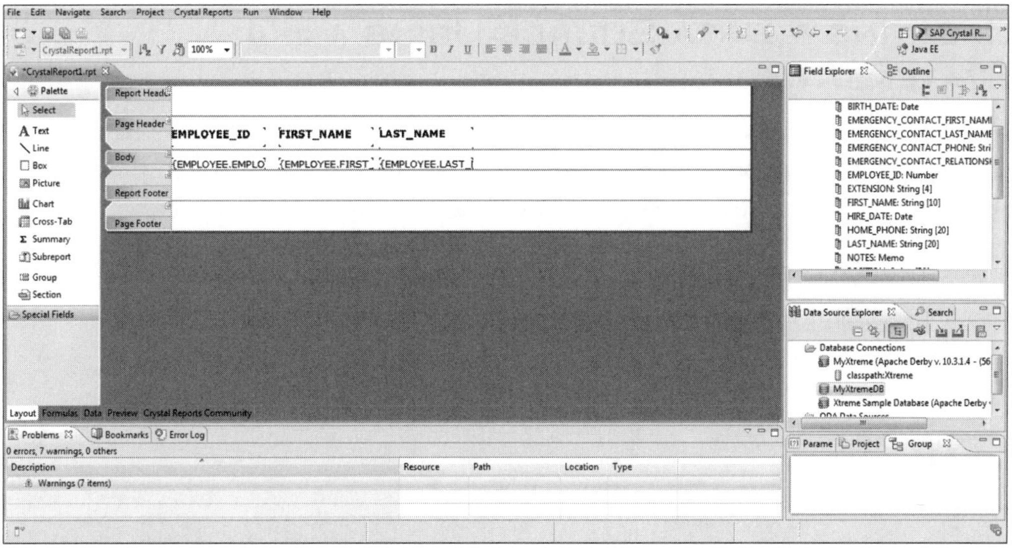

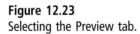

Figure 12.22
Inserting fields on the layout design window.

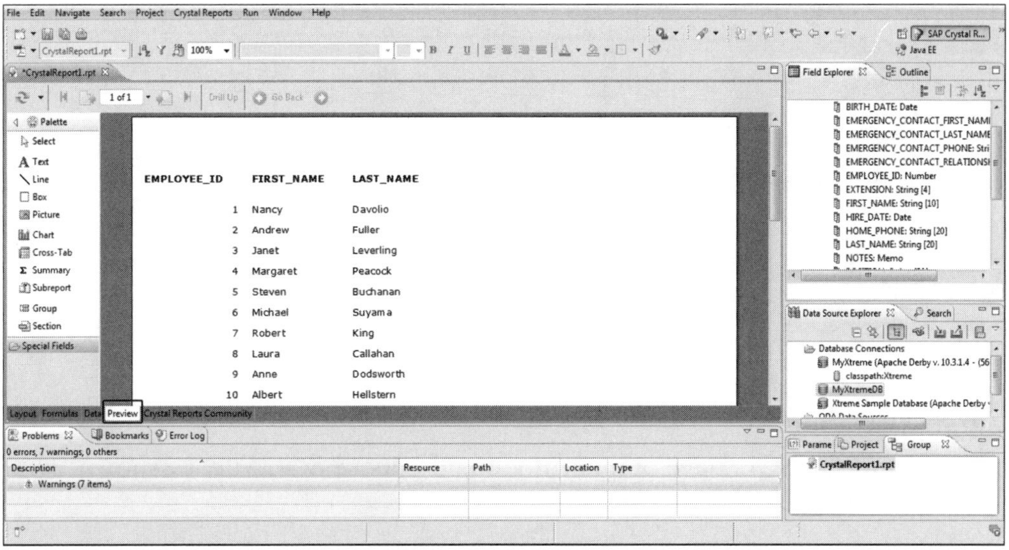

Figure 12.23
Selecting the Preview tab.

CREATING A DATA SOURCE USING A SQL STATEMENT

Using a SQL command is more efficient than dragging and dropping tables onto the Data Explorer. You can create your own SQL command through the use of a SQL file. Use the following steps to create an ad hoc SQL statement.

1. Open the desired project.

2. Choose File > New > Other, as shown in Figure 12.24.

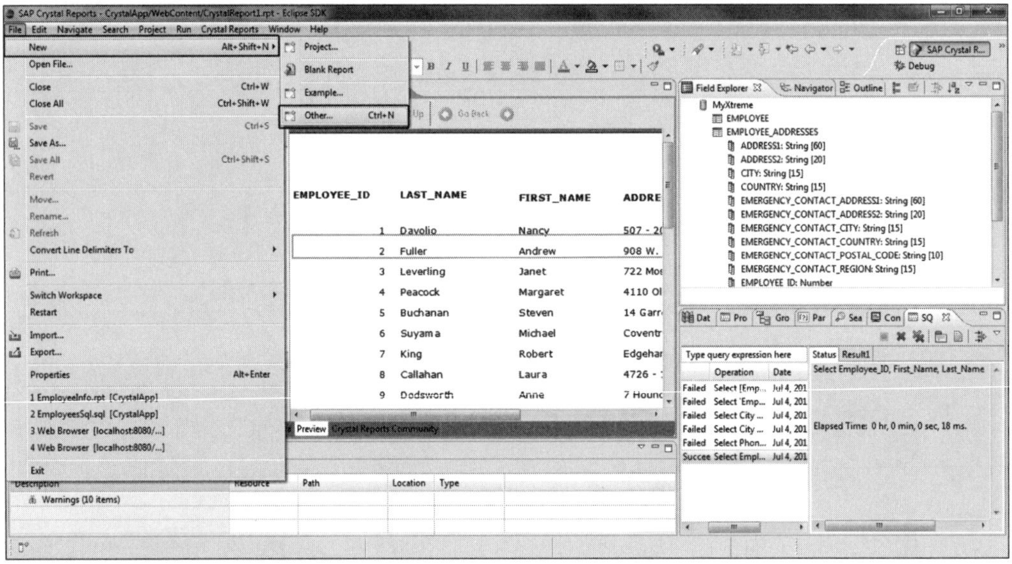

Figure 12.24
Creating a new SQL file.

3. Expand the SQL Development node and choose SQL File, as shown in Figure 12.25.

4. Click Next. The New SQL page opens, as shown in Figure 12.26.

5. Select the project name to which the SQL file should be added or create a new project.

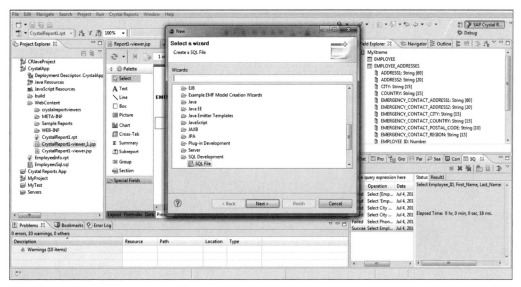

Figure 12.25
Selecting a SQL file.

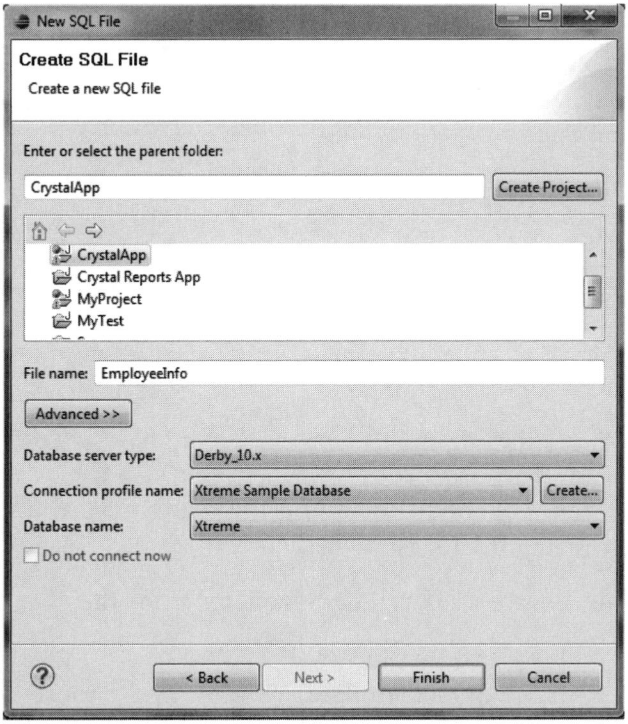

Figure 12.26
Naming the new SQL file.

6. Enter a name for the SQL file.

7. Select the database server type from the drop-down list.

8. Select a connection profile name from the drop-down list.

9. Select a database name based on the connection profile name.

10. Click Finish. The SQL window opens in the project, as shown in Figure 12.27.

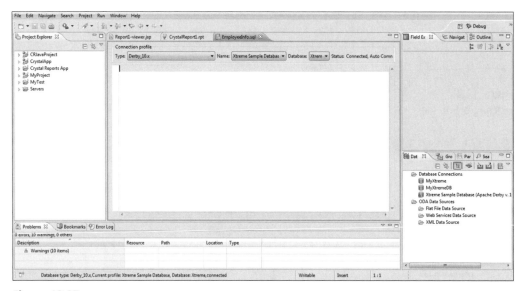

Figure 12.27
The SQL window.

11. Using SQL syntax, create a SQL statement including the fields from the appropriate table, as shown in Figure 12.28.

12. Save the file by selecting File > Save or click the Save icon from the toolbar.

13. To test the query, right-click in the SQL command window and choose Execute All or Execute Text, as shown in Figure 12.29.

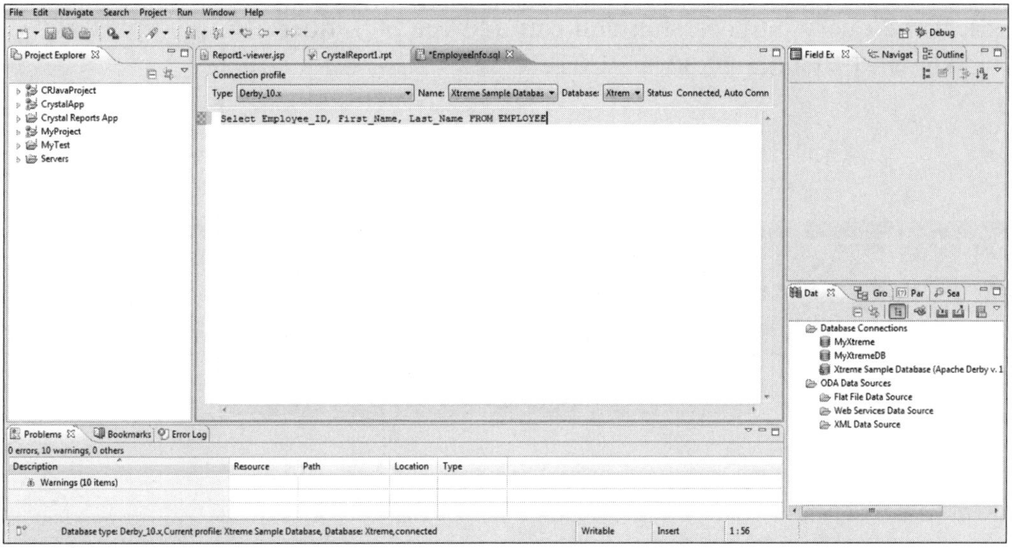

Figure 12.28
Creating a SQL statement.

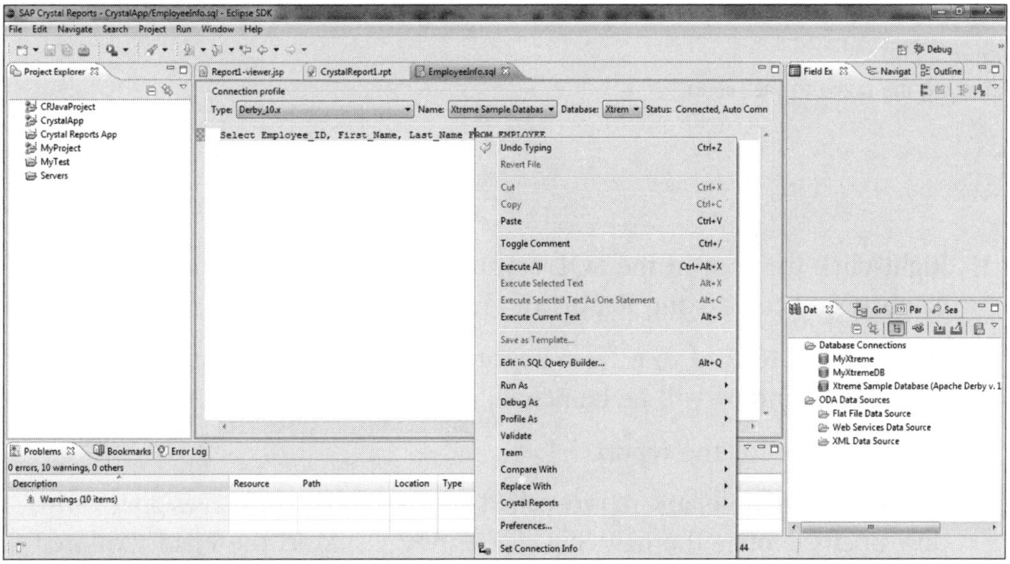

Figure 12.29
Testing the query.

14. If the query is successful, you can add the SQL query to the report as shown in Figure 12.30.

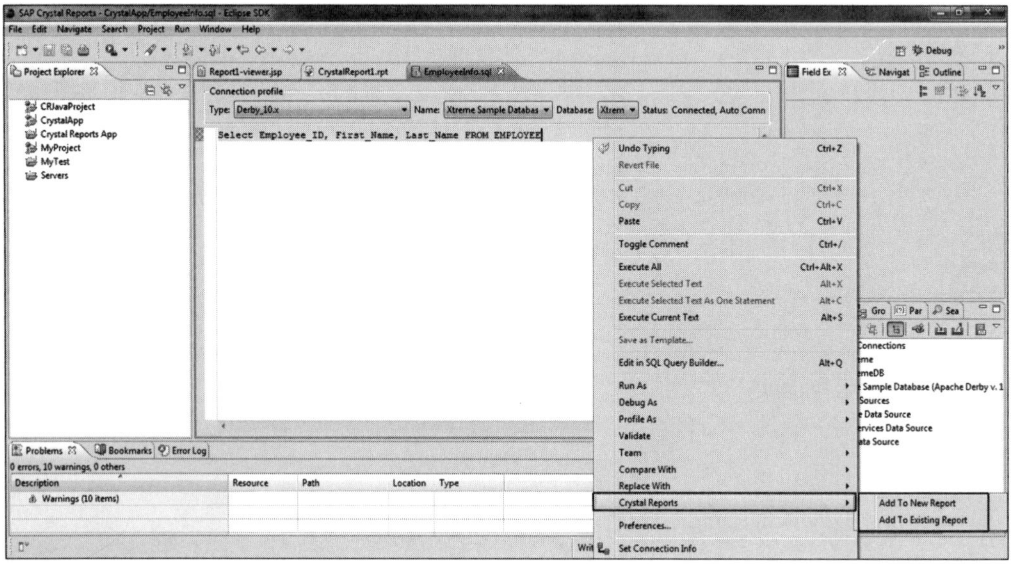

Figure 12.30
Attaching the query to the report.

15. Right-click the area in the SQL command and select Crystal Reports. Choose Add to Existing Report or Add to a New Report.

16. If the option to Add to a New Report is selected, the Create a New Crystal Report window will be launched, as shown in Figure 12.31.

17. Enter a name for the report.

18. Click Finish. The blank report called "embedded Report Designer" window opens. Notice the new SQL file is now listed in the Field Explorer as the data source, as shown in Figure 12.32.

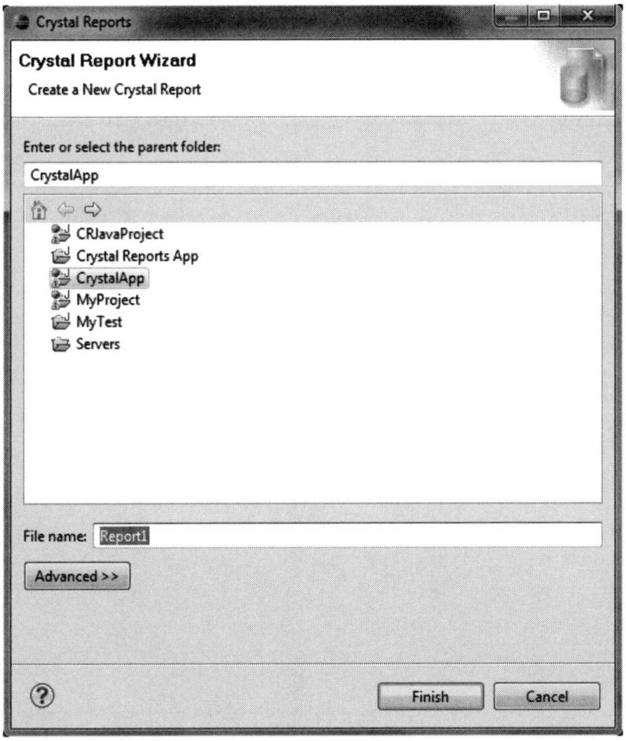

Figure 12.31
Naming the new report.

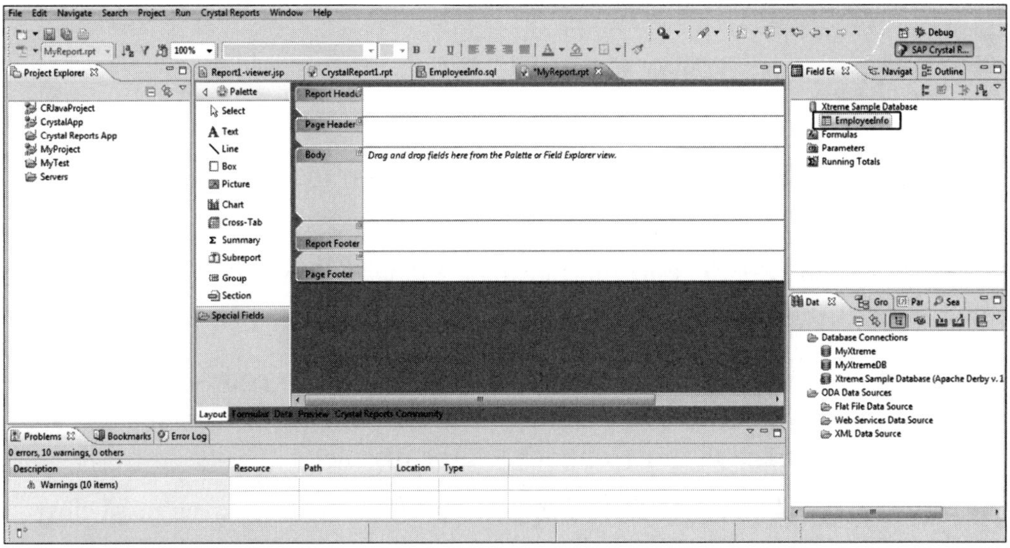

Figure 12.32
The SQL file is added as data source.

CREATING A JSP PAGE

You need a JSP page in order to view your report in the DHTML viewer supplied with Crystal Reports for Eclipse. The JSP page can be created by using the JSP wizard, as specified here:

1. Right-click the report's name in the Project Explorer and select Crystal Reports > Create Report Viewer JSP, as shown in Figure 12.33.

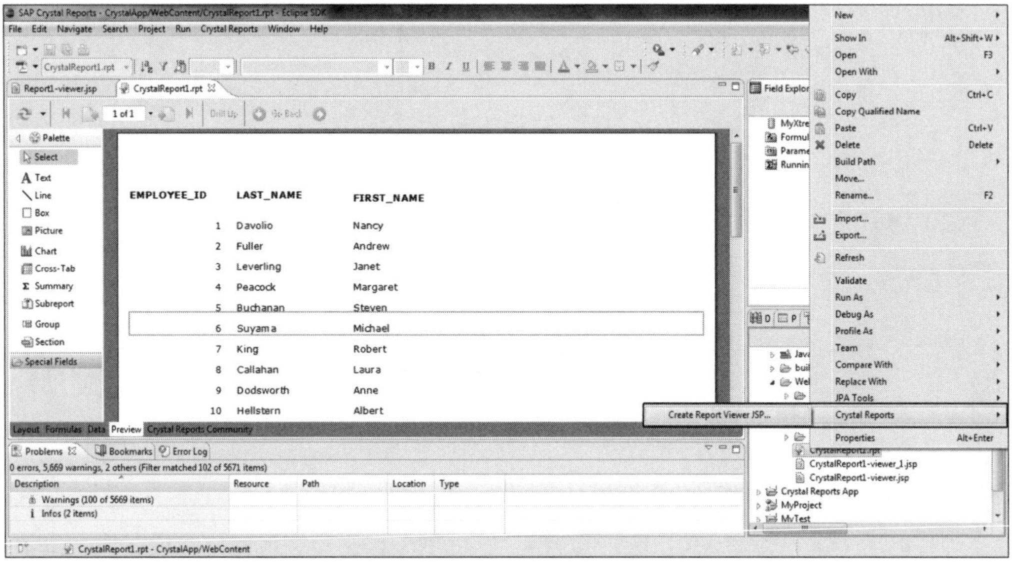

Figure 12.33
Creating a JSP page.

2. The Create JSP page wizard launches, as shown in Figure 12.34.

The wizard options allow you to access viewers programmatically or use the automatic option without knowing Java code. The options are broken down in two categories in the wizard:

- **Insert standard Crystal Reports viewer Tag library code**—This option automatically generates Java code to populate the XML tags. If this option is chosen, all other options will be disabled.

- **Insert Crystal Reports code snippets to**—This option is the most flexible of the two options and allows the developer to customize the viewer

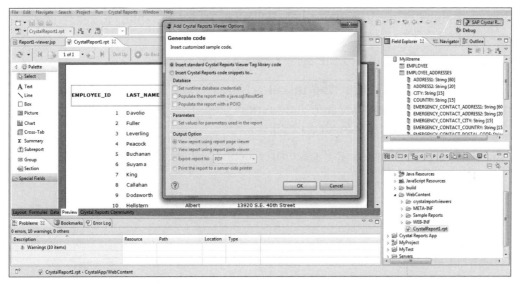

Figure 12.34
The Create JSP page wizard.

experience. For example, if the report should be exported to a certain format, it can be set using this option. If this option is selected, additional options can be set, including database login information, parameters, and output of the data.

The additional options include:

- **Database**—This section allows you to establish security information for the data source.

  - Sets runtime database credentials.
  - Populates the report with `java.sqlResultset`.
  - Populates the report with POJO.

- **Parameters**—Allows you to set the values for the parameters in the report if desired.

- **Output Options**—Allows you to set the printer, export format, and options for the page viewer.

  - View report using the report page viewer.
  - View report using the report parts viewer.

- Export report to: PDF (default), RTF, RTF (Editable), Excel (Data Only), CSV.
- Print the report to the server-side printer.

4. Click OK. If you chose the Install a New Crystal Report option in the install sample database and new report step, the new JSP page will appear, as shown in Figure 12.35.

5. Enter a name for the JSP page or accept the default.

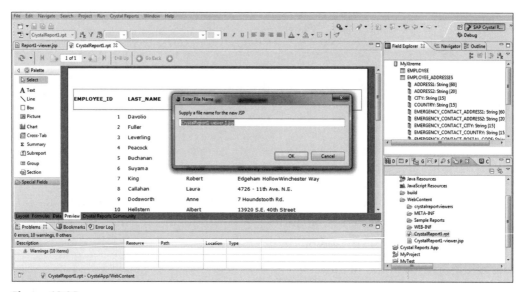

Figure 12.35
Naming the JSP page.

6. Click OK. The JSP page will be created and opened in the perspective, as shown in Figure 12.36.

The JSP page name will be displayed in the Project Explorer. To preview the report in the web browser, follow these steps:

1. Right-click the JSP page in the Project Explorer and choose Run As > 1 Run on Server, as shown in Figure 12.37. The Run on Server wizard will launch, as shown in Figure 12.38.

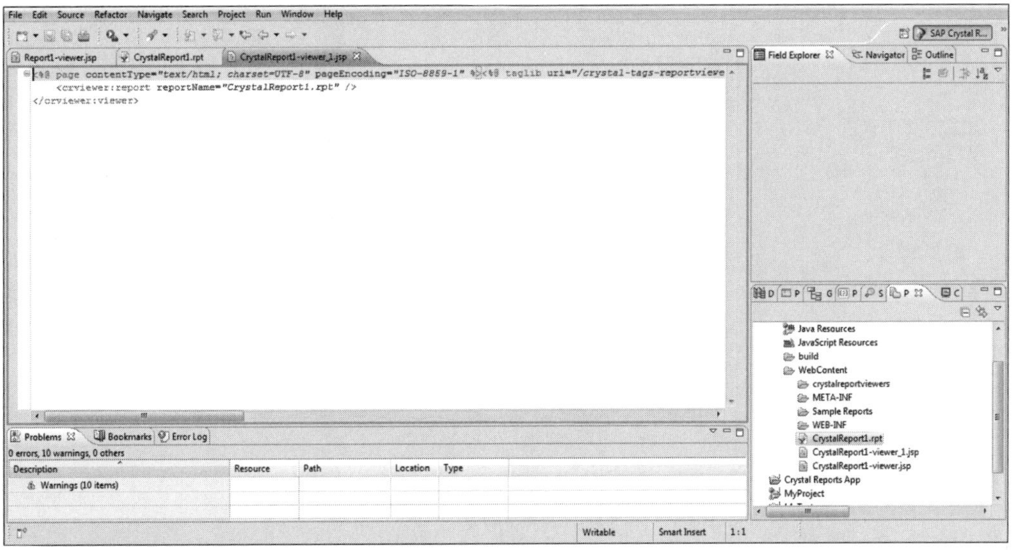

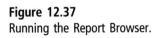

Figure 12.36
The JSP page.

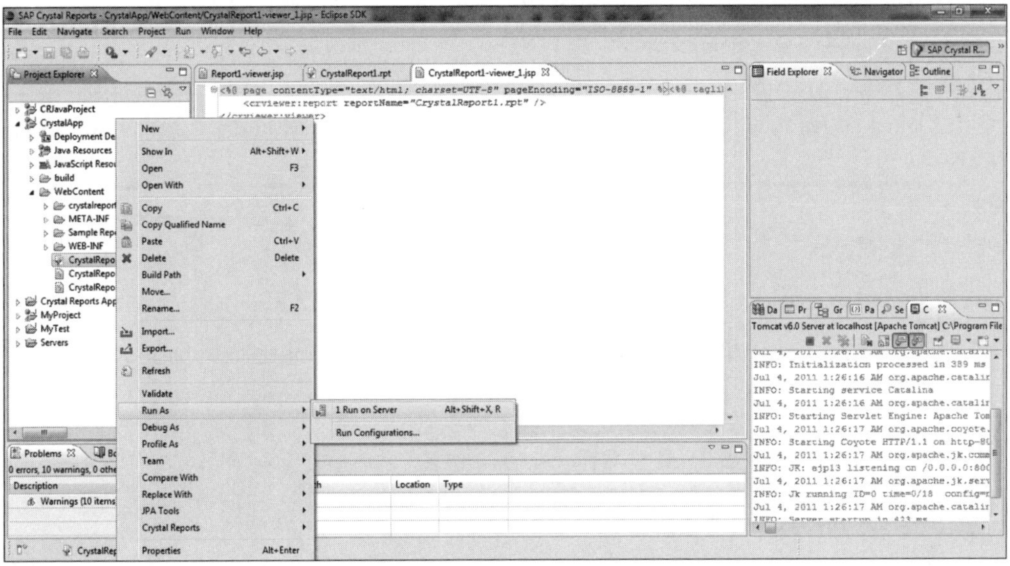

Figure 12.37
Running the Report Browser.

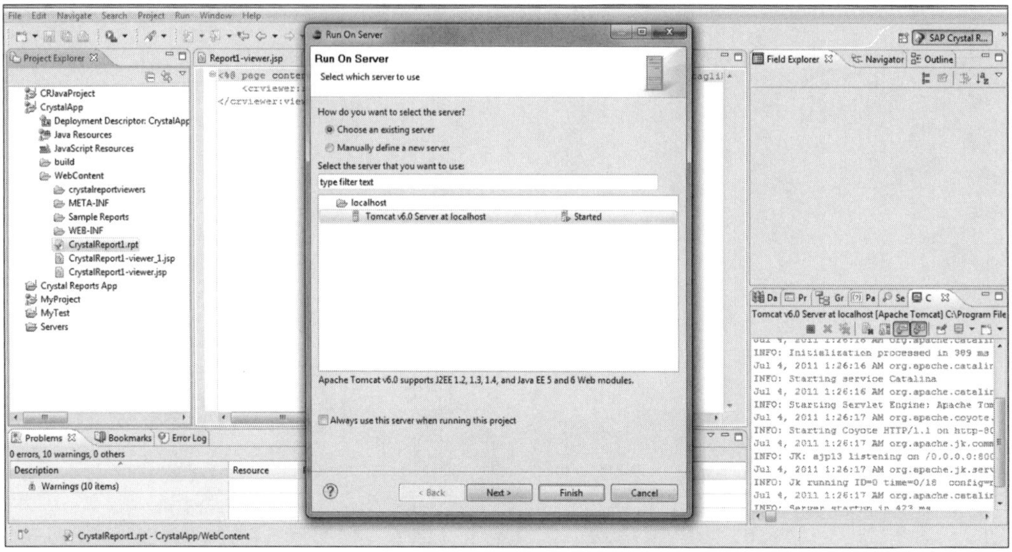

Figure 12.38
Selecting a server.

2. Select the web server to run the report on. If you have multiple servers, you can select the appropriate server at this point. You can also manually define a server. You can also define the default server to be displayed.

Tip

The initial server status may be reflected as stopped. Once you click next the option, the server will start.

3. Click Next.

4. Select the project to include, as shown in Figure 12.39.

5. Notice the project, including the JSP page you executed, will be selected by default.

6. Click Finish.

USING PARAMETERS

Parameters are used to give users control of the data being retrieved from the data source as well as control of titles and formatting features. To create a parameter field, open your Field Explorer and then follow these steps.

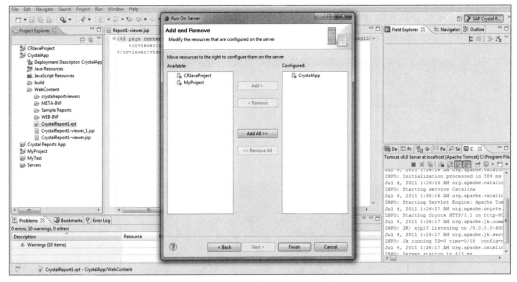

Figure 12.39
Selecting a project.

1. Right-click on the Parameters node in the Field Explorer and choose New, as shown in Figure 12.40.

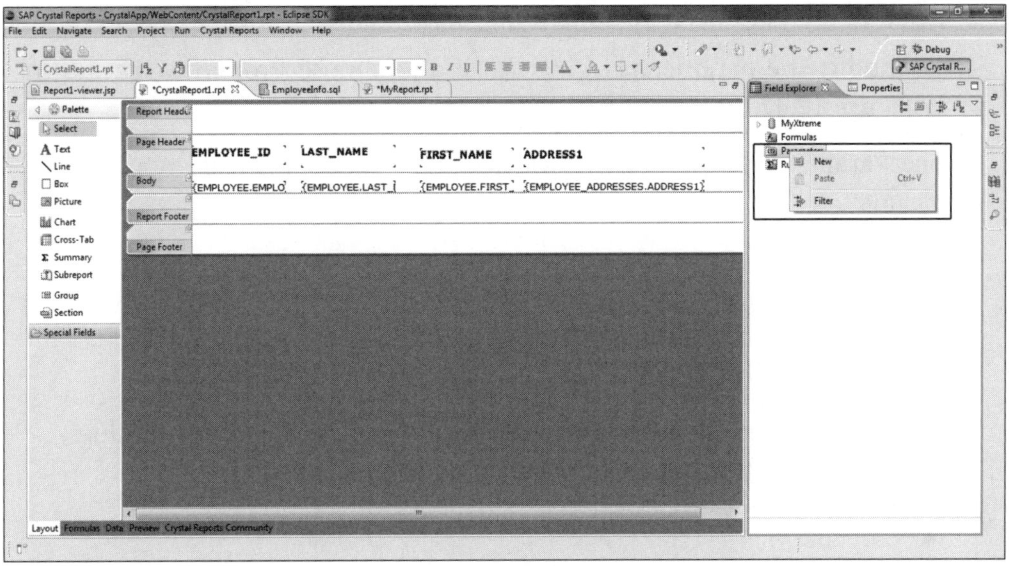

Figure 12.40
Creating a new parameter.

2. The New parameter will be created with a default name of MyParameter1..2, as shown in Figure 12.41.

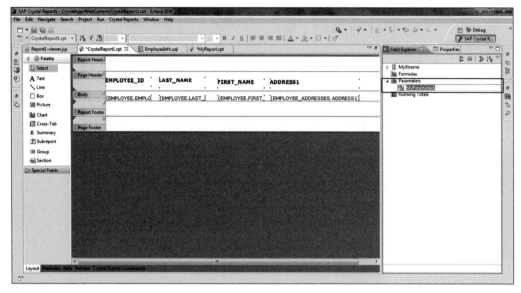

Figure 12.41
Name the parameter

3. Rename the parameter to something meaningful.

4. To modify the parameter, right-click it and choose Properties, as shown in Figure 12.42.

The Parameter properties (shown in Figure 12.43) you can modify include:
- Name
- Type
- Prompt text
- Allow custom values
- Allow multiple values
- Value range kind
- List of values (Figure 12.44 shows the list where you enter values, and Figure 12.45 shows the resulting populated list.)
- Prompt with description
- Edit mask
- Min length
- Max length

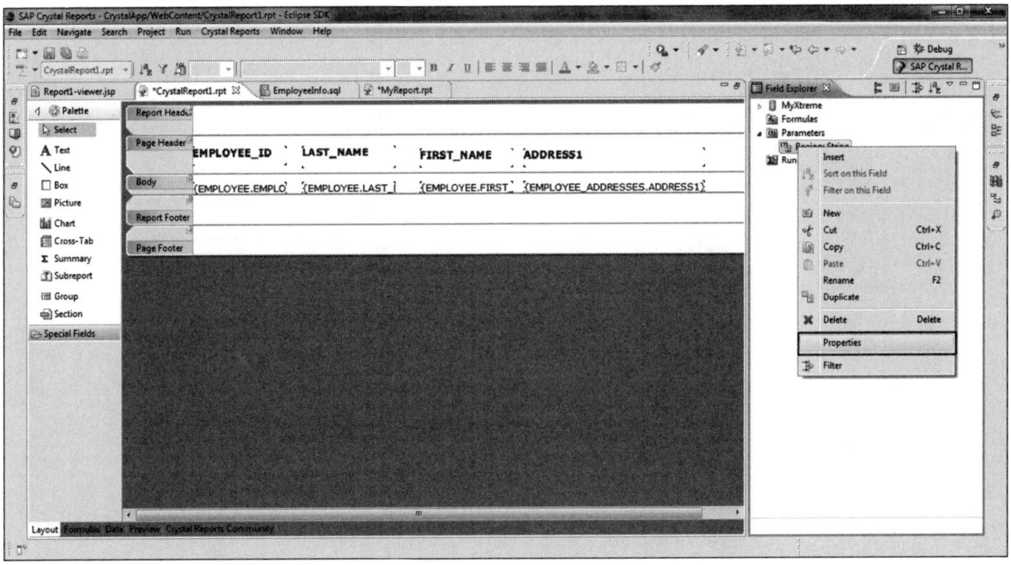

Figure 12.42
Modifying the Parameter.

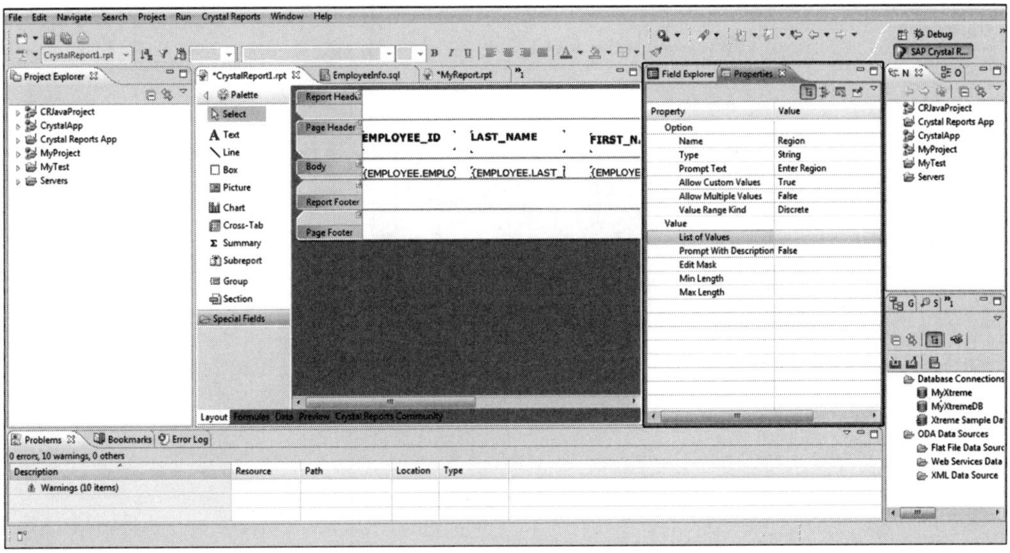

Figure 12.43
The Parameter properties.

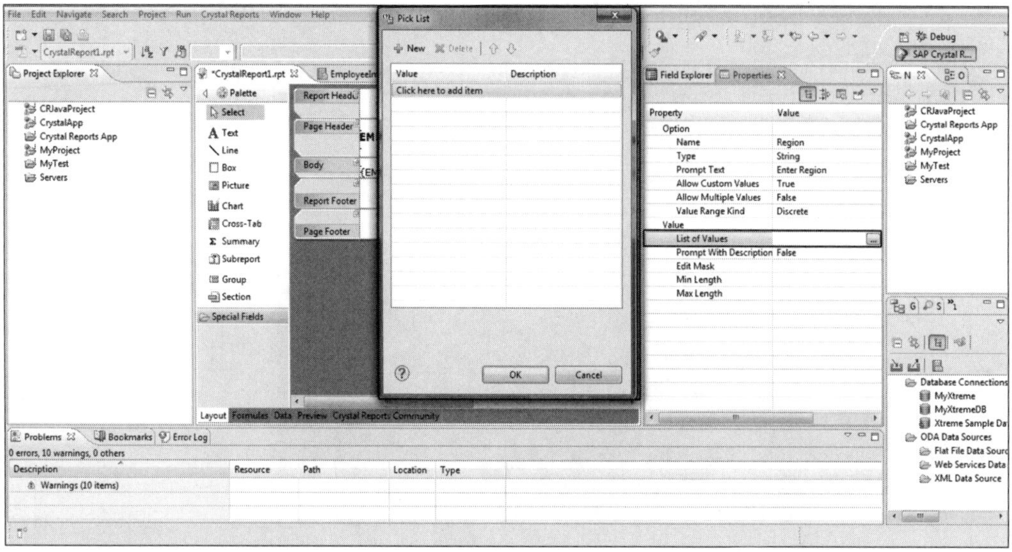

Figure 12.44
Enter a list of values for the parameter drop-down list.

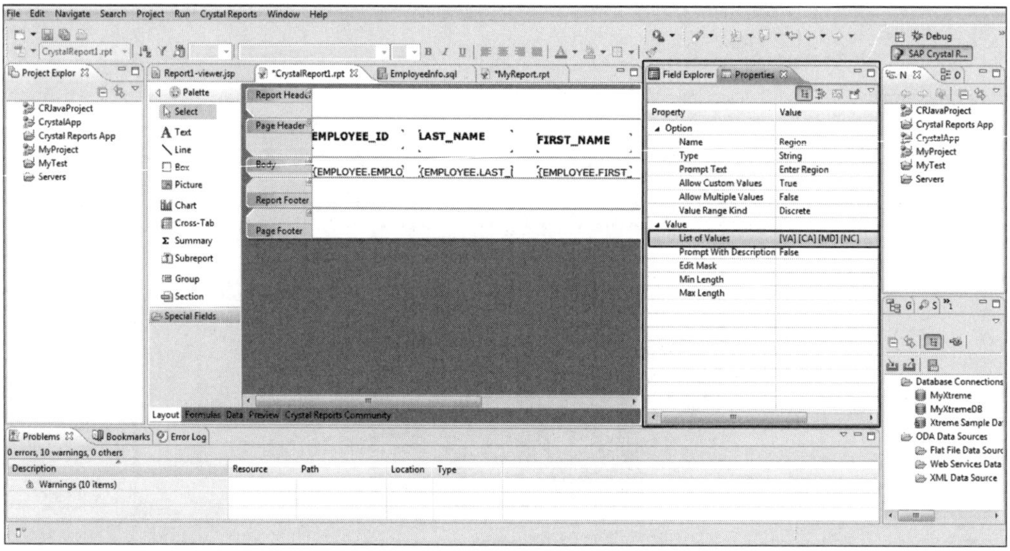

Figure 12.45
List of values.

5. Close the Property dialog box. In order for the parameter to be used, you must reference the parameter in the field formula.

6. Open the Record Filter from the Crystal Reports > Record Filter. The Record Filter window opens, as shown in Figure 12.46.

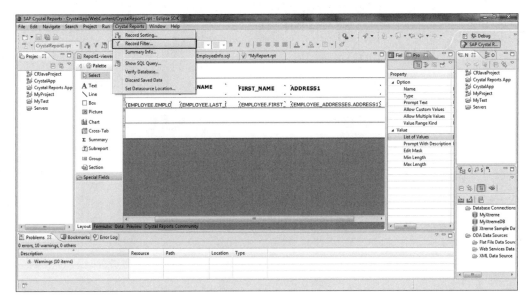

Figure 12.46
Applying the parameter to the field.

7. Click the Add Filter button, as shown in Figure 12.47.

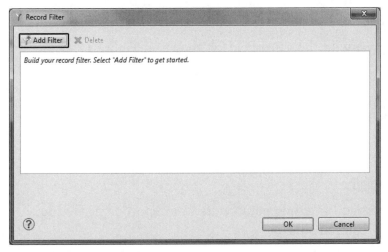

Figure 12.47
Adding a filter.

8. Select the field to filter the report data on, as shown in Figure 12.48.

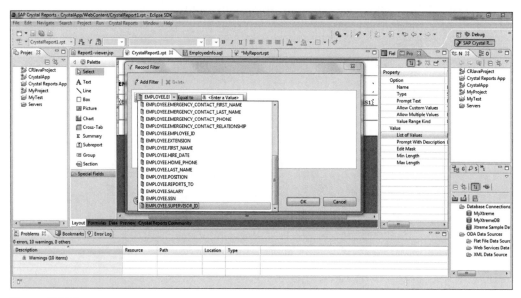

Figure 12.48
Selecting a field.

9. Choose an operator to use in the filter such as Equal to, Not Equal to, In List, Not in List, and so on.

10. Enter or select a value in the third field, as shown in Figure 12.49.

11. Click OK.

12. Click the Preview tab to view the data. If the data has been previewed, you may need to refresh the parameter prompt by selecting the drop-down arrow next to the Refresh button, as shown in Figure 12.50. The parameter prompt dialog box will be displayed as shown in Figure 12.51.

13. Enter or select a value.

14. Click OK. You can add multiple parameters to a report as needed to meet your user's requirements.

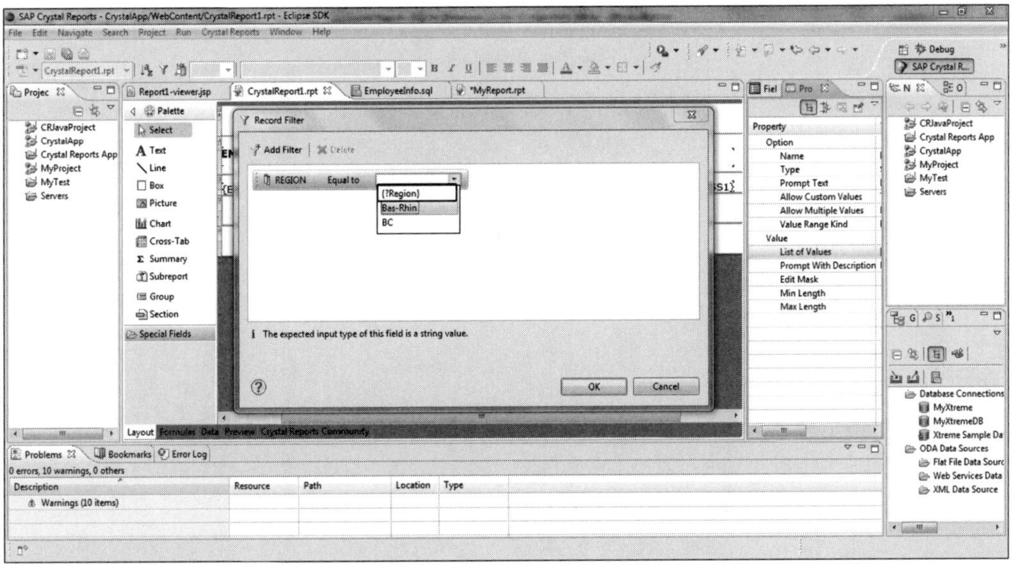

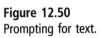

Figure 12.49
Enter a filter value.

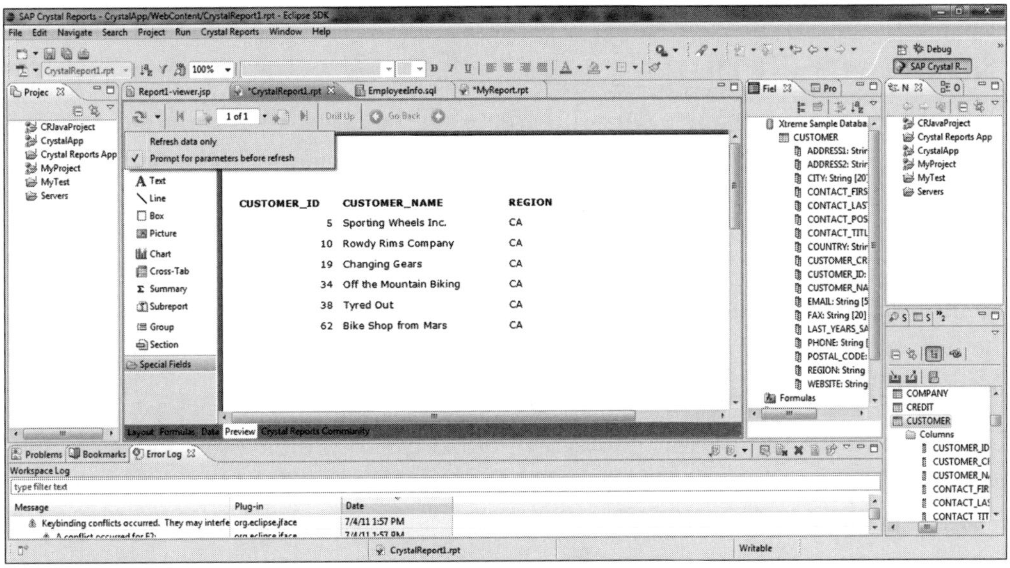

Figure 12.50
Prompting for text.

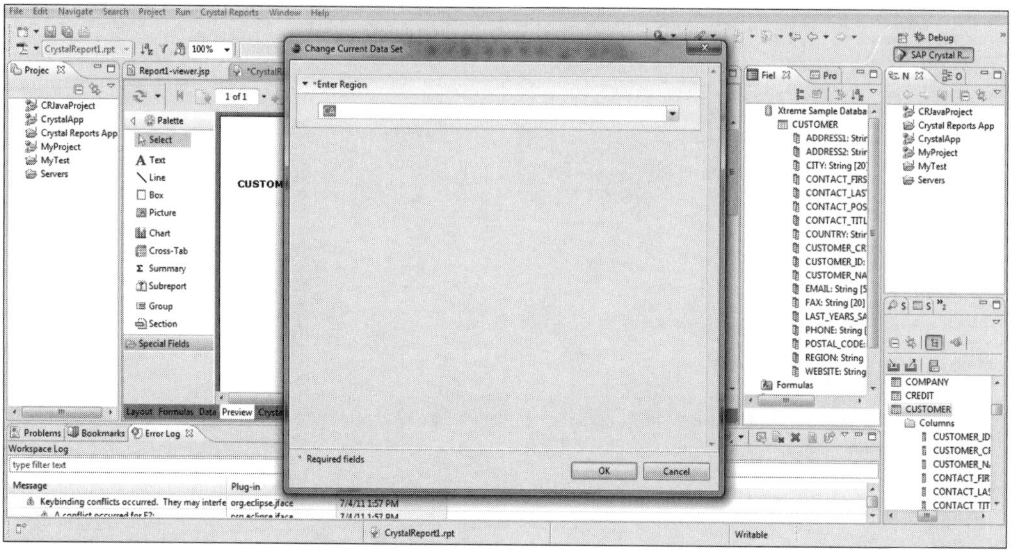

Figure 12.51
The Parameter dialog box.

INSERTING GROUPS

Groups are used to organize data and create aggregations. You should determine your grouping needs during the report requirements gathering session.

Fields do not have to be placed on your report in order to create a group based on that field.

To insert a group, you right-click on the field in the body of the report or select the field from the data source in the Field Explorer and select Group on Field, as shown in Figure 12.52.

The group header and group footer will be added to the Layout view, as shown in Figure 12.53.

INSERTING SUMMARIES

Often summaries are needed to get subtotals, averages, minimums, maximums, and other aggregations to meet your report requirements. Inserting summary fields is very easy in Crystal Reports for Eclipse.

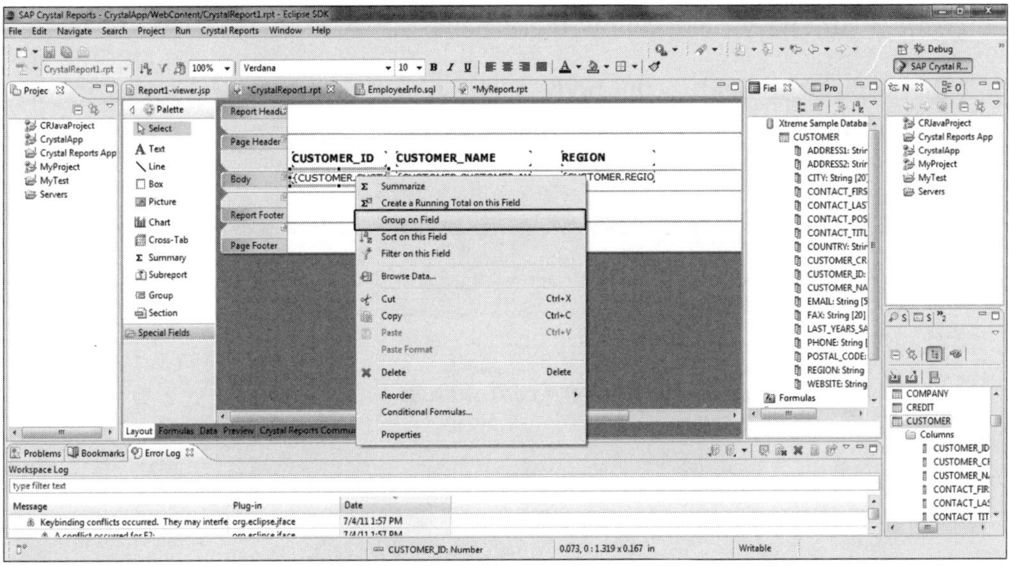

Figure 12.52
Creating a group.

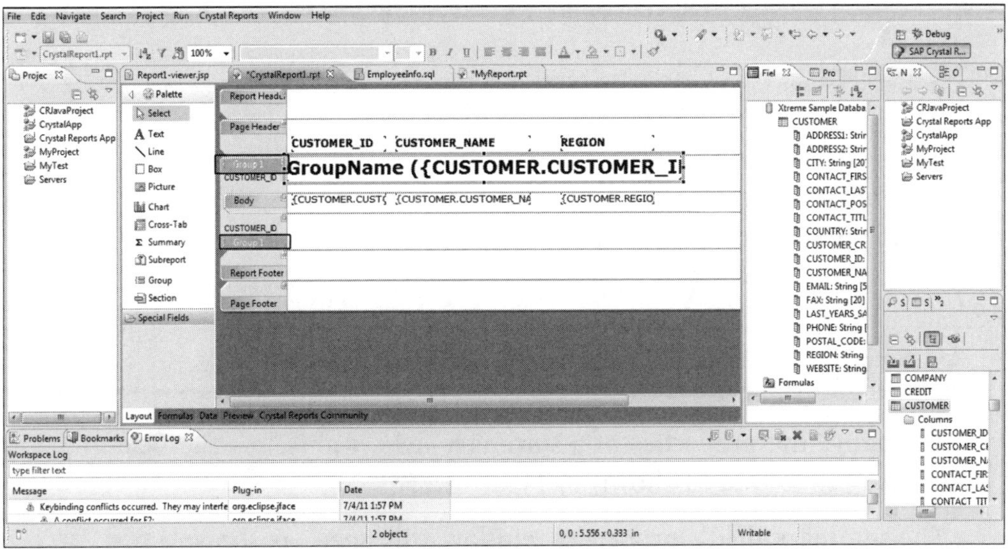

Figure 12.53
Additional group sections.

To create a summary field, follow these steps:

1. Right-click the field in the body of the report and choose Summarize, as shown in Figure 12.54.

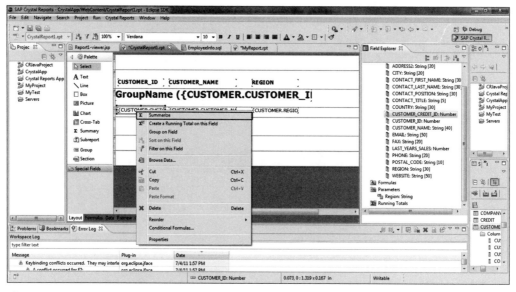

Figure 12.54
Summarizing a field.

A summary field will be placed in the Group Footer of the corresponding group, as shown in Figure 12.55.

Note

A numerical field's summary operation defaults to the SUM option.

2. To change the properties of a summary field, right-click the field and choose Properties, as shown in Figure 12.56.

The summary field's properties window will open, as shown in Figure 12.57. You can change properties such as the summary operation, font face, font style, and number format.

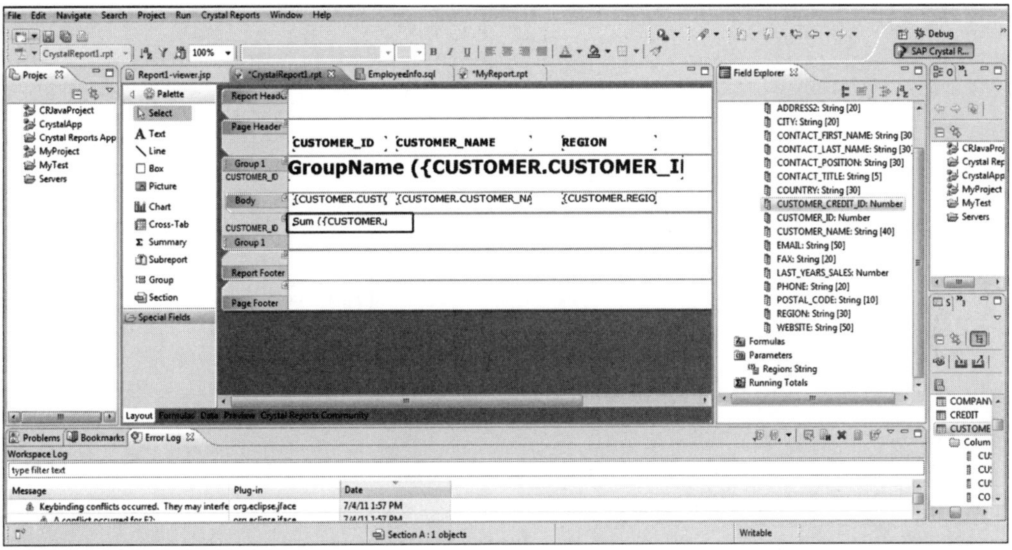

Figure 12.55
Summary field in group footer.

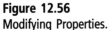

Figure 12.56
Modifying Properties.

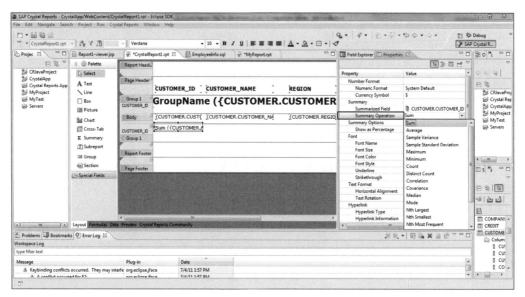

Figure 12.57
Summary field properties.

INSERTING FORMULAS

You need formulas in order to perform mathematical calculations, concatenate text, do comparisons, and include conditional formatting. Formulas can be accessed from the Formulas tab of the designer window, or by accessing the Formula node of the Field Explorer.

1. Right-click the Formulas node in the Field Explorer or click the drop-down list next to the New button on the Formulas tab, as shown in Figures 12.58 and Figures 12.59. The Formula Editor window will appear as shown in Figure 12.60.

2. Rename the formula.

3. Click on the first blank line and enter the data source field or type an opening curly brace ({) to display the available data source tables, views, or SQL, as shown in Figure 12.61.

4. Double-click the appropriate table or source.

5. Double-click on the field to be used in the formula.

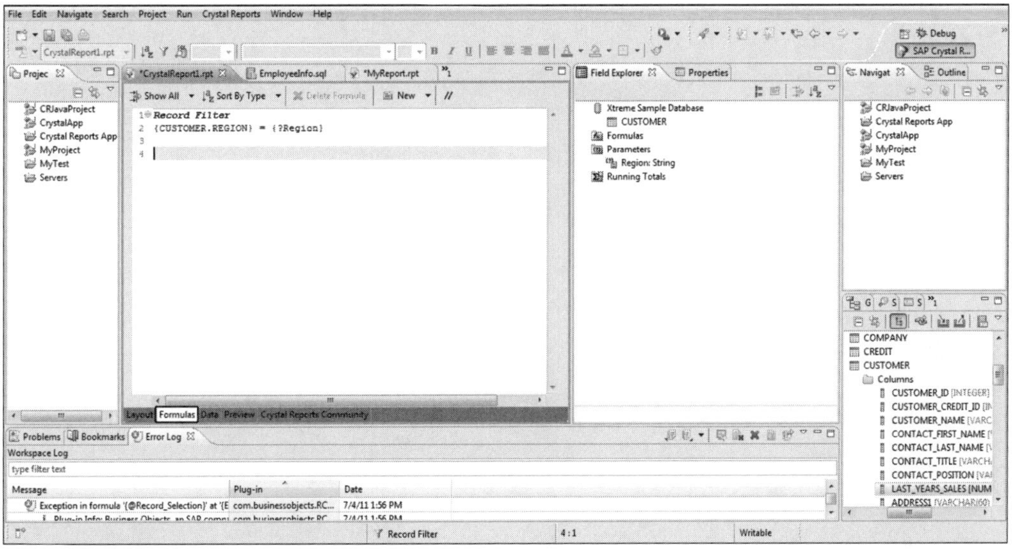

Figure 12.58
Creating formulas from the Formula tab.

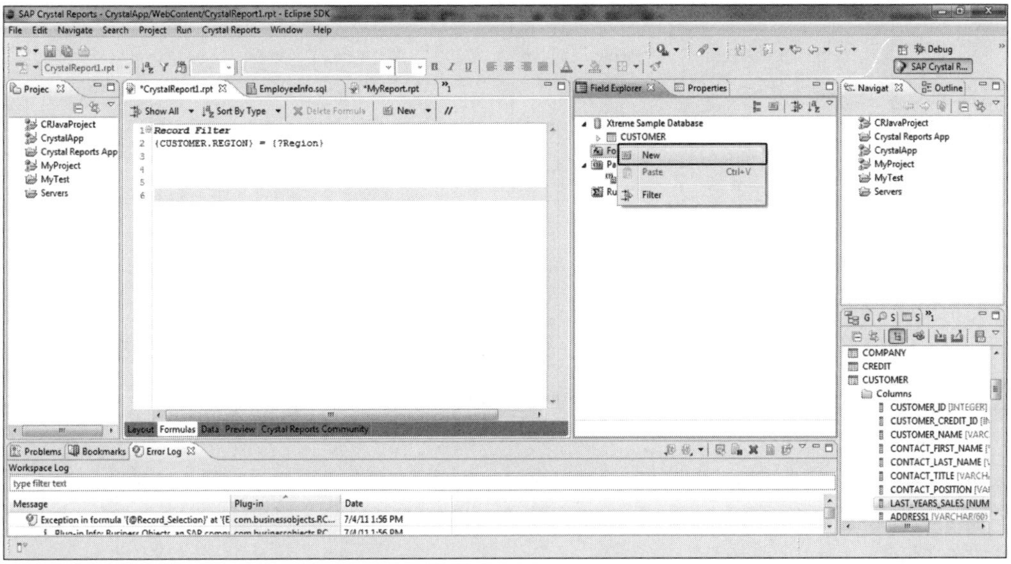

Figure 12.59
Creating formulas from the Field Explorer.

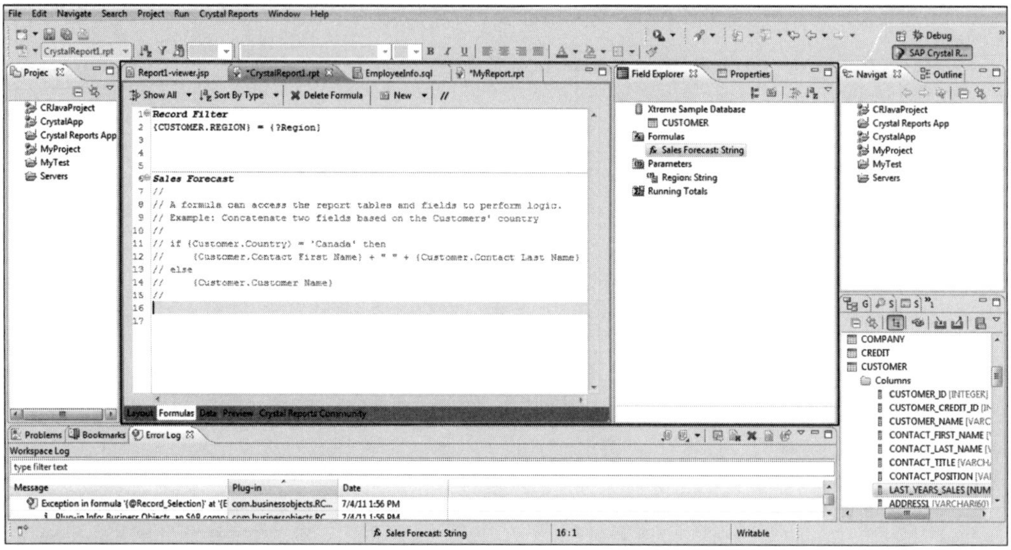

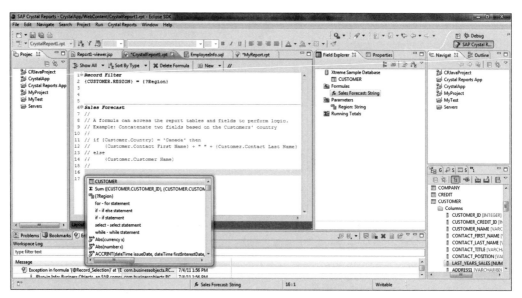

Figure 12.60
The Formula Editor window.

Figure 12.61
Using Formula IntelliSense.

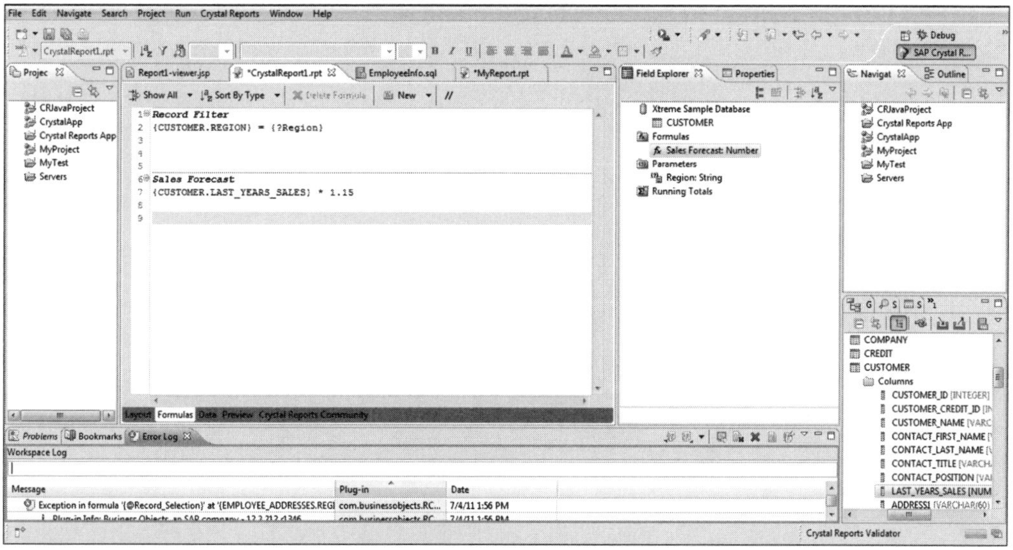

Figure 12.62
Entering a formula.

6. Enter the mathematical operator, such as * for multiplication or / for division.

7. Enter a value or select another data source field, as shown in Figure 12.62.

8. Add the formula field to the Layout view as desired.

Summary

Crystal Reports for Eclipse was developed to assist with Java report development. The SDK and this version of Crystal Reports for Eclipse allow users with minimal Java programming experience to create powerful applications. This chapter was written to give you a brief introduction to the Crystal Reports for Eclipse environment. This is a powerful program that will give beginner and advanced developers tools that can enhance a user's experience.

INTRODUCTION TO SAP CRYSTAL REPORTS FOR ENTERPRISE XI 4.0

CHAPTER 13

INTRODUCTION TO CRYSTAL REPORTS FOR ENTERPRISE XI 4.0

The objectives of this chapter are as follows:

- Getting to know Crystal Reports for Enterprise XI
- Connecting to a data source
- Understanding multi-source Semantic Layers
- Designing a report
- Exploring the Crystal Reports for Enterprise XI user interface

As a developer, it is important to choose the version of Crystal Reports that best meets your organization's business requirements. There are data connectivity limitations between both applications that should be considered prior to choosing between Crystal Reports 2011 and Crystal Reports for Enterprise. The available data connections are listed in Table 13.1. You should keep in mind that you can run both versions on the same machine and migrate to the advanced semantic layer capabilities at your own pace. SAP has compiled a list of recommendations for the versions based on some common data connections, as listed in Table 13.2.

The depth of the changes in the Crystal Reports for Enterprise version is so wide; it is impossible to condense it into a few chapters. The coverage in this book gives you a brief introduction into getting started with Crystal Reports for Enterprise.

Table 13.1 Data Connectivity

Data Source	SAP Crystal Reports 2011	SAP Crystal Reports for Enterprise XI 4.0
Direct Data Access Drivers (RDBMS)	Allowed	Not Allowed
Direct Data Access Drivers (OLAP)	Allowed	Limited (Allowed for BEx queries only)
ODBC, JDBC	Allowed	Allowed (with unx only) universes
Legacy universes (unv)	Limited	Not Allowed
Universes (unx)	Not Allowed	Allowed
Business Views	Allowed	Only for Cascading Prompts
Analysis Views	Not Allowed	Allowed

Table 13.2 SAP Recommendations

SAP BusinessObjects BI 4.0 relational universe (unx), OLAP universe (unx)	SAP Crystal Reports for Enterprise
SAP NetWeaver BW 7	SAP Crystal Reports for Enterprise
Analysis Views	SAP Crystal Reports for Enterprise
SAP NetWeaver BW 3.5	Crystal Reports 2011
Business Views	Crystal Reports 2011
Direct RDBMS or OLAP Access	Crystal Reports 2011
SAP ERP	Crystal Reports 2011
Live Office	Crystal Reports 2011

MIGRATING REPORTS TO ENTERPRISE

You can easily convert your existing reports by opening them in Crystal Reports for Enterprise XI 4.0 and launching the Upgrade wizard.

To convert your report to the new Semantic Layer, follow these steps:

1. Click the Browse Report option from the Start page, shown in Figure 13.1, and locate the report that you want to convert.

2. Choose to back up the report prior to migration. It is checked by default, as shown in Figure 13.2. Click Next.

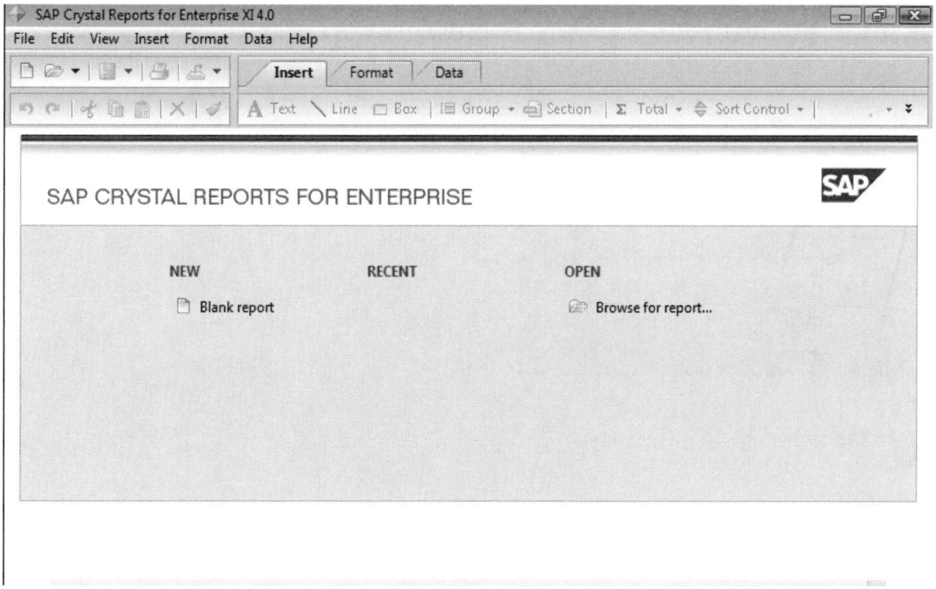

Figure 13.1
Upgrade wizard.

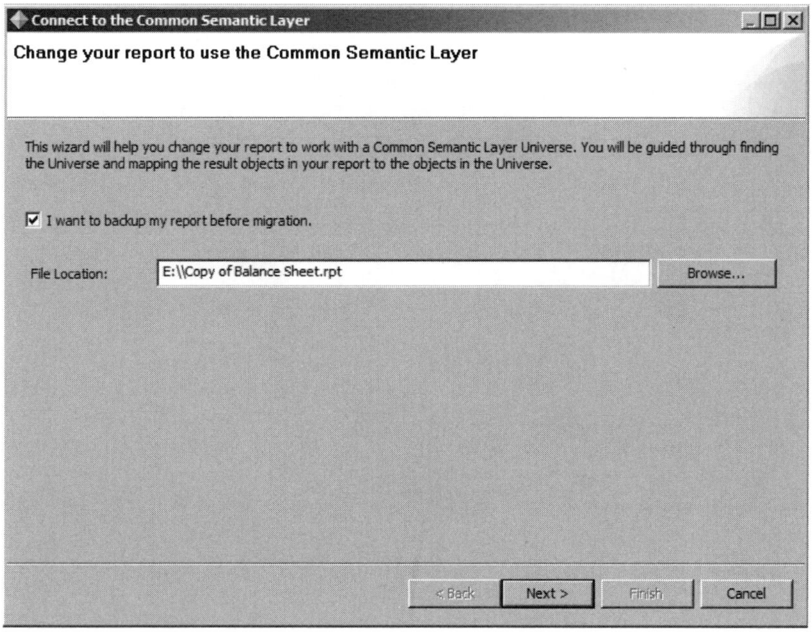

Figure 13.2
Backing up the report.

3. Log on to the SAP BusinessObjects Enterprise XI server, as shown in Figure 13.3.

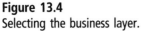

Figure 13.3
Logging on to the server.

4. Click OK.

5. Select the business layer object to connect to data sources such as a universe or BEx query, as shown in Figure 13.4.

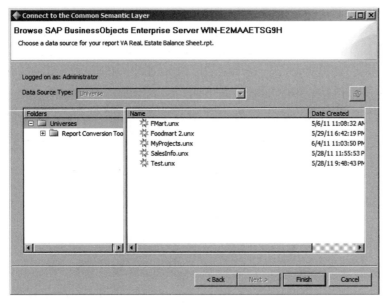

Figure 13.4
Selecting the business layer.

6. Click Finish. The system will convert the report and automatically open it in Crystal Reports for Enterprise XI 4.0.

The Crystal Reports for Enterprise platform has been completely revamped in a bold move to make the program more effective with business layer-type applications using the Semantic Layer. In the initial release of version XI 4.0, the Crystal Reports Enterprise version does not allow direct access to a database. Any reports requiring direct access must be developed and run using Crystal Reports 2011. Crystal Reports 2011 and Crystal Reports for Enterprise XI 4.0 can run simultaneously on the same machine. Therefore, you will be able to convert your existing reports to the new Enterprise platform at your own pace while designing new reports on the new platform.

Tip

I recommend installing Crystal Reports for Enterprise XI 4.0 on the computer first before installing the Crystal Reports 2011 version.

Crystal Reports for Enterprise XI 4.0 takes full advantage of the semantic business layer. SAP's semantic business layer hides the back end of the data sources from the end user and displays a visual representation of the required data. This prevents the end users from viewing the complexity of the data source and gives them minimal objects to work with. The business layer can read any type of data source and can combine multiple sources into one working object that can be read into any application using web services.

Crystal Reports for Enterprise XI 4.0 introduced the Information Design tool, which allows you to create a universe, a data foundation, a business layer, as well as publish the object to the repository for secured and shared use from one central location. The Information Design tool's environment is used to define, extract, and manipulate information from relational or OLAP data sources to create and publish a SAP universe. The new version allows you to create a universe based on multiple sources that was not available in previous versions. The creation of these data connections will be made on the SAP BusinessObjects Enterprise side of the server and not through Crystal Reports. You must create the data connection storing the objects you will need in the report prior to attempting to make a connection in Crystal Reports for Enterprise XI 4.0.

Although this book is not intended to teach you how to use the BusinessObjects Enterprise Server, I want to introduce you to the Information Design tool, which you will use to create a universe. This is only a brief introduction to the tool.

CREATING A UNIVERSE WITH THE INFORMATION DESIGN TOOL

In order to create a new universe in SAP BusinessObjects Enterprise XI 4.0, open the Information Design tool. It's located on the program menu, under the SAP BusinessObjects Enterprise Client Tools submenu, which is located under the SAP BusinessObjects Enterprise XI 4.0 menu. The Information Design window will open and look similar to Figure 13.5.

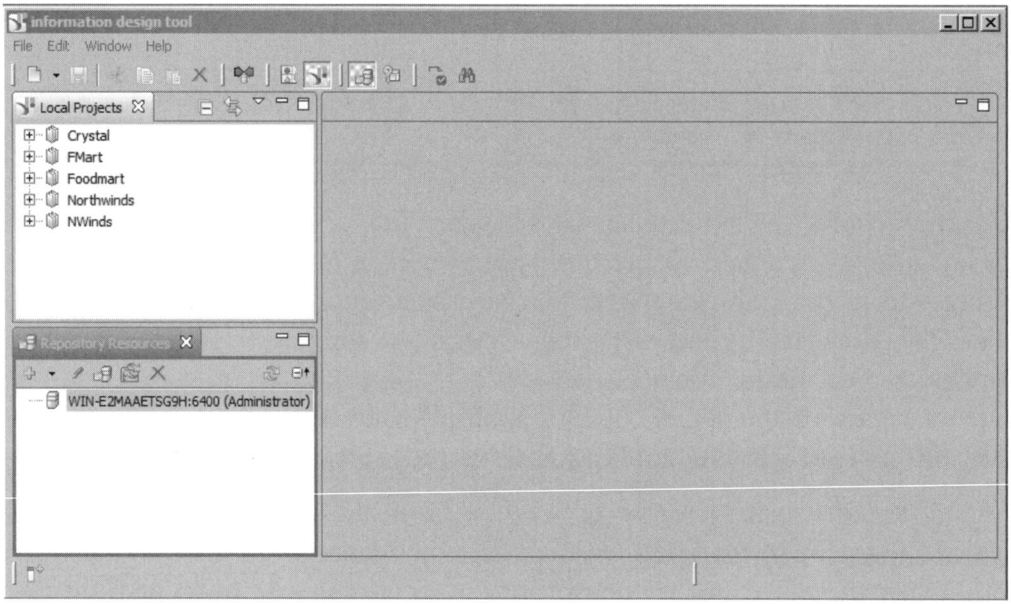

Figure 13.5
Using the Information Design tool.

Note

You must have the Northwinds Access database installed and the connection set up on the BusinessObjects Enterprise server in order to follow this exercise.

You must first create a local project to store the data source objects. You can use the Information Design tool to create a universe or other semantic layer connections.

1. Choose File > New > Project, as shown in Figure 13.6.

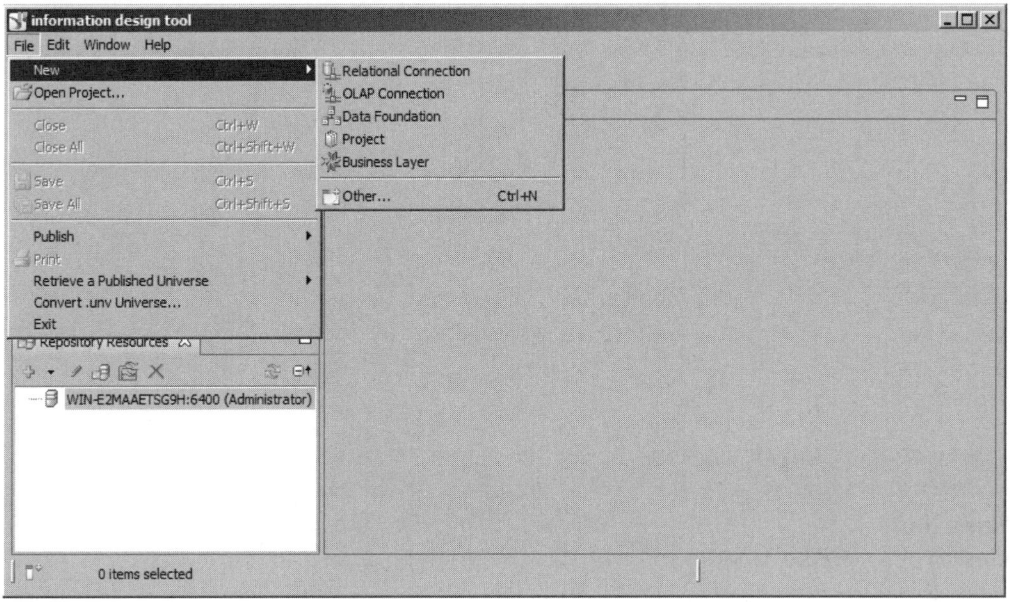

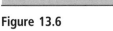

Figure 13.6
Creating a new project.

2. Enter a name for the local project. This example uses MyProject as the name.

3. Click Finish. You should see something similar to Figure 13.7.

4. Now that the project has been created, the next step is to create a relational connection. To do so, right-click on the MyProject object in the Local Projects pane and choose New > Relational Connection, as shown in Figure 13.8.

5. Enter a name for the connection. Description is optional.

6. Click Next. The Database Middleware Selection window will open. This is where you select the driver used to connect to the database based on the type of data source being used, as shown in Figure 13.9. This exercise uses a Microsoft Access database.

7. Expand the Microsoft item and choose Microsoft Access 2007 > ODBC Driver.

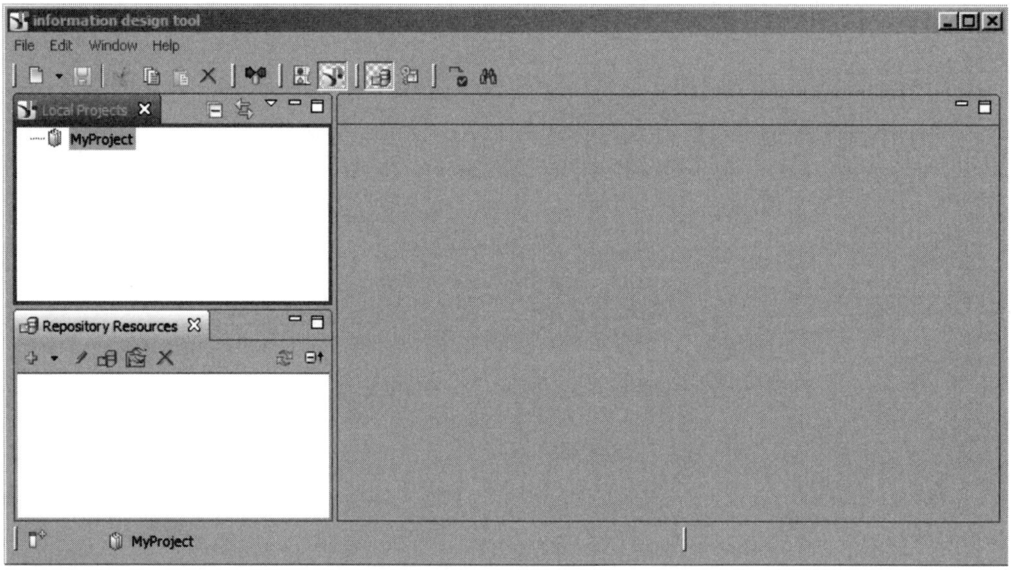

Figure 13.7
Creation of a new local project.

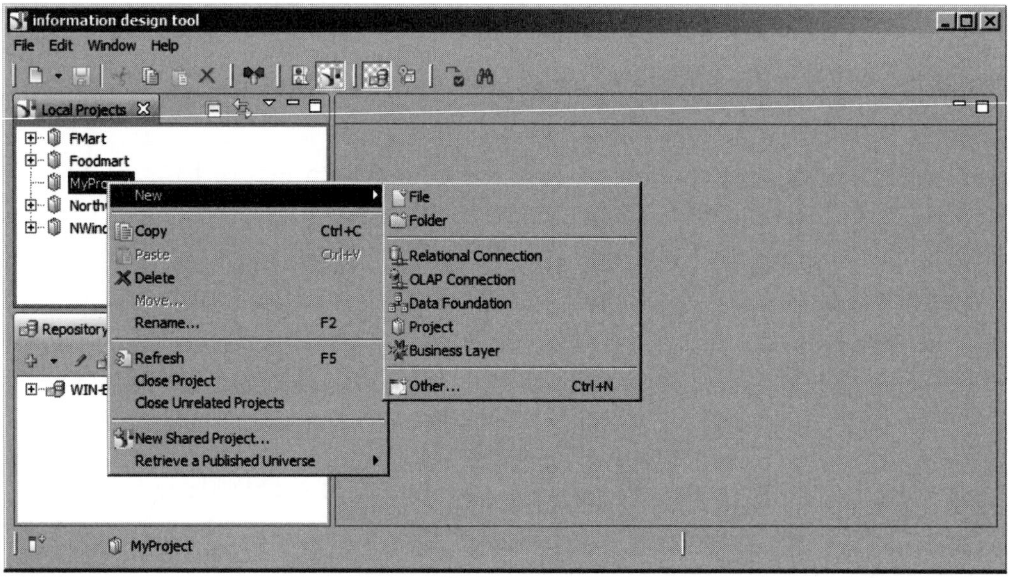

Figure 13.8
Creating a connection to a relational database.

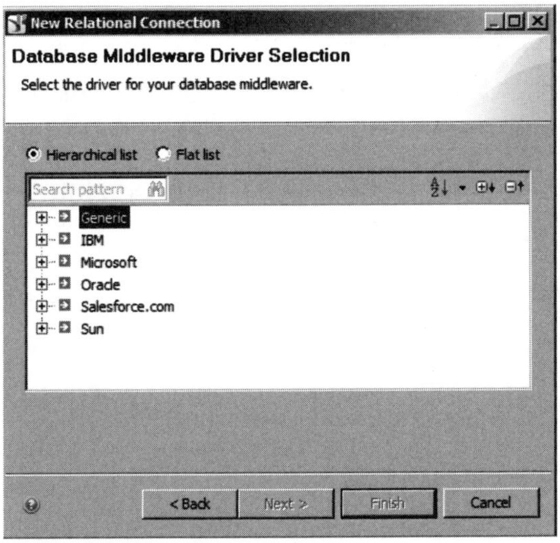

Figure 13.9
Selecting a data source driver.

8. Click Next. The Parameters for Access 2007 Connection will open. This
window allows you to enter the authentication type, the username and
password if the database is secured, and the ODBC connection, as
shown in Figure 13.10.

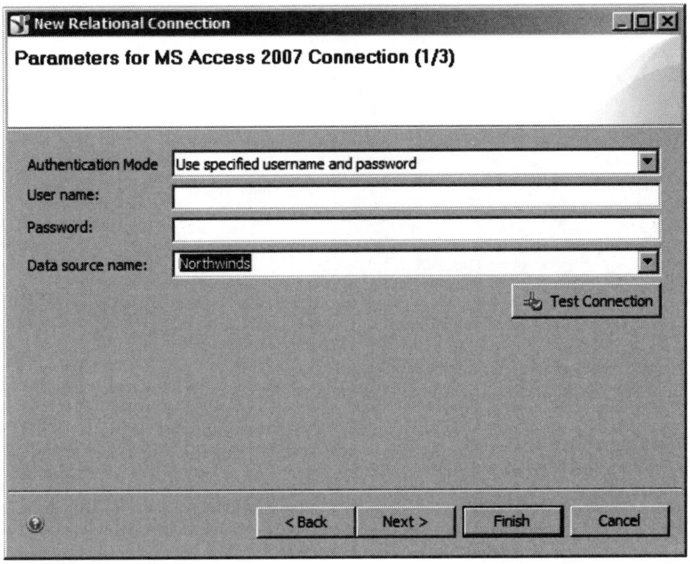

Figure 13.10
Connection parameters window.

9. Use the following options:

Authentication Type—Leave as the default option of Use the Specified Username and Password.

Username—Leave blank. Populate this box only if your database requires a username and password to log on to the database.

Password—Leave blank. Populate this box only if your database requires a username and password to log on to the database.

Data source connection—Select the ODBC connection name previously set up on the BusinessObjects Enterprise server. For the purpose of this exercise, choose the Northwinds connection.

10. Click the Test Connection button to ensure the proper credentials have been set and you can connect to the intended data source, as shown in Figure 13.11. Once the test is complete, close the Test Results window.

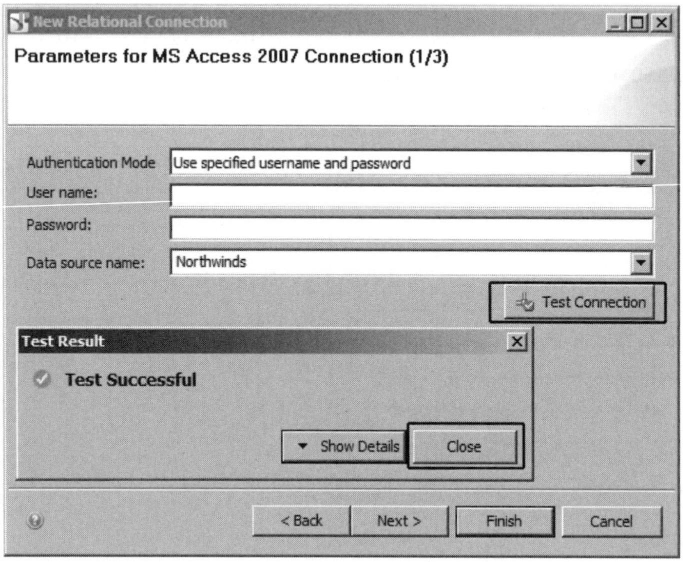

Figure 13.11
Establishing connection parameters.

11. Click Next. The next connection parameter's window allows you to establish the connection time settings, as shown in Figure 13.12.

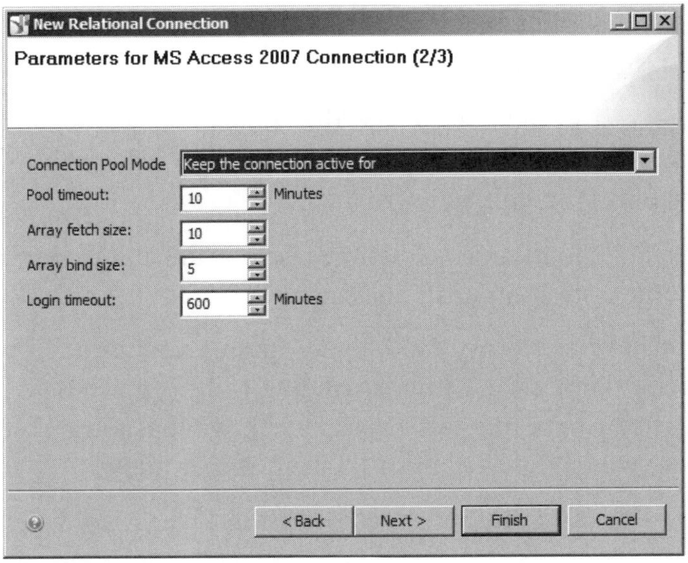

Figure 13.12
Last connection parameters window.

You may want to work with your BOE administrator on this option. The best options are going to depend on the type of database you are connecting to. For example, the SAP Netweaver database versus a Microsoft Access database. The options are:

Connection Pool Mode—Determines whether the universe will maintain a constant connection to the database, disconnect after each transaction, which is normally an expensive option, or maintain the connection throughout the entire user session. The default is to keep the connection active for ten minutes. SAP recommends this option. However, you should test the performance of each type of connection on live data to determine the best performance options for your organization.

Pool Timeout—Depending upon the connection pool mode chosen this option may be disabled. It allows you to set the number of minutes the connection is to stay active.

Array Fetch Size—Establishes the number of rows to retrieve during a fetch. The default value is 20. The default setting returns to the database and retrieves records in increments of 20, which may cause the system to return to the database multiple times to retrieve all records. The greater the value, the faster your records will be retrieved.

Array Bind Size—The area in memory where the connection server stores a batch of data to be sent to the repository. The higher the number, the better performance you will achieve.

Login Timeout—Specifies the number of seconds before the connection attempt will timeout and display an error message.

12. For the purposes of this exercise, leave the default options and click Next. The last parameter connection settings window will open. These settings are optional. If you have any initialization settings that must be set prior to connecting, you should establish them in this window.

13. Leave the parameters as is and click Finish, as shown in Figure 13.13.

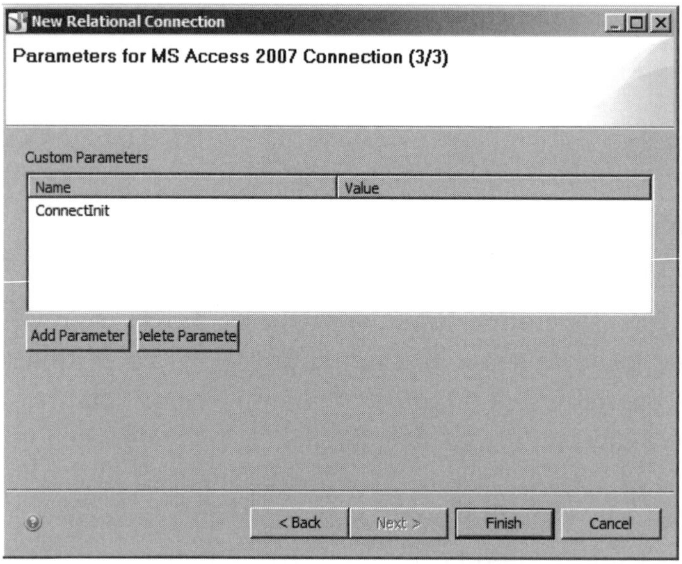

Figure 13.13
Creation of a relational connection.

Securing the Connection

In order to publish a business layer to the repository, the connection must be secured. A connection is only secure after it has been published to a public location and not saved in the local folder. The default option saves it at the local level. The connection is local if the extension ends in .cnx. It is a secured connection if the extension is .cns.

1. In order to secure the connection, right-click the connection under the local project name and select Publish Connection to a Repository from the context menu, as shown in Figure 13.14.

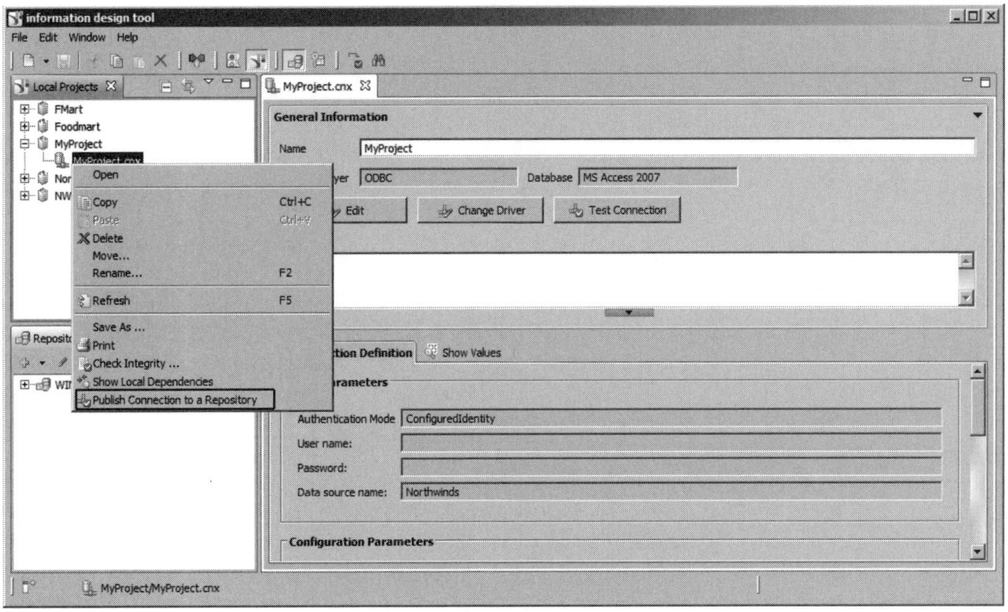

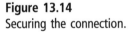

Figure 13.14
Securing the connection.

2. Verify the correct server is being referenced in the session option or create a new session, as shown in Figure 13.15. Click Next.

3. Define a repository folder to store the secured connection, as shown in Figure 13.16. There is a Common Connections folder by default. However, you can organize your connections as you desire by creating a new folder in this window. For the purpose of this exercise, select Common Connections and then click Finish.

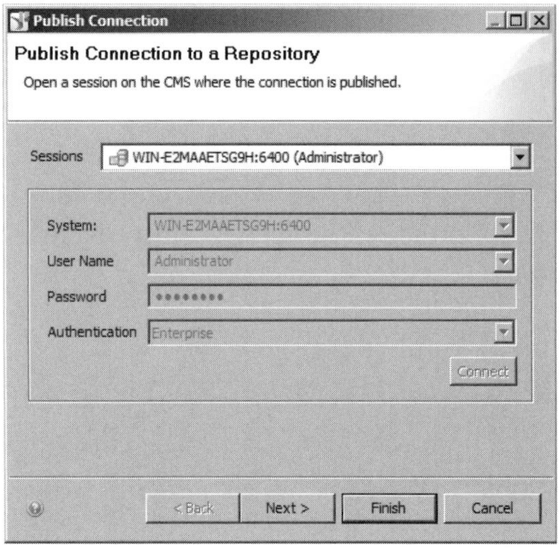

Figure 13.15
Verify Server Session.

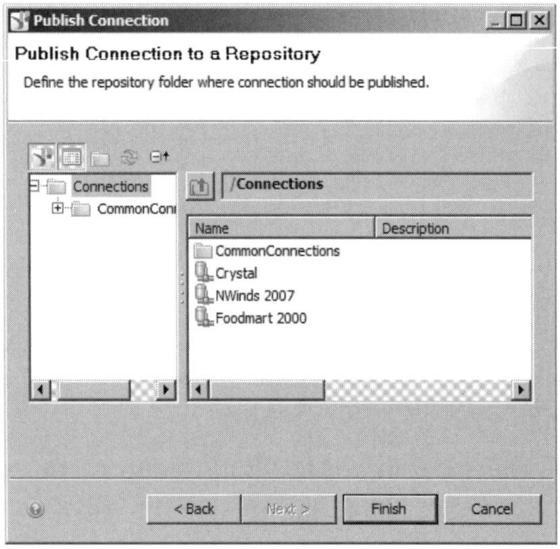

Figure 13.16
Selecting the repository folder.

Figure 13.17
The connection was published.

The Publication status window will appear indicating whether the connection could be published successfully. The message will appear asking if you want to create a shortcut to the secured connection in the local folder. I recommend selecting Yes. See Figure 13.17.

4. If the connection shortcut was successfully created, the success window will appear, as shown in Figure 13.18. Click Close to exit the window.

Figure 13.18
Creation of shortcut to the secured connection.

You should now see two connections in the Local Projects pane under your project name. As mentioned previously, the secured connection will end with the extension .cns, as shown in Figure 13.19.

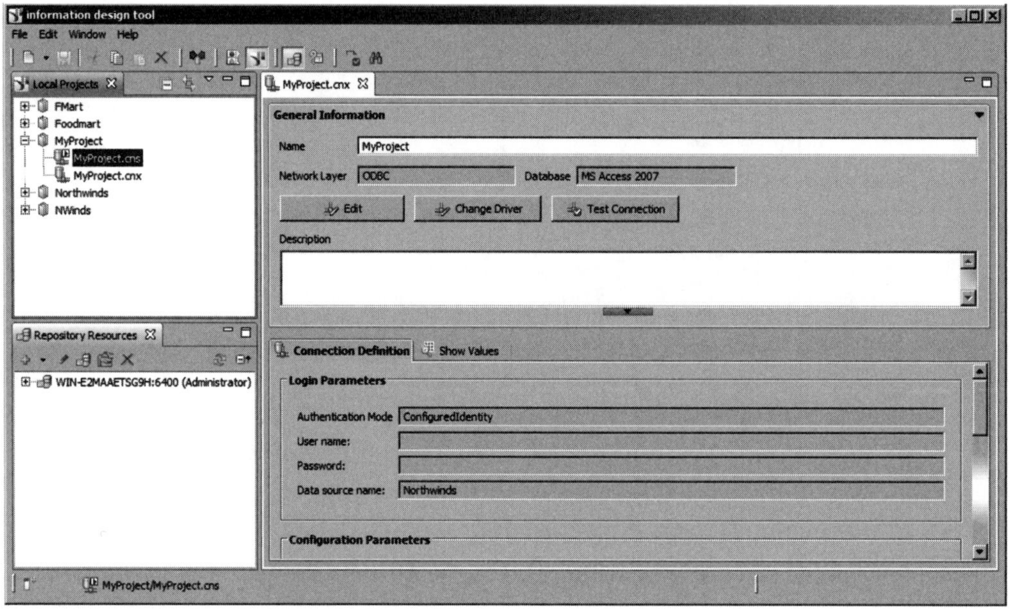

Figure 13.19
Secured (.cns) and non-secured (.cnx) connections.

Creating a Data Foundation

A *data foundation* is a schema of tables and joins from one or more relational databases. You must create a data foundation before you can build a business layer. Many business layers can be built from one data foundation. Building a data foundation is similar to building a query by selecting the tables and joining them via a common field. Depending on the data foundation type, you can also build calculated columns and alias tables; and create new derived tables, prompts, and other objects. You can seek more information relating to data foundations from the BusinessObjects Enterprise user guides or books focused on the topic.

To create a data foundation, use the following steps. (Note that this exercise is a continuation of the previous one. Therefore, you must have completed the previous exercise before starting the data foundation exercise.)

1. Right-click the local project you are working with. For this exercise, right-click the MyProject object and choose New > Data Foundation, as shown in Figure 13.20.

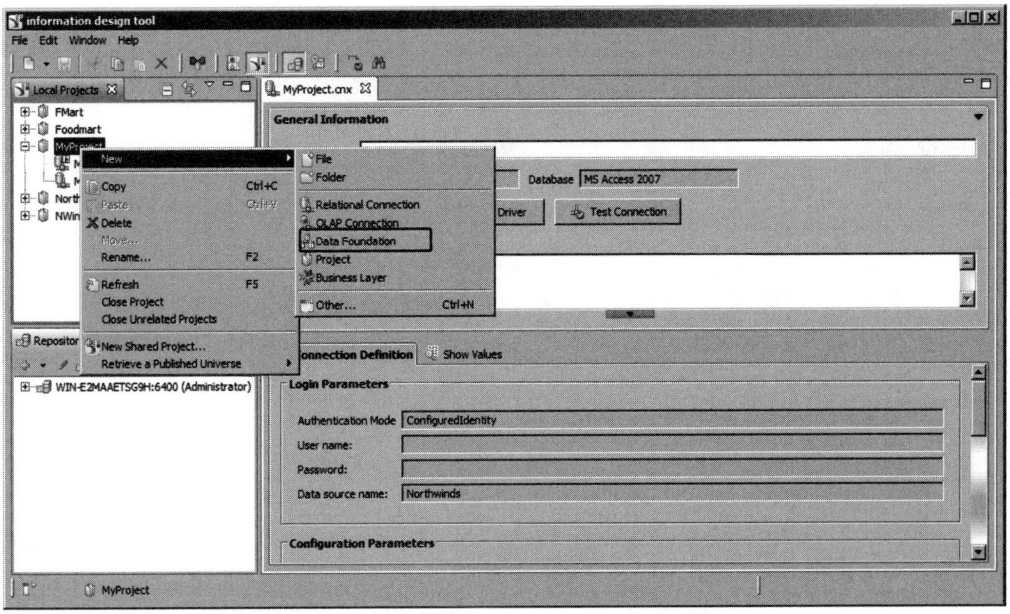

Figure 13.20
Creating a new data foundation.

2. Enter a name for the data foundation, such as MyProject, as shown in Figure 13.21. The description is optional.

3. Click Next. You can select a single source connection or connect to a multi-source foundation that includes two or more database connections, as shown in Figure 13.22.

Note

You can publish a universe to a local folder or to the repository using a single source; however, with a multi-source connection you can only publish to the repository.

4. Select the single source connection and then click Next.

5. Select the appropriate connection. For this exercise, select MyProject.cns.

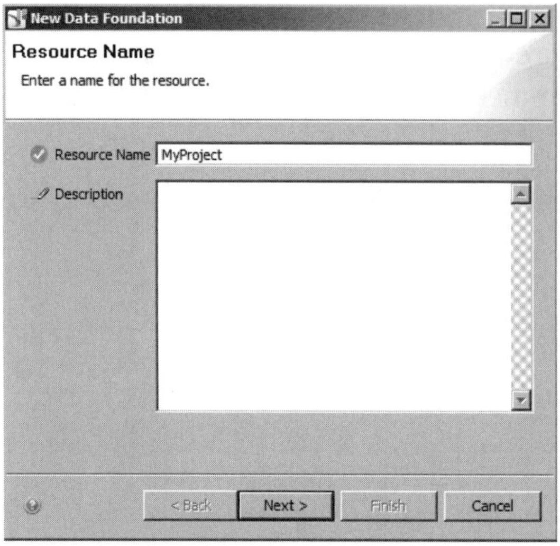

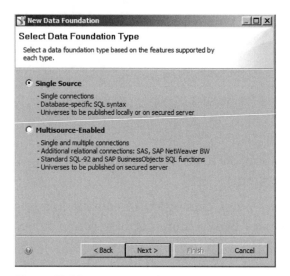

Figure 13.21
Naming the data foundation.

Figure 13.22
Selecting single or multi-source foundation.

Note

If you intend to publish the universe to the repository, you must select a secure connection as shown in Figure 13.23.

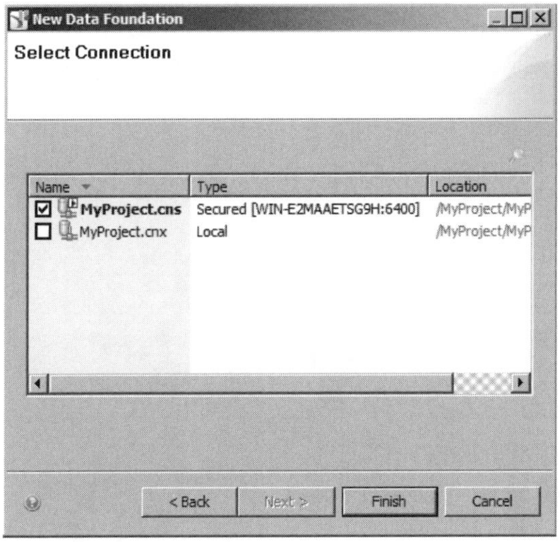

Figure 13.23
Selecting a secure connection.

6. Click Finish. You should now see an entity under the Local Project tree with an extension .dfx for the data foundation as shown in Figure 13.24.

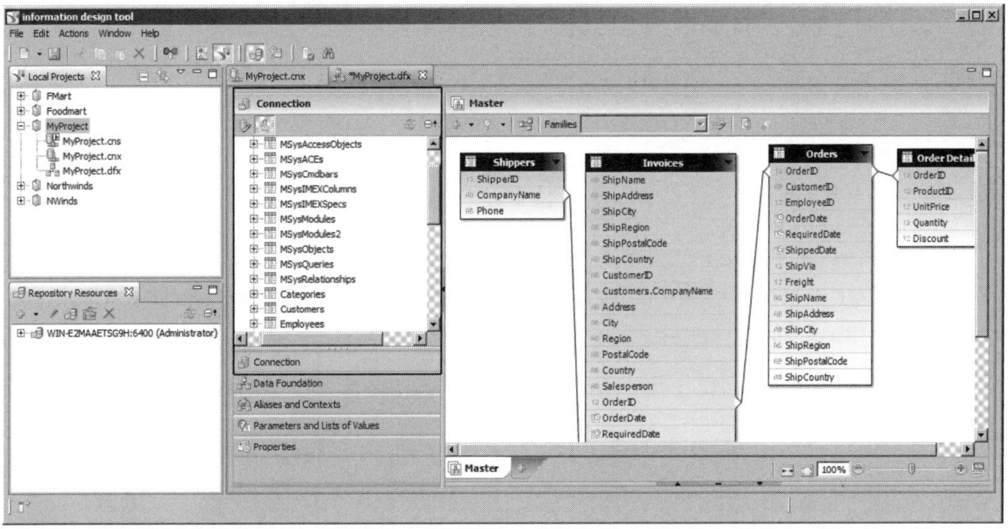

Figure 13.24
Completed data foundation (.dfx).

7. In the Connection pane, expand the appropriate connection and locate the tables, queries, stored procedures, or views that you would like to base the business layer on.

8. Select the table and double-click or drag and drop the table to the Master section, as shown in Figure 13.25.

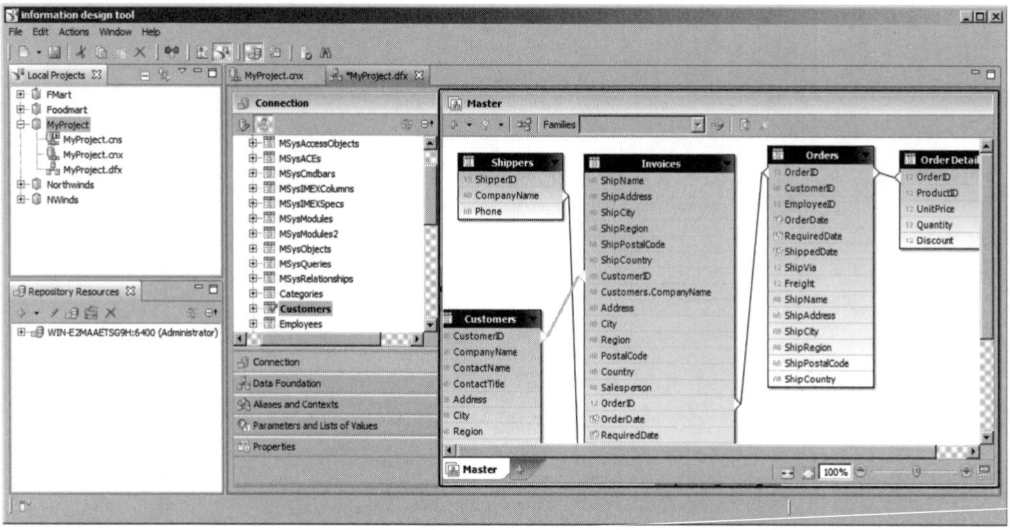

Figure 13.25
Adding tables and joins to the data foundation.

In this view you can create parameter prompts, a list of values, alias tables, and other properties by changing the views located below the Connection pane, as shown in Figure 13.26.

9. Click the Save button on the toolbar or choose File > Save.

This section has only touched on a brief part of the data foundation. To learn more about the data foundation, see the BusinessObjects Enterprise XI 4.0 Users guide.

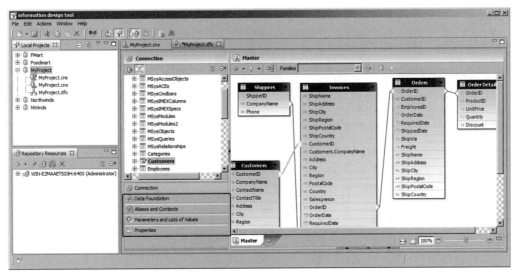

Figure 13.26
Creating data foundation properties and settings.

Creating a Business Layer

A *business layer* is a collection of metadata objects that map to SQL or MDX definitions in a database. A business layer can be created on an OLAP cube or on a data foundation built on a relational database. The primary role of the business layer is to organize the metadata objects before the universe is published.

To create a business layer, follow these steps:

1. Right-click on the local project and select New > Business Layer, as shown in Figure 13.27.

2. Select the business layer type. You can create a business layer type on a Relational Business Layer or on an OLAP Business layer. For the purpose of this exercise, select the Relational Business Layer, as shown in Figure 13.28.

3. Click Next.

4. Enter a name for the Business layer resource, as shown in Figure 13.29. For this exercise, enter **MyProject** as the resource name. Description is optional.

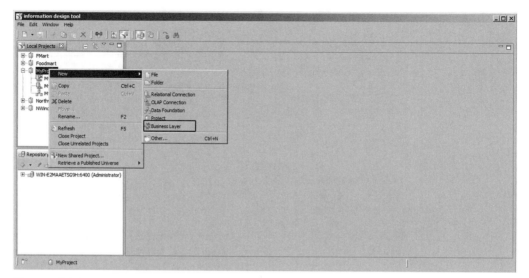

Figure 13.27
Creating a new business layer.

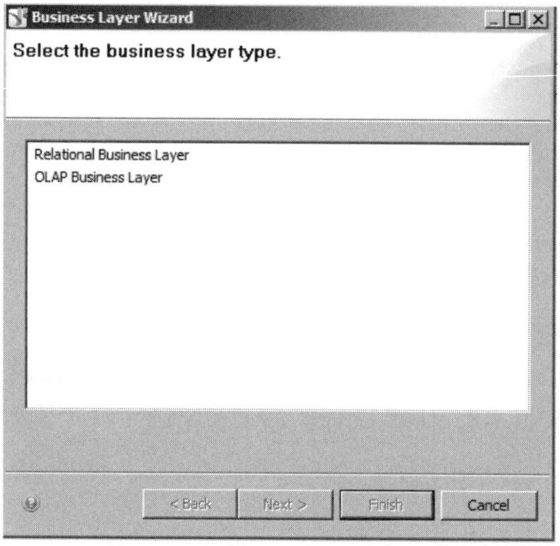

Figure 13.28
Selecting the business layer type.

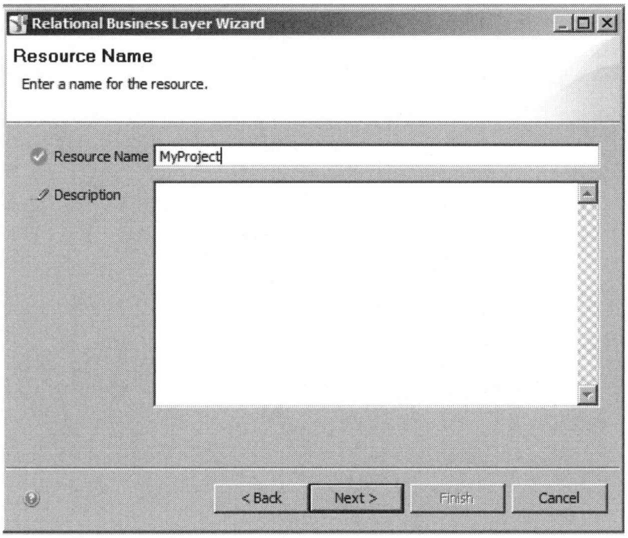

Figure 13.29
Naming a business layer.

5. Click Next and then click the ellipsis, as shown in Figure 13.30. You will see a list of data foundations connected with the local project you are working with, as shown in Figure 13.31.

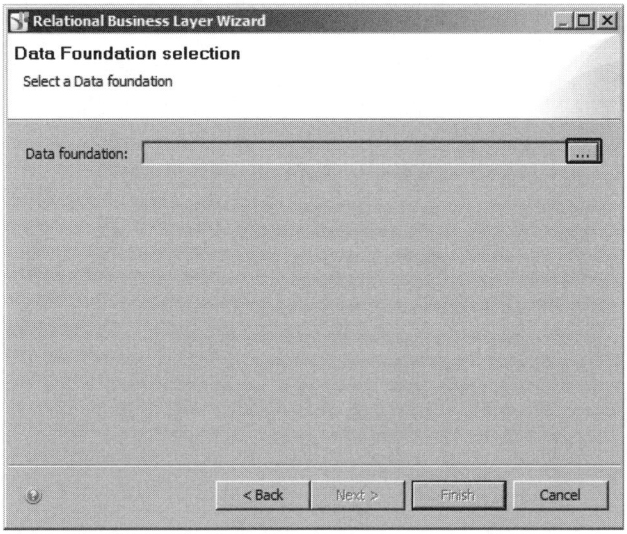

Figure 13.30
Selecting a data foundation.

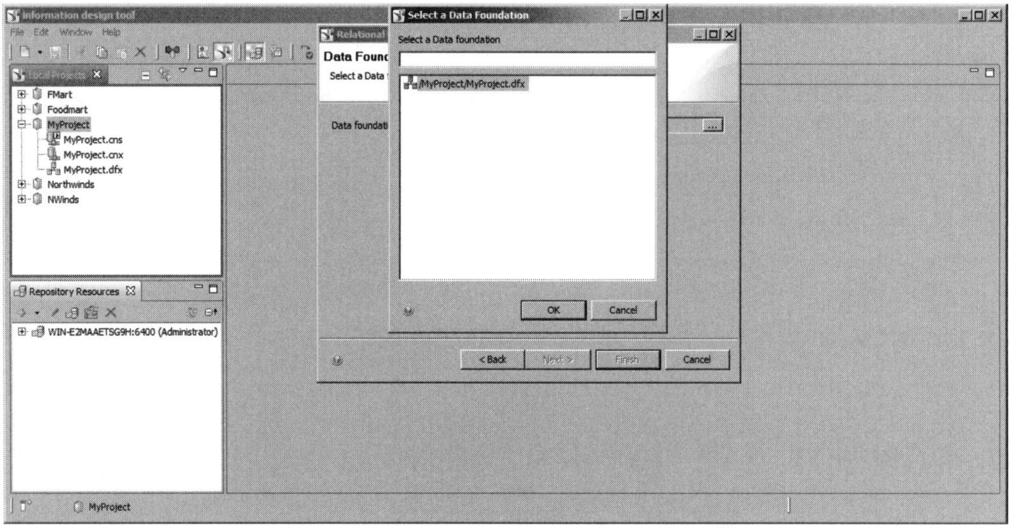

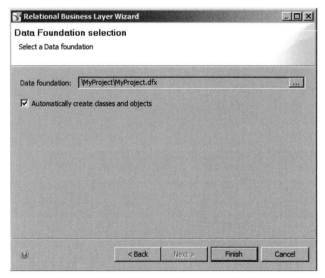

Figure 13.31
List of data foundations.

6. Select MyProject.dfx.

7. Click OK.

8. Click Finish, as shown in Figure 13.32.

Figure 13.32
Completing the business layer creation.

You should now see your business layer in your local project tree under the specified project. The business layer extension is .blx. You are now ready to create a universe and publish it to the repository.

Publishing the Universe

To publish the universe, follow these steps:

1. Right-click the business layer entity. For the purpose of this exercise, right-click the MyProject.blx object and choose Publish > To a Repository.

2. Select the Integrity Rules to check. You can select All Rules or select individual rules to check before publishing the universe, as shown in Figure 13.33.

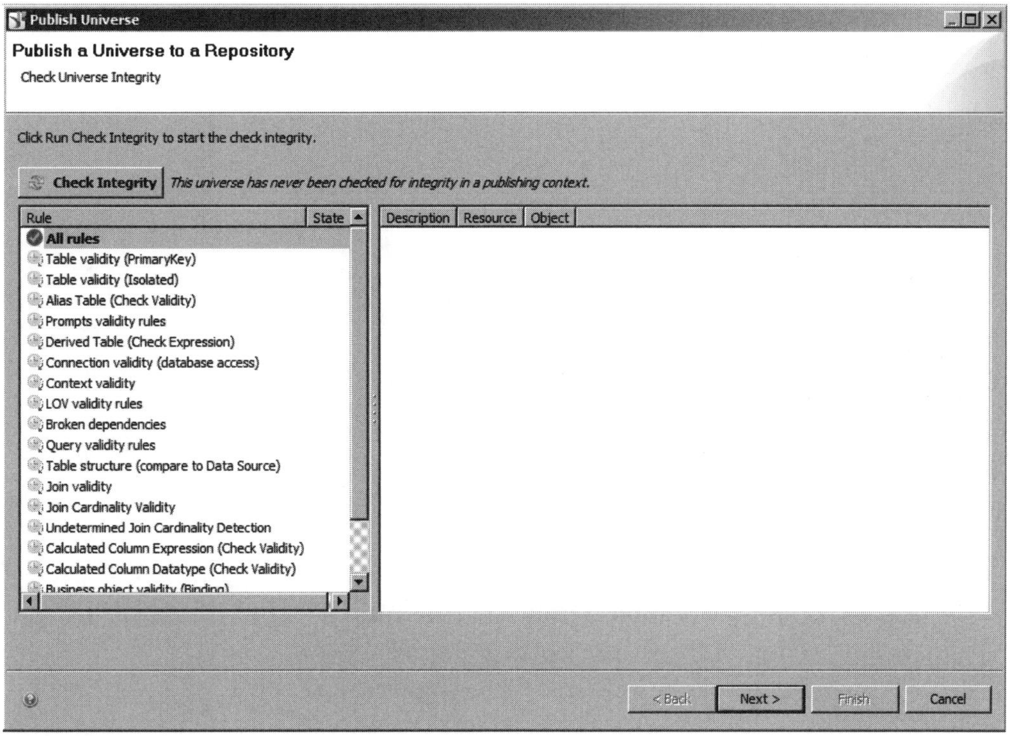

Figure 13.33
Selecting integrity rules to check.

3. Click Next.

4. Select the repository folder to store the universe, as shown in Figure 13.34. For the purpose of this exercise, select the Universes folder and click Finish.

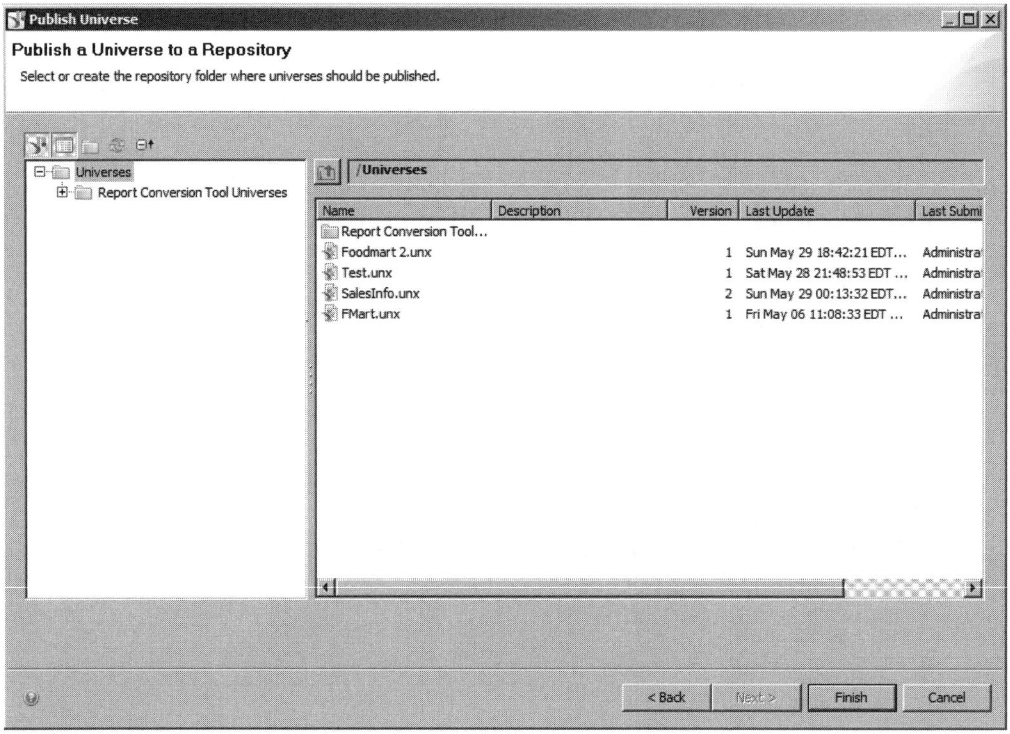

Figure 13.34
Saving the universe to the repository.

A status window will appear notifying the user whether the universe was published successfully, as shown in Figure 13.35.

5. Click Close. You are now ready to create a report with the new universe.

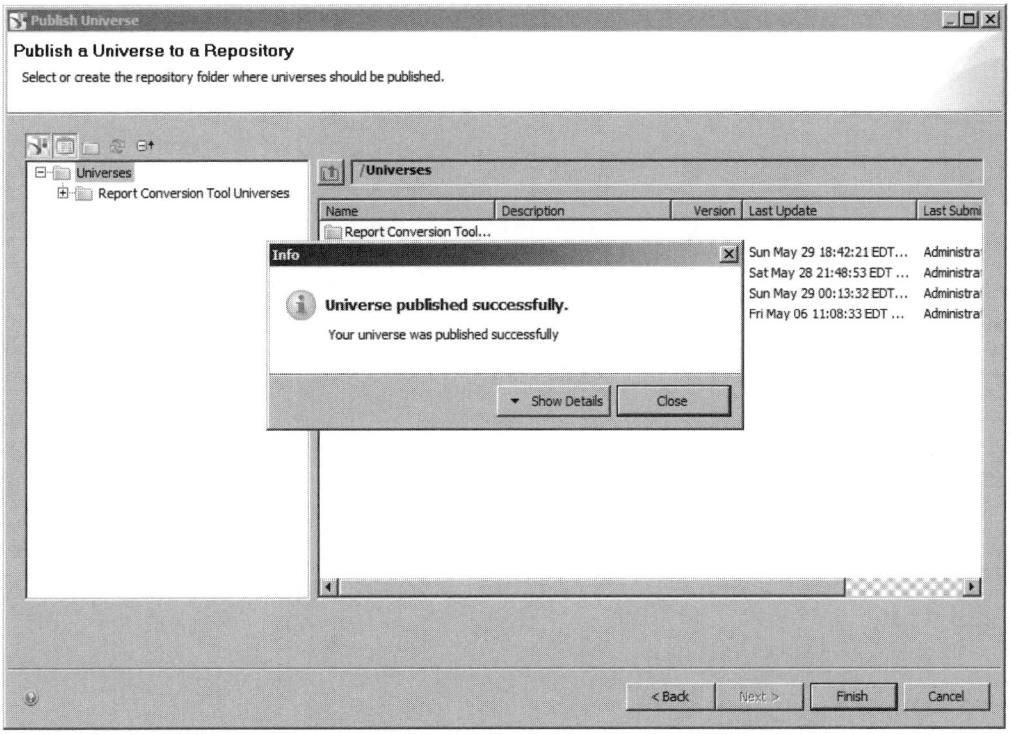

Figure 13.35
Universe published successfully.

SAP CRYSTAL REPORTS FOR ENTERPRISE START PAGE

The Crystal Reports for Enterprise XI 4.0 graphical user interface and platform has changed from previous versions. From the Start page, shown in Figure 13.36, you can create a blank report, access recent reports, or open an existing report. If you have created a universe connection and published to the repository, they will also be available.

Customizing the Environment

Customizing the system will enhance your ability to create efficient reports in a timely manner. To customize the Enterprise environment, select the Edit > Preferences option on the menu bar. You'll then see the Preferences window, as shown in Figure 13.37.

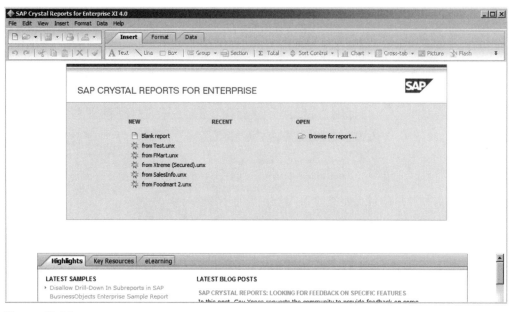

Figure 13.36
BusinessObjects Enterprise Start page.

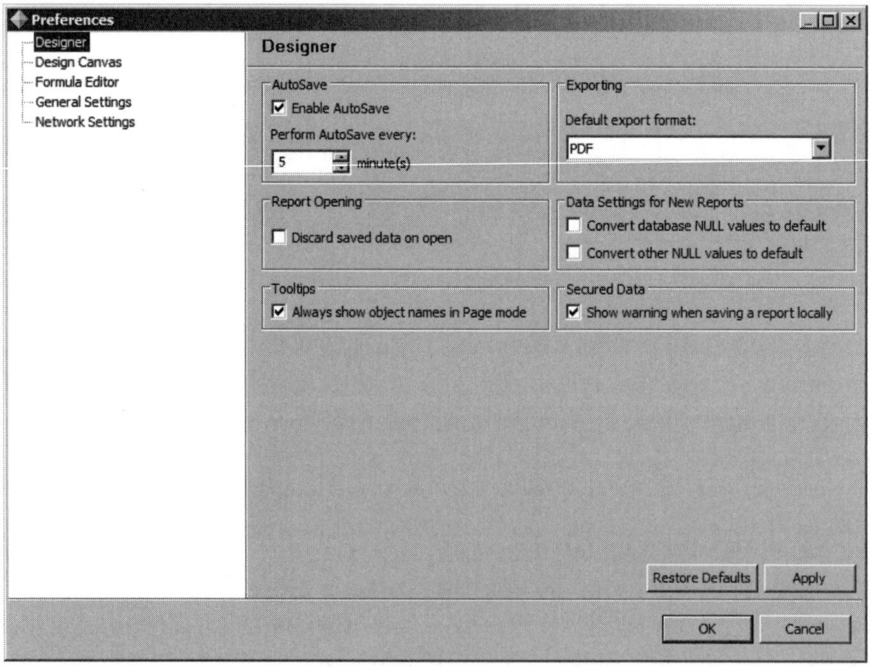

Figure 13.37
Customizing Preferences window.

Designer Tab

The Designer tab is equivalent to the Reporting tab in Crystal Reports 2011, standalone version. The Designer tab allows you to customize options such as the auto-save, default export options, and other features that are listed in Table 13.3.

Table 13.3 Designer Tab Options

Feature	Description
Enable Autosave	Turns on the auto-save feature in the background and automatically saves your report after the defined number of minutes.
Perform Autosave every:	Used in conjunction with the Enable Auto-Save feature. Sets the number of minutes to have the program auto-save the report.
Discard saved data on open	Allows you to force a refresh of the data upon opening the report. Necessary only when the Saved Data with Report is turned on.
Always show object names in Page mode	Turns on/off the tooltip displaying the field name in Page mode.
Default export format	Allows you to set the default export format for all reports generated.
Convert database NULL values to default	Converts database values to default values. Zero for a numeric field and a blank for a non-numeric field. Note: Affects database fields only.
Convert Other NULL values to default	Converts other field values to default values. Zero for a numeric field and a blank for a non-numeric field. Note: Affects non-database fields only.
Show warning when saving a report locally	Ensures a warning message is displayed if the report is saved to the local computer instead of the repository or server.

Design Canvas Tab

The Design Canvas tab, shown in Figure 13.38, is equivalent to the Layout tab in Crystal Reports 2011. This tab allows you to customize the options of the canvas and the elements placed in the design window, such as the grid measurements, snap to grid options, and other layout options listed in Table 13.4.

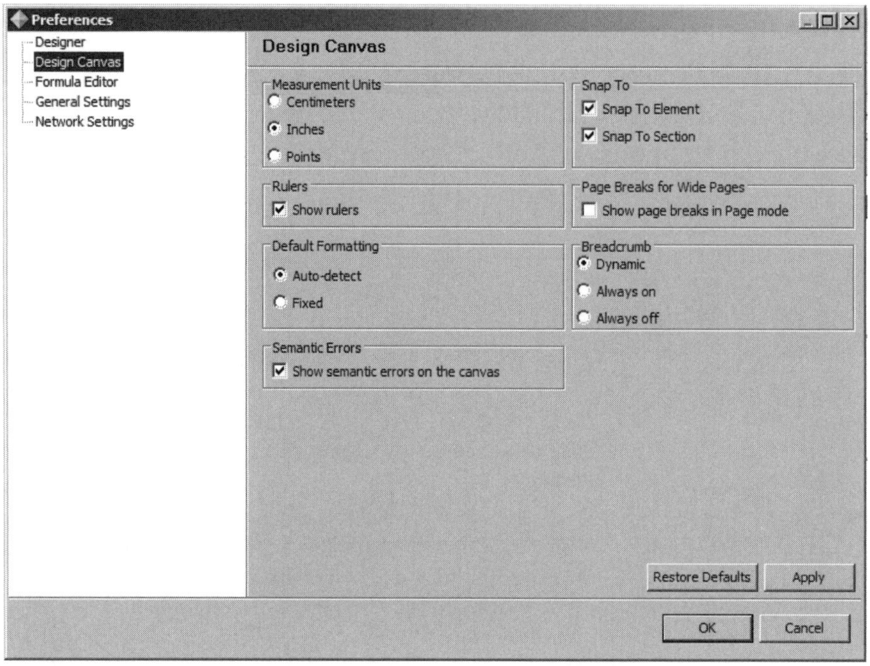

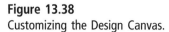

Figure 13.38
Customizing the Design Canvas.

Table 13.4 Design Canvas Tab Options

Features	Description
Measurement Units: Centimeters Points Inches	Allows you to set the unit of measure on the Design Canvas in centimeters, points, or inches.
Show Rulers	Turns on/off the vertical rulers in the Structure and Page modes.
Auto-detect (Default Formatting section)	Allows the program to format objects placed in the same section as existing objects. For example, if all of the fields placed in the detail section are bold, the addition of a new field in the section will automatically be bold.
Fixed (Default Formatting section)	Maintains the format of the field as in the database when placed on the report.

Table 13.4 *(Continued)*

Features	Description
Show semantic errors on the canvas	Turns on/off the feature to display an error message if an object is placed in a section that will generate incorrect data.
Snap to element	Snaps the object to the element.
Snap to section	Snaps the object to the section.
Show page breaks in Page mode	Turns on/off the display of page breaks in Page mode. It is turned off by default.

Formula Editor

The Formula Editor, shown in Figure 13.39, allows users to customize the font color of the functionality of the Formula Editor. For example, in Crystal Reports 2011, the font color for comments automatically defaults to green. In Crystal

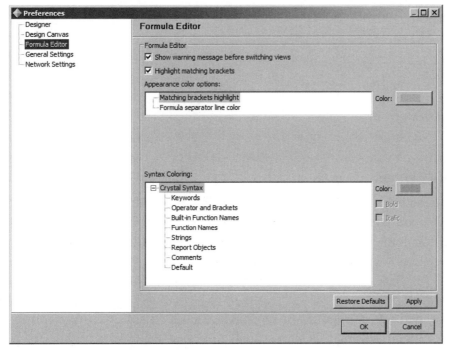

Figure 13.39
Customizing the Formula Editor.

Reports for Enterprise, you can customize it. See Table 13.5 for more about the available options.

Table 13.5 Formula Editor Options

Features	Description
Show warning messages before switching views	Turns on/off the message notifying that you are about to switch views in the Formula Editor. The options are Simple view and Advanced view.
Highlight matching brackets	Displays the opening or closing brackets.

Appearance color options:
    Matching bracket highlight
    Formula separator line color
	Allows you to set the default color for the matching bracket highlight and the formula separator line.

Syntax coloring
Crystal Syntax Options:
    Keywords
    Operators and Brackets
    Built-in Function Names
    Function Names
    Strings
    Report Objects
    Comments
    Defaults
	Allows you to set the default color for the Crystal Syntax options when creating the formula.

General Settings

The General Settings preferences, shown in Figure 13.40, allow you to set custom export configurations for the SAP BusinessObjects Enterprise Server XI 4.0. Setting this configuration options may require a reboot.

Network Settings

The Network Settings configuration settings are used to set the proxy configuration and any SSL settings, as shown in Figure 13.41.

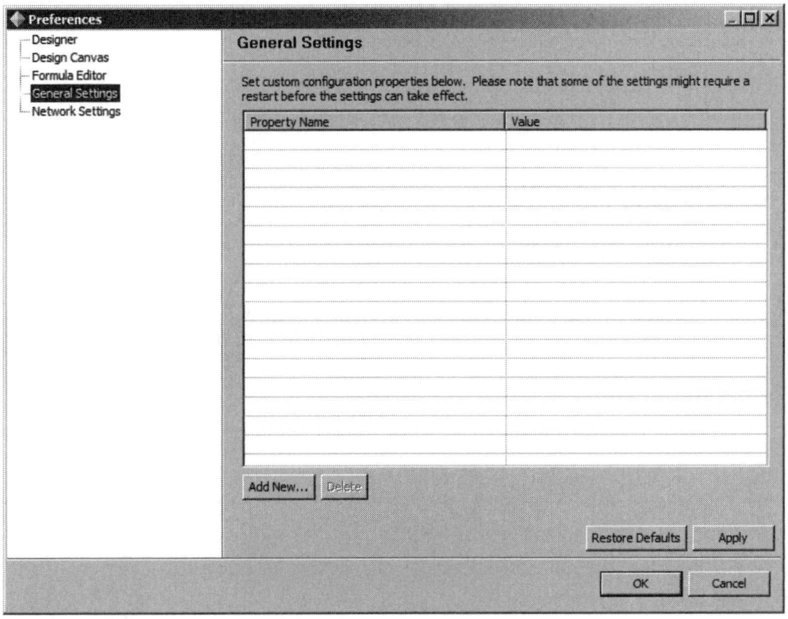

Figure 13.40
Configuring the General Settings.

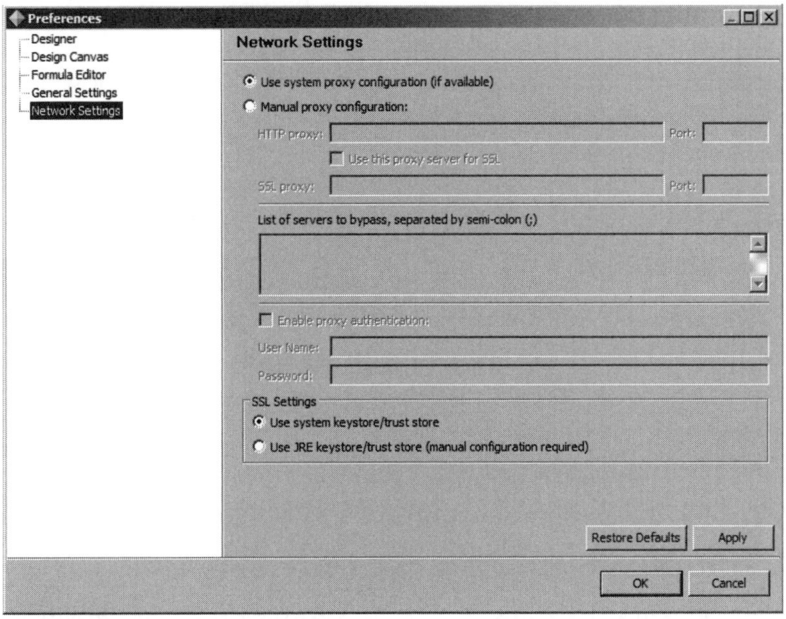

Figure 13.41
Configuring the Network Settings.

Connecting to a Data Source

With the new platform of the Enterprise XI 4.0 version release 1, you cannot connect directly to a relational database. Crystal Reports for Enterprise XI 4.0 can only be connected to a universe, SAP BEx query, or an analysis view. Due to this fact, you can install the Crystal Reports 2011 standalone version on the same computer as the Crystal Reports Enterprise XI 4.0. This allows you to use the standalone version for those systems that you cannot create a business layer for at this time and also gives you time to migrate all of your reports at your own pace. You must be connected to a SAP BusinessObjects Enterprise server before you can connect to a data source.

Note

> The appropriate type of data access connections must be set up on the BusinessObjects Enterprise server. Setting up data access connections on the Enterprise server is beyond the scope of this book. See the BOE Administrator for questions.

Data access connections are now able to connect to multiple data sources from relational databases. Previously, the data federator was used to compile data from two different data sources in order to make the report run more efficiently. The release of Crystal Reports Enterprise XI 4.0 has unleashed more power to control the processing of your data.

Creating a Report

To create a new report, select a blank report or an existing data connection from the Start page. For the purpose of this book, you will be connecting to a universe. The SAP BusinessObjects Enterprise Server logon window will appear. See Figure 13.42.

1. Log on to the server.

2. Enter your username and password, as shown in Figure 13.43.

3. Click OK. The New Data Source Connection window will open.

4. Choose the datatype from the Data Source Type drop-down, as shown in Figure 13.44.

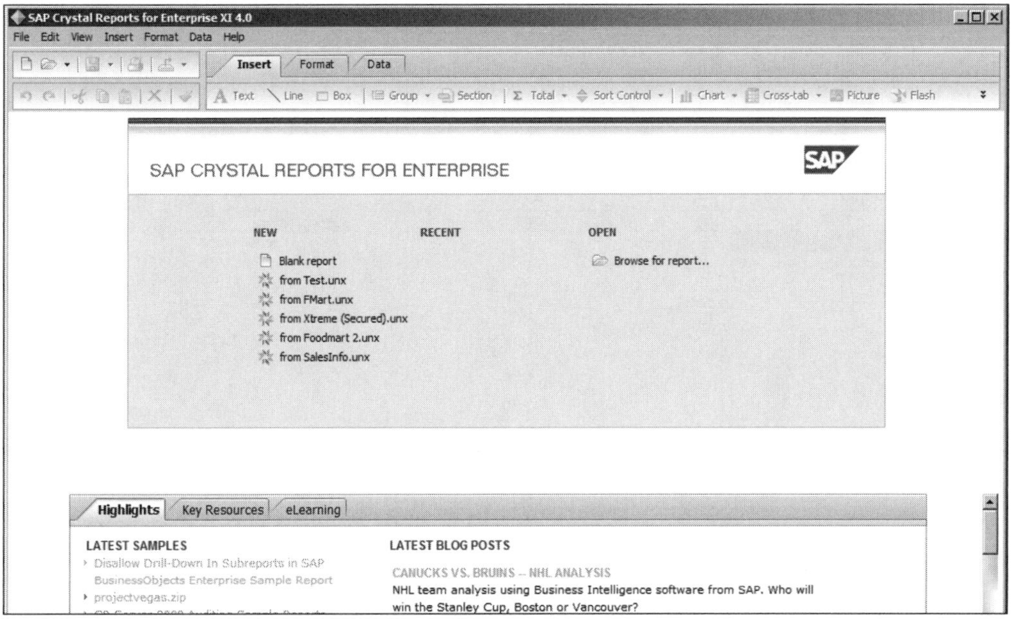

Figure 13.42
Creating a new report.

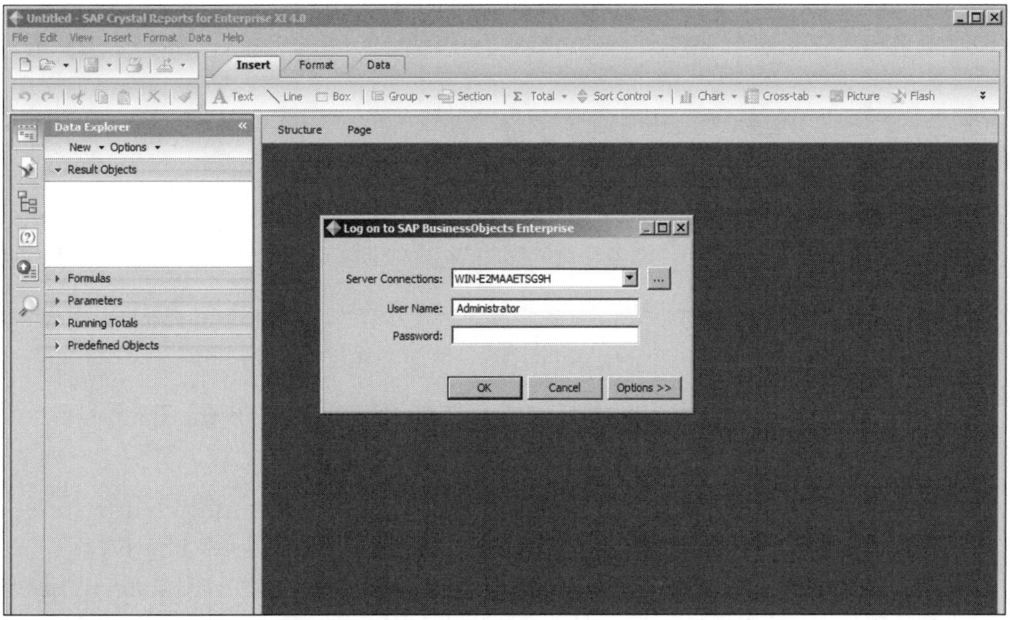

Figure 13.43
Logging on to the Enterprise server.

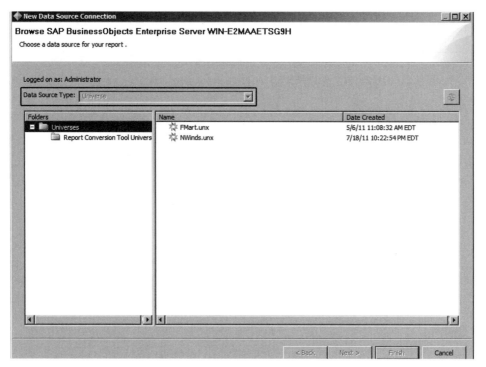

Figure 13.44
Choosing the datatype connection.

Note

You must have at least two connection datatypes set up on the SAP BusinessObjects Enterprise server for this data source type drop-down menu to be enabled. Otherwise, it will default to the one datatype available.

5. Select the appropriate connection from the list based on the datatype connection you selected previously, as shown in Figure 13.45.

6. Click Next. The system will begin the retrieval process indicated by the progress indicator box in the lower corner of the window. The Edit Query will appear allowing you to choose fields from the available objects stored in the universe created in the SAP BusinessObjects Information Design tool or the Universe Design tool, as shown in Figure 13.46.

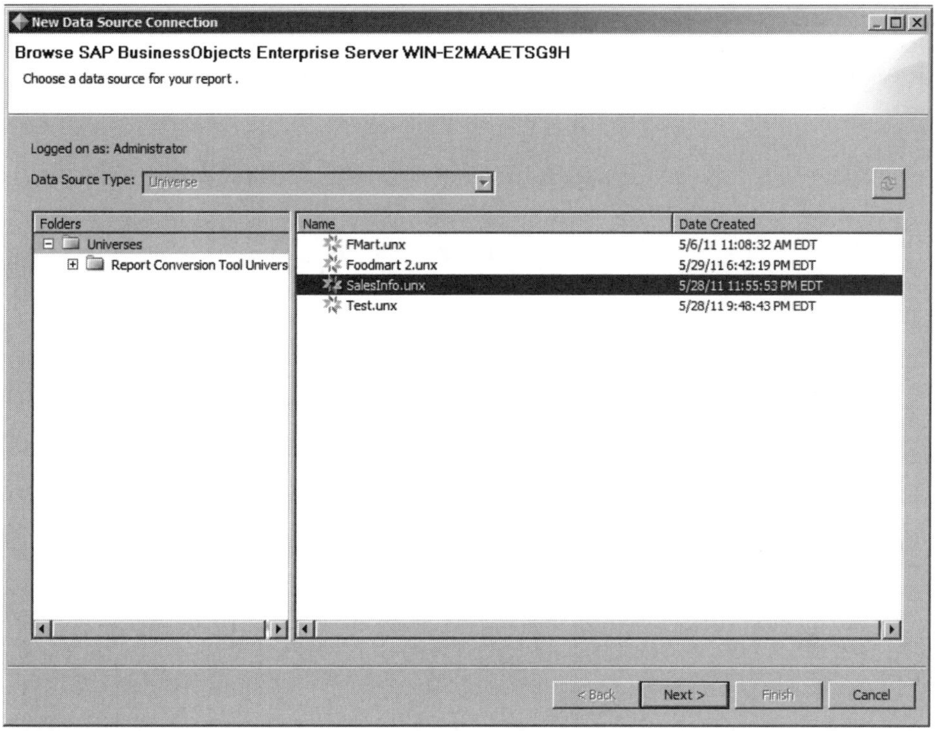

Figure 13.45
Selecting a universe connection.

The Edit Query window allows you to add the fields to the report, create or modify a filter on the query, and create or modify the existing query. The Edit Query window has a myriad of valuable tools; I want to take the time to introduce you to the functionalities of this window.

The Edit Query window has its own toolbar, as shown in Figure 13.47. The buttons found on the Edit Query toolbar are defined in Table 13.6.

The Query properties enable you to set the following features:

- Retrieve duplicate rows
- Retrieve empty rows
- Max retrieval time
- Max rows retrieved

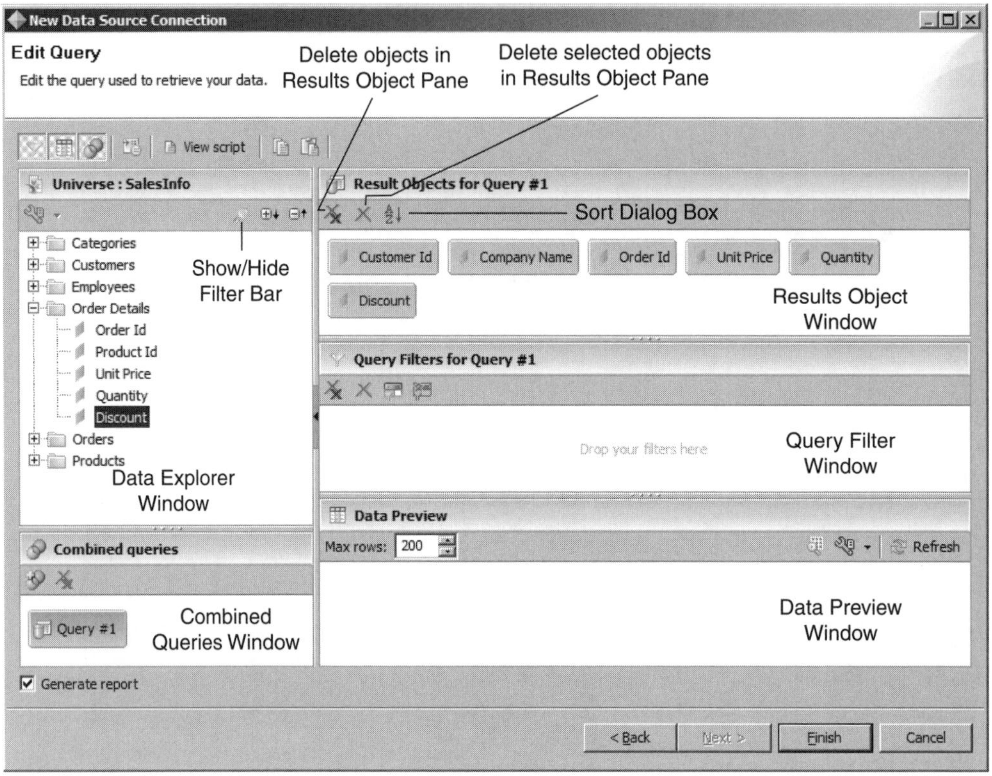

Figure 13.46
The Edit Query window of the Create Data Connection wizard.

Figure 13.47
The Edit Query toolbar.

- Sample result set
- Context

The View Script options allow you to view the script generated by the objects placed in the Results Objects pane or create your own query using a SQL query, as shown in Figure 13.49. You can choose from these options:

- **Use the query script generated by your query**—Objects placed in the Results Objects pane are used to create the query.

Table 13.6 Edit Query Toolbar Buttons

Icon	Name	Description
	Show/Hide Filter Panel	Hides or displays the panel that allows you to add a filter to your query for the report.
	Show/Hide Data Preview Panel	Hides or displays the pane used to view the data derived from the query.
	Show/Hide Combined Queries Panel	Combines two or more queries on your relational database. Cannot be used on an OLAP database.
	Query Properties	Displays options to set for the query. See Figure 13.48.
 View script	View Script	Displays the query generated by adding objects from the Data Explorer and gives you the ability to create your own custom query.
	Copy query specification to clipboard	Copies the query specifications from the Results Objects pane to the clipboard in .xml format. Query based on the objects you have added to the Results Objects pane.
	Paste query specification from clipboard	Pastes the query specifications from the clipboard to the Results Objects pane. Can be used in lieu of adding objects to the Results Objects pane.

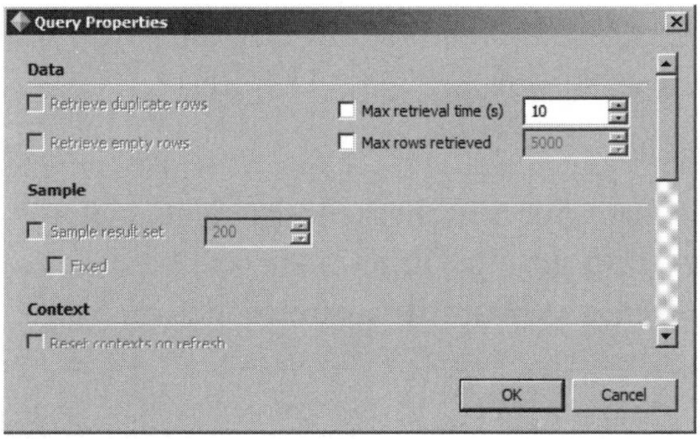

Figure 13.48
Working with Query properties.

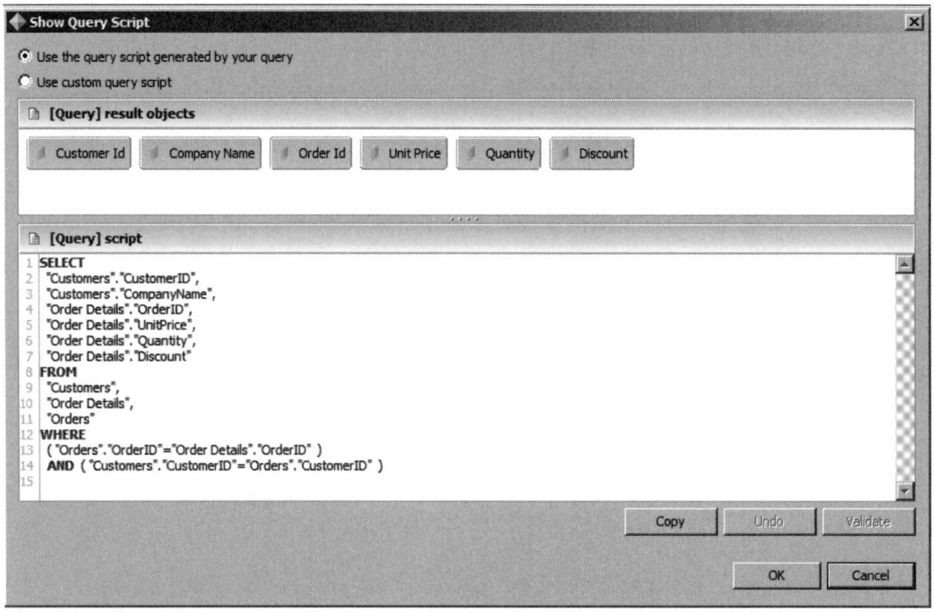

Figure 13.49
The View Script options.

- **Use custom query script**—Used when you create your own SQL statement using SELECT, FROM, GROUP BY, WHERE, and ORDER BY.

Continue to follow these steps to create the report:

1. Expand the Table folders and double-click the field or drag-and-drop the field in the Results Objects pane, as shown in Figure 13.50.

2. Add a filter to the query if desired.

3. Click Finish. If the Generate Report option is checked, the fields will automatically be placed on the report and the Page mode will be displayed. If the option is not checked, the blank structure mode will be displayed for you to design your report.

Before you can design your report, you should become familiar with the Crystal Reports for Enterprise XI 4.0 design environment, which you'll do in this next section.

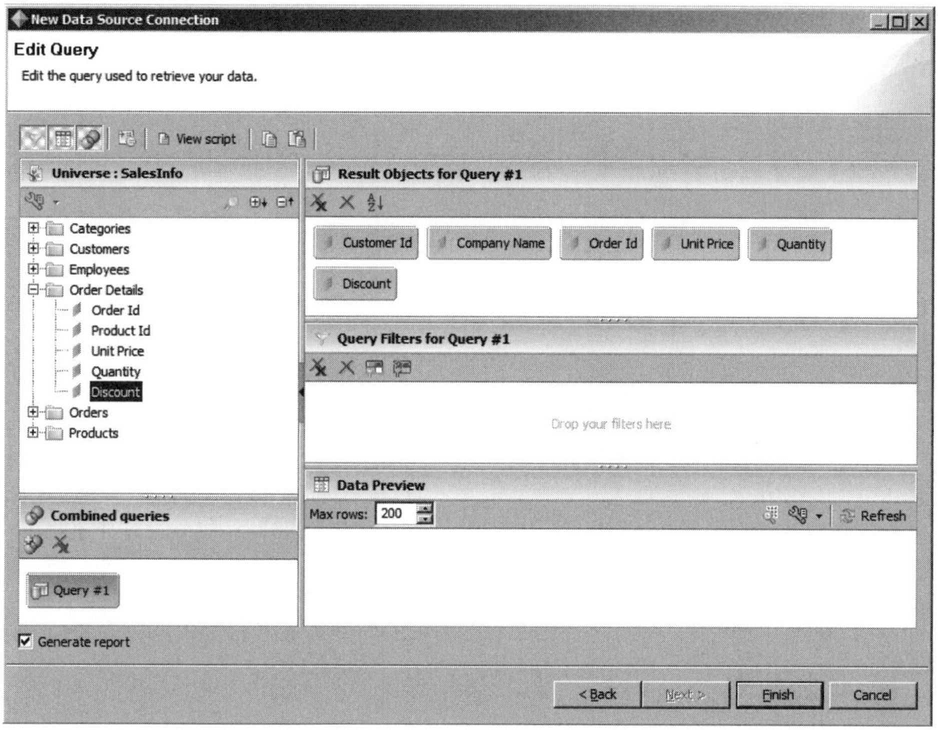

Figure 13.50
Adding fields to the report through a query.

Exploring the Crystal Reports Enterprise User Interface

The user interface for Crystal Reports Enterprise XI 4.0 has been completely revamped from previous versions. SAP developers have created a more intuitive user interface that promises to give users a better experience developing reports. Figure 13.51 shows the Report Development window.

Using the Toolbars

Many of the functions on the toolbars have been placed on tabs, similar to the Ribbon approach in the Microsoft Office suites. The remaining objects on the toolbars consist of the basic New, Open, Save, Print, Export, Undo, Redo, Cut, Copy, Paste, Delete, and Format Painter options, as shown in Figure 13.52.

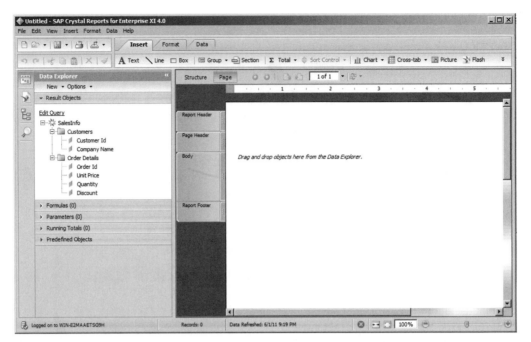

Figure 13.51
The Report Development window.

Figure 13.52
Basic options on the toolbars.

Note

The Export button is enabled only in the Page mode.

Using the Ribbon Tabs

The Ribbon tabs replace the Insert, Formatting, and Expert toolbars. The Insert toolbar's options are listed in Table 13.7.

Table 13.7 Insert Toolbar's Buttons

Icon	Purpose
A Text	Used to insert text object.
\ Line	Used to insert a line into the report.
☐ Box	Used to insert a box around the desired object.
{⊟ Group ▾	Used to insert a group.
⊡ Section	Used to insert a section in the report based on the section you have selected.
Σ Total ▾	Used to total a field. Allows you to insert the summary field in the group header or footer, report footer, or any other place of your choosing.
⇕ Sort Control ▾	Used to give the user ad hoc sorting capabilities on the predefined fields.
⑋ Chart ▾	Used to insert a chart.
▦ Cross-tab ▾	Used to insert a crosstab chart into the report.
⌸ Picture	Used to insert a picture into the report.
⅄ Flash	Used to insert a Flash object into the report.
⊡ Subreport	Used to insert a subreport into the main report.
⊞ Page Number ▾	Used to insert a page number into the report in the desired location.

Using the Format Tab

The options previously located on the Formatting toolbar have been placed on the new Format tab, shown in Figure 13.53. The formatting options allow you to set the font face, style, size, alignment, and borders. You can set these options by right-clicking on the object and choosing Format Result Object Element or Format Text, based on the object that you have selected.

Figure 13.53
Format tab's options.

Using the Data Tab

The Data Tab, shown in Figure 13.54, allows you to manage the data retrieved from the data source. You can edit the query generated by the data source, create groups and group sorts, set the record sort, create multiple types of formulas, and add or create subreport that links to the main report. The Data Tab options are listed in Table 13.8.

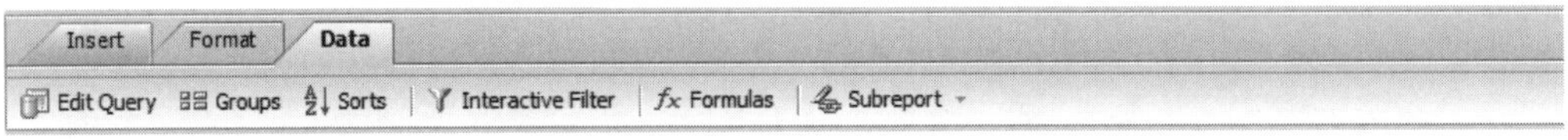

Figure 13.54
The Data Tab options.

Table 13.8 Data Tab Options

Icon	Purpose
Edit Query	Use this option to edit the existing report query generated in the Data Connection wizard.
Groups	Use this option to insert and sort groups.
Sorts	Use this option to create record sorts.
Interactive Filter	Use this option to filter the data retrieved from the database. This option is equivalent to the Select Expert in the standalone version.
ƒx Formulas	Use this option to create record, group, or save data filters through selection formulas. You will be able to access all formulas from this dialog box.
Subreport ▾	Use this option to set the options to pass data between the main report and the subreport or create the links between the main report and subreport.

Using the Data Explorer

The Data Explorer, shown in Figure 13.55, replaces the Field Explorer in SAP BusinessObjects Enterprise XI 4.0. The Data Explorer displays the objects that are available based on the type of data connection used in the report. From the Data Explorer, you can create formulas, parameters, running totals, and predefined objects previously known as the special fields.

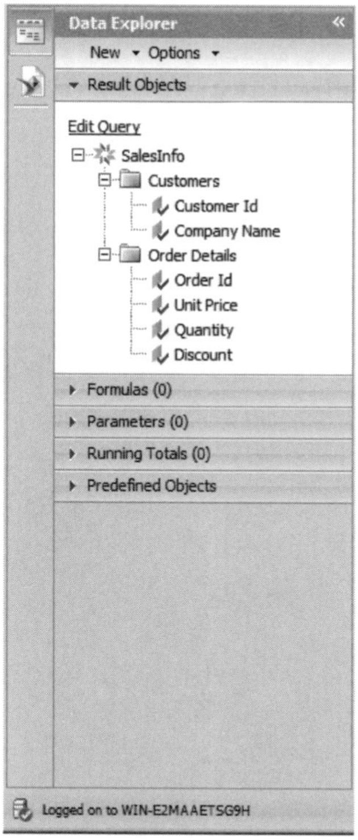

Figure 13.55
The Data Explorer.

The Data Explorer icons you see on the left side of the pane allow you to view different aspects of the report, as listed in Table 13.9.

Table 13.9 Data Explorer Icons

Icon	Purpose
	Data Explorer View—Displays data, formulas, parameters, and predefined objects to be used in the report.
	Outline View—Displays the sections and the fields included in each section. Replaced the Report Explorer in the standalone version.
	Group Tree—Displays the list of groups in the report.
	Search—Allows you to search the report for any word(s).

Using the Views

The Design Canvas (see Figure 13.56) consists of two views, the Structure mode and the Page mode.

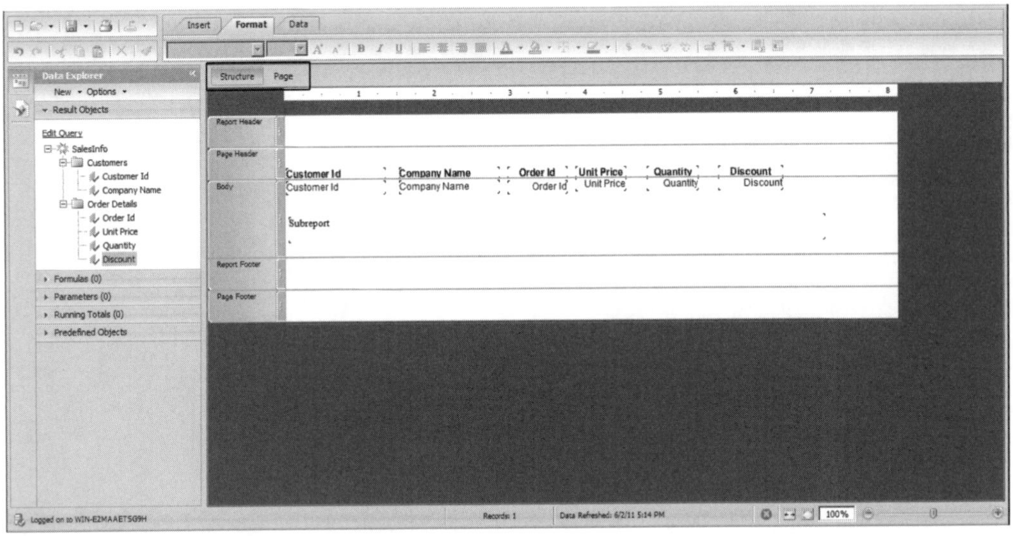

Figure 13.56
Design Canvas views.

- **Structure mode**—Replaces the Design view in previous versions. The Structure mode is the place where you organize and design your report and perform any initial formatting.

- **Page mode**—Replaces the Preview view in previous versions. The Page mode allows you to see how the report will look when printed.

Using the Sections

The Design Canvas consists of five standard sections. If a group has been inserted, a group header and group footer will be added to the Design Canvas.

- **Report Header**—Objects placed in this section will print one time on the first page of the report.

- **Page Header**—Objects placed in this section will print at the top of each page.

- **Body**—Objects placed in this section will print for every record retrieved from the database. This section is the equivalent of the Details section in Crystal Reports 2011.

- **Report Footer**—Objects placed in this section will print on the last page of the report such as a grand total or summary section.

- **Page Footer**—Objects placed in this section will print at the bottom of each page such as page number or print date and time.

- **Group Header**—The header for a group contains objects such as a group name or information relating to a group such as a chart or crosstab chart. This section appears only if a group has been inserted into the report.

- **Group Footer**—The group footer can contain objects such as a summary field or an object relating to the group information such as a chart or crosstab. This section appears only if a group has been inserted into the report.

Using the Smart Guidelines

Smart guidelines are intuitive and allow for easy report column format. The smart guidelines allow you to move the column and all objects within the column, as shown in Figure 13.57. They allow for easy rearranging of the

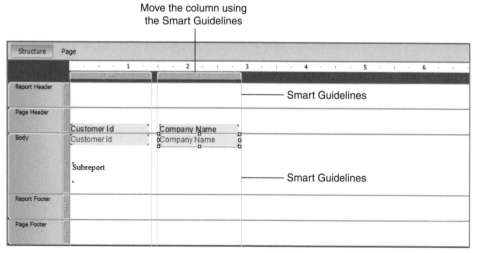

Figure 13.57
Using smart guidelines.

columns. The smart guidelines replaced the triangular guidelines that are used in the Crystal Reports 2011 version and prior versions. With a field selected, the column becomes visible and can be moved using the smart guideline. The field can be resized using the smart guidelines.

Summary

Crystal Reports for Enterprise XI 4.0 has unleashed a more powerful, intuitive platform. Evaluating the features of Crystal Reports 2011 and Crystal Reports for Enterprise and data connectivity options will allow you to intelligently make a decision on which software to purchase. You should perform the transition to Crystal Reports for Enterprise XI 4.0 at your own pace while considering all of the ramifications of using the new version, including the data source connectivity. Therefore, running Crystal Reports 2011 side by side on the same desktop client can be a beneficial practice.

CHAPTER 14

FORMATTING AND ORGANIZING REPORTS

The objectives of this chapter are as follows:

- Formatting fields
- Inserting groups
- Sorting groups
- Inserting summaries
- Sorting records
- Filtering records

Now that you've learned the basics of creating a simple report in SAP Crystal Reports for Enterprise XI 4.0, this chapter will cover some of the basic formatting options needed to create more than a list report. Formatting and organizing your reports are crucial aspects to developing useful, visually appealing reports. In the next few sections, you'll take a look at organizing reports through filtering records and sorting groups.

FORMATTING FIELDS

The ability to format the fields on the report gives you control over how the fields are displayed. You can change some of the format options from the Format ribbon, which replaced the Formatting toolbar in previous versions. You can also format your data source objects from the new Format Result Object Element option, which is accessible by right-clicking the object or choosing Format > Format Result Object Element from the menu.

You can format labels and other text objects by right-clicking them and selecting Format Text. Depending on the object type you have selected, the context menu and options will change.

The Formatting ribbon allows you to quickly control the following formatting properties of an option, such as:

- Font face
- Font size
- Increase font
- Decrease font
- Font Style—Bold, Italicized
- Underline style
- Alignment
- Font color
- Background color
- Borders
- Border color
- Use Currency symbol
- Use Percentage symbol
- Increase decimals
- Decrease decimals
- Hide (Suppress)
- Align Multiple Fields
- Conditional formatting
- Format subreport

USING THE FORMAT RESULT OBJECT ELEMENT

The Format Result Object Element maintains all of the options necessary to format the field to fit your reporting requirements. To format a data source object, you right-click the data source object and choose Format Results Object Element, as shown in Figure 14.1.

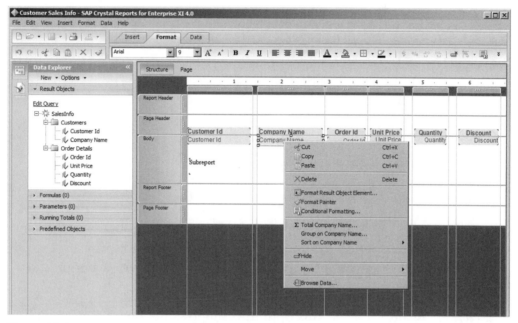

Figure 14.1
Formatting a field.

The options of the Formatting Element window are the same as in the Crystal Reports 2011 version; however they are categorized in multiple sections in this version, giving the window a streamlined look. The sections are General, Font, Appearance, and Paragraph. Each of them is discussed in the following sections.

The General Page

The General page (shown in Figure 14.2.) has the following options:

- **Data source**—Defines the name of the data source field from the database.

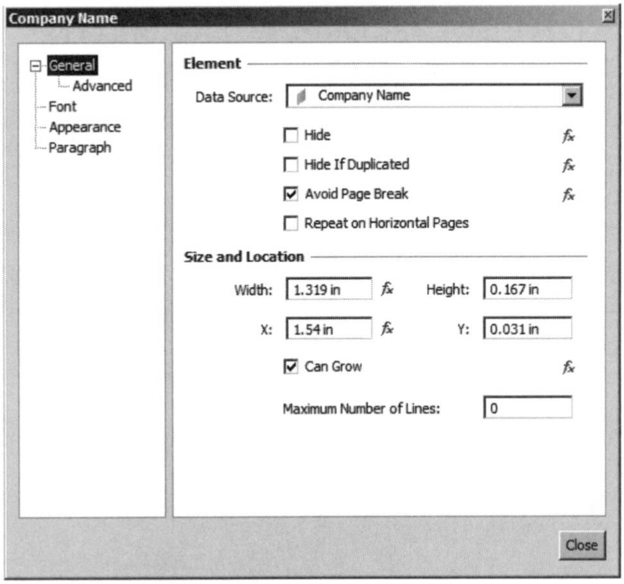

Figure 14.2
The General page of the Formatting Result Object Element.

Hide—Use this option to suppress the object. It will not print on the report. This option can be conditionally set by using the *fx* button next to the option.

Hide if Duplicated—Use this option to suppress the object if it is duplicated on the report. This option can be conditionally set by using the *fx* button next to the option.

Avoid Page Break—Use this option to keep the object together. If there is not enough space to print the entire object on the page, it will stop printing at that point and start printing the entire object on the next page. Use of this option may cause wasted white space on your report. This option can be conditionally set by using the *fx* button next to the option.

Repeat on Horizontal Pages—Use this option to repeat the object on the next page if the data spans multiple pages horizontally.

■ **Size and Location**—Allows you to set the width and height of a field and the location of the field on the report. The options are:

Width—Allows you to numerically program the width of the field. This option can be conditionally set by using the *fx* button next to the option.

Height—Allows you to numerically program the height of the field. This option can be conditionally set by using the *fx* button next to the option.

x—Allows you to set the horizontal placement of the field on the report. This option can be conditionally set by using the *fx* button next to the option. Setting the option conditionally will allow you to place the field in different columns based on defined criteria.

y—Allows you to set the vertical placement of the field on the report.

Can Grow—Allows the field to grow vertically if the text is greater than the height of the data source object. This option is similar to the Wrap Text feature. This option can be conditionally set by using the *fx* button next to the option.

Maximum Number of Lines—This option is used in conjunction with the Can Grow option. It gives you the ability to specify how many lines of text you want to display from the data source object. For example, when you want to show only the first five lines of the data source field such as a memo field.

- **Advanced Settings**—These are several advanced settings, as follows:

Name—The name of the field in the data source. You can change the name of the field.

Tooltip Text—Use this option to describe the field to the users. When users hover their mouse pointers over the field, the tooltip will appear. This option can be conditionally set by using the *fx* button next to the option.

CSS Name—This option specifies a Cascading Style Sheet name used to consistently format the same type of fields in every report.

Display String—This option is set by using the *fx* button. It allows you to specify a custom format for your string fields.

Hyperlink Type—The available hyperlink options will depend on the object selected and its location on the report. You can choose from these hyperlink types:

- No Hyperlink—This is the default option. Select this option to not have the field displayed as a hyperlink.
- A Website on the Internet—Use this option to have the object point to a website address.
- An Email Address—Use this option to have the object point to an email address.
- A File—Use this option to point to a file that is accessible to the users of the report. It must be stored in a shared location.
- Current Website Object Value—Use this option to turn the current selected field into a website hyperlink. The field value must be formatted as a website in order for the option to be enabled.
- Current Email Object Value—Use this option to turn the current selected field into an email hyperlink. The field value must be formatted as an email in order for the option to be enabled.
- Another Report Element—Use this option if you want to create a hyperlink to another object on the report, such as to a chart or summary.

The Font Page

The font options allow you to format the font face, size, style, and other effects that can also be quickly set from the Format ribbon tab.

The Font page consists of the following options, as shown in Figure 14.3:

- **Font**—Use this option to set the font face of the object. This option can be conditionally set by using the *fx* button next to the option.

- **Size**—Use this option to set the font size of the object. This option can be conditionally set by using the *fx* button next to the option.

- **Color**—Use this option to set the font color of the object. This option can be conditionally set by using the *fx* button next to the option.

- **Effects Style**—Use this option to set the style of the text in the object. Examples include regular, bold, italic, and bold italic.

  Strikethrough—Use this option to place a strikethrough effect on the object.

  Underline—Use this option to underline the value of the object.

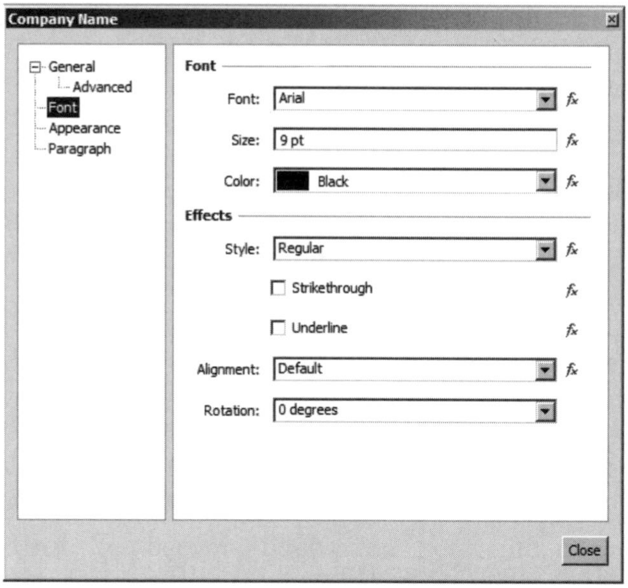

Figure 14.3
The Font page options of the Formatting Results Object Element.

Alignment—Use this option to set the horizontal alignment of the object. The options are default, left, right, justified, and centered.

Rotation—Use this option to rotate the text of the object.

The Appearance Page

The Appearance page, shown in Figure 14.4, includes options relating to the border and background color.

The Appearance page replaces the Border tab in previous versions of the Format Editor and consists of the following options:

The Border options are as follows:

- **Left**—Use this option to set a border on the left side of the field. This option can be conditionally set by using the *fx* button next to the option.

- **Right**—Use this option to set a border on the right side of the field. This option can be conditionally set by using the *fx* button next to the option.

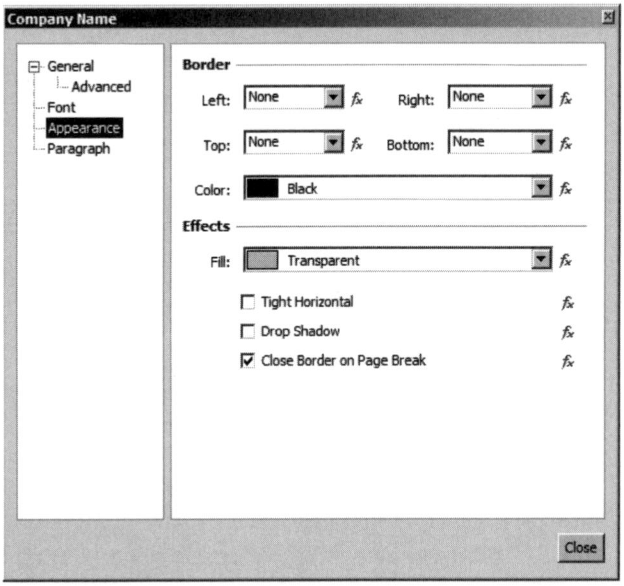

Figure 14.4
The Appearance page of the Formatting Results Object Element.

▪ **Top**—Use this option to set a border on the top of the field. This option can be conditionally set by using the *fx* button next to the option.

Tip

The top border can be used as a total line indicator on a field instead of inserting a single line above the total field. The border line is the length of the field and stays with the field if exported.

▪ **Bottom**—Use this option to set the bottom border of the field. This option can be conditionally set by using the *fx* button next to the option.

Tip

The bottom border can be used as the double line at the end of a financial report instead of inserting a double line below the total field.

▪ **Color**—Use this option to set the border's line color. This option can be conditionally set by using the *fx* button next to the option.

The Effect options are as follows:

- **Fill**—Use this option to set the background color of the object. This option can be conditionally set by using the *fx* button next to the option.

- **Tight Horizontal**—This option trims the space around the border. Use caution when using this option, because it will resize your fields. The borders will be tight around the length of the value in the field, not the original size of the field. This option can be conditionally set by using the *fx* button next to the option.

- **Drop Shadow**—Use this option to print a drop shadow on the object. The drop shadow prints across the bottom and to the right of the object. This option can be conditionally set by using the *fx* button next to the option.

- **Close Border on Page Break**—This option prevents any field or object that has a border around it and spans multiple pages from printing partial borders. This option ensures that each page the field is printed on has a full border around all partial text. This option can be conditionally set by using the *fx* button next to the option.

The Paragraph Page

The Paragraph page, shown in Figure 14.5, displays the options related to spacing and other paragraph attributes.

The Paragraph options are described here.

- **First Line**—Use this option to set the exact measurement in inches that the first line should be indented in a paragraph. If your report is measured in units, pixels, or centimeters, the measurement you enter here should match that unit of measure.

- **Left**—Use this option to set how far the paragraph should start from the left margin.

- **Right**—Use this option to set how far the paragraph should start from the right margin.

- **Line**—Use this option to set the exact line spacing or to set it as a multiple of your font size.

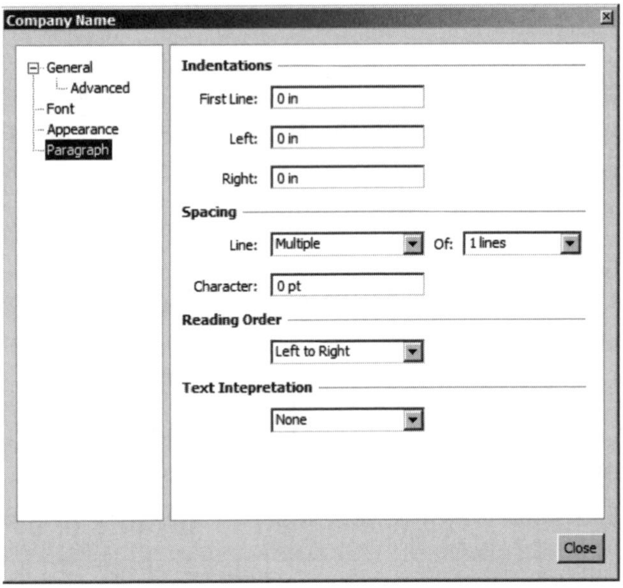

Figure 14.5
The Paragraph page of the Formatting Results Object Element.

- **Of**—If you chose Exact in the Line option, you need to enter the exact number. If you chose Multiple, enter the multiple of the line spacing.

- **Character**—Use this option to set the character spacing between the characters.

The Reading Order formatting options are:

- **Left to Right**—Use this option to ensure that the system reads the text from left to right.

- **Right to Left**—Use this option to ensure that the system reads the text from right to left.

You use the Text Interpretation option to select the type of preformatted text. You can choose from the following options:

- **None**—The text is read as plain text.

- **RTF**—The text is read in Rich Text Format.

- **HTML**—The text is read as HTML data.

Numeric Formatting Options

The Format Number page is shown in Figure 14.6.

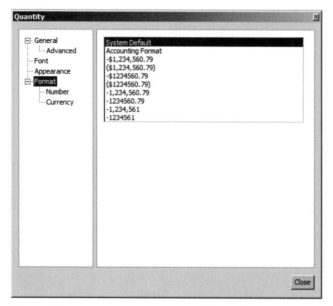

Figure 14.6
Numerical format options of the Formatting Result Object Element.

The Format page of the Formatting Result Object Element allows you to specify the numerical format of the object. The system default number format is the default setting. When the format does not fit your requirements, you can customize the number format from one of the following format pages shown in Figures 14.7 and 14.8.

The Format Number page allows you to specify attributes relating to decimals, rounding, and the handling of zeroes and negative numbers. It has the following options:

- **Decimals**—Use this option to set the number of decimal places. This option can be conditionally set by using the *fx* button next to the option.

- **Rounding**—Use this option to determine how values are rounded. This option can be conditionally set by using the *fx* button next to the option.

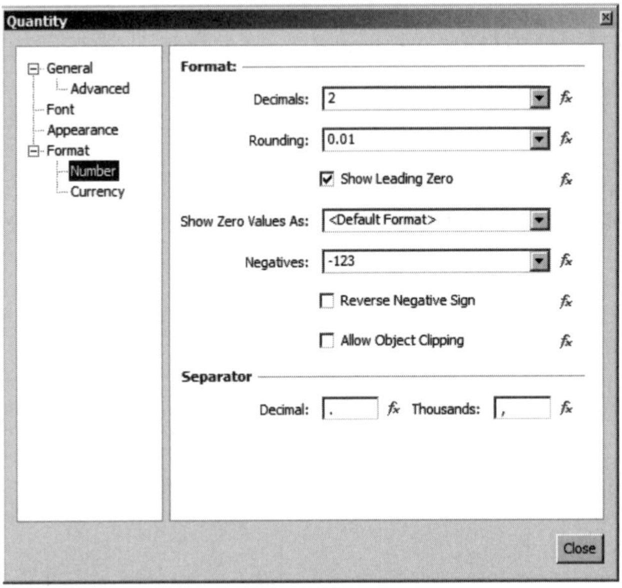

Figure 14.7
The Format Number options.

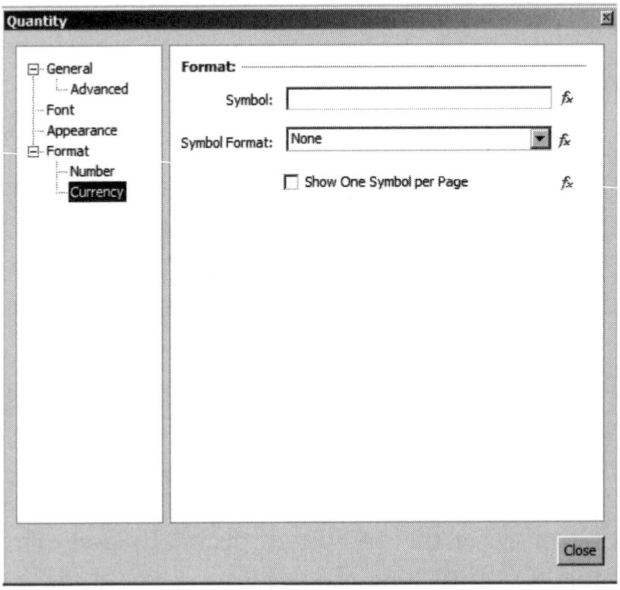

Figure 14.8
The default currency options.

Show Leading Zero—Use this option to ensure a single digit is preceded by a 0. This option can be conditionally set by using the *fx* button next to the option.

- **Show Zero Value As**—Use this option to set the value as a−, 0, or Hide. This option can be conditionally set by using the *fx* button next to the option.

- **Negatives**—Use this option to set the way you want the negative values to appear. This option can be conditionally set by using the *fx* button next to the option.

- **Reverse Negative Sign**—Use this option to reverse the signs for debits and credits in a financial report. This option can be conditionally set by using the *fx* button next to the option.

- **Allow Object Clipping**—Use this option to determine whether the number truncation sign is visible. If the field is not wide enough to show the whole number, the field will display on the report as ########. If this option is chosen, it will show only the number of characters the field is wide enough to show, with no truncation indicators.

Caution

It is recommended that you not use this option because it can have severe undesired results. Numbers are by default right-aligned; therefore, a field with the value of $1,231,567.89 that is wide enough to show only six characters will display as 567.89. If the field is left aligned it will display as $1,231. Either way, you can see the need for caution when using this option.

- **Decimal Separator**—Use this option to specify the symbol to separate the decimal digits. This option can be conditionally set by using the *fx* button next to the option.

- **Thousands Separator**—Use this option to specify the symbol for the thousands character. This option can be conditionally set by using the *fx* button next to the option.

The Format Currency page's options are used to set the currency symbol and its location. This enables you to display foreign currency in the correct format. The options are context-based, which means they change based on the attributes that are set. The default currency options are shown previously in Figure 14.8.

- **Symbol**—Enter the currency symbol desired for the object. This option can be conditionally set by using the *fx* button next to the option.

Note

If you enter a currency symbol, the Symbol Position option will be enabled, allowing you to specify inserting the currency symbol in front or behind the dollar value.

- **Symbol Format**—This option defines the format of the currency symbol in relation to the value of the object. The options are fixed, floating, or none. The fixed position as a default will always align the currency symbol to the far left of the width of the object, keeping all symbols aligned. A floating currency symbol will appear immediately to the left of the value of the object. This option can be conditionally set by using the *fx* button next to the option.

Tip

I recommend using Fixed for the Symbol Format. The Fixed position is more visually appealing and seems to give a cleaner, more professional appearance. However, it should be based on your organization's normal format.

- **Symbol Position**—Use this option to define the location of the currency symbol. This option is available only after you enter a currency symbol in the Symbol option. See Figure 14.9.
- **Show One Symbol per Page**—Use this option to enable a currency symbol on the first record on each page only. This option can be conditionally set by using the *fx* button next to the option.

Boolean Type Formatting Options

Boolean type fields will have a Boolean page in the Formatting Results Object Element, as shown in Figure 14.10. Boolean fields are fields that result in a True or False, Yes or No, or 0 or 1 values.

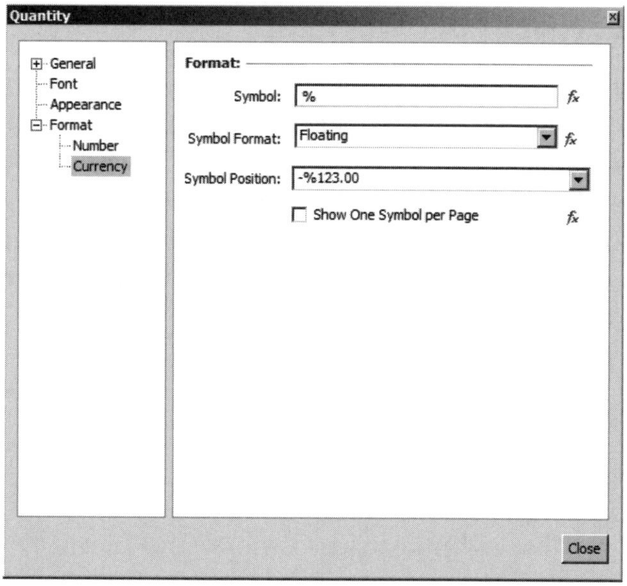

Figure 14.9
Setting the currency symbol position.

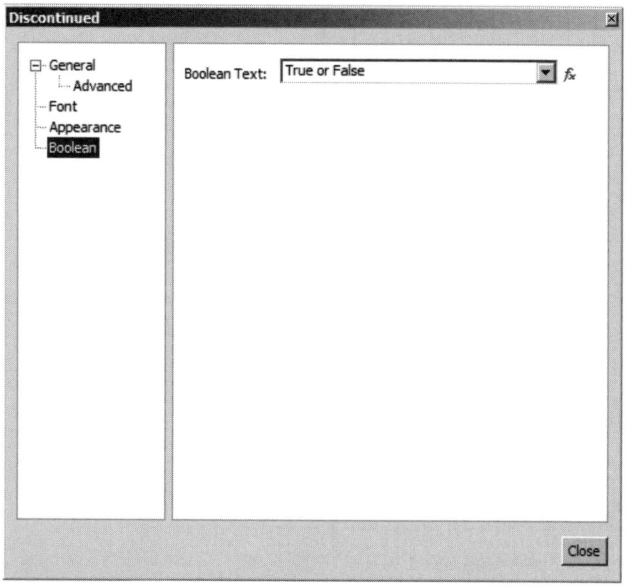

Figure 14.10
The Boolean options.

CONDITIONAL FORMATTING

Conditional formatting allows you to establish formatting under certain conditions. Conditional formatting replaces the Highlighting Expert in previous versions. You can access the Conditional Formatting dialog box in one of three ways—by right-clicking the object and selecting Conditional Formatting, by using the Format > Conditional Formatting menu, or by clicking the Conditional Formatting icon on the Format tab. You can format the font style, color, border style and color, and the background color, as shown in Figure 14.11.

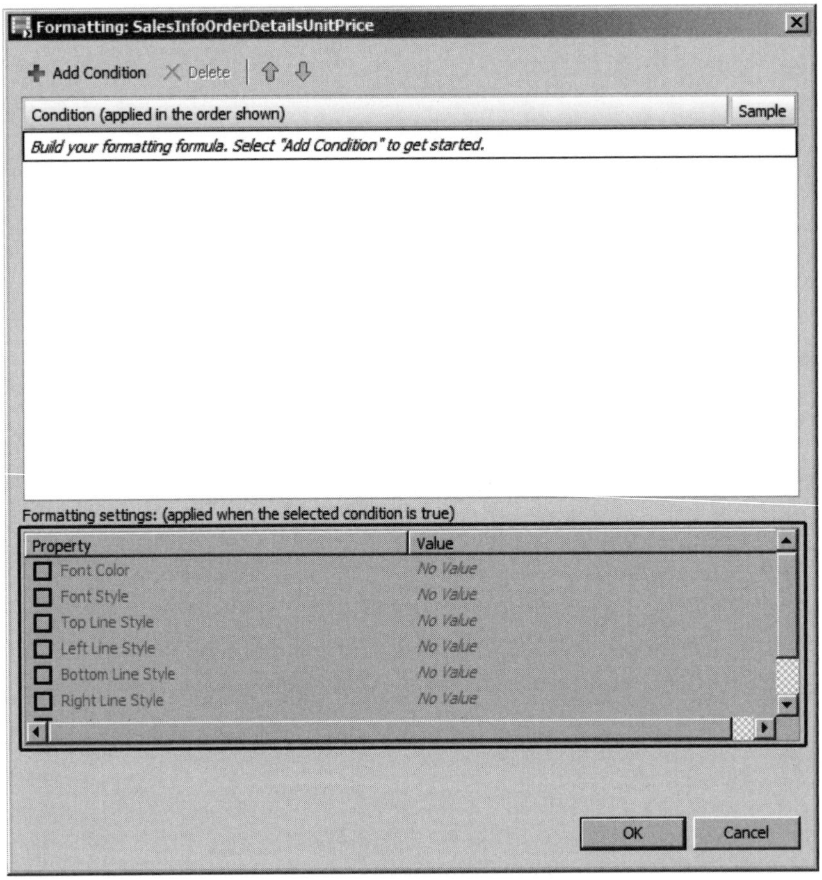

Figure 14.11
The Conditional Formatting dialog box.

To create conditional formatting criteria follow these steps:

1. Open the Conditional Formatting dialog box via one of the methods discussed previously.

2. Click the Add Condition button, as shown in Figure 14.12.

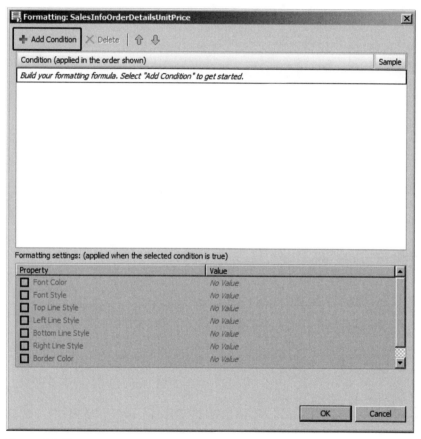

Figure 14.12
You insert conditional criteria using the Add Condition button.

3. The first option includes the fields available in the universe associated with the report. If you had a field selected when you opened the Conditional Formatting dialog box, the drop-down menu will default to that field. You can choose any field that is available, as shown in Figure 14.13.

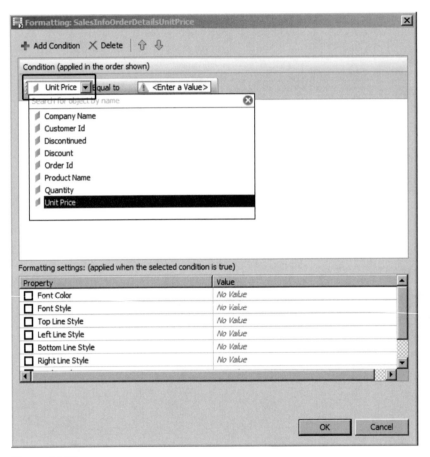

Figure 14.13
Selecting a conditional formatting field.

4. Using the list of operators, select the one that best fits your requirement. For example, if you were setting a criteria to highlight all records in which the unit price is greater than $45.00, you would use the operators, Greater Than or Greater Than or Equal To, as shown in Figure 14.14.

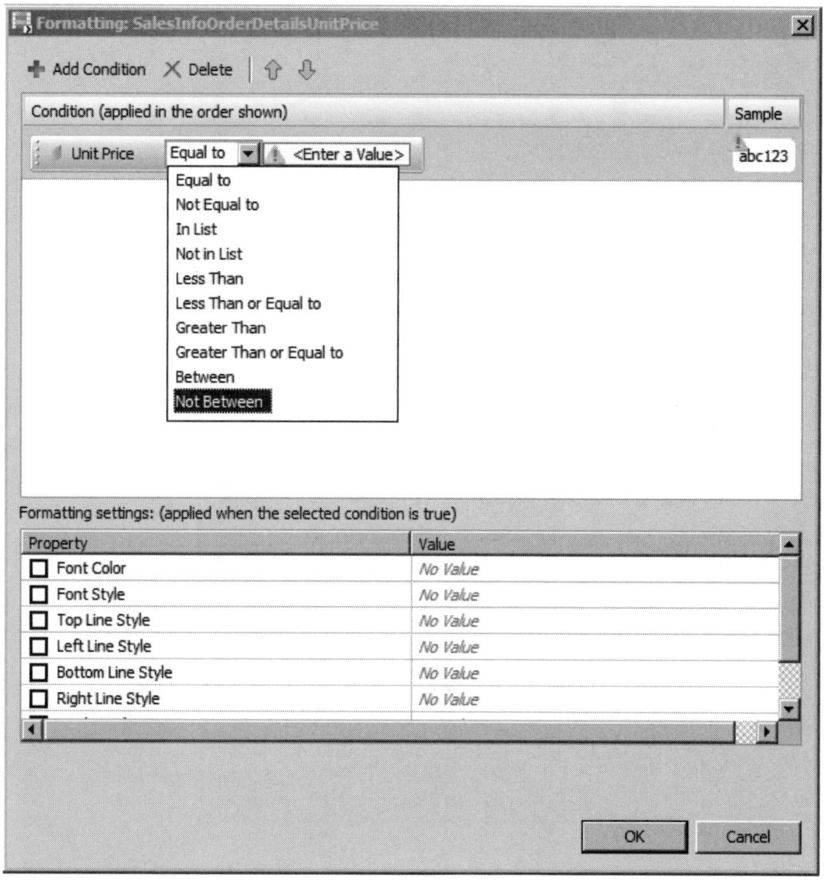

Figure 14.14
Using an operator to set conditions.

5. Enter a value to complete your criteria. You can also click the drop-down arrow and select a value in the database or you can create a new parameter to choose the value on an ad hoc basis, as shown in Figure 14.15.

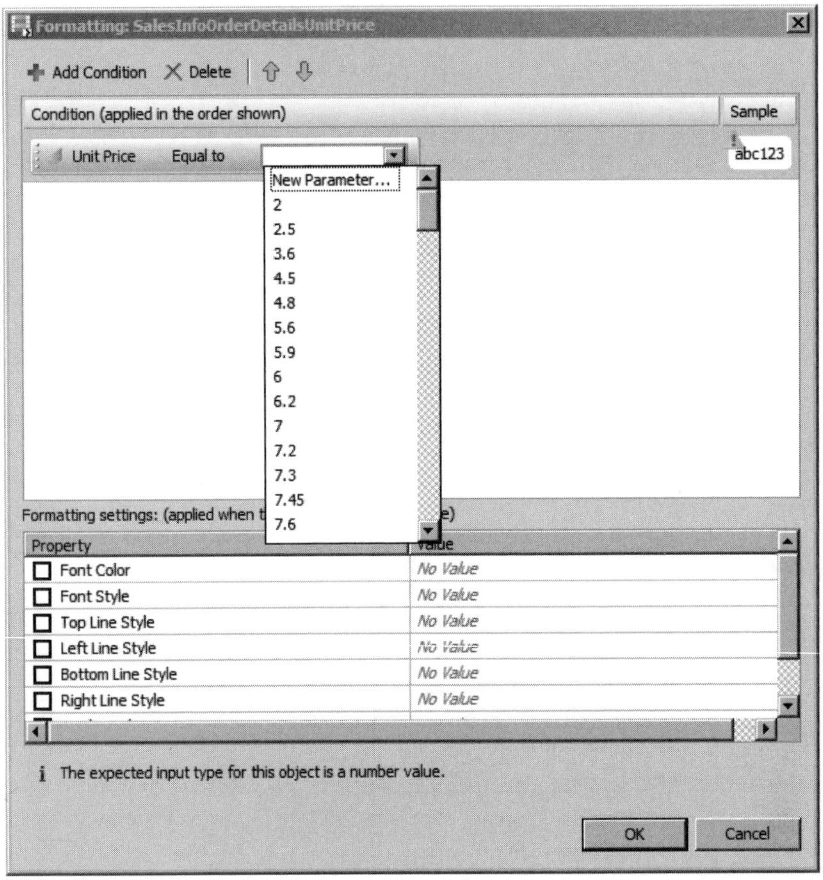

Figure 14.15
Entering a value.

6. Select the Formatting Settings check boxes that define your desired format. For example, click the Font color checkbox and set the value, as shown in Figure 14.16.

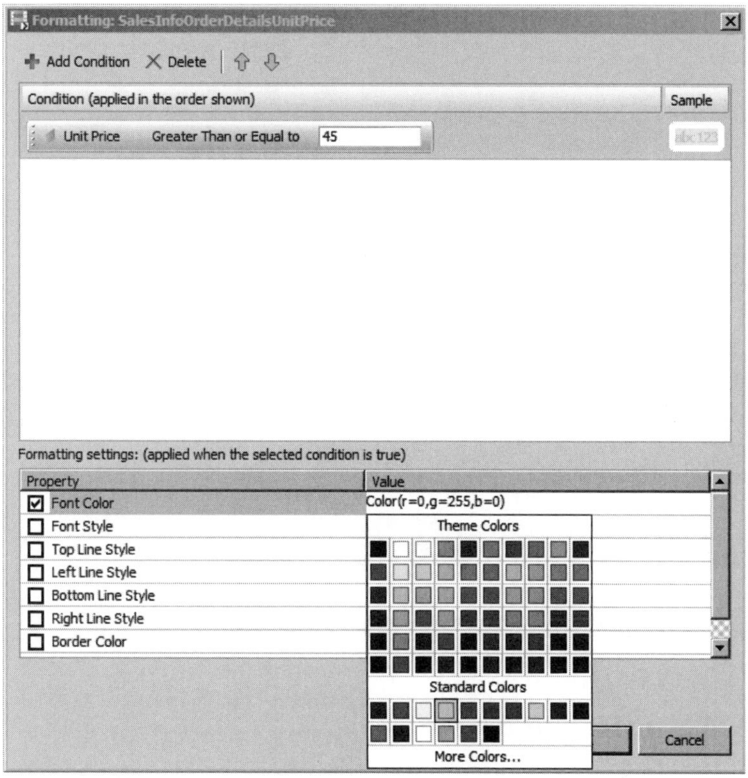

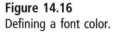

Figure 14.16
Defining a font color.

7. You can set as many options as you desire. Click OK when you're done.

You can also create multiple criteria. However, you must have the highest value in the hierarchy shown first or the formatting will be incorrect. If you have multiple criteria established, you can reorder any of the criteria by using the up and down arrows shown in Figure 14.17.

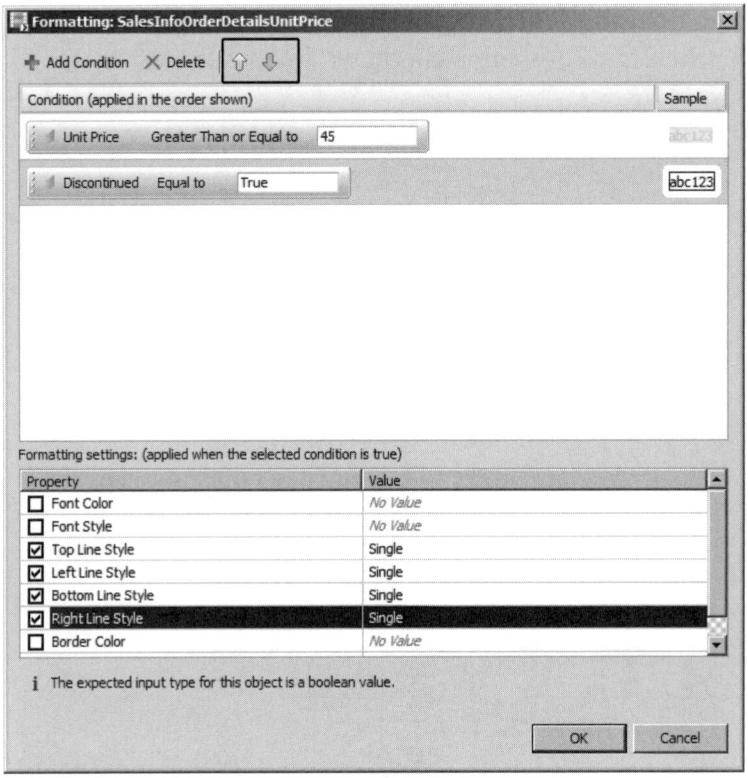

Figure 14.17
You reorder your criteria using these arrows.

WORKING WITH GROUPS

As discussed in Chapters 2 and 4, a report developer will determine if any grouping is needed based on the specifications documented during the Report Gathering Requirements discussion. One of the keywords used that indicate you must have one or more groups is the word "by." If the user specifies that she needs a report by month, you should group the report on a date field. If at any time, an aggregation (average, summary, minimum, maximum, and so on) has to be made, you must group the report by the subject of the aggregation.

The Insert Group option has drastically changed from the Insert Group feature in Crystal Reports 2011 version. To access grouping options from Crystal Reports for Enterprise XI 4.0, you can choose Insert > Group from the Insert menu or choose the Group button on the Insert ribbon tab, as shown in Figure 14.18.

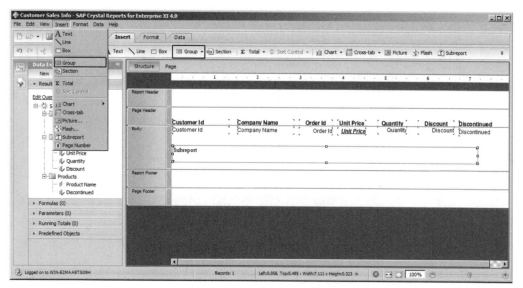

Figure 14.18
Accessing the Insert Group option.

The Group dialog box will open. The first drop-down list displays all available fields from the data source. The second drop-down list enables you to set the group order. If this is the first group created in this report, the only option in the drop-down will be At Group Level 1. If you have existing groups, you will have additional options, such as At Group Level 2 and At Group Level 3. This option enables you to reorder your groups at the time of creation.

Creating a Group

Follow these steps to create a group:

1. Choose Insert > Group. The Group dialog box will open, as shown in Figure 14.19.

2. Choose the field to group on; for this exercise, choose Customer ID.

3. Leave the sort order at Ascending.

4. Click the Insert button. The Group header and footer will be inserted into the report, as shown in Figure 14.20.

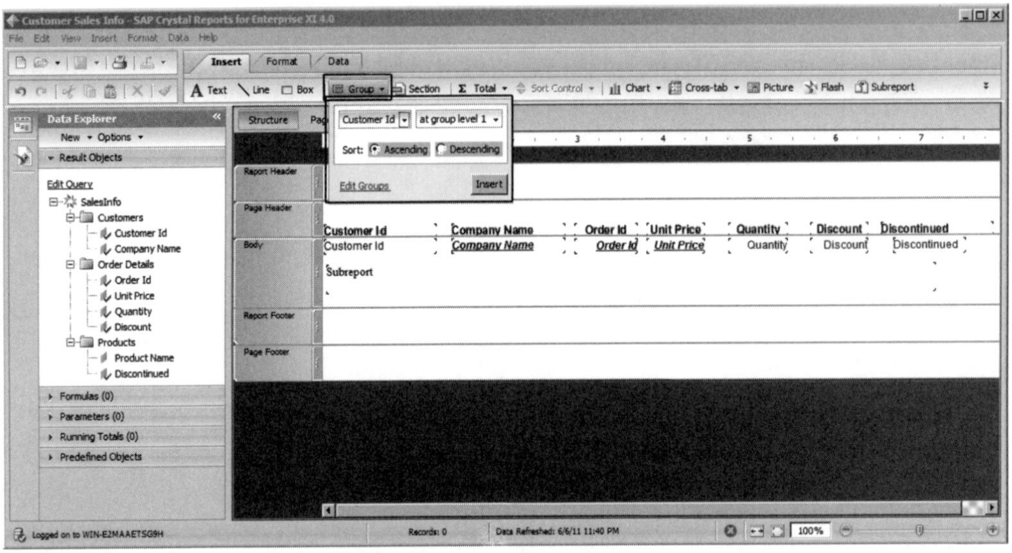

Figure 14.19
The Group dialog box.

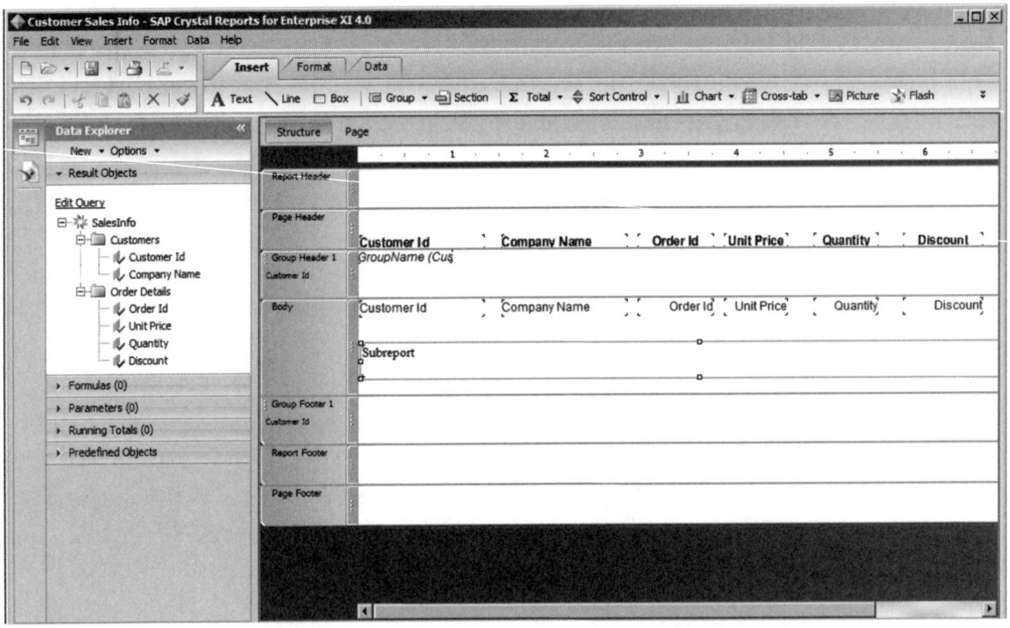

Figure 14.20
Inserting a group.

You can also create a group using the shortcut menu on the object. Right-click the field that you want to group on and choose Group on [Field], as shown in Figure 14.21.

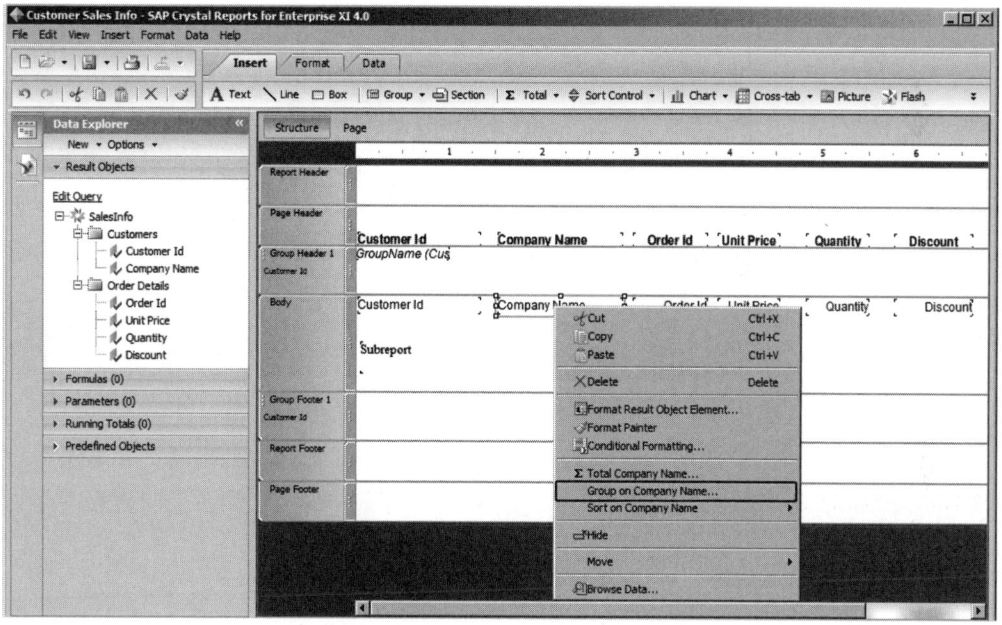

Figure 14.21
Creating a group using the shortcut menu.

Editing a Group

The Edit Group option holds the options needed to create a hierarchical group, to create a Top N/Bottom N group, to customize a group and group name, and to set the sort order for the group. To edit a group, right-click on the blue section area of the group header or footer, as shown in Figure 14.22, or click the Insert or Change Group button on the Insert tab, as shown in Figure 14.23.

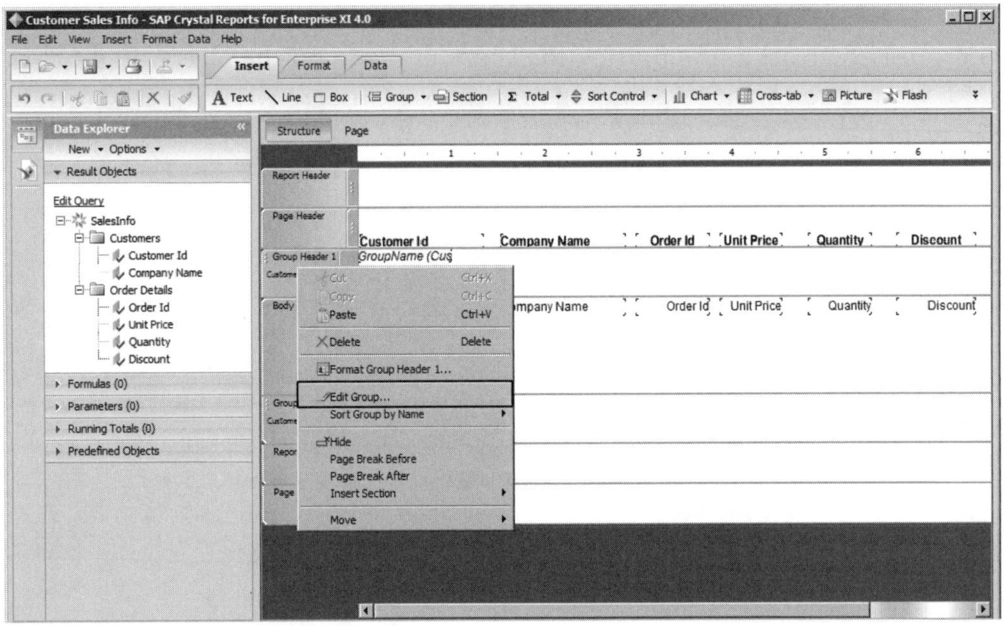

Figure 14.22
Editing a group by right-clicking it.

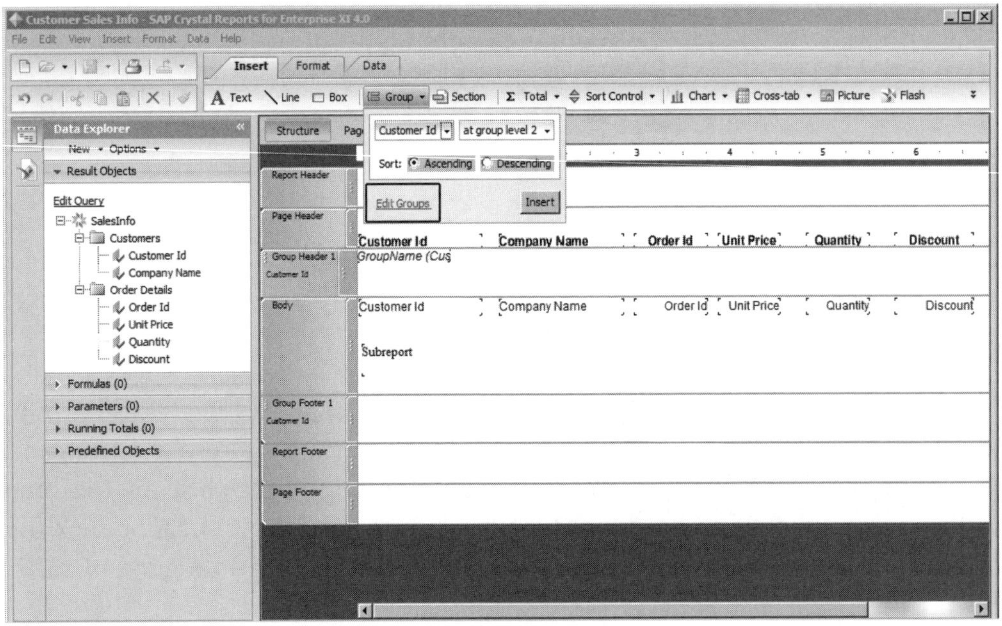

Figure 14.23
Editing a group using the Insert and Change Group button.

Creating a Custom Group

The Edit Group dialog box allows you create a custom group, which is the equivalent to using the In Specified Order option in Crystal Reports 2011 and prior versions.

To create a custom group, click the Custom Group button, as shown in Figure 14.24. Select the values from the drop-down menu or click New to create a custom group, as shown in Figure 14.25.

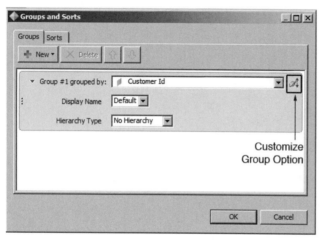

Figure 14.24
The Edit Group dialog box.

Customizing the Group Name

To customize the group name, from the Edit Group dialog box, change the Display Name drop-down box from Default to one of the existing data source fields, as shown in Figure 14.26 or choose Formula to create a custom name, as shown in Figure 14.27.

Creating a Hierarchical Group

Using the Edit Group, you can create a hierarchical level in a group by changing the Hierarchy type, as shown in Figure 14.28. The options are No Hierarchy and Hierarchical Group Parent. This option is equivalent to the Create Hierarchical Group option in Crystal Reports 2011 and previous versions.

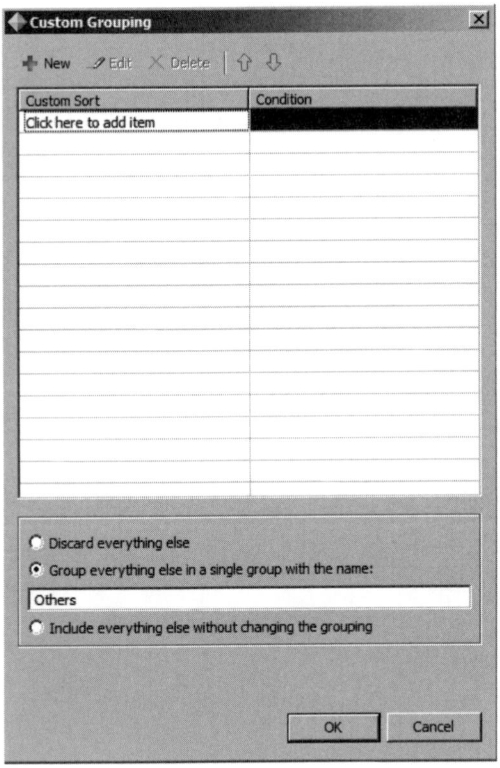

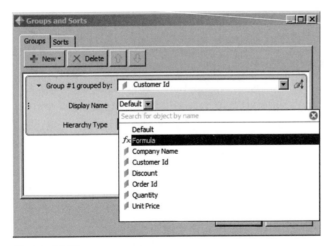

Figure 14.25
Creating a custom group.

Figure 14.26
Customizing a group name.

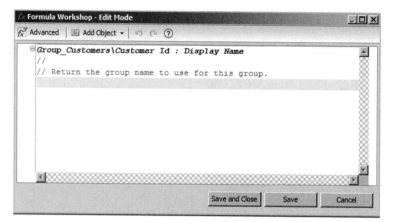

Figure 14.27
Creating a group name using a formula.

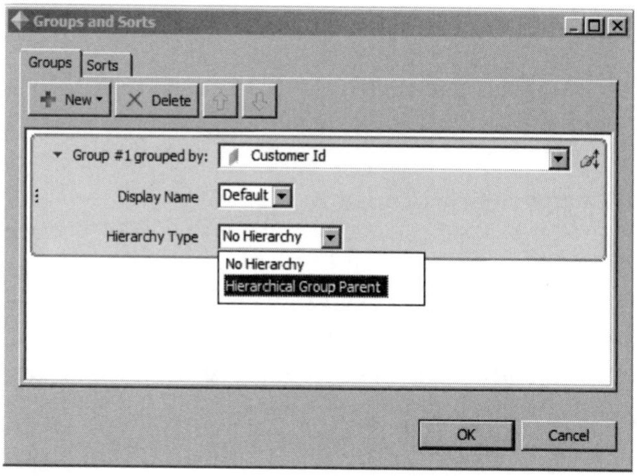

Figure 14.28
Creating a hierarchy.

Creating a Group Sort

The Group Sort option is available on the Sort tab of the Edit Group dialog box. The new features in the Group Sort option allow you to sort the groups and create a total operation at the same time. The Top N and Bottom N feature is now accessible from the Sort tab in the Edit Group dialog box, as shown in Figure 14.29.

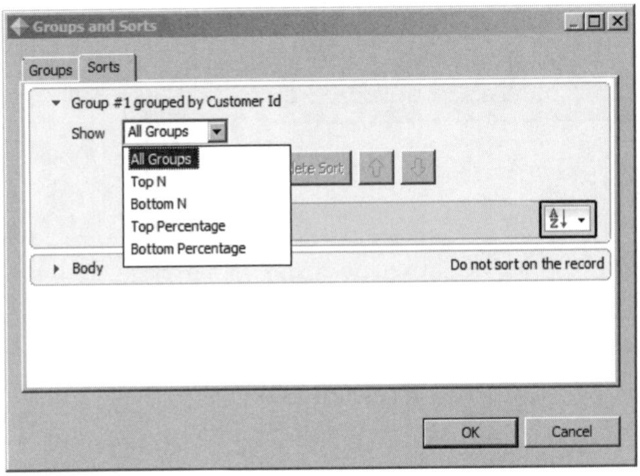

Figure 14.29
Creating a group sort.

Creating a total operation with a group sort can be accomplished by selecting the Add Sort button. This option will allow you to create a summary operation based on the datatype of the grouped field. Click the Custom option to open the Edit Custom dialog box, as shown in Figures 14.30 and 14.31.

Formatting Group Header

Many of the Group options have been moved to the corresponding Format Group Header or Footer dialog box.

You can access options such as Customizing Group Name and Repeat Group Header on Each Page by right-clicking on the blue section area of the group header or footer and selecting Format Group Header, as shown in Figure 14.32. You can also set the page break options, including specifying the number of

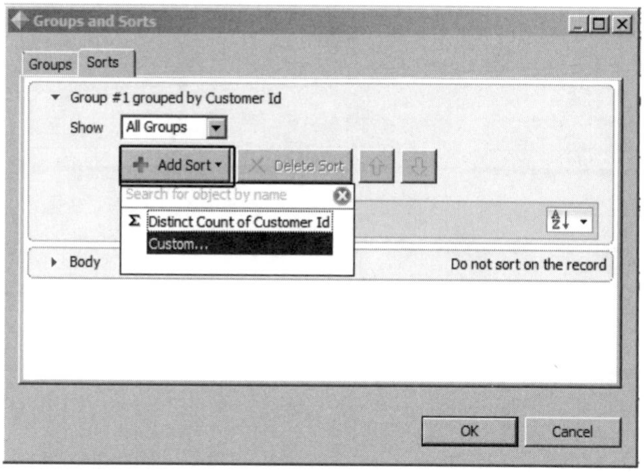

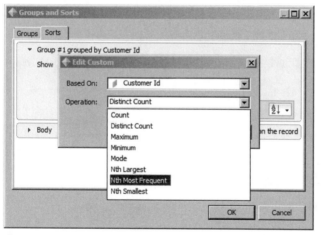

Figure 14.30
Creating an additional sort option.

Figure 14.31
Creating a total operation with a group sort.

groups to display on the page, by right-clicking on the blue section area of the group header or footer and selecting Format Group Header.

The Group header format option can also be accessed by selecting the Format > Group Header option from the menu, as shown in Figure 14.33.

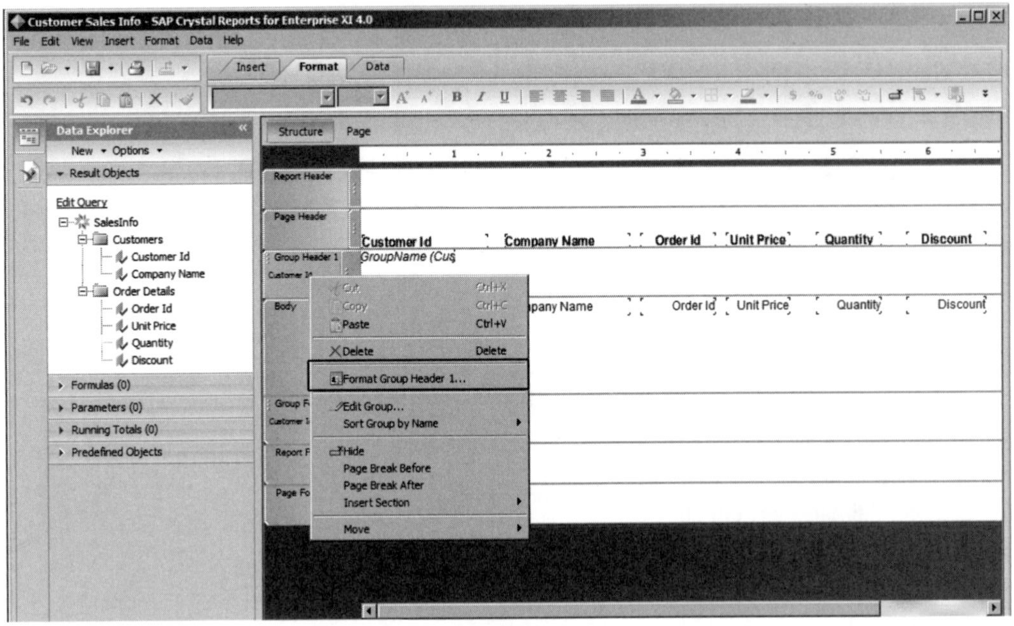

Figure 14.32
Selecting the Format Group Header from the shortcut menu.

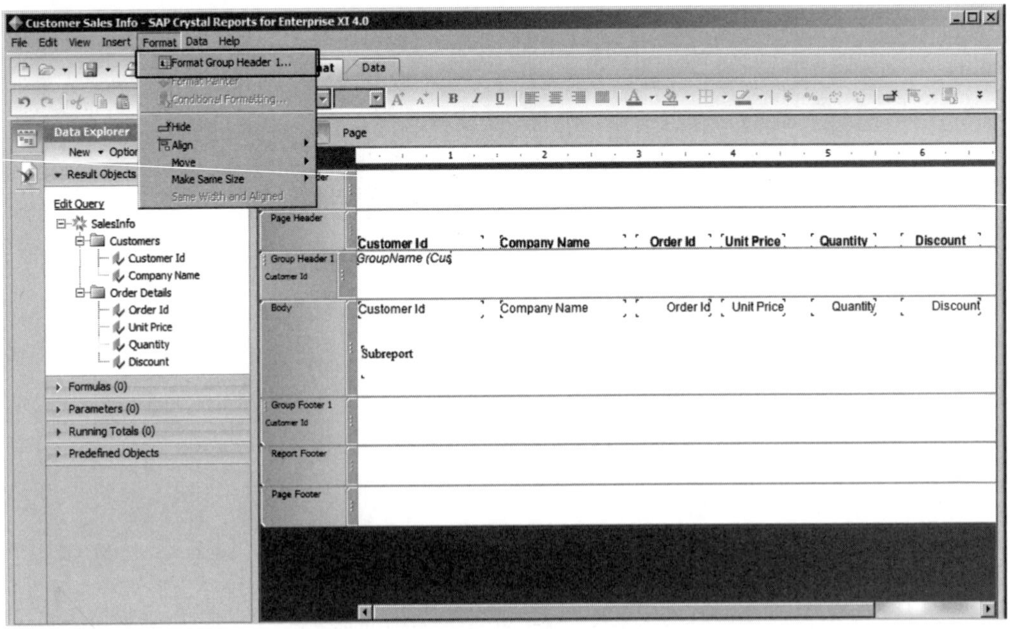

Figure 14.33
Selecting the Format Group Header from the standard menu.

USING INSERT SUMMARIES

Generating a summary field is often the reason groups are created in the first place. The summary operations that are available depend on the datatype of the field. You can create summary fields by accessing the Insert > Total menu or by right-clicking on the field and selecting the Total field option from the shortcut menu, as shown in Figure 14.34. The dialog box to select the summary operation and total location will open, as shown in Figure 14.35.

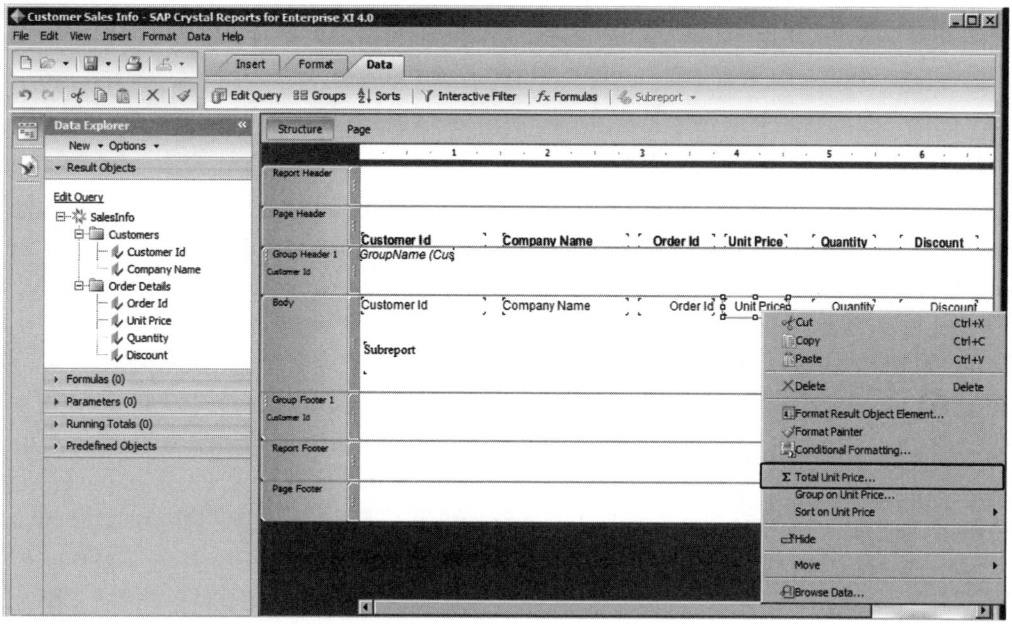

Figure 14.34
Inserting a summary field from the shortcut menu.

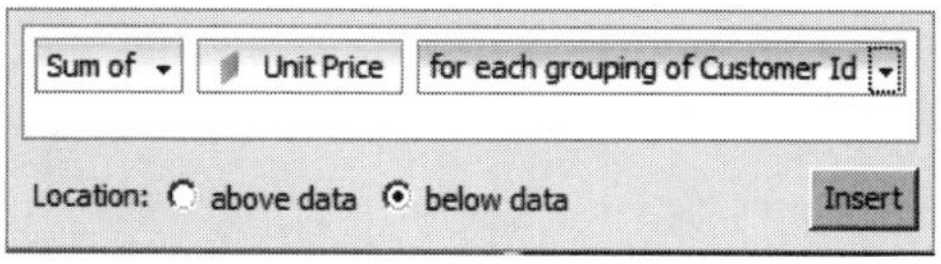

Figure 14.35
The Total dialog box.

The new insert summary option allows you to place the summary field in the header or footer by choosing the Location options shown in Figure 14.36.

The new total option also allows you to insert the summary in any custom location that you desire by selecting the Custom Location option from the Total option, as shown in Figure 14.36.

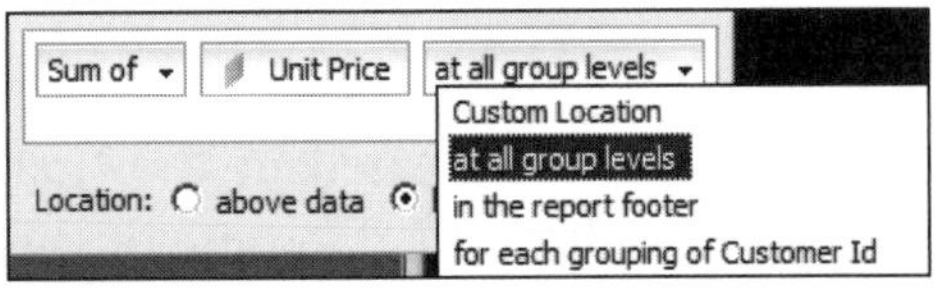

Figure 14.36
Changing the summary field location.

When the Custom Location option is chosen, you have total free-form placement of the field. After the Insert button is selected, the summary field is attached to your mouse cursor. Place the field in your desired location such as in the Page Header or Footer.

Filtering Records

Rarely do your report requirements request that you view all of the records in the data source tables. It's necessary to filter your database records to speed up the processing of your report and only present the data the users need. The Select Expert has been replaced with the Interactive Filter option in SAP Crystal Reports for Enterprise XI 4.0. The Interactive Filter can be accessed from the Data > Interactive menu or by selecting the Interactive Filter button on the Data tab, as shown in Figure 14.37. The Interactive Filter option limits the records listed on your report based on the values selected in the prompts. The criteria is based on parameter values. You can create parameters in the Interactive Filter window.

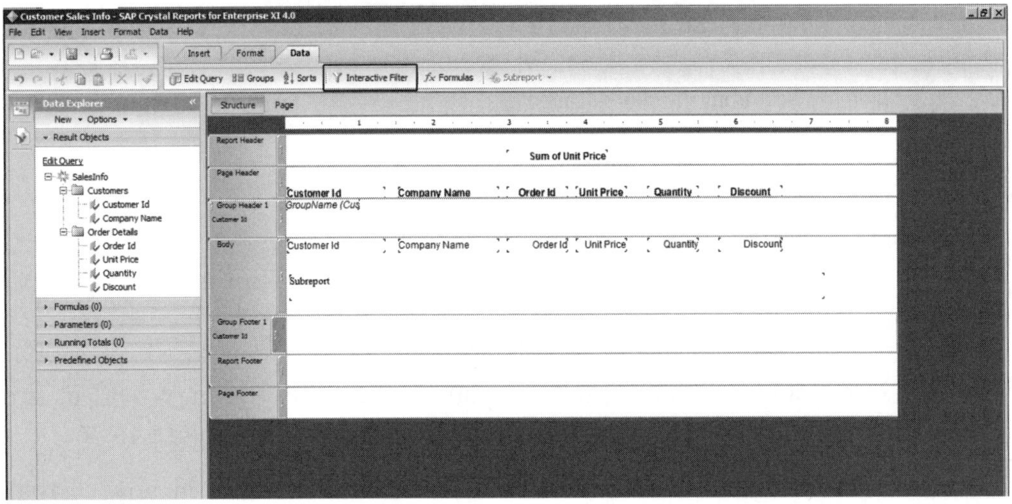

Figure 14.37
Accessing the Interactive Filter button.

Click Add Filter, as shown in Figure 14.38.

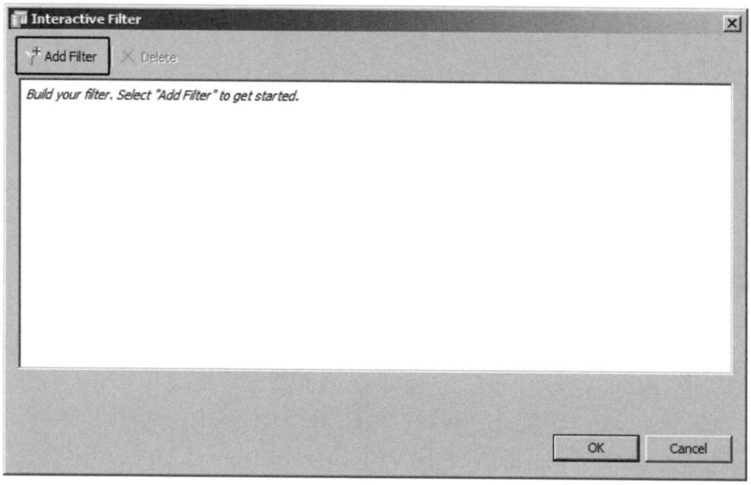

Figure 14.38
Accessing the Interactive Filter dialog box.

The first drop-down list allows you to select the field to filter the data, as shown
in Figure 14.39.

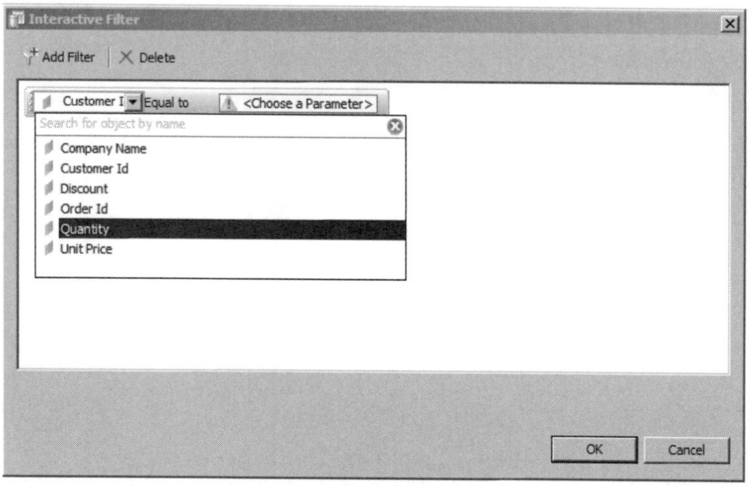

Figure 14.39
Selecting the filtering criteria.

The second drop-down list allows you to select the operator for the criteria, as shown in Figure 14.40.

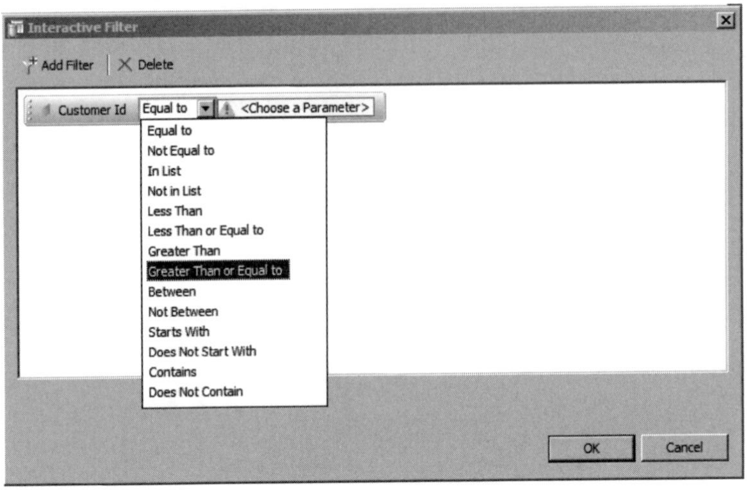

Figure 14.40
List of operators in the Interactive Filter dialog box.

The third option allows you to enter or select the criteria value via a parameter. If no parameters have been created, you can select the Choose a Parameter option, as shown in Figure 14.41.

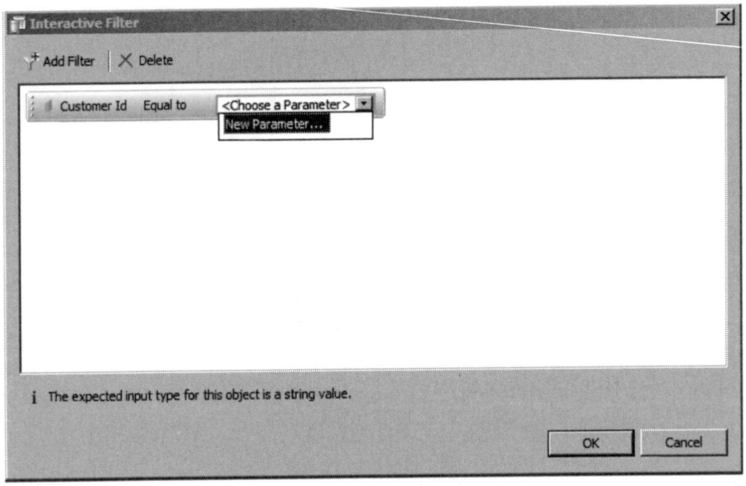

Figure 14.41
Choose parameters in the Interactive Filter.

If no parameters exist, choose New Parameter. The Create Parameter window will open, as shown in Figure 14.42. Follow the next steps to create a parameter:

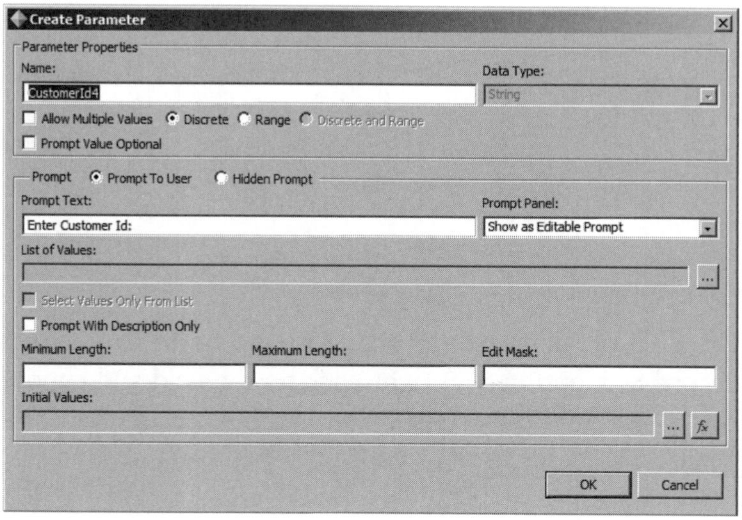

Figure 14.42
Creating a new parameter.

1. Enter a name for the parameter. The datatype will be grayed out because it is derived from the datatype you selected to filter on.

2. Select the parameter value options:

   Allow Multiple Values

   Discrete

   Range

   Prompt Value Optional

3. Select the Prompt value:

   Prompt to user—A prompt will be displayed for the user.

   Hidden prompt—The value is passed programmatically.

4. Enter the prompting text.

5. Select the options for the Prompting panel.

6. Enter, select, or import the list of values if desired.

7. Select or enter the parameter options such as:

Prompt with description only

Min and Max field length properties

Edit mask

Initial values

USING RECORD SORT

The Record Sort option sorts the database records in ascending or descending order. To access the Record Sort option, you right-click on the field and choose Sort on Field Name, as shown in Figure 14.43. You can also select the Sorts button from the Data tab.

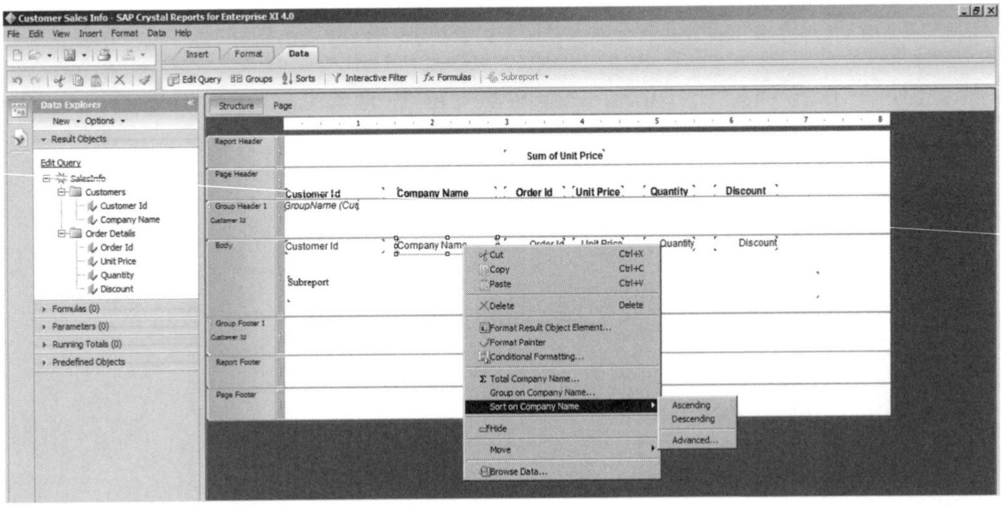

Figure 14.43
Selecting the Record Sort option.

If you used the Sorts button, the Sorts tab will open, as shown in Figure 14.44.

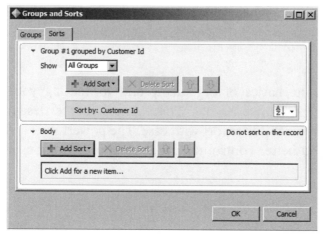

Figure 14.44
Using the Sorts tab.

To create a record sort, follow these steps.

1. Double-click on the Body section of the window. The Groups and Sorts window opens, as shown in Figure 14.45.

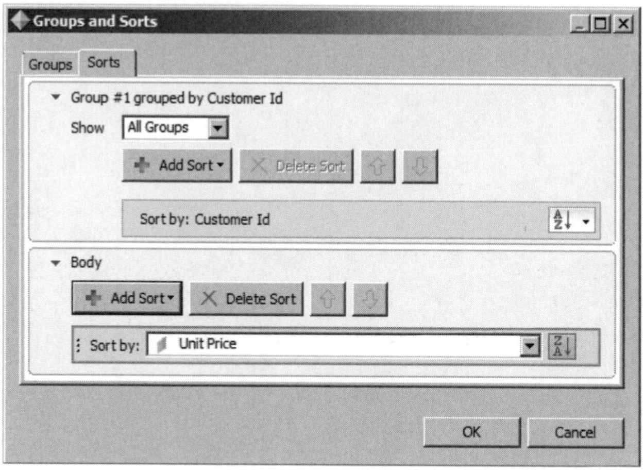

Figure 14.45
Creating a record sort.

2. Choose the Add Sort drop-down menu.

3. Select the field from the data source list to sort the records on.

4. Click OK.

SUMMARY

You have been introduced to the basics of organizing and formatting your reports in Crystal Reports for Enterprise XI 4.0. The changes in the design environment will allow you to format your report with ease. The powerfulness of the formatting changes gives you better control over the visual presentation of your data.

APPENDIX A

FORMULA FUNCTIONS

There are many predefined functions in Crystal Reports. Some of the more common functions are defined in this section.

DATE AND TIME FUNCTIONS

Date functions allow you to convert numbers to dates and convert dates to numbers. Some functions have arguments that allow you to format the field as desired.

CurrentDate

Returns the print date of the report.

The CurrentDate function can be used in Basic or Crystal syntax.

Example:

CurrentDate

Returns:

6/30/2011

CurrentTime

Returns the print time of the report.

The CurrentTime function can be used in Basic or Crystal syntax.

Example:

CurrentTime

Returns:

11:39:18

CurrentDateTime

Returns the current print date and time of the report.

The CurrentDateTime functions can be used in Basic or Crystal syntax.

Example:

CurrentDateTime

Returns:

6/30/2011 11:39:18

Date

The Date() function is equivalent to the CDate() and DateValue() function. The Date() function can be used only in Crystal syntax.

Date Functions

Date (number)—The number argument represents the number of days from the date December 30, 1899.

Example:

Date (300)

Returns:

10/26/1900

Date (string)—The string argument requires you to reference a date field in a string format, such as June 30, 2011.

Example:

Date ("June 30, 2011")

Returns:

June 30, 2011

Date (datetime)—The datetime argument requires you to reference a datetime field such as June 30, 2011 11:39:18.

Example:

Date (#June 30, 2011 11:39#)

Returns:

June 30, 2011

Date (YYYY, MM, DD)—The date argument requires you to enter a four-digit year, two-digit month, and two-digit day.

Example:

Date (2011, 06, 30)

Returns:

06/30/2011

Time Functions

The Time() function is equivalent to CTime() and TimeValue() functions. The Time () function can only be used in Crystal syntax.

Time (number)—This function requires a number that can be fractional, positive, or negative.

Example:

Time (.75)

Returns:

6:00:00PM

Time (string)—This function requires a time in string format.

Example:

Time ("11:39am")

Returns:

11:39:00AM

Time (dateTime)—This function requires a date and time field that returns only the time.

Example:

Time (DateTime(2011, 06, 30,   11, 39, 18))

Returns:

11:39:18AM

Time (HH, MM, SS)—This function requires the time to be entered in numerical format.

Example:

Time(11, 39, 18)

Returns:

11:39:18AM

The DateTime Function

The DateTime function converts a date or dateTime field into a date and time field.

DateTime(date)—This function requires a date field or date value in the argument.

Example:

DateTime(2011,06,30)

Returns:

06/30/2011 12:00:00AM

DateTime (number)—This function requires a positive, negative, or fractional number based on the number of days since December 30, 1899.

Example:

DateTime (100)

Returns:

4/9/1900 12:00:00AM

DateTime (string)—This function requires a date field in a string format.

Example:

DateTime ("December 31, 2010")

Returns:

12/31/2010 12:00:00AM

DateTime (date, time)—This function requires a date value in one argument and the time value in the second argument.

Example:

DateTime(2011, 06, 30, 12, 00, 00)

Returns:

6/30/2011 12:00:00AM

DateTime (YYYY, MM, DD)—This function requires a four-digit year, two-digit month and two-digit day in this argument.

Example:

DateTime(2011,06,30)

Returns:

6/30/2011 12:00:00AM

DateTime (YYYY, MM, DD, HH, MM, SS)—This function requires a four-digit year, two-digit month, and two-digit day, as well as a two-digit hour, minute, and second.

Example:

DateTime (2011, 06, 30, 11, 15, 30)

Returns:

6/30/2011 11:15:30AM

DateValue Functions

The DateValue() function converts the field to a date value.

DateValue (string)—This function converts a string date field into a date field.

Example:

DateValue ("June 30, 2011")

Returns:

June 30, 2011

DateValue (number)—This function returns a date value given the number of days starting from December 30, 1899. The number can be positive, negative, or a fraction.

Example:

DateValue (35)

Returns:

2/3/1900

DateValue (dateTime)—This function requires a `dateTime` field.

Example:

DateValue (#June 30, 201112:00PM#)

Returns:

6/30/2011

DateValue (YYYY, MM, DD)—This function requires a date field.

Example:

DateValue (2011, 06, 30)

Returns:

6/30/2011

TimeValue Functions

The time value function converts a field into a time value.

TimeValue (number)—This function returns a time value given in a 24-hour format.

Example:

TimeValue (.65)

Returns:

3:36:00PM

TimeValue (string)—This function converts a string `datetime` or `time` field into a `Time` value.

Example:

TimeValue ("June 30, 2011 11:30pm")

Returns:

11:30:00pm

TimeValue (dateTime)—This function requires a `dateTime` field to be referenced in the argument. This function will convert the value into a `Time` format.

Example:

TimeValue (#June 30, 2011 11:45AM#)

Returns:

`11:45:00AM`

TimeValue (HH, MM, SS)—This function requires the time value to be entered into the argument.

Example:

`TimeValue (11, 45, 30)`

Returns:

`11:45:30AM`

DateTimeValue Functions

The `DateTimeValue` function converts a field to a date and time value.

DateTimeValue (date)—This function converts a date field into a `DateTimeValue`.

Example:

`DateTimeValue("10/24/2010")`

Returns:

`10/24/2010 12:00:00AM`

Example:

`DateTimeValue({Orders.OrderDate})`

DateTimeValue (date, time)—This function requires two arguments. The first argument requires a date value and the second argument requires a time field. This function converts a field into a date and time field.

Example:

`DateTimeValue ( CDate ("June 30, 2010"), CTime ("3:30 pm"))`

Returns:

`June 30, 2010 3:30:00PM`

DateTimeValue (number)—This function allows you to represent a number of days from December 30, 1899.

Example:

DateTimeValue (30)

Returns:

1/29/1900 12:00:00AM

DateTimeValue (string)—This function converts a string field into a date and time value.

Example:

DateTimeValue ("October 15, 2010 8:15am")

Returns:

October 15, 2010 8:15:00AM

DateTimeValue (YYYY, MM, DD)—This function converts an absolute four-digit year, two-digit month and two-digit day into a date and time value.

Example:

DateTimeValue(2011, 05, 21)

Returns:

May 21, 2011 12:00:00 AM

DateTimeValue (YYYY, MM, DD, HH, MM, SS)—This function converts an absolute four-digit year, two-digit month, two-digit day and hours, minutes, and seconds into the date and time value.

Example:

DateTimeValue (2011, 06, 10, 4, 30, 15)

Returns:

6/10/2011 4:30:15AM

Year (x)

The Year () function extracts the year from the date specified field.

Example: Order Date = 7/12/2009

Year ({Orders.OrderDate})

Returns:

2009

Month(x)

The `Month()` function converts the month of the field to a numerical value.

Example: `Order Date = June 30, 2010`

`Month({Orders.OrderDate})`

Returns:

`6`

Day (x)

The `Day()` function extracts the day from a date field.

Example: `Order Date = June 30, 2010`

`Day({Orders.OrderDate})`

Returns:

`30`

WeekDay

This function converts the day of the week into a numerical designation. Crystal Reports considers the first day of the week to be Sunday.

Example: `Order Date = July 4, 2011`

`WeekDay ({Orders.OrderDate})`

Returns:

`2`

The result returned 2 because July 4, 2011 was a Monday.

There may be times when you need the first day of the week to be a day other than Sunday. You can use `WeekDay (x,y)`, which has two arguments to specify the first day of the week in the second argument.

Example:

`WeekDay({Orders.OrderDate}, crMonday)`

Returns:

`1`

The result returned 1 because the example specified that the first day of the week is Monday.

DayOfWeek

The DayOfWeek function is equivalent to the WeekDay function. It converts the day into a numerical value—from 1 to 7—with Sunday being the first day of the week.

Example: Order Date = July 4, 2011

DayOfWeek({Orders.OrderDate})

Returns:

2

Hour (x)

The Hour () function extracts the hour portion of a time value.

Example: Time: 6:34 PM

Hour(CTime (06,34,00))

Returns:

6

Minute (x)

The Minute () function extracts the minutes from a time value.

Example: Time 6:34 PM

Minute (CTime(06, 34, 00))

Returns:

34

Second (x)

The Second (x) function extracts the seconds from a time value.

Example:

Second (CTime((06, 30, 12))

Returns:

12

MonthName ()

The MonthName() function converts the numerical month value with the string name. The MonthName() function can be used with one argument or two arguments, which specify whether to abbreviate the name. The `MonthName` function can be used in conjunction with the `Month()` function.

Example:

`MonthName(6)`

Returns:

`"June"`

Example: `OrderDate = 6/30/2011`

`MonthName(Month({Orders.OrderDate}))`

Returns:

`"June"`

WeekDayName

The `WeekDayName ()` function converts a numerical day of the week to the string value of the week. This function can be used in conjunction with the `WeekDay ()` or `Day ()` function.

Example: `OrderDate = July 4, 2011`

`WeekDayName(WeekDay({Orders.OrderDate}))`

Returns:

`Monday`

Timer

The `Timer()` function calculates the number of seconds that have elapsed since midnight.

Example: The time is 11:00:00 pm.

`Timer`

Returns:

`82,800.00`

DateAdd (intervalType, nintervals, startDateTime)

The `DateAdd()` function adds a specified number of intervals to a specified date. For example, you want to know the end date when you add six months to a project inception date.

It's important to know the abbreviations for the interval types, as shown in the following table.

Interval Type	Description
Yyyy	Year
Q	Quarter (three-month period)
M	Month
Y	Day of year
D	Day
W	Weekday
Ww	Week (seven-day period)
H	Hour
N	Minutes
S	Seconds

Note

The w interval is slightly misleading. The assumption is that it refers to Monday—Friday as weekdays. However, it functions the same as the d function in a calendar day. The interval types are case-sensitive.

Example: The following function adds six months to June 30, 2011.

```
DateAdd("m", 6, #6/30/2011#)
```

Returns:

```
12/30/2011 12:00:00 AM
```

DateDiff

The `DateDiff()` function allows you to calculate the difference between two dates based on the intervals that you specified.

```
DateDiff (intervalType, startDateTime, endDateTime)
DateDiff (intervalType, startDateTime, endDateTime, firstDayOfWeek)
```

Example:

```
DateDiff("d", #7/1/2011#, #7/15/2011#)
```

Returns:

```
14
```

Example: Calculate the number of weeks between two dates.

```
DateDiff("ww", #7/1/2011#, #10/15/2011#, crMonday)
```

Returns:

```
15
```

The function calculates how many Mondays are between 7/1/2011 and 10/15/2011.

DatePart

The `DatePart()` function extracts the specified part of the date from a `DateTime` field. This function can be used in conjunction with other functions to create a user-defined ID. For example, a project ID that is made of characters from the customer name, the date, and project type.

Example:

```
DatePart("n", #11:25 am#)
```

Returns:

```
25
```

Date Ranges

Date range functions are preset date ranges that can be used in formulas.

WeekToDateFromSun

The `WeekToDateFromSun` function includes transactions with dates from last Sunday to the current date.

Example:

```
If {RequiredDate} in WeekToDateFromSun  then count({OrderID}) else 0
```

MonthToDate

The `MonthToDate` function includes transactions from the first day of the current month to the current date. This date range can be used to eliminate the need for users to have a date prompt.

Example:

```
If {Orders.OrderDate} in MonthToDate then {Orders.OrderAmount}
```

YearToDate

The YearToDate function includes records from the first day of the current year to the current date.

Example:

```
If {Orders.OrderDate} in YearToDate Then Sum({Orders.OrderAmount})
```

Last7Days

The Last7Days function includes all records from the last seven days to the current date. The current date is included.

Example:

```
If {Orders.OrderDate} in Last7Days then Sum({Orders.OrderAmount})
```

Last4WeeksToSun

The Last4WeeksToSun function includes all records from the last four weeks from the previous Sunday based on the current date. For this function, a week begins on Monday.

Example:

```
If {Orders.OrderDate} in Last4WeeksToSun then Sum({Orders.OrderAmount})
```

LastFullWeek

The LastFullWeek function includes all records from the last full week. For example, if you run the report with a Tuesday's date, this function will ensure that data from last Monday through Sunday is included.

Example:

```
If {Orders.OrderDate} in LastFullWeek then Sum({Orders.OrderAmount})
```

LastFullMonth

The LastFullMonth function includes all records from the last full month. For example, if you ran the report on July 1, 2011, the report would include data for the full month of June.

Example:

```
If {Orders.OrderDate} in LastFullMonth then "Last Month" else ""
```

AllDatesToToday

The AllDatesToToday function includes all records up until the current day.

Example:

`If {Orders.OrderDate} in AllDatesToToday then {Orders.OrderAmount} else 0`

AllDatesToYesterday

The `AllDatesToYesterday` function includes all records up until yesterday.

Example:

`If {Orders.OrderDate} in AllDatesToYesterday then {Orders.OrderAmount} else 0`

AllDatesFromToday

The `AllDatesFromToday` function includes all records from the current day that may have a future date. This is a beneficial function when looking for future posted transactions.

Example:

`If {Orders.OrderDate} in AllDatesFromToday then {Orders.OrderAmount} else 0`

AllDatesFromTomorrow

The `AllDatesFromTomorrow` function includes all records from today that may have a future date.

Example:

`If {Orders.OrderDate} in AllDatesFromTomorrow then {Orders.OrderAmount} else 0`

Aged0To30Days, Aged31to60Days, Aged61To90Days

The aging functions are used to categorize records in a time period. A prime example would be an Accounts Receivable report.

Example:

`If {Orders.OrderDate} in Aged0To30Days then {Orders.OrderAmount}`

Over90Days

The `Over90Days` function is used to present aging reports.

Example:

`If {Orders.OrderDate} in Over90Days then {Orders.OrderAmount}`

Next30Days, Next31To60Days, Next61To90Days, Next91To365Days

Additional aging functions categorize transactions based on a time period. A prime use of these functions would be a forecasting report.

Example:

```
If {Orders.DueDate} in Next30Days then {Orders.OrderAmount}
```

Calendar1stQtr, Calendar2ndQtr, Calendar3rdQtr, Calendar4thQtr

These quarter aging functions are used to categorize records by quarters of the current calendar year. The first quarter refers to January 1st through March 31st. The second quarter refers to April 1st through June 30th. The third quarter refers to July 1st through September 31st. The fourth quarter refers to October 1st through December 31st.

Example:

```
If {Orders.OrderDate} in Calendar1stQtr then {Orders.OrderAmount}
```

Calendar1stHalf, Calendar2ndHalf

These functions include records for the first or second half of the current calendar year. The first half includes dates from January 1st to June 30th. The second half includes July 1st to December 31st.

Example:

```
If {Orders.OrderDate} to Calendar2ndQtr then {Orders.OrderAmount}
```

LastYearMTD

The `LastYearMTD` function includes records from the previous year that match the current month to date. This function is used to analyze annual data comparisons by month.

Example:

```
If {Orders.OrderDate} in LastYearMTD then {Orders.OrderAmount}
```

LastYearYTD

The `LastYearYTD` function includes all records with dates in the last year up to the current date from the previous year. This function is used to analyze annual data comparisons.

Example:

```
If {Orders.OrderDate} in LastYearYTD then {Orders.OrderAmount}
```

DOCUMENT PROPERTY FUNCTIONS

Document property functions return results about document attributes.

PrintDate

The `PrintDate` function inserts on the report the date that it was printed. The `PrintDate` function is equivalent to the `CurrentDate` function.

Example:

```
PrintDate
```

Example:

```
If {Orders.OrderDate} < PrintDate then {Orders.OrderAmount}
```

The previous code prints all orders that have been placed prior to the print date.

PrintTime

The `PrintTime` function inserts the time the report is printed on the report. The `PrintTime` and `CurrentTime` functions are equivalent.

Example:

```
PrintTime
```

ModificationDate

The `ModificationDate` function inserts the date the report was last modified. Note this date is going to be the last time the report was saved. Often, you open a formula to review it but will not make any changes. Once you close the report, you may be asked to save the changes. If you choose Yes, the modification date will be updated. The `ModificationDate` can also be accessed from Special Fields.

Example:

```
ModificationDate
```

ModificationTime

The `ModificationTime` function inserts the time the report was last modified. The `ModificationTime` can also be accessed from Special Fields.

Example:

```
ModificationTime
```

DataDate

The `DataDate` function returns the date the report was last refreshed.

Example:

`"The report reflects data as of " & DataDate & "."`

The previous code may be printed in a formula in the Report Header or Page Header to give the user information about the data. It is particularly useful when data is saved in the report.

MATH FUNCTIONS

Math functions are used for mathematical calculations and operations.

Abs (x)

The `Abs ()` function returns the absolute value of a number.

Example:

`Abs (-2.5)`

Returns:

`2.5`

Sgn (number)

The `Sgn ()` function returns the sign of a specified number. Returns 1 if the number is greater than 0; 0 if the number is 0; and −1 if the number is less than 0.

Example:

`Sgn (-5)`

Returns:

`-1`

Int (number)

The `Int ()` function returns the integer value of a number. This function is beneficial when you need to return the whole number.

Example:

`Int ( 145.387)`

Returns:

145

Round

The Round () function rounds a number to the specified decimal places.

Arguments: Round (number to be rounded, # of decimal places)

Example:

Round(2.590)

Returns:

3

RoundUp

The RoundUp () function rounds a number up from zero.

Arguments: RoundUp (number to roundup, # of decimal places to round up)

Decimal places:

- If the number of places is greater than zero, the number is rounded up to the number of decimal places specified.

- If the number of places is zero or unspecified, the number is rounded up to the next integer.

- If the number of places is less than zero, the number is rounded up to the left of the decimal point.

Example:

RoundUp (4.14)

Returns:

5
RoundUp (40.34, -1)

Returns:

50

Truncate

The Truncate () function deletes the characters to the right of the decimal point unless the number of decimal places is specified.

Example:

`Truncate (124.56)`

Returns:

`124`

`Truncate ({ExtendedCost} / 5)`
Returns:
`4 where 23/5 = 4.60`

Ceiling

The `Ceiling ()` function rounds the number up to the multiple that you specify.

Example:

`Ceiling (4.55)`

Returns:

`5`

Floor

The `Floor ()` function rounds the number down to the multiple that you specify.

Example:

`Floor (4.55)`

Returns:

`4`

Remainder (num, denom)

The `Remainder ()` function returns the remainder after the numerator is divided by the denominator.

Example:

`Remainder (31, 3)`

Returns:

`1`

STRING FUNCTIONS

String functions are used for the evaluation, manipulation, and conversion of text strings.

Len (str)

The Len () function indicates the length of a string field. This function is very useful when the length of a field is important, such as when converting to a new system. The new system field might not be as long as the legacy system; therefore, the value needs to be modified.

Example:

Len ("Crystal Reports")

Returns:

15

Length (str)

The Length () function indicates the length of a string field. This function is equivalent to the Len () function.

Example:

Length ("Crystal Reports")

Returns:

15

Trim (str)

The Trim () function removes leading and trailing spaces from a string field.

Example:

Trim (" Crystal Reports   ")

Returns:

"Crystal Reports"

LTrim (str)

The LTrim () function removes all spaces stored to the left of the string field. This function should be used to remove any leading spaces that can interfere with a formula.

Example:

LTrim (" Crystal Reports   ")

Returns:

`"Crystal Reports    "`

TrimLeft (str)

The `TrimLeft ()` function is equivalent to `LTrim ()`. The `TrimLeft ()` function removes all spaces to the left of a string field.

Example:

`TrimLeft (" Crystal Reports")`

Returns:

`"Crystal Reports"`

RTrim (str)

The `RTrim ()` function removes all trailing spaces from the right of the string field.

Example:

`RTrim ("Crystal Reports    ")`

Returns:

`"Crystal Reports"`

TrimRight (str)

The `TrimRight ()` function is equivalent to the `RTrim ()` function. The `TrimRight ()` function removes all trailing spaces from the string field.

Example:

`TrimRight ("Crystal Reports    ")`

Returns:

`"Crystal Reports"`

UCase (str)

The `UCase ()` function converts the string to all uppercase characters. The `UCase ()` function is preferred in Basic.

Example:

`UCase ("jones")`

Returns:

"JONES"

UpperCase (str)

The UpperCase () function is equivalent to the UCase () function. The UpperCase () function is preferred in Crystal syntax.

Example:

UpperCase ("jones")

Returns:

"JONES"

LCase (str)

The LCase () function converts the string field to all lowercase. The LCase () function is preferred in Basic.

Example:

LCase ("Crystal Reports")

Returns:

"crystal reports"

LowerCase (str)

The LowerCase () function converts the string field to all lowercase. The LowerCase () function is preferred in Crystal syntax.

Example:

LowerCase ("CRYSTAL REPORTS")

Returns:

"crystal reports"

ProperCase (str)

The ProperCase () function capitalizes the first letter of each word in the string field and converts all others to lowercase letters. This is particularly useful when users enter data in different cases but must be consistent on the report.

Example:

ProperCase ("MICHAEL JONES")

Returns:

`"Michael Jones"`

ToNumber

The `ToNumber()` function converts a number, currency, string, or Boolean value to a number. The function may be necessary when you need to include the field value in a formula.

Example:

`ToNumber("13.45")`

Returns:

`13.45`

Example:

`ToNumber(Maximum({Employee.EmployeeID})) + 1`

The previous example can be used to find the next available Employee ID.

ToText()

The `ToText()` function converts Booleans, Numbers, Currency, Date, Time, and DateTime fields to strings. Each argument is different based on the datatype of the field.

Arguments:

`ToText(x)`

`ToText(x,y)`

`ToText(x,y,z)`

`ToText(x,y,z,w)`

`ToText(x,y,z,w,q)`

Datatype	Description
Boolean	x is a Boolean value.
Number and Currency Values	x is a Number or Currency value.
	y is a whole number indicating the number of decimal places to carry the value in x to. (This argument is optional.)

Datatype	Description
(Continued)	
	z is a single character text string indicating the character to be used to separate thousands in x.
	w is a single character text string indicating the character to be used as decimal separator in x.
Number and Currency Values (formatting)	x is a Number or Currency value to be converted into a text string.
	y is a text string used to indicate the format for displaying the value in x.
	z is a whole number indicating the number of decimal places to carry the value in x to.
	w is a single character text string indicating the character to be used to separate thousands in x.
	q is a single character text string indicating the character to be used as a decimal separator in x.
Date values	x is a Date value to be converted into a text string.
	y is a text string that defines how the value in x is to be formatted.
Time values	x is a time value to be converted into a text string. (optional)
	y is a text string that defines how the value in x is to be formatted. (optional)
	z is a text string to be used as a label for A.M. hours. (optional)
	w is a text string to be used a label for P.M. hours. (optional)
DateTime values	x is a DateTime value to be converted into a text string.
	y is a text string of characters that indicate how the resulting text string will be formatted. (optional)
	z is a text string to be used as a label for A.M. hours. (optional)
	w is a text string to be used a label for P.M hours. (optional)

Example: `Employee Id--123 John Smith`

```
ToText({Employee.EmployeeID}) + "—" + {Employee.FirstName} + " " + Employee.
LastName}
```

Returns:

```
123-John Smith
```

ToWords

The `ToWords()` function converts a number or currency field to words so it can be used for purposes like a check.

Example:

```
ToWords(1500.50)
```

Returns:

```
One Thousand Five Hundred and 50/100
```

Reports Requirements Documents

Requested Date: Requestor: _____

Purpose of document needed:

_____

_____

_____

_____

_____

_____

_____

Audience: _____   **Report Delivery Method:**   □ PDF file

Sample report included: □ Yes   □ Email

                              □ No   □ Scheduled

                                                                                      □ WORD Document

Date Needed: _____   □ OTHER

Database/Application Report Based On:

_____

Database Tables (if known):

_____

_____

_____

_____

Fields Requested:

_____

_____

_____

_____

Grouping: _____

_____

Summaries: _____

_____

Frequency: _____
(when will the report be run)

What is the intended use of the report?

_____

_____

_____

_____

INDEX